A HOUSE MADE OF LIGHT

A HOUSE MADE OF LIGHT

essays on the art of film

GEORGE TOLES

WAYNE STATE UNIVERSITY PRESS   DETROIT

CONTEMPORARY FILM AND TELEVISION SERIES

*A complete listing of the books in this series can be found
at the back of this volume.*

Library of Congress Cataloging-in-Publication Data

Toles, George E.
A house made of light : essays on the art of film / George Toles.
    p. cm. — (Contemporary film and television series)
Includes bibliographical references and index.
ISBN 0-8143-2945-4 — ISBN 0-8143-2946-2
1. Motion pictures—Psychological aspects. 2. Motion pictures. I. Title. II. Series.
PN1995 .T59 2001
791.43'01'9—dc21
                                                        00–012780

TO MY MOTHER
ROSE TOLES

CONTENTS

ACKNOWLEDGMENTS

This book has been too long in the making. For that reason I have accumulated an unusually large number of intellectual and personal debts which demand some brief recognition here. I would like to thank Edgar Dryden, Joseph Fradin, Fred See, Irving Massey, and Leslie Fiedler for teaching me how to respond more fully and keenly to literature during my undergraduate years at the University of Buffalo. Buffalo's English Department, in that charmingly tumultuous Albert Cook era, was the most heady, stimulating, and welcoming academic environment I have ever known. At the University of Virginia, I had the good fortune to spend office and classroom time with Alan Howard, Alistair Duckworth, Anthony Winner, Philip Fisher, Del Kolve, Gary Lindberg, and William Kerrigan. With enormous forbearance they revealed to me how far I was from achieving the critical voice and critical aims that I frantically proclaimed as my prerogative. Their diversely efficacious examples led me to strive for less arid and congested language and for thinking that took genuine risks. Pauline Kael's and Manny Farber's film criticism abundantly demonstrated how crucial it is that scenes and details be presented vividly on the page. Randall Jarrell's and Robert Warshow's essays provided me with impressive models of how aesthetic, ethical, and personal concerns could be integrated with minimal preciosity and posturing. They also give evidence of how crammed to overflowing with striking ideas and impressions a single paragraph could be. (These examples seem as far from my own powers now as when I first set out to emulate them.)

André Bazin's writing taught me how to approach images in film—more than that, convinced me that I'd never really looked at the screen in the course of thousands of hours of movie watching. Andrew Sarris, Robin Wood, and Jonathan Rosenbaum led me to share their passion for the directorial signature and sensibility. Stanley Cavell, William Rothman, Anne Carson, Marina Warner, T. J. Clark, Edward Snow, Michael Wood, Leo Braudy, Gilberto Perez, Helen Vendler, and James Naremore have encouraged me, through the imaginative brilliance of their own responses to film and related arts, to keep faith with the view that traditional aesthetic and humanist concerns continue to matter, and gave me questions about the purposes and effects of the art experience that have nourished me for decades. A number of friends and colleagues have graciously read through one or more of the essays in this book and offered me searching, constructive comments as well as a persuasive level of interest and support. They include Michael Silverblatt, Faye McIntyre, Evelyn Hinz, Lew Layman, Robin Hoople, Carl Matheson, Herb Weil, Charles Baxter, Bart Testa, Brenda Austin-Smith, Pamela Perkins, Chris Johnson, Mark West, Carolyn Williams, Greg Klymkiw, Doug Constable, and Elise Moore. Many excellent editors have significantly improved the quality of the essays through their careful readings, recommendations for revision, and tactful pruning of my stylistic excesses. Obviously, the imperfections that remain are no fault of theirs. I am especially indebted to Richard Poirier (*Raritan*); Ralph Cohen (*New Literary History*); Laurence Goldstein (*Michigan Quarterly Review*); Michael Anderegg (*North Dakota Quarterly*); Ann Martin (*Film Quarterly*); Edgar Dryden and Susan White (*Arizona Quarterly*); Paul Bové (*boundary 2*); Barry Grant (*post script*); and Howard Curle and Eugene Walz, for their invitations to write on Vittorio De Sica and Jean-Claude Lauzon. I wish to thank these editors for permission to reprint the essays that appeared in their journals (or books) in a somewhat different form. Marilyn Loat has typed and proofread many versions of this manuscript, and has displayed boundless patience with me as I returned to her, time and again, with indecipherable handwritten pages of nervous additions and deletions. Helen Osman also agreed, on very short notice and with no adequate incentive, to retype two of the chapters. El Jones prepared a remarkably full index during the busiest time in her academic year. My editors and copy editor at Wayne State University Press—Jane Hoehner, Kristin Harpster, Adela Garcia, and Tammy Oberhausen Rastoder—have been meticulous, patient, supportive, and swift in the final editing and preparation of this book. I am grateful for their sensitive handling of both word and image.

Steve Snyder, Ross McMillan, and Guy Maddin, in addition to being sympathetic readers of most of what I have written, have offered me rich, sustaining friendships over a great many years, with steady infusions of new art enthusiasms and dependably exciting perspectives on old ones. Each has taught me far more than I usually dare to admit, as well as making me laugh easily and often. My students at the University of Manitoba have been a wonderful ongoing reminder of how remarkably divergent viewing and reading experiences of the same texts can be. Trying out my ideas in the classroom (and so often being confronted there with better ones) has been my strongest impetus to return to the writing desk. The student voices in the back of my mind oblige me to exchange, repeatedly, the sense of knowing something beforehand for the preferable spirit of happy "unknowing." Les Brill, in faraway Detroit, has been tirelessly supportive of my scholarly work and was chiefly responsible for my decision to gather my scattered occasional pieces together and make a book of them. Les's lightly worn erudition, his wit, his taste and judgment are everywhere in evidence in his own indispensable studies of Hitchcock and Huston, and continue to push my thinking forward. His numerous acts of kindness have left me rather dazed with gratitude and disbelief.

My beloved, skeptical brother, Tom, has played "William" James to my "Henry" throughout my years as a critic, forever reminding me to come down to earth and reacquaint myself with the sorts of things *real* moviegoers are interested in. Gretchen Toles has provided me with a work space every summer in Hamburg, New York, for as long as I can remember needing one. Insofar as I find room in my writing for an occasional reference to gardens or, more generally, *any* "green thought in a green shade," it reflects her influence. As a child, I was awakened every weekday morning by the thunderous sound of my father George's venerable Royal typewriter one floor above me. I owe to him my early acquired sense of writing as a pleasurable daily activity and, equally important, the value of persisting at it, whatever the difficulties. My grand-mother, Rosena, announced to me when I was five years old that I might follow her example and become a teacher, adding that there were many worse things one could do with one's life. And that was that. My mother, Rose, in addition to being the most generous person I have ever known, instilled in me both her love of reading and her belief that there was nothing in life more exciting and necessary to pursue than ideas. (Except possibly humor.) My movie-enamored, creative, unrepentantly eccentric children, Sam, Rachel, and Thomas, make it possible for me to view Frank Capra's *It's a Wonderful Life* unironically, in every season. As is the custom with acknowledgments, the most important and difficult to express tribute is reserved for last. My partner, Melissa, has made it possible for me to experience the joy and saving power of a great love. All of these essays are continuations of our never-ending discussion of the interrelationship of art, ethics, and the enticing mysteries of human behavior. She is my best friend, my ideal reader, and the one I am most concerned to occasionally surprise or delight with a fresh turn of thought or phrase. Melissa knows the way to the house made of light.

INTRODUCTION:
A HOUSE MADE OF LIGHT

It's extraordinary how one must always shield oneself, against
the world, against oneself, against everything.

She was sleeping with an obstinate expression on her face, as if
she knew that it was light but did not want to wake up.

—Emmanuel Bove, *A Man Who Knows*

When I go to the movies, I eagerly accept the first condition of my
presence there: I am the one in the dark. Moreover, I am choosing to
be in the dark. The film's field of light will, if the encounter proves
a memorable one, vouchsafe glimpses of beauty and seize me with
feeling-filled shapes that I only partially understand and need to bring
closer. From there to here—the screen above, and me, when I can select
my seating, at least slightly below. Part of my critical inquiry involves a
re-creation of the components of my original viewing situation: diffuse-
ness, intensified presence (at key moments), and dependence.

Let me provisionally declare what I take to be the central element
in my most significant film experiences: a condition of healthy psychic
dependence on the work itself. The faces and forms inhabiting certain
films keep turning toward me, demanding fuller, more intimate acknowledgment, like the enigmatic beloved who somehow makes necessary a whole series of sonnets. Here I recklessly throw down the impressionist's tainted gauntlet. I am summoned to draw a series of verbal
sketches, as precise as close study will allow, of what certain images in
a film—bound together in a strangely trustworthy narrative sequence—
are striving to reveal to me. I am most imaginatively receptive to art that
seems, in ways that are worth pursuing, stronger than I am within its
spheres of knowing, and of composed, achieved being. What does form
contribute to this *welcome* seduction by authority? The poet Richard
Wilbur has proposed an apt metaphor for the hidden resources of the
confining structure: the genie's strength comes from being enclosed in
the bottle.

Roslyn (Marilyn Monroe) and Gay (Clark Gable) survey the morning from the doorway of Guido's unfinished house in *The Misfits*.

Surely the best times to offer a defense of art and aesthetic modes of response are times like our own when the aesthetic has fallen into disrepute. I think that it is fair to say that any impassioned talk about art values in the current critical scene is difficult to carry out without a certain degree of defensiveness, and even embarrassment. To declare a continuing trust in what Sven Birkerts calls "the transformative power of artistic vision" is almost tantamount to an admission of theory ignorance, and an accompanying retreat from the daunting complexity of our present cultural situation.[1] Claims for what art can do, unless lengthily qualified and voluntarily quarantined in the run-down tenements assigned to rhetoric and formalism, are bound to be construed as backward-looking. (Formalism now seems as wedded to the word "empty" as peanut butter is to jelly.) Art purchases its suspect authority, we have often been told, by seeking an ahistorical, utopian hiding place from material conditions and the inexhaustibly intriguing flow of power within capitalist culture. Though many critics have periodically attempted to "reclaim the aesthetic" from those who have misunderstood or dismissed its imaginative and ethical uses, it can nonetheless seem

14

disheartening that so little measurable progress has been made in this debate.[2] The fear of being judged conservative, in some culpable sense, infiltrates many critics' attempts to speak forcefully on art's behalf. As with so many of the recurring questions of philosophy, discussions about art keep returning us to the beginnings, to an unsettled wilderness, where very little is named and known for certain, and where there is much disagreement about how to proceed (and, in fact, about the actual value of proceeding). The way to get things right in an argument for art's importance may be to concede, happily, a paucity of secure reference points, and to embrace a permanent doubt about what would be required to get art and the imagination to a state of "rightness."

In an essay appealingly entitled "Not-Knowing," Donald Barthelme argues that what the artist is looking for is "the as-yet unspeakable, the as-yet unspoken" but that, paradoxically, (s)he never loses touch with the external world in this search. "Art is a true account," Barthelme declares with attractive confidence, "of the activity of mind. Because consciousness, in Husserl's formulation, is always consciousness *of* something, art thinks ever of the world, cannot not think of the world, could not turn its back on the world even if it wished to."[3] To imagine "true accounts of the mind" necessarily in and of the world seems to provide so much larger and less encumbered a perspective than that entailed by the disciplinary maxim, "everything is political." Barthelme's affirmations match up with those of the visionary film theorist, André Bazin, whose highest hope for the cinema was that it would find ever more luminous, penetrating ways of giving the world viewed by the camera back to us, and hence restoring our continually endangered sense of living connection to things. He believed in the camera's power to reopen our eyes and ears to mystery, which for him inhered most thrillingly in the spectacle of ordinary existence. Bazin saw the ordinary as a realm forever vanishing to habitual perception, and therefore, even in its incontestable nearness, belonging to the as-yet unseen, the "as-yet unspoken."

The essays collected in this book are the record of an ongoing love affair with the movies from someone whose first allegiance has always been to literature. I am inclined to ignore the standard boundaries separating the various art forms, and those art forms from the domains of psychology and social history.[4] Although all of the essays display a prominent interest in psychology (especially the complex interactions of character and spectator psychology), I never felt that my choice of subject was dictated by the availability within certain films of a fertile psychoanalytic terrain. Moreover, while I am agreeably indebted to the patterns traced out by Freud, Lacan, Kristeva, Melanie Klein, D. W. Winnicott, Ernest Becker, Adam Phillips, Alice Miller, and others who share my preoccupation with the secrets and surprises of human behavior, I am a fickle ally and promiscuous disciple, seemingly incapable of systematizing my own views or of pledging myself, by an act of critical faith, to an already consolidated method.

Few critics presently feel tempted to bring back visions from their experience of art, to document the tumult that comes with being carried away. This task seems to have passed entirely into the realm of advertising—with its formulaic rapture about whatever fantasy object has just been engineered to captivate "young eyeballs." As a means of reconsidering what has been sacrificed, I shall now resurrect the unguarded rhetoric of a nearly forgotten great essayist, R. P. Blackmur, describing an early reading encounter with Henry James. The altar-of-art assumptions underlying this excerpt will undoubtedly bring every sensible objection to the well-known excesses of New Criticism thunderously to mind. Even the most extravagant tributes to beauty drafted in ancient Greece may seem less removed from our current sense of things than this resplendent outpouring:

> The day was hot and muggy, so that from the card catalogue I selected as the most cooling title *The Wings of the Dove*, and on the following morning, a Sunday, even hotter and muggier, I began, and by the stifling midnight had finished my first elated reading of that novel. Long before the end I knew a master had laid hands on me. The beauty of the book bore me up; I was both cool and waking; excited and effortless; nothing was any longer worthwhile and everything had become necessary. A little later, there came outside the patter and cooling of a shower of rain and I was able to go to sleep, both confident and desperate in the force of art.[5]

Blackmur's ecstatic testimony of mental and emotional awakening is echoed by Jim Burden, the narrator of Willa Cather's novel, *My Antonia*, as he tries to describe his new life as a receptive reader: "When one first enters that world [the world of art and ideas] everything else fades for a time, and all that went before is as if it had not been."[6]

One of the more dubious accomplishments of theory over the last thirty years is the triumphant removal of utterances of this sort from serious intellectual debate, and a simultaneous denial of the value of passing on to others the sort of experience which Blackmur and Cather's narrator attest to. Both excerpts are instantly identifiable as florid remnants of what Charles Taylor, in *Sources of the Self,* calls "the Romantic ideal of self-completion through art."[7] We have been trained to regard with suspicion and condescension any transcendent or quasi-theological discourse about the impact of art. We are expected to have outgrown our need for the faith of the high modernist fathers, for whom the aesthetic became an anxious substitute for failed religion. Not only have we been weaned away from any alarming conviction of art's "redemptive" force; we have also surrendered, after a surprisingly brief struggle, our public attachment to that antiquated "self," which once required discovery and slow, arduous realization. At this juncture, the astonishingly porous and malleable term "culture" engages the mapping energies and imaging power of the most adventurous, forward-looking critics. Only yesterday, it seems, "ideology" was omnipresent, but it has gracefully ceded most of its territory to culture, possibly because ideology could not quite shed its affiliations with a now too debilitated and static Marxism. (When a god decisively fails, what remains most visible is a rusting theological apparatus.) The term "power" still retains its aura and allure, but to perform well on the data-glutted playing field of culture, it is presently selling off its stock in the Foucault panopticon, or all-purpose surveillance tower. If "power" is to survive as a key term in the cultural studies glossary, Foucault's estate must be deprived of ownership. Finally, the role of "film," in this aggressive exchange district of terms, has also been devalued, out of misplaced respect for the new godhead of commodity and information culture. The word "product," which twenty years ago was industry insider shorthand for movie marketing, has recently emerged as an almost benevolent term for general use, less pretentious and worrisomely elitist than "film." It feels right, somehow, to embrace film's status as "product" without further fuss, instead of holding onto "film" and its messy entanglement with the lost cause of art. "From the *respect* paid to property [and, I would add, commodity]," Mary Wollstonecraft acutely noted in *A Vindication of the Rights of Woman,* "flow, as from a poisoned fountain, most of the evils and vices which render this world such a dreary place to the contemplative mind" (emphasis mine).[8]

I wish to return now to the Blackmur quote and raise some questions about its assumptions and implications, questions that bear directly on the approach to film I have taken throughout this book of essays. First of all, is the experience Blackmur describes, however associated with a particular phase in the history of literary criticism, one that we would recognize as possibly true? Did the act of reading Henry James's novel *The Wings of the Dove* actually unsettle, disorient, and overwhelm Blackmur in the way that he claimed? If so, is the kind of revelation that he received (and was susceptible to receiving) merely carrying forward the customary—and perhaps insidious—work of cultural construction? Had Blackmur possessed in 1921, the year he discovered Henry James, a more theory-based understanding of literature, one which managed to safeguard him against the storm of sensations and painfully vivid impressions that comprised his highly "subjective" experience, would he have been better off missing it? Are there still a large number of readers (and, by extension, filmgoers) who have comparable experiences, and if so, how might they and we best deal with them? Is it possible, perhaps even beneficial, for a culture effectively to eradicate such experiences, by no longer sanctioning them or encouraging the development of a vocabulary, a set of shared reference points, that might make the "awakening" to art intelligible or valuable to others? Is Blackmur less capable of interpreting Henry James thoughtfully and precisely by virtue of starting his relationship with the writer as a willing, grateful apprentice? "Long before the end I knew that a master had laid hands on me." Does the full acceptance of the novelist's authority blunt Blackmur's critical judgment, limit his imaginative responses, or demonstrably impair his "instruments of reading"? Does acceptance deprive one of the freedom to be skeptical?

I consider it always a piece of rare good fortune to find a narrative that I trust enough or experience so strongly that I desire to submit, for the happy time being, to its authority. As a reader of film—or literature or painting—it is never the task I set myself to *master* the narrative I am interpreting. It is more a matter of trusting the film to show me things—in its own terms, terms that I do not initially have at my disposal, living as they do within the form of the work itself. One views these terms, from an enchanted distance, as an initiate. As Peter Brooks states in his essay, "What Happened to Poetics?": "One cannot claim to speak for the text until one has attempted to let the text speak through oneself."[9] The trust I'm capable of, admittedly, is seldom absolute. If it were, I would find it next to impossible to interrogate the work with much cogency or flexibility. Moreover, I have no ability (and no desire) to rule out of bounds whatever I think I know about a work's larger context. (The attempt to keep art and culture separate, by denying the usefulness of each other's language, strikes me as the joint madness of New Criticism and cultural studies.) Yet context remains secondary for me to the concentrated act of engagement with resonant particulars, and with the attempt to fathom—without finalizing—the articulate, mysterious form of the work as a whole. I admire what Edward Snow has to say on this topic. He is confronting the unevadable contextual milieu of the painter Bruegel and wondering how that milieu can most productively enter into his slow, deliberately inconclusive book-length meditation on one Bruegel canvas, *Children's Games*. He decides that context is best treated as a "complicating factor, a fund of possible connotations rather than a controlling frame."[10] Snow also draws attention to a remarkable endorsement by Nietzsche of slow reading, of the process-oriented gathering of "particular knowledge" as one endeavors to move, with expansive empathy, *inside* an artist's form. Here are the most provocative lines from Nietzsche's 1856 preface to *Daybreak*: "this art does not so easily get anything done, it teaches to read *well*, that is, to read slowly, deeply, looking cautiously before and aft, with reservations, with doors left open, with delicate eyes and fingers."[11]

What is the appropriate spectator balance of trust and skepticism, no easier to achieve perhaps in our relation to art than in our relation to other people? I would respond to the oft-repeated fear of giving art more right and room to control us than it deserves by citing a passage from the Mary Gaitskill story, "Orchid": "And that feeling of not quite trusting but at the same time trying to trust is the best."[12] Can one learn anything useful about trust from those earliest film spectators who were so unsure about the limits of visual representation, so credulous about the power of images to reach out and penetrate them that they cowered before a train rapidly approaching a camera? Folklore tells us that many were convinced they would be run over if they didn't clear out of the train's path. Perhaps the recurring impulse to go to the movies is sustained by something as primitive as the fear of being "run over," and the desire for it—placing oneself in the path of forces that may prove larger than one's capacity and need for self-protection. Movies are arguably one of the last refuges of the sublime in a culture progressively deprived of ways to express its longings for awe, nobility, beauty, terror. The sublime emerges not from a rational contemplation of what we already know, in its familiar order, but from a productive confusion of the senses. The power the sublime manifests may be greeted by a not altogether unwelcome recognition that we are made smaller by what we behold. The moving picture screen has so often been described as "haunted" because film so readily involves a lost-in-the-woods dimension, conjoined with an experience of Presence—of being intensely present at or in something that transcends us—that exceeds what the steady work of daily living brings to light.

We can fully comprehend and endorse the view that film is nothing but representation and "feigning" and that our engagement with its sounds and images is always mediated, but still. . . . But still. The "still" allows for the fact that we do not remain steadily fixed in one identity position as we observe the swift moving image stream in front of us. How easy it is for the adult to metamorphose into an unrestrained child, heedlessly slipping from the safe bank into the strong current and being borne along, who knows where? And I think we can become this wayward and helpless child without instantly punishing him with the too knowing labels of "regression" and "masochism." I prefer a description of the child psyche which is more attuned to the experience of being alternately confident and adrift, powerful and purely vulnerable, in response to the turnings and returnings of a forcefully composed film.

The Portuguese poet Luiz de Camoes speaks the truth of film, with appropriate ambiguity, centuries in advance of the medium's arrival: "A truth there is that moves in things, / living in the visible and the invisible."[13] Film's most arresting claims to truth, it seems to me, are inseparable from the facts of its nature: a fixed, enclosed form that is experienced always through the inescapable force of movement. However sedate the rhythm of a film, its meaning is formed, processed, and imaginatively recovered in the constancy of motion. Image particulars, unlike poetic phrases on the page, declare their presence and vanish; they do not mean to stand still, not for long, seldom long enough to let us be clear about what exactly we've taken in and how it has affected us. The movement of film energizes us by spreading us out over an ever-widening surface, spatial and temporal. We feel in the presence of film, not altogether inaccurately, that we have gained a greater proficiency at being many places, many things at once. We are both Proteus and the nimble proprietor of seven league boots. A successful film creates a beautiful tension between pleasurable dispersals of the spectator self and abrupt summonings to convergence. Astonishingly potent and confounding emotional effects can be built up in the space of a few film moments, as compressed as a perfect line of verse, and then promptly dissolved back into a wider, more diffuse landscape of feeling—where we can again flow freely, relieved of the burdens of this prior tightness.

What the spectator already knows, and naturally relies upon, going into any film is, of course, the history of his previous engagements with the medium, and the cultural signs everywhere inscribed in it. This preliminary knowledge is by no means negligible. We cannot watch a film without drawing ceaselessly upon our familiarity with movie conventions, and our highly developed intuitions about the narrative patterns these conventions will most likely generate. Nevertheless, I would argue that the function of conventions is to prepare the ground for what the filmmaker aspires to bring to light; convention is not itself the sum total of revelation. Film satisfies and awakens us most fully when it outwits the conventions it employs, finding means to go beyond what conventions can be said to "know" and what we know in our settled relation to them. Something singular and arresting is suddenly at work in an actor's expression or gesture or in the words that are spoken or left unspoken; something in the look or sound of an environment, of a movement of a tree in the wind *just then*, or the perfectly timed intrusion of a mirror reflection or window or doorway into a space that had previously appeared sufficient to contain what was going on. This is the art language of cinema, composed—as art language always is—of shifty, perishable particulars, often as difficult to catch and properly engage with as our own sensations, feelings, memories, and continents of amnesia.

The charge that is always brought against talk that goes too far athwart the presumably solid basics of conventions and genres, of production history and "collective" reception—in other words, talk about anything that resists sober categorization or deflating (because invariably skeptical) cultural commentary—is that we have succumbed to subjectivity of an extreme and unproductive sort. The subjective "elements" in our film viewing are unproductive, critically speaking, because there is little likelihood of their being felt and evaluated by other spectators in the same manner. What hope is there of a meaningful consensus? Placing primary emphasis on aesthetic perception, many would argue, serves the cause of mystification or promotes a naive indulgence in reveries that consecrate the individual sensibility. Instead one could (should) be addressing the pressing needs and dismaying defects of the always ailing body politic. There is a world of lies to dismantle, and so little time. Recall the rhetoric and faith of soviet artists immediately following the Russian Revolution. Can we not detect an echo of their commitments in the present veneration of culture as the source of all pertinent meaning? Let us "overthrow the old worlds of art and create a new world, a new building, new structures of a new culture, a culture for all, in accordance with the new forms of the commune" (M. Kunin, *"Partiinost* in Art," 1920). Or, in the pithy phrase of a collectivist street flyer: "Direct your creative work in line with Economy!" (And your analytic work as well.)[14] Once again the quarrel appears to be between those who feel that art is there to be interpretively controlled or denied its distinctiveness (in either case, put in its place) and those who feel that art is entitled to whatever "higher" authority we freely grant it. I know that the word "freely" is always under suspicion. How much should we guard ourselves against the myriad things that we regularly experience in art but truly *cannot* say that we know? How are such things to be accounted for, and properly valued?

I have returned most often in my writing on film to the work of Alfred Hitchcock. What is endlessly instructive about Hitchcock is the paradoxical fate of his fierce commitment to the idea of control—both at the level of form and of spectator response. The enormously diverse critical commentary that continues to be produced in response to his narratives would suggest that spectators have found remarkable freedom to maneuver and generate fresh discoveries within his tight, "mechanical" designs. No film artist has ever expended more labor and ingenuity than Hitchcock in preparing a space for the spectator within each meticulously designed scene, the purpose of which space is to accurately gauge and carefully manipulate the spectator's emotions. But so many separate registers of feeling are accommodated by Hitchcock's imaginatively rich contexts that the viewer determined to proceed slowly scarcely knows where to begin. Moment by moment shifts in emotional emphasis and in the linkage with character point-of-view can remarkably complicate Hitchcock's apparently clear-cut narrative logic. The more we attend to our responses and what has possibly produced them, the more Hitchcock's guidance seems to multiply possibilities rather than reduce them. The deceptive clarity of his narrative intentions— signaled by the ABC diagrammatic precision of his shot progressions— keeps altering and realtering as our gaze follows his. (Perhaps this is what every film we deem interesting as art has the cunning to do: to slip away from the sense of completed pattern we provisionally create for it and assign to it, in our quest for meaning. A memorable film unravels enough of our interpretive design when we go back to it so that we can be lured once more into a naive submission to its power.)

Each of my three essays on Hitchcock, for all of the continuity I at one time imagined giving them, reveals conspicuously divergent images of the Hitchcock entity and of what his narrative forms enable us to bring, morally and emotionally, to life. Hitchcock is also prodigiously gifted at turning, again and again, in the shocking span of an instant, even the most theatrically exaggerated, patently "unreal" situations to an imperatively personal mode of address. Any figure in his designs can emerge, for a brief interval, as a tantalizing, credible "you" and then regain the face of a stranger.

Henry James, as obsessed as Hitchcock with shifting perspective, has famously described, in his preface to *The Portrait of a Lady*, the "house of fiction" as a dwelling with countless "possible windows" to accommodate a host of dissimilar artists and their widely divergent points of view on the "human scene."[15] James is also describing the architecture of his own fiction, though he doesn't press the connection here. What better way to encapsulate the Jamesian situation than to imagine a set of characters, mute and still, within window apertures, intently observing and speculating on an ambiguous action unfolding at twilight in a spacious garden? It is difficult to ascertain, from James's elaborate rendering of the double metaphor, where we, as readers, are best situated—inside or outside the house? Is the position we seek one of intimate proximity to the characters and artist arranger peering out, or one of detachment, where we stand at some remove from the house proper, and calmly contemplate the composite arrangement of the figures (characters and artist alike) in their private window compartments? Perhaps the confusion of our placement in the passage is James's most finely conceived effect. Readers are continually in both positions, as well as in others "not quite" specified. Our shifts from inside to out and back resemble the apparitional film technique known as the lap dissolve. We are still here, but already halfway there, and somehow the transition feels effortless.

Given the number of important houses (usually family dwellings) that I almost compulsively attend to in each of my film essays—from the cottage in *Random Harvest,* to the homes of Marge Gunderson, Boo Radley, and Norman Bates—I would like to propose a modified Jamesian metaphor for the House of Film. This house faces us, from a traversable distance, in a form both uncannily familiar and estranged. It is equally connected to what we already think we know, given what we have been and done in that "plural being" that is our scattered family origin, and what we do not know, by virtue of all we have still not confronted and achieved in separation from it, "on our own." The house of film is a frame we long to enter in the spirit of homecoming, but that we cannot possess any more securely than the lost home of our beginnings. The interior of the dwelling is everything that film can reveal to us by way of *presence,* privileged enclosure, and the successive vanishings that are always the cost of film's forward movement. Viewed in certain lights, it seems clear that the house is situated, as *Random Harvest* shows us, in the suburbs of death, where one cannot linger too long or form too strong an attachment without becoming a shade oneself. What the house of film withholds from us is exactly congruent with what it so effortlessly and profusely yields, as we caress its particulars: what we know and what we desire. Is this habitable frame a utopia? Yes, but only if one keeps postponing the possession date and the moment of true arrival. Like Marilyn Monroe's Roslyn in *The Misfits*, we keep crossing and recrossing the threshold by way of a makeshift front step, exclaiming each time with a mixture of playfulness and wonder, "I can go in and I can come out; I can go in and I can come out." Or we are Giuletta Masina's Cabiria in *Nights of Cabiria*, trying to find a point of entry to a home we claim as ours but that is senselessly locked against us; someone we loved has, in true-to-form betrayal, stolen our keys. The truth of our placement, when film works as art, is a continuous sense of drawing nearer to a place we seek, with some last vital task or piece of business not yet accounted for. Any moment, perhaps, things will be sorted out, and we can finally set our bags down. But until then, let us keep ourselves in a fine pitch of readiness. The house lives, as we do in relation to it, as the imagination's movement between the visible and invisible. It all looks very familiar, but we're sure we've never been there.

I

SENTIMENTS OF
WAR AND PEACE

1

Being Well-Lost in Film

What we call place is only that detail of it which we understand to be ourselves.

—Eavan Boland

Longing, we say, because desire is full of endless distances.
—Robert Hass, "Meditation at Lagunitas"

Greta Garbo, in *Queen Christina* (1933), is silently exploring the upstairs room of the snowbound cottage where she and John Gilbert have become lovers. She rests her hand on the mantel by the fireplace, then touches a candlestick. Peering into a mirror, she discovers a small reflection of Gilbert, who is reclining on the floor and looking back at her with a mixture of delight and wonder. As she continues her slow journey around the room, we see her contemplating and stroking a variety of objects: an unopened oval box, a spinning wheel, and a cascade of flax, each of which shimmers under the light of her gaze with a fairy-tale delicacy. Now she moves to a large curtained bed (the room's center of gravity) and spreads herself full length across it, pressing her cheek against a pillow and absorbing its sensations in a close-up view so profusely unguarded that one feels momentarily stunned by the breach of a lover's privacy.

Garbo rises, drawn to the faded painting of a Madonna on the wall, and takes it in as her finger comes to rest on it. Her attention returns to the bed. She leans forward to embrace the bedpost in a transport of melancholy joy, closing her eyes when her face makes contact with it. As long as this object bears her weight, as long as it confirms her presence here, there is no deception or obstacle to love. After watching this lengthy ritual unfold in perfect, wordless contentment, Garbo's lover finally asks her, with such gentleness that he does not dissolve the spell she has woven: "What are you doing?" Her reply is both revelation and confirmation of the truth her gestures have already spoken. "I have

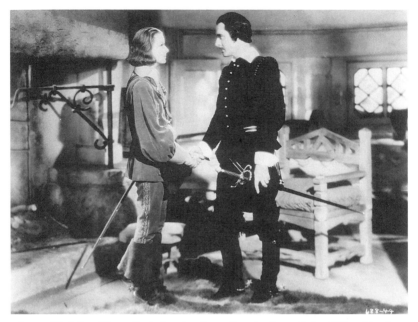

Queen Christina (Greta Garbo) saying farewell to her lover (John Gilbert) in the room she has committed to memory. (*Queen Christina*)

been memorizing the room. In the future, in my memory, I shall live a great deal in this room."

What must be clearer to those of us who see *Queen Christina* now than to its original audiences in 1933 is the fixed quality of Garbo's life in that chamber. The details of her existence there are established with a finality far beyond the capacity of even Christina's formidable romantic memory. Whenever an unspoiled print of this film is screened, Garbo's upstairs bedroom returns to its viewers intact, and she once again embarks on her enchanted tour of it, in an order that never varies or grows weary of itself. What does such effortless repeatability in film signify?

The idea of fated, endless repetition is commonly associated with the realm of curses, and terrible acts of propitiation. In contrast, one exact repetition of a perfect moment or memory-consecrated experience seems a reasonable thing to hope for; it has the quality of miracle. An extraordinary isolated experience sometimes leads us to beg for recurrence as the only way to reduce (or explain) its power over us. The

The Monster offers Mary a flower as part of their "forbidden game" in James Whale's *Frankenstein*.

structures of folktales, myths, and even ordinary fictions have nurtured our belief in the possible retrieval of essential moments from time's heartless, chaotic flow. Such moments achieve their poetic truth as they are relived by a fortunate hero in the precise form of their first occurrence. However, even comic literature is wary of a second repetition. The potent logic of romantic return and reenactment does not easily accommodate a character's desire to make a *third* visit to a scene of past happiness. At what point does one's need to go back become a dishonorable sign of weakness? The determination to settle for nothing less (or different from) what one has already had is a condition akin to madness. It is isolating, in a frightening sense. I am reminded of Sisyphus eternally rolling his rock; perfect repetition, turned meaningless, has become a tragic ordeal, his punishment for inexpiable crimes against the gods. The hell of Sisyphus is one where repetition has put an end to singularity as an attribute of experience. Memory has no function there. Perhaps Sisyphus should be understood as one who has sinned

29

against memory. What might an ethics of memory require of us? Being true to one's memory could mean perhaps to have faith in the sufficiency of the unrepeatable moment. If an experience returns to us to be relived, it cannot be the result of an impatient or desperate willing. The consciousness must always be taken by surprise if a lived action is to gain a second, deeper life in memory.

What sort of habitation then is possible in film, where perfect repeatability is not a curse but the inevitable—indeed, natural—way of things? The emotional power of Garbo's efforts to memorize her room in *Queen Christina* arises in part, I think, from our sense of their beautiful redundancy. The camera has already sealed the chamber and the two lovers into its imperishable frame of light and shadow. While Garbo mourns the imminent loss of the room's presence, the fact of its necessary vanishing, the camera is claiming the space and all of its visualized contents as its own. The camera remembers in advance of Garbo's moving pledge that her own memory will be equal to the challenge of keeping everything just as it was (is).

Film scenes do not, as a rule, so openly acknowledge that the movement of time, and hence the movement toward death, have been suspended in them. On the one hand, film documents a time that was once immediate (we can imagine a "historic" moment of shooting) but is now lost, except for the photographic remains. Time leaves its mark on deteriorating, heavily spliced prints of once whole films; colors inevitably fade, the texture and gradations of light and shadow sadly diminish. On the other hand, the time the camera has captured through the sorcery of its gaze *does* live on as a continuous present. Film is a place where fixity flows, visibly contradicting at every moment the fact that what happens now has already happened, that what is attended to with such palpitating force is over and gone. The figures that "live" on film, having no burden of memory to carry beyond the instant of recording, do not succumb, like Pirandello's six characters, to the fatigue or recriminations of the half-real. There is no chance of their coming to recognize themselves (over time) as mere images. It would be more accurate to characterize each living photograph as an ever-deepening thought of belonging, by necessity, to one set of appearances and no other.

As a popular film ages, it loses its easy continuity with the world of its audience. The many taken-for-granted points of contact and of automatic communication can become blurred, and perhaps fade away altogether. A movie is eventually cut loose from its grounding in familiar, convention-defined experience. In their first release, most movies aspire to leap the divide separating the film image from our mind's eye. In effect, they reach out, and come to us. In a matter of years, however, screen images can seem to reverse direction—receding further and further into a palpable condition of temporality, as though more timid recipients of light. The spectator must work harder to clear a path to the "interior" of older film images, entering them somewhat contemplatively and self-consciously, over a felt (albeit precious) distance.

One is more likely to assimilate movie narratives of the 1930s, say, fragmentarily, as they alternately close off and open themselves to us. Time is like a veil which obscures certain scenes to the point of unintelligibility, and then magically grows transparent in the presence of a setting, exchange of dialogue, series of gestures, or face that somehow feels more intensely illuminated. There is a special salutary shock of pleasure when a moment of film penetrates us with undiluted force and immediacy from a world that has so irrevocably passed from view. One sifts through the celluloid ruins like an archaeologist, searching for the living artifact that releases what is gone from the shadows and provides connection. The found link or "spot of time" (which, of course, sometimes lasts for an entire film) makes room for us in a world where we are utterly unknown and where our presence can alter nothing; it is as though the possibility of our coming into being is something a movie is capable of dreaming.

Garbo, in the famous closing shot of *Queen Christina,* stands at a ship's prow looking out over the sea as she absorbs the knowledge of her lover's death. His body lies behind her; she has turned away from it, just as she had earlier turned away from his resting form in the cottage bedroom so that she could find her love reflected in all the consecrated objects of their sanctuary. Now, as the narrative ends, the camera gradually closes in on her impassive, wind-stroked face until it fills the screen. Her expression is unreadable, and our steadily enlarging view of it oddly forestalls emotional identification even as it strengthens the invitation to probe. Her gaze recedes, in other words, in the act of moving toward us. The camera possesses and relinquishes the image of Garbo in the same motion. It is perhaps the archetypal face of memory we are confronted with, striving to complete its journey back to where it came from. Garbo's face lingers, as Roland Barthes once described it, between mortal flesh and a Platonic idea of it.[1] Her features here seem on the verge of surrendering their protected status as memory image for something more tangible but also more perilous. Garbo reverses the usual direction of film metamorphosis, which elevates flesh out of the mutable real into the stasis of dream. Her gaze in this shot appears to begin outside of time, then wills a voyage back into it. In such moments as this one and the earlier memory scene in the bedroom, one of the secrets of cinema time—what it means to "live" in the image—is *almost* revealed to us. Thus we are given a perfect illustration of Jorge Luis Borges's definition of the aesthetic phenomenon: "this imminence of a revelation which does not occur."[2]

Garbo's unyielding expression seems already to be repeating itself (happening over and over again) while she stands motionless, an actress waiting to be photographed. As we try to find the person within the face, we are thrust back by the invincible (and plainly visible) fact that Garbo's appearance is a likeness, not a substance. What is the precise relation of this likeness to the woman who bears it, and who is vanishing before our eyes as the image conveys her to us? Either the image mourns the face that it leaves behind, or the face looks out on a world where the image cannot follow, and gives itself to realities, including death, which the image (already memory) cannot know. Or both things at once.

In the central episode of Rudyard Kipling's 1904 short story, "Mrs Bathurst," a moving picture, one of the novelty exhibits in a small traveling circus, is viewed by a group of British seamen on shore leave in Cape Town. The film, entitled *Home and Friends,* consists of a random assemblage of familiar urban scenes photographed in England. One of the men in the group, a warrant officer named Vickery, has already seen the movie the previous night. He has brought an acquaintance with him to confirm his belief that a woman they have both known in New Zealand, Mrs. Bathurst, makes a brief appearance in a segment filmed at a railway station. Vickery, who is white with apprehension before the screening begins, does not tell his comrade, Pyecroft, in advance about the woman he expects him to recognize. The two men sit together in the front row of the small theater. This is how Pyecroft recalls the film years later, while trying to piece together the odd facts of Vickery's tragic story:

> "We saw London Bridge an' so forth an' so on, and it was most interestin'. I'd never seen it before. You 'eard a little dynamo like buzzin, but the pictures were the real thing—alive and movin'."
>
> "I've seen 'em," said Hooper. "Of course they [movies] are taken from the very thing itself—you see."
>
> "Then the Western Mail came in to Paddin'ton on the big magic lantern sheet. First we saw the platform empty an' the porters standin' by. Then the engine come

in, head on, and the women in the front row jumped: she headed so straight. Then the doors opened and the passengers came out and the porters got the luggage—just like life. Only—only when anyone came down too far towards us that was watchin', they walked right out o' the picture, so to speak. I was 'ighly interested, I can tell you. So were all of us. I watched an old man with a rug 'oo'd dropped a book an' was tryin' to pick it up, when quite slowly, from be'ind two porters—carryin' a little reticule an' lookin' from side to side—comes our Mrs Bathurst. There was no mistakin' the walk in a hundred thousand. She come forward—right forward—she looked out straight at us with that blindish look that Pritch alluded to. She walked on and on till she melted out of the picture—like—like a shadow jumpin' over a candle."[3]

As soon as the film ends, Vickery asks Pyecroft if he would come to see it again with him the following evening, "'Willingly,' I says, 'it's like meetin' old friends.' 'Yes,' he says, openin' his watch, 'very like. It will be four-and-twenty hours less four minutes before I see her again.'"[4] Vickery spends the rest of the night making a tour of the Cape Town pubs with Pyecroft in tow, scarcely saying a word as he drinks, perspires, and attempts to escape the pain of consciousness. For five consecutive evenings, Vickery and Pyecroft return to the movie theater and wait for Mrs. Bathurst to reappear, then complete their ritual by getting drunk. Utterly taciturn for most of these outings, Vickery is briefly roused to attention once during their final late-night walk when Pyecroft directly alludes to the woman in the film: "'I wonder what she's doin' in England,' I says. 'Don't it seem to you she's lookin' for somebody?' That was in the Gardens again, with the South-Easter blowin' as we were makin' our desperate round. 'She's lookin' for me,' he says, stoppin' dead under a lamp."[5] When the traveling circus leaves Cape Town the next day, taking the movie with it, Vickery becomes a deserter, and there are rumors that he has journeyed "up country" to find the circus and see Mrs. Bathurst one more time before he too disappears altogether.

Kipling wrote this story just after the turn of the century, when moving pictures were still so fresh an addition to our cultural life that he had no need to reconstruct the awe or disorientation of its first audiences. Movies were in no sense domesticated yet, nor were they generally regarded as casual diversions. The nature of the illusion required a preliminary explanation, of the sort that the characters in "Mrs Bathurst" excitedly provide. What is repeatedly insisted upon is that the pictures are taken from the "real thing," and that they are "alive and movin'." Kipling seizes upon the common early response to film as an extension of the necromancer's art. Mrs. Bathurst seems conjured up on the "magic lantern sheet" like the spirit of a departed loved one at a seance. The setting Kipling provides for this alarming disinterment of the "dead" past is a circus tent, exotically planted in a seaport at the southern tip of Africa, half a world removed from London (*Home and Friends*). The movie has, in effect, pursued Vickery to the ends of the earth, and there confronted him with a repeating image of a lost woman (one he has presumably betrayed, perhaps abandoned) searching for him.

The question that Kipling most vividly puts before us is why Vickery returns to the movie theater night after night, to behold the same sequence of images. Vickery strives to keep his mind empty or numb (that is to say, free of competing actualities) in preparation for the "perhaps forty-five seconds" each night when he can observe "Mrs B. walking down toward (him) with that *blindish* look in her eyes an' the reticule in her hand." Does Vickery believe that his faithful attendance might somehow make a difference to the outcome of the film? Perhaps he has persuaded himself that he can prove something to the image of Mrs. Bathurst by waiting so patiently for her "arrival" at the station, even under these impossible circumstances. Vickery both knows and doesn't know that *Home and Friends* is a movie, that its progress is as fixed as the hours of the day, that Mrs. Bathurst will never be at liberty to perform other actions on screen than those he has already memorized. And yet why does she walk so purposefully toward the camera and look toward it, as though she could see the audience facing her? Her seeming search of her immediate surroundings, with her recognizable "blindish" expression, includes, potentially, everything in front of her. Before "melting" out of the picture light, she has, like Garbo's Christina, grown to immense size in the frame, so that Vickery, for an agonizingly prolonged moment, can be engulfed by the totality of her presence. Mrs. Bathurst, in Anne Hollander's words, "comes to claim (this) viewer, acknowledging no barrier between the action and his inner life."[6]

The random bits of filmed reportage at the train station become a linear narrative in response to Vickery's emotional recognition of one of the disembarking passengers. Everything preceding her appearance in the film seems to transcend mere contingency, and to assume a fated order, like the steps in a classical tragedy. The arrival of the train at Paddington now must take place at its appointed time if she is to materialize. The doors opening and the porters handling the luggage are electrically charged anticipatory movements, a strategic prelude to an eagerly awaited star's entrance on the scene. Even the congestion on the platform is metaphorically linked to the idea of a gradually revealed central personage; the other passengers serve as collective camouflage whose sole function is to mask, then disclose, the figure that gives them meaning.

Immediately prior to Mrs. Bathurst's theatrically unobtrusive first appearance in the frame, slowly coming into view behind two porters, the camera seems to attend with heightened specificity to the tiny drama of an old man with a rug, trying to pick up a book that he'd dropped. This old man achieves an identity apart from that of the crowd by virtue of his picturesque mishap and gesture of recovery, but he is still more sharply defined by the proximity of his accident to the moment that Mrs. Bathurst finally emerges, almost by sleight-of-hand, behind him. It is as though we are *meant* to be watching the gentleman bending over to retrieve his book so that we will be all the more surprised by her sudden illumination in our midst. She is *already* at the center of things when the viewer notices her, stepping out of nowhere to fill the frame. The old man's dropping and picking up of the book, because they repeated themselves with haunting exactness in every screening just before Mrs. Bathurst is unmistakably revealed, seem to be tied to her presence by intractable laws of cause and effect. Because the old man "remembers" to perform his gesture just then, Mrs. Bathurst is permitted to find her predestined place in the narrative, and thus come into being. If, however, this nameless stranger fails on one occasion to drop his book and continues walking, the world flickering on the magic lantern sheet would perhaps lose touch with what inevitably follows it. Mrs. Bathurst is not to be released from her place of concealment in a world which fails to include a falling book.

The return of the woman's searching form asserts, with equal force, its necessity and perfect arbitrariness. Her arrival seems imbued with the one-chance-in-a-million flavor of things ungraspably fortuitous: the result of a recording camera's improbable conjunction with one capricious sliver of temporal reality. And yet, Vickery's transfixed gaze tells him that everything, simply everything, has conspired to bring Mrs. Bathurst back to him in the unconditional form of this almost living encounter. He watches the movie as though its contents were a life-and-death riddle, the solution of which might remove the scales from Mrs. Bathurst's eyes, so she could acknowledge him.

She must repeat her search at the station until she discovers the absent loved one she expects to meet there. Vickery, in turn, keeps coming back to the film in the moving, desperate hope that his continued "keeping of his appointment" may gradually reduce to nothing the duplicitous time and space that divide him from her wandering shade. Vickery perhaps believes that his chastened, purified vision will at last achieve the power to *heal* the suffering that Mrs. Bathurst's image conveys to him. His eyes must, against all logic, do the work of the helpless hands, which can only reach out to the air. It is the eyes which must carry the whole of Vickery into the image if he is ever to touch her face, make restitution, console her.

The films that make a difference to us seldom begin at their beginning. Like Vickery, we are passively absorbed in a spectacle that corresponds, in all sorts of *external* ways, to life; then suddenly we are arrested, however briefly, by experience of another order, which somehow manages to invade and unsettle our privacy. An image or scene *demands* a stronger response from us, and we are helpless in the face of it because we don't know what such a response means or entails. Movies typically afford the viewer the pleasure of feeling secretly curtained off from both the "real world" and her own pressing difficulties. In place of the tense entanglements and discords of these realms, from which the viewer longs to gain some distance, comes the joy of furtive, risk-free possession. One does not simply observe the framed space of an effective movie fantasy, one aspires to *own* it, to be the lord of the dominion, as a child owns the secret spaces she reserves for play. However, when the movie image asserts with unaccustomed force its own claims over *you* (shattering the illusion that the movie is obedient to your will, and comfortably knowable), the terms of ownership shift. The generalized "you" of the audience (what Norma Desmond in *Sunset Boulevard* calls "you beautiful people out there in the dark") suddenly becomes a specific vulnerable you—addressed with the imperative intimacy of a lover's "I know you."

Vickery loses himself to the movie *Home and Friends* the moment he is convinced of Mrs. Bathurst's presence in it. He struggles to regain possession of the film experience by making Mrs. Bathurst's appearance the center of the movie's "story," though objectively it has no more weight or narrative significance than any of the film's other casually linked visual episodes. Another spectator might not recall seeing the woman at all; his memory might be of the train entering the station, or even the old man dropping and picking up the book. But Vickery henceforth can only conceive of the film as the story of Mrs. Bathurst's sad, ongoing search for him. It is, of course, possible (even likely) that Mrs. Bathurst is *not* looking for him at the train station, and that he occupies no space in her thoughts at this time. But Vickery cannot be deterred from making himself (the fact of his physical presence in the theater) the proper ending of the story—the happy resolution of her quest—as his obsessive vigil at every screening attests.

Similarly, whenever any of us encounters a fragment of film that penetrates some orphaned region of the heart—leaving us helpless because our swift, extreme, involuntary internalization of it precedes an act of conscious recognition—our natural defense is to devise a story within the movie's larger, overt story to come to terms with it. As we elaborate it further after the screening, this second story imperceptibly fuses with the larger story until it distortedly becomes one with it. In telling the plot of the film to someone else, one will find that all narrative roads lead naturally toward or away from the scene that forms one's primary memory image of the whole. The imagination gradually transforms the crucial segment of film, as the latter works its way closer and closer to the emotional memory that the scene echoes and elusively embodies. If considerable time elapses before a second viewing of the film, or if there is no second viewing, everything extraneous to the story arising from the spectator's psychic need is likely to fall away. The actual narrative is frequently supplemented (or even replaced) by invented scenes and details that support the logic of one's private vision. These imaginary segments can easily achieve a clarity in our memory far beyond anything that the film literally contains. How startling it is to discover that what one most vividly remembers from a movie is missing not only from other people's versions of it but also from the work itself. It seems unthinkable that we could have dreamed something so unambiguously clear and present into existence.

In Victor Erice's 1973 film, *Spirit of the Beehive,* a little girl named Ana attends a screening of *Frankenstein* in a remote Spanish village in Castille. World War II has just begun, though Spain is not officially involved. The ghastly outcome of Spain's own recently concluded civil war seems somehow continuous with the European war raging just beyond the country's borders. *Frankenstein* has entered the village by cinema truck, and the ritual unloading of the tin cases bearing the magic reels is an occasion for excited conjecture by a group of children, who appear to have been waiting for hours for the truck's arrival. This movie, or almost any movie, offers them astonishing proof of the wonders available in the larger world. The boundaries and possibilities of that unknown reality far from their isolated village are so mysterious that even a stylized horror film, worn and faded from a decade of circulation, furnishes plausible documentation of how life is being lived elsewhere. As a woman from the village writes to her long absent lover, "the tidings we get from the outside world are so scarce and so confusing." The world *must* contain places less paralyzed than this one, less dominated by an atmosphere of privation and defeat.

We catch our first glimpse of Ana, the child protagonist of the narrative, during the showing of *Frankenstein* in the village hall. Ana sits next to her slightly older sister in an audience made up entirely of women and children. She is not even a conspicuous face in the crowd for us until after the film has begun. The camera is gradually drawn to her as though in response to her singularly intense absorption in the monster's plight. Because we have no prior associations with her life outside this darkened, makeshift theater, her psyche (her imaginative existence) seems somehow to be born here, at this instant, just as the monster undergoes his abrupt, unnatural "birthing" in the doctor's laboratory.

On-screen, a father who might have come from a village like Ana's urges his young daughter, Mary, to go and play with her cat while he returns to his work. Father and daughter clearly have a close relationship. The child asks her father if he will be back soon and bids him an affectionate goodbye. He, in turn, smiles at her from behind the gate that separates them before he departs. Even when he tells her to behave herself, his voice is kind and not at all reserved or authoritarian. Mary immediately walks to the riverbank, which is but a short distance from her home, and sits down to play. There are bushes along the path, which begin to part as soon as she passes them. Frankenstein's monster emerges from his hiding place, and the child, who is holding a flower, looks at him, strangely unafraid. She approaches him without hesitation, and after telling him her name, takes him by the hand and leads him to the riverbank, where she offers him a flower like her own. The monster's face, painfully beautiful in its fear and uncertainty, seems to take on some of the ethereal light of Mary's trusting presence as he accepts her gift. The water behind the pair appears to radiate innocence as well, forming an entire possible world of soft, warm, delicately fluent feelings for them to retreat to.

Ana's rapt expression as she watches this scene in the theater is distinguished from her sister Isabel's. Isabel is tense and wary during the monster and child's game of tossing flowers into the water to make them float. (There is a close-up image of the flowers slowly drifting toward one another in the water, in perfect, enchanted stillness. Their brief coming together marks the union of the child's and monster's souls.) For Ana, the monster is entirely credible in his goodness. He is released from both his suffering and his ugliness by Mary's simple gestures of acceptance, and is tenderly initiated into a realm where playing, imagining, and sharing are natural. Ana, unlike her sister, has no suspicion that the past will return or that the monster's history of affliction will have any further power over him.

In Ana's eyes the movie's true narrative begins in this scene: in this unexpected but completely appropriate reprieve for the monster as he discovers that he has a friend (a friend, moreover, that Ana imagines herself turning into, as she becomes lost in the scene). For the rest of this episode Ana is totally identified with Mary, and no protective distance remains between them. Here is what Ana's expressions while watching the film convey to me: "Perhaps I could be an even better friend to the monster than Mary is. Mary likes him, but I would be able to love him with all my heart. I would know how to make him happy. Mary, after all, has a perfect father already. He is probably waiting for her with a big smile on his face behind the garden gate. The monster is a lonely creature, and a little girl who is lonely too is the right person to take care of him."

In the next segment of *Frankenstein* that we view with the two girls, the sympathetic father, now grief-stricken, carries the lifeless form of his dead child through the village streets. Ana, no doubt stunned by this abrupt termination of the movie's "real story" (the one she has given her heart to) has a question for her sister that *must* be answered, that cannot wait until the movie is over: "Why did he kill her?" Isabel impatiently replies that she knows why but will not tell Ana until later. We are shown no more of the monster's story. This version of *Frankenstein* ends, in effect, with the unsteady, traumatic advance of the father bearing his terrible burden amidst a crowd of onlookers—as if he were searching, without end, for a fit place to lay his daughter's body to rest.

Ana's unanswered question hovers in the air as we rejoin her and her sister in their bedroom after night prayers. In a chamber lit by a single candle Ana and Isabel whisper back and forth over the space separating their two beds. Ana accuses Isabel of not knowing why the monster killed the little girl or why the monster himself was killed later on. In order to preserve her fragile position as an authority on all difficult life questions, Isabel insists that neither the little girl nor the monster was really killed. When pressed on how she knows this for a fact, Isabel interestingly proposes both that everything in the movie is a lie *and* that she has actually seen the monster alive. Isabel's proof that movies are a lie and a trick is her claim of possessing a secret knowledge of the monster's present whereabouts. After all, if the monster still lives, then in all probability the little girl Mary was herself only pretending to be dead, thus alleviating Isabel's own anxiety about the monster's inexplicable need to turn against the child who befriended him. As Ana continues to interrogate her about the nature of the monster, Isabel, gaining fresh confidence with each bit of fabricated lore, assigns him the status of a spirit. He only appears to have a body, as in the movie, "when he puts on his disguise to go out." She concludes her interpretation by telling Ana that *because* he's a spirit, if you are a friend of his you can talk to him whenever you want to. "You close your eyes and you call him. 'It's me, Ana. It's me, Ana.' "

What is most impressive about Ana's relationship to the movie she has seen is her ability to formulate direct questions about the episodes in which she has most clearly beheld herself, and to hold on to them after she has left the theater. She does not conceal from herself or others the depth of her emotional involvement (and belief). Neither is she embarrassed to speak aloud the worries that arise from these suddenly glimpsed mysteries, which her own knowledge and experience of life cannot yet reach. Like Vickery in "Mrs Bathurst," Ana does not flee from the power of the spectacle she has witnessed. The images that have wholly absorbed her inside the theater continue to absorb her when she returns to her smaller world outside. It is fair to say that she remains lost in the narrative of *Frankenstein,* though not in a manner which proves disabling. The ending she seeks, like all true endings, is rather something invisible and unutterable. The eyes are not meant to see it, and it dwells in a silence as deep and fittingly inviolate as the enclosed "chambers of being" painted by Vermeer. The true ending perhaps lies somewhere in the "missing" footage following the encounter of the monster and the young girl at the riverbank. (Censors, both in Spain and the United States, removed the scene of the monster actually killing the child.) What prompted the monster to misunderstand the child's friendly intentions and stop listening to her? If he picked her up and she cried out, why did he not comprehend her fear and pain, since these are the emotions he has most often experienced and craves relief from? Did he hold her gently, like he held the flower, or did he savagely kill her? Ana cannot understand how he could possibly have turned brutal on this occasion. Furthermore, if the child fell in the water, could he not see her struggle? Did he make no attempt to rescue her? Perhaps there was a mistake, and someone else attacked the girl, knowing that the monster would be wrongly blamed for it. In which case it was also a mistake for him to be killed before he could make the villagers see whatever they needed to be shown to recognize his innocence. Why

40

does the goodness that is so visible and tangible to the child Ana remain hidden from the villagers, whose distracted fury settles for nothing but blood? Surely the answers are to be found back at the riverbank, where the monster and Mary have found a secret, ideal refuge from humiliation and punishment. The riverbank is not, nor will it become, a ravaged Eden in Ana's imagination. The monster and child remain there just as they were, smiling and casting flowers into the glowing water.

The portions of Isabel's interpretation of *Frankenstein* that Ana accepts are those which enable her to annul the official story of the film and keep faith with the possibility of reparation that is for her the intensely desired, just, and therefore necessary outcome of the tale. Is her refusal of the monster's and the child's death an act that could reasonably be termed *escapist?* We tend to think of escapism as something that adults or adolescents consciously seek out at films. It is as though one must first possess a conception of reality as something hard *and* escapable before one chooses to go to films with that sort of painless deliverance as one's goal. Young children go to movies without a sense of what the limits of movie experience are, or the ability to protect themselves against the unpleasant surprises of a visual narrative whose contents have as much validity as anything else that happens to them. They cannot easily make distinctions between the things that belong to the artifice of story-telling and the life they are returning to. (Perhaps we exaggerate our own capacity to make better, more meaningful distinctions.) But without some such security and understanding, movies are not a reliable means of escape.

Older viewers who use the word *escapist* believe they know what they are escaping from (their reality sense) and what they are escaping *to* (romance, comedy, adventure). Yet, to be satisfying, an escape (even for the least demanding spectator) must still correspond, at some level, to something one wishes to believe about the world, or still hopes for in one's own existence. As I suggested earlier, a memorable movie experience is a partial story that completes itself through a productive confusion with genuine psychic needs. It either triumphantly confirms or disturbingly disrupts that feeling/dreaming part of ourselves that we have surrendered to the film, in a condition closely resembling early childhood dependence. "*Escapists*" go to the movies to lose in an unthreatening environment the map that locates them in a determined world and a defining set of life circumstances. The plot of the movie is designed to help them find their way back home without the aid of this map. By *home* I mean an ending, which can be situated almost anywhere within the narrative, that either recalls a lost dimension of the past or provides, momentarily, a place of security, well-being, plenitude. The longing to be *inside* the film can be construed positively, in Steve Snyder's words, as an effort "to combat the emotional and imaginative impoverishment" that so often preys upon "the average life."[7]

Movies (as yet another crude, immoderate form of T. E. Hulme's "spilt religion"[8]) continually promise us secret glimpses of essential things. This is perhaps their most primitive and efficacious power. Sometimes on the periphery of even the most ordinary narrative we may suddenly come into contact with a near totem image of "mother," "father," "friend," "home," "community," "solitude," "privation" that is inescapably alive for us. We are given back to ourselves as creatures who feel connected, *are* connected, to what they see. Memories we can hardly bear are transfigured for us (like Garbo's face at the end of *Queen Christina*), coming out of hiding, as it were, and bidding us to look at them. In their new guise, these memories more willingly stand separate from us, having given up the power to look back at us and know (or harm) us. They have become objects of vision, for our sake, and wait to reenter us until we step forward to meet them. ("Its me, Ana. It's me, Ana.")

In the presence of certain indelible movie images I feel that I am just now beginning to see, and that this is precisely where I should always be in relation to sight: at the beginning. Our eyes are closed to so much (as a learned strategy of survival) that we must somehow find ways to take rejected images back again, in less menacing forms, in order to be able to see further. Film images are, of course, an intensely mediated vision but afford a kind of mediation that is potentially enabling—giving us a protected route back to an openness that may at one time have been easier for us and that may with luck be partially reclaimed. When the cinema altogether loses this restorative capacity (a welcome by-product of our superficial escape) I would contend that the medium goes bad for a spectator. It then achieves, ironically, its literal status as mechanism, boring us or binding us to reflections of our isolation, numbness, captivity.

In *Spirit of the Beehive,* Ana cannot stop seeking out evidence in her home and village that the monster, indeed, lives. She hears him in the creaking floorboards of the room above her bed, where her unhappy father restlessly paces back and forth. She sees him in the sad, withdrawn look of her mother, who has become bewilderingly remote from her husband's and children's lives. She touches him in any object that has even a vague association with death. When Ana's sister teases her one afternoon by pretending to be dead, Ana finds the sight of her "corpse" both frightening *and* reassuring. The monster has possibly left her sister's body as a message that he is nearby and will soon be making his way to her, so that she will finally have her chance to save him.

The desolate buildings in and around her quiet village, vacated and stripped of valuables during the civil war and its unreal aftermath, are now potential sanctuaries for a persecuted creature in flight from society. The decaying houses seem dolorous and expectant—the life within them unnaturally interrupted. Their shrouded, dust-filled rooms call out to even the most abject presences to enter and abide a while, as if yearning for their whispers and rustling and lonely sighs to restore to these forsaken dwellings a semblance of vitality. The silence and emptiness of the fields surrounding the village also bode well for the life-in-hiding of the monster's shy, tormented spirit. Out in the countryside, Ana listens for him in the depths of a well and seeks out his reflection in its shadowy waters. On another occasion, like Robinson Crusoe, she discovers a solitary footprint freshly made for her in a patch of earth; placing her own foot inside it, she appears to be securely contained by its immensity. The monster, however invisible, encloses her life in the same way, and fills her imagination to overflowing with his barely hinted intentions.

To say that the movie *Frankenstein* becomes one with Ana's whole existence (its sustaining order and its occasionally ascertainable meaning) is not to diminish the quality or density of her relations with the world. She projects onto Frankenstein's "hideous progeny" everything she fears she can lose and at the same time an infinite power to make amends. The monster she seeks has come back from the dead in a confused, hopelessly difficult quest for forgiveness and *true* self-disclosure. Disfigured by all the terror he has endured, he yet longs to put his vast strength in the service of one who will love him and accept his pain. A single nervous gesture or thoughtless word in the monster's presence, however, might be sufficient to kill his trust forever. The young girl Mary, after all, did die (whether by his own hand or someone else's), and, whatever the circumstances, the creature seemed to lose all memory of her afterwards. When he materializes again, Ana must try to be even more careful with his feelings and more protective of him than Mary was.

Through her efforts to bring back the monster, Ana is paradoxically hoping to rescue her family and herself from the deep sadness and extreme emotional isolation which oppress them—all of which she keenly feels, none of which she can give a name to or resolve. If the monster, whose entire being carries death and innocence like a flower, can be coaxed out of hiding and led to rest once again by the riverbank, to smile and stretch out his arms, then the rest of his tragic history, past and future, might dissolve. The good father at the gate (and the absent mother) might look for the daughter where she is still playing and find her before evil has swallowed her up. They might see the monster in the same light she does and, at that moment, see each other in the way they need to in order to get back home.

The movie that Ana continually replays in her imagination, as I have noted, is one where death, however fearsome, has no finality, since Ana herself has not made up her mind what death is. She is like the child F. Gonzalez-Crussi recalls himself being in his book of essays, *The Five Senses*. After he is made to look at his father's cadaver in "precisely the attitude in which death had surprised him,"[9] he secretly attempts for a long period to reproduce his father's expression exactly in front of a mirror: "I thus tried to reconstruct by a retrospective method, as it were, the possible meaning behind the visage: 'Given a man with this facial expression, what thoughts, what feelings would seem most appropriate to attribute to him?' The answer, of course, never came. But I achieved a perfect imitation by dint of continued practice. His gesture I made mine in the process."[10] This boy is old enough to know that his father is never going to come back and to feel his absence as "an emptiness at the core of my being."[11] Yet the mirror game defies this certainty, as though death were simply a dreadful thought his father's expression was condemned to hold, and if his grimace could be duplicated somehow (and understood), the father's face as well as the son's might escape death's consequences and move on to other matters. (I am also reminded of the elderly man in the film *Cinema Paradiso*, who suffers a fatal heart attack in a movie theater while watching a gunfight. Why does it seem odd that the movie he has been watching can continue so effortlessly without him? His ending precedes the film's. If he could somehow catch up with the narrative and find his place in it, he might perhaps leave his death behind—a dramatic moment whose intention he misunderstood.)

The ending of *Frankenstein*, for Ana, lacks the authority to bring the monster's life to an absolute close. Her private version of the story is, paradoxically, both fixed in her mind as something static (with the truth and solidity of myth) and continually metamorphosing. She allows her story to "forget" (or nearly forget) the bad things that have happened in it, and to move backward and forward in its temporal sequence to correct past errors or to halt right at the threshold of disaster. The movie's story is granted the freedom to wake up from its own worst nightmare, to remember *in time* to avoid painful recurrences, and by this means to recover its true identity. And yet for the monster to be convincingly healed, Ana's own actual life circumstances must show healing as well. As long as she feels unsheltered and lost within her own family, and *outside* nearly everything she sees and touches in the larger world, the monster cannot quite shed his death or the dark dream of a child floating in a stream. He waits for her patiently to give him the ending that belongs to him—a way into the world, so that the love inside him might illuminate her, and free both of them.

At the end of Jean Renoir's *Grand Illusion* (1937), a company of German soldiers train their rifles on a pair of French officers who have recently escaped from a German prisoner-of-war camp. Though the Germans, halting on a ridge above a large, snow-filled valley, are a considerable distance from the enemies they have just sighted, it seems very likely that if they commence fire, the Frenchmen will be killed. The two French officers, Rosenthal and Marechal, are making slow, stumbling progress through the heavy snow, and they seem to have been discovered well before they could move safely out of range. After a preliminary shot rings out, the German officer commanding the soldiers on the ridge orders his men to desist. He announces that the Frenchmen have crossed over the Swiss border, where his troops (and the war that they serve) have no right to pursue them. "Lucky for them!" one of the German recruits exclaims. Then we watch from above and at what feels like a great distance as the two former prisoners, their backs turned to us, cautiously work their way across the unbroken expanse of snow.

There are a few moments in film that affect me as strongly as this one does, and though I have seen it many times, familiarity has not dulled its power in the least. If the closing image of *Queen Christina* brings a human presence as close to the camera and its revelatory power as it seems possible to go, the *Grand Illusion* ending places its human figures almost beyond the camera's reach, at the blurred edge of visibility. They are still held within the frame, but at any moment they will be taking leave of the only world in which this film and its viewers can have knowledge of them. We have been told that Marechal and Rosenthal have arrived in Switzerland. They have successfully crossed a border which, in World War I, means the difference between life and death, freedom and captivity. But the viewer cannot see this border. It is an invisible line existing somewhere beneath a whiteness that covers everything. The only boundary that is apparent to us here is that of the frame, which declares itself most emphatically when a narrative comes to an end, and our visual connection to it is suddenly broken. The guns have not fired, the two men are still walking, having entered the space of freedom. In all likelihood, they are unaware that they have reached it yet. Their progress has not quickened. They do not pause even for an instant to mark the fact that they have reached their destination.

The complex emotion I experience as I watch them passing out of view has something to do with my knowing that they have already said goodbye to one another. Before they began their walk across the mountain valley they made arrangements to separate shortly after crossing the border. Their destinations lie in different directions. Both intend to return to their respective regiments so that presumably they can engage in further battles. The war is far from being over, and neither of them even briefly considers walking away from his military duties. The last third of *Grand Illusion* is filled with movingly restrained farewell scenes, and we know as we watch Marechal and Rosenthal warmly embrace each other that theirs is to be the final image of parting in the film. The emotional logic of their narrow escape a few moments later from the Germans' guns is that they have received permission (through this piece of good fortune) to stay together. The enemy has spared their lives. Does this action not revoke the need for the goodbye they have just spoken? Then we remember Marechal and Rosenthal's larger plan, and understand that the seemingly critical decision of the German officer to abide by the rules of war and grant them safe passage to Switzerland alters nothing beyond the dangers of this moment. The French officers will remain together only for as long as we see them stepping carefully through the deep snow. The implied next image will be their agreed-upon separation, when each will take a solitary path away from this suddenly essential visual emblem of brotherhood.

It seems unreasonable to assume that the two men are only together (in this closing glimpse of their journey) by accident, or for temporary convenience, or as a result of strange, war-defined circumstances. At the same time, though, we must feel that freedom is as much behind them, in what they have already been to each other, as in front of them. They have recently left behind a German widow and her child in a farmhouse. In this temporary refuge they have been fed, restored to health, sheltered from their foes, and loved, as though these things are as natural and within reach as the battlefield or further flight. Since their goal is escape, however, they dare not linger there too long. Marechal and Rosenthal have turned away, with equal finality, from the farmhouse sanctuary, from the file of German soldiers with the power to kill them, from the spectators of *Grand Illusion,* and—very shortly—from each other, replacing their vital companionship with the loneliness and uncertainty of a private search for their place in the war. The war, in turn, offers a world scheme of infinite further sunderings. The narrative does not extend much hope that the two men will find their way back to the farmhouse, or to each other as fellow wayfarers, a condition which has taught them to respond with beautiful plainness and directness to one another's basic needs.

In 1937, the year of *Grand Illusion*'s release, Marechal and Rosenthal seem to be walking not only in the direction of the still-unfinished hostilities of World War I (which was then safely part of history), but into the terrifying unknown of an even larger struggle, taking shape "right now," as it were, behind it. And yet, possibly because there is such a massive array of conscious and unconscious ironies working to qualify, or even eradicate, our belief in the meaningfulness of *Grand Illusion*'s final image—two friends, who have miraculously escaped death, crossing the border to Switzerland and freedom, *together*—the image unequivocally retains its positive force. In the face of so much comprehensible opposition, why does it seem both natural and necessary to attach my faith to the dwindling shapes of two soldiers in the snow? I cannot reduce such repeated depth of assent on my part to a sentimental gesture. But neither can I explain what exactly my faith consists of or what warrants it.

This leads me back to the questions I have dealt with throughout the essay. What can "blind" repeating images on film give us that is not an impoverished semblance of actual living? Why, and on what terms, do we wish to inhabit living pictures that seem to demand our emotional dependence as the price of our "being there"? Since we can in no way alter, or remedy, the sequence of events in a film narrative by the fact of our presence, what is it we hope to secure from fictions that we often yield to with far more conviction and commitment than the beckoning realities of our own lives? What things of consequence do films gain the authority to give us in the act of taking other things away?

The habitable space that belongs to film can best be thought of as a ceaseless dialectic between open and closed environments. I will conclude by talking about this dialectic, very briefly, in terms of two specific dwellings in the movie adaptation of Harper Lee's *To Kill a Mockingbird*. The open environment can be represented by the home of Atticus Finch. When we are invited to regard things from the perspective of this idealized domestic space, and imaginatively enter into it, we have the illusion of seeing actions and intentions clear and whole. (Everything that happens here becomes an extension of Atticus himself, who is, quite simply, openness personified.) In this environment, we find an almost total harmony of the visible and moral realms, and both manifest the contained splendor of a quiet, well-lighted room viewed by a homesick stranger through a window late at night. The living details such a window-world contains can easily achieve, through the force of memory and longing that the stranger imparts to it, a clear, piercing proof that security exists, at least for others. Atticus himself, viewed by a reminiscing narrator (his grown daughter) through just such a window in the film's closing moments, is described for us as faithfully keeping watch by his injured son's bedside while the boy sleeps. Atticus "would be in Jem's room all night. And he would be there when Jem waked up in the morning." We actually *see* Atticus through the window as the narrator speaks these words, from her poignant temporal distance. He is powerfully, consistently, luminously there, and dependably himself, as long as we can keep him in view.

But *To Kill a Mockingbird* is concerned to form a traversable path from this house, where there are no secrets or confounding contradictions, to a darkened dwelling further down the street, whose front gate is never opened and whose windows always have their shades pulled down. This is the home of Boo Radley, who survives somehow in its cloistered recesses, and who is reputed to be a kind of monster. The Radley house is one that guards its privacy fiercely. It is entirely mysterious. Even the camera is not permitted access to its interior. It can move no closer to it than Atticus's daughter, Scout, is able to. On two occasions she stands briefly on its front porch, feeling the force of locked doors. Those who live here remain, for most of the film, beyond our knowledge and our sight. Only for a few minutes, late in the movie, does Boo Radley become visible to us; as a rescuer of children (one who must kill to save), and as someone deeply afraid of even the most subdued and sheltering social light. He is anxious to return as quickly as possible to the dire closed space of the Radley house, where we can no longer *have* him (as a source of reassurance). It is, in fact, strongly implied that once back there he will never reemerge. Boo shares with Atticus a strong instinct to protect what he loves, and both men happen to love the same two children. However, neither Atticus's goodness nor his profound commitment to justice is able to save Boo from the pain of his life, to relocate him by narrative sleight-of-hand to the open space which is Atticus's home and identity. Boo is led back to the darkness of the Radley house by everything that is inside him. There is nowhere else for him to go, and we have no choice but to watch him disappear. He is taken away from us, turned into the "heart" of absence, so that Atticus's continued *presence* can have a meaning that does not make false claims about the world.

The characters and memory geography of all the film episodes we have considered seem to dwell in ghostly proximity to these absent and present spaces in *To Kill a Mockingbird*. Vickery stands outside Atticus's lighted window, gazing at the lost image of Garbo, who is available to him in romantic memory as one who will never change, never depart. Meanwhile, the child, Scout (Ana), leads Boo Radley (the Frankenstein monster) to the darkened dwelling that is his proper home. He has saved her life, this time, after many earlier failed attempts and proved finally, beyond question, his love for her. It is the love of a deeply maimed victim, who has been granted one night's reprieve for a killing that is, like the monster's drowning of Mary, out of his hands. Let us call the path between the two houses that these soon to be parted friends travel the Swiss border—the life of the imagination, in its freedom and determinism.

The hidden must remain hidden in film, in a place where images cannot (will not) take us, if the well-lighted spaces that remain are to offer a comfort that endures. What is open to us in film owes its light to a neighboring darkness we are still able to feel.

2

No Bigger than Zuzu's Petals: Dreaming the Real in *It's a Wonderful Life*

> What we know beforehand we don't know.
> —Mark Rudman, "A Response to Heidegger"

The spirit of Frank Capra's 1946 film, *It's a Wonderful Life*, is akin to that expressed in the tumultuous VJ Day celebrations of the previous year. On August 14, 1945, with the pressures of nearly four years of war suddenly removed, America's collective response was momentarily that of an undivided family. The frantic demonstrations of joy that everywhere spilled forth were in exact ratio to the degree of emotional stress that Americans felt they had the need to overcome. What we discover in the newsreels and magazine pictorials which documented the festivities is a powerful "selective focusing" of those activities and those qualities in the nation's character that affirmed its solidarity. It is as though the regenerative force one associates with Capra's persistently wonder-struck immigrant's vision of the American landscape for once magically coalesced with its object, and was exceeded by it.

Life magazine ran a feature with the charming heading, "The Camera Records the Varied Pattern of American Life in the Days of Victory."[1] This title will serve equally well for the following list of phantasmagoric snippets I've compiled from *Life* and other sources. Obviously, the photographers covering this singularly charged "episode" of transition—a *moment*, like the Kennedy assassination, stretched over a number of days—sought out images that not only identified what was happening but that also might recover for Americans a long absent sense of how to see themselves functioning in a state of peace. In one famous photograph of Times Square, the "greatest throng in New York's history" jubilantly parties in the darkness, with the only visible movie marquee brightly advertising "A Thousand and One Nights." In another part of

George Bailey (James
Stewart) and Mary
Hatch (Donna Reed)
joined and separated
by a telephone in *It's a
Wonderful Life.*

New York, the caption on a *Life* photo reports, Little Italy "bedecks
itself with flags and bunting. Tenement-house fire escapes and windows
were jammed with joyful people watching the dancing and listening to
the sound of exploding firecrackers. Everybody offered free beer and
wine to everybody." In a newsreel clip filmed in the city on the following
day, an unidentified man, viewed only from the back, erupts into a fan-
tastically elaborate dance down Broadway, waving his hat to the crowds
on either side of him amidst the citywide cacophony of air-raid sirens,
marching bands, honking horns, singing, and shouting. Near the San
Francisco civic center, two nude blondes who had left their clothes in a
waiting taxi, went for a brief swim in a lily pond, cheered on by a large
group of GIs who, after taking some pictures, "politely offered the girls
towels as they returned to their taxi."

As the orgiastic enthusiasm of the first days diminished, "spot"
photographs and accompanying anecdotes from various sections of the
country endeavored to maintain an emotional continuity with the exhilarating craziness and effusive camaraderie of the not quite vanished
festival atmosphere. In the *Life* "days of victory" pictorial, for example,

most of the peculiar assortment of juxtaposed items have a consciously eccentric tinge. Clearly, the principal aim of the article is to reinitiate Americans into the "mysteries" of ordinary experience, to stimulate their appetite for a fresh involvement with that experience by releasing the startling or fantastic element lurking in the small occasion, the familiar place. So, we learn that a perpetual dominos game continues in a San Marcos, Texas, smithy; that two concrete dinosaurs erected before the war "lay in wait for tourists on their way to nearby Mt. Rushmore"; that vast quantities of pink lemonade were consumed when Russell Brothers Pan-Pacific Circus played two performances in Walla Walla, Washington; and that "twin girls were delivered to Mrs. Frank Miley of Brooklyn by two policemen pressed into service at the last minute."

There is an understandable attempt here to blur the line at which the difficult crossover into America's postwar reality must take place. It is suggested that the spirit of celebration is one to which we can rebound naturally and without undue effort, once the regular activity of life resumes, and that if we properly measure the scenes and define the drama in which we participate, we will continue "to hear the ring of urgent presentness"[2] in all of our experiences as clearly as we did on VJ Day. The quality of perception revealed in the human interest items I've cited, needless to say, is hardly adequate for such a task. But the lemonade vendors in Walla Walla and the concrete dinosaurs (already visibly defaced in the photo by the painted names of unsung tourists) are significant because of the kind of homely magic with which the magazine attempts to invest them. One is invited to approach the native landscape as though it were under a spell and (if one sharpens up one's sight) perhaps to see, in the words of Grace Paley, "through the appearance of things right to the apparition itself."[3]

After any calamitous enterprise like World War II, so totally underwritten by death, it is exceedingly difficult to appeal to mere unaided reality for strength or reassurance. One's imaginative sympathy recoils from the actual since it fails to induce a quickened sense of life. Instead of giving one a pattern shaped to one's hopes, the actual (with senselessness in the ascendant) supplies a pattern shaped to one's increasingly rational fears. The jubilation at war's end was a collective push against the long-term schooling in privation and dread, and when the nationwide party subsided, the search for other openings on the trail of causality (through which saving apparitions might enter in) began. The case of the bartender in Columbus, Ohio, who devised and marketed a potent elixir called the "Atomic cocktail," thereby giving his customers a chance to safely digest the tremors of Hiroshima, is paradigmatic. Those that have just escaped from death require the most emphatic kind of proof that they, indeed, live. Like Kafka, in one of his diary entries for 1921, they look for confirmation of their own possible rebirth in the capacity of the world around them to be made new, and to show itself inclined to befriend them: "It is entirely conceivable that life's splendour forever lies in wait about each one of us in all its fullness, but veiled from view, deep down, invisible, far-off. It is there, though, not hostile, not reluctant, not deaf. If you summon it by the right word, by its right name, it will come. This is the essence of magic, which does not create but summons."[4]

Each of these elements of the short-lived postwar jubilation has a vital relation to Frank Capra's achievement in *It's a Wonderful Life*. The fantasy framework Capra employs in the film does not provide a secure, anxiety-free perspective for the narrative, as it might at first appear to do. It functions rather to move his story further in the direction of death than it might otherwise go. Capra shares in the nation's heavy preoccupation with destruction and loss, and he turns, perhaps for reasons similar to those I've described above, to fantasy as a means of assimilating that loss, and also of establishing some sort of control over it. Somewhat unexpectedly, however, when the fantasy elements are brought actively into play in the film, they are used not to release us from a consciousness of death but to maintain and heighten death's presence.

No sooner has George Bailey's provident angel diverted his thoughts from suicide than he plunges him into the utter darkness of Pottersville where he is permitted to see his world as it would have been had he never existed. All the faces George encounters there bear the imprint of death, if we can reasonably regard death as the obliteration of every remembered point of contact one has with another person. Capra obviously believes, with infinitely less difficulty than Kafka, that life's "glows and glories" lie in wait about each one of us, yet he looks for the magic to summon them in death's dark country. One cannot discover what it is that forms the splendor that one has been waiting to see, until one comes to the place where one loses the power of visioning not the impossible but the actual. Capra deftly reverses the terms which we associate with the act of dreaming, implying that to dream our way out of ourselves is the true closure of possibility, and that the light of fantasy obscures the stronger light of real things. The highest use of our dreaming faculty is to learn how to dream what is already there.

It is Capra's intention to show that an accommodation to one's given circumstances is not automatically synonymous with dull acquiescence. He seems to be arguing with everything we know about desire—that it depends, always, on a keen sense of not-yet-having, but requiring. Desire tells us that our real life, the one that finally answers to our true needs, will commence as soon as we find the right escape route: become someone else, arrive somewhere else, make an entirely new set of arrangements. Many critics have tried to account for *It's a Wonderful Life*'s commercial failure in 1946 by arguing that Capra was out of touch with the sour, disenchanted postwar mood. The film's plot surely owes its resonance, however, to the culture-wide experience of soldiers returning home only to discover in dismay that home had vanished in their absence, that it had become emotionally unrecognizable. The life so many veterans "knew" they could come back to, if they just managed to survive the war, often seemed, when they arrived to reclaim it, an impenetrable dream. They could recall the outward forms of things, but these familiar outlines strangely bore little resemblance to what they'd imagined so vividly while they were away. Everything stood at the wrong distance, more remote, ironically, than when the soldiers were overseas.

Capra's creative challenge, therefore, is to address Americans' lost sense of connection to the postwar present. George Bailey's miraculous return to his own life, with its ordinariness and hardship not removed, but convincingly transformed, is predicated on the belief that one's achieved relation to things is prodigious, but almost always hidden from view. Most of the time (not only in the aftermath of war) our senses are sealed to the present reality we think we occupy; we do not "hear the urgent ring of its presentness." We cannot see where we are. We cannot quite see our way to others, no more than they can see their way to us. Suppose, as a possible remedy to this common plight, one were able to make a proper homecoming. What might that involve? Perhaps one might find oneself spiritually ready, in the manner of George Bailey, not only to submit to the full demands of the present but to embrace them unreservedly.

If life chooses to answer such a willingness, as so often in Capra, with a joyous explosion of fellow feeling, it does not, in my view, compromise the meaning of Bailey's "coming back to life" in any way. It seems to me a structural necessity that as much of George's accustomed reality as possible be brought before him after his deliverance at the Bedford Falls bridge so that, for the first time, he can be pierced to the depths of his being with an awareness of what his life holds for him. No less importantly, *It's a Wonderful Life* is a film that is concerned at every level with a "sharing of the wealth." A victory achieved in isolation from the community, whether we are referring to George's escape from

Pottersville or Americans' equally narrow escape from the Great Depression and the War, is both a victory incomplete and unnatural in
terms of the dialectic the film has established. George has repeatedly
dreamed of fleeing from this community, but he is always "awakened to
himself" in its presence. And so the tearful euphoria, as he finds himself
standing alive among others who affirm that this is so, builds and
spreads. Capra has found a way to retrieve a more enduring image of
the spirit released in the end-of-the-war rejoicing from the defeat of
George Bailey's dreams.

Paul Goodman once wrote that "you cannot create a work [of art] with
a false attitude,"[5] and while I remain skeptical of his or anyone else's
ability to explain conclusively what such an attitude consists of, I think
I know what he was getting at. A film like *It's a Wonderful Life* is immediately susceptible to the charge of "false attitude." One need only
allude to the fact that the narrative chooses to take seriously a whim-
sically conceived guardian angel named Clarence to give those unfamiliar with it a way of "placing" it, of getting a handle on its likely
deficiencies. What is felt to be "false" in Capra's attitude toward his
subject is that he is telling us less than he knows about reality in order
to be able to invest it with the final illustriousness that he wishes it to
have. It has been argued that he shrewdly employs familiar conventions,
in which he has next to nothing at stake, in order to secure the emotional
response he is after. If he possesses a vision, according to this view, it is
not one continuously resubmitted to inner shaping. Like the device of
the angel, his material consists of imposed forms, "done for effect," in
the manner of a breezily confident salesman, rather than of forms that
come unbidden, discovered as they unfold.

I would argue, quite to the contrary, that the prevailing impression
one receives of Capra's method in *It's a Wonderful Life* is that it is always
risking total failure, that he allows himself no sure way of getting from
one moment or scene to the next. This uncertainty about how one is to
proceed has nothing to do with intricacy of plotting, for Capra's stories,
without exception, have fallen to pieces when "retold" by other directors.
The plot, beyond supplying the narrative with its volatile forward motion, functions for Capra, in each of its separate phases, "as a net of
successive moments," to quote C. S. Lewis, in which he is trying to
catch "something that is not successive."[6] Capra addresses this problem
briefly in his autobiography when he recounts his first, disastrous attempt to tell the completed story of *Wonderful Life* to his principal actor,
James Stewart. "The story evaporated into thin air," he recalls, "like one

of those fragile, gentle things that 'if you touch them they vanish.' Frustration hit me. I leaped to my feet. 'Goddammit, Jim, I haven't got a story. This is the lousiest piece of cheese I ever heard of. Forget it, Jimmy. Goddammit, forget it! Forget it!' "[7]

Capra, to be sure, makes extensive use of the conventions of established Hollywood genres, and unlike, say, Preston Sturges, does so mostly in an uncynical manner. But it has generally escaped notice that once his scenes have gotten under way (at least in *It's a Wonderful Life*) the supports that these conventions might be expected to supply—for example, the motivating information for our emotional reading of a situation—rapidly drop away. Capra seizes upon conventions as the quickest route into a scene, just as Astaire sidles his way into a dance by a series of simple, orthodox steps, which are minimally communicative about the flights of invention that his motions will inscribe later on. Conventions bring the *ground* for scenes into preliminary focus, but the scene-structures that feel their way into being on that ground are meant to shed this easy affiliation with the usual setup and become self-sustaining. Capra is not at all interested in the habitual, somewhat protected mode of response that conventions necessarily bring with them. What he consistently strives to distill out of them is a moment that effectively bursts the bounds of the familiar situation. His goal is to powerfully transcend convention without undermining it.

If this is the case, the question arises why he needs to rely so heavily on these ready-made forms, not only in *It's a Wonderful Life* but in all his major films. He does so, I believe, because his creative temperament is neither naturally well-suited nor attracted to the slow, patient buildups required for a fully particularized rendering of individual psychology or environment. For his major scenes to work properly, Capra believes that they must be made to feel highly compressed. Convention allows Capra to bring the viewer swiftly into the midst of a strong dramatic situation. His best scenes are typically planned as short-distance assaults on a privileged moment of vision, and if Capra starts at a point too far away from the moment, or stays with it too long once he has arrived at it, he knows he is likely to lose it. It must never seem as though the thing that is aimed for is forecasting itself or that, once we have hit it, the privileged moment is eager to prolong itself and have us become accustomed to it. Hence, in the Gower Drugstore scene early in the film, in George and Mary's love scene by the telephone, in Uncle Billy's collapse at his office desk, or in George's visit to his daughter Zuzu's bedroom, to cite only a few examples, there is a close-checked concentration of feeling at exactly the point where it is wanted, with no spillover.

I am freshly astonished each time I return to *It's a Wonderful Life* at how Capra manages to crystallize whatever is important to him in relationships, events, or spaces in a matter of instants, without an effect of diminishment or hasty abbreviation. In his wonderfully imagined book, *Eccentric Spaces*, Robert Harbison writes that "the better we know a place the less we want it reduced,"[8] a statement that surely applies as well to characters and their defining actions. Nevertheless, Capra repeatedly demonstrates that the contrary may also be true. Now, while a typical Capra frame is as crowded with jostling life as a Brueghel canvas or, less grandiloquently, Moon Mullins's boardinghouse, the expressive significance of any element in *Wonderful Life* is usually proportionate to the smallness of the space or the sliver of time into which it is squeezed. Like Zuzu's flower petals absentmindedly tucked in George's pants pocket, which eventually convey to us, in Rilke's words, that "the very fact that (she's) not there is warm with (her) and realer and more than a privation," Capra counts on our imaginatively holding on to the things that he most quickly relinquishes. For it is chiefly in their absence that things demand to be known more intimately, and that we begin to give them the weight and value that belong to them. (I shall have more to say about this in my chapter on *Random Harvest*.)

There should be little surprise in the fact that the depth of Capra's emotional understanding isn't more widely acknowledged in a period like our own when it is generally assumed that emotions, after so much abuse in the world of buying, selling, and healing, have no reliable value. We might regard it as another case of what Walter Pater once described as "preponderating soul, embarrassed, at a loss, in an era of preponderating mind." Pater goes on to make an interesting, if too simple distinction between the categories, one that I consider pertinent to our examination of Capra. "By mind, the literary artist reaches us through static and objective indications of design in his work, legible to all. By soul, he reaches us, somewhat capriciously perhaps, one and not another, through vagrant sympathy and a kind of immediate contact. Mind we cannot choose but approve where we recognise it; soul may repel us, [and] not because we misunderstand it."[9]

When Capra's instincts don't fail him, the act of paying heed to something—which I guess I take to mean attending to it in the same spirit that so many commonplace entities in the Capra world seem to inspire—is also, quite naturally, a way of paying emotional homage. The not unfamiliar complaint of "too much-ness," directed, for instance, against the conclusion of *Wonderful Life*, is more than an objection to probability (which is invariably a stalking horse for other, less easily articulated dissatisfactions). Perhaps the objection translates to the more difficult awareness that "too much" is *demanded* from us. One is not used to having one's sympathies forcibly activated over so wide a field, and the fact that the thing has been done, and maybe done legitimately, is necessarily a little alarming, and quite possibly feels *wrong*. Some form of violation has taken place. Paradoxically, that which has the greatest force to release us often carries within it the greatest power of violation, and it is this tension, which I will subsequently explore, that gives Capra's art in *It's a Wonderful Life* "its natural full-bodied rise and fall."

A brief comparison of *Wonderful Life* and Vincente Minnelli's *Meet Me in St. Louis* (1944) might prove helpful in identifying the hazardous sort of struggle present in Capra's rendering of community life that is not to be found in the many other American films of the period that similarly set out to reaffirm family and small-town values. The Minnelli film proceeds on the assumption that it is rather an easy matter to locate imagery corresponding to popular conceptions of a secure and tranquil home environment. Minnelli approaches the turn-of-the-century Smith household with the same confident air one would have in preparing a shop window for the holidays, aware that he is reproducing a well-known pattern, free of troubling perplexities. One's attitude toward all the separate features of this world seems preordained.

In our initial leisurely journey through the Smiths' dwelling, various members of the family are introduced to us, singing the title song and cheerfully passing it, beanbag fashion, upstairs and down until nearly the entire domestic establishment has been accounted for. This is a charming musical conceit, and if the cumulative effect is somewhat awkward and earthbound, it may be because the number permits no loosening or freeing up of the family's literal situation; conceivably it even tightens it, since the song makes it clearer than it perhaps would have been otherwise that what these characters are *about* are their un-thinking functions in a stable home system. In effect, the refrain affords each of them an opportunity to "dance" to his or her assigned place within the household, a place which necessarily proves, in a phrase George Herbert once used to describe his stanza lengths, "a strict but welcome size."

Apart from the remarkable Halloween sequence (where we accompany the child Tootie on a "dare" visit to the home of a lonely, embittered recluse) and the climactic episode where Tootie, in a fit of displaced rage, destroys the "family" of snow people after her older sister, Esther, sings to her about the pain of wishing and waiting, Minnelli regularly halts at the border of any experience whose meaning cannot be absorbed instantly by the rhetoric of "family occasions." There is an unintended pathos in the fact that Tootie, the Smiths' youngest child, is at times permitted to "disobey" this rhetoric. She is endowed with the "overactive imagination" appropriate to small children, with the implicit understanding that it is a thing apart from the *real* concerns of the family, and, as such, it doesn't count for anything. It doesn't pose a challenge that requires serious or sustained acknowledgment. The family benevolently regards imagination as a phase to be passed through, and so, with a mixture of patience and friendly exasperation, endeavors to check it back whenever it seems to run "a little wild." Tootie has not yet learned to keep her world at a reassuring distance; it enters into her on all sides, and she cannot help cleaving to its outsized images with passionate conviction.

This quality of conviction forms no part of the rest of the family's approach to their affairs or of Minnelli's approach to them. The kind of stylization Minnelli solicits from his performers serves to make the mood of each episode in the seasonal round a matter of assertion rather than of testing. It is never the actual source (always elusive) of another's delight or enthusiasm that Minnelli tries to put in touch with in his scenes; he is after the *look* of a "happy gathering," not the volatile complex of *feelings* that brought it into being. For example, when the Smith children hear their parents singing and playing the piano downstairs following a family dispute and individually feel compelled to join them, what seems at issue in the scene is not, as one might at first conclude, the mysterious power of the music to lead the children, almost involuntarily, to an expression of solidarity. That is the given of the scene; the logic of the situation, rather than the palpable pressure of the moment, is what is called upon to make the desired gathering happen. Minnelli refuses the deeper operations of enchantment which might give to the occasion the quality of inevitability. Instead, his main concern is with the *pictorial* harmony of the completed tableau. As each child enters the room, she moves, with Trapp family prescience, to a position that further extends the anticipated symmetries of the whole.

Whether the narrative places us in the kitchen, to spy out dinner preparations and the cozily old-fashioned business of ketchup making, or at the dinner table, where father's mock-temper is agreeably overruled by mother's mock-gentle remonstrances or the girls' mock-impetuosity, predigested ritual ungrounded in observation is encouraged to fill up every available space. One is invited to *appreciate* the choreographed bustle whose unvarying rhythms have the clacking emphasis of a broom-tapping session but not to participate in an atmosphere of conviviality that is so busy keeping itself alive that it never thinks to inquire where it comes from or what purpose it fulfills. Contrary to the well-known dictum that begins *Anna Karenina,* happy families, at least in film, are not all alike.

Frank Capra's attitude toward the possibilities for idealization in the Bailey family and Bedford Falls is closer to that expressed by John Updike in his preface to a collection of Oscar Wilde's fairy tales. "And is it not to some extent so, that things become what we wish them to be? But only 'to some extent,' for the resistance of the real world is very real."[10] Like Minnelli, Capra announces at the outset of his narrative the moral direction in which he wants things to point, but unlike him he does not expect the familiar context in which he's working to supply ready-made the meanings he desires to express. If the small town is the context Capra hopes to elevate, he regards it for that very reason as the area of greatest natural resistance to his imaginative urges.

It is Capra's ambition to recover, through his vision of Bedford Falls, a primal manifestation of that dim, hovering promise "deep in the race" from which the community ideal first took hold of men's minds. To get at it, he knows he must break through the stale, habit-diminished forms that long familiarity with corrupt or emptily "nice" variants have bred into our perceptions, and do so not once, but a multitude of times. In virtually every scene, he is obliged to find a fresh means of holding the viewer in a state of heightened responsiveness since Capra is, in effect, arguing with what the viewer already thinks he knows, and an argument of this sort must be won over and over again. Thus, Bedford Falls is never there for Capra ready to hand, complete and inviting comfortable habitation. It is to be seen rather as the hidden epiphany element in every situation which, when struck, produces the chord (oddly unforeseen) that we have been waiting for, and that extends the authentic life of the place by the length of its own duration.

These successive relocations of the same truth must be drawn forth by a continuous exertion of will—a passionate will to believe in which strain is ever visible. There is always imminent danger that a misstep or a miscalculated appeal for acceptance will return the intensely focused clarity of the dream to formlessness. (The physical appearance and behavior of Mary in front of the library during the Pottersville sequence, which adds up to a clichéd negative image of her, is the one serious miscalculation of this kind in the film, and it throws the conclusion of the nightmare segment off balance.) Our ongoing sense of the tremendous stakes riding on each of George Bailey's decisions is steadily reinforced by an awareness of Capra's simultaneous daring in plotting the course of his fantasy through a wilderness of snares. Part of what we feel is propelling his scenes along is the reckless, slightly lunatic energy of the high-risk gambler: what we're involved in has the dizzying slam of an all-or-nothing proposition. To win, in Capra's or George Bailey's terms, means one is merely holding one's own; it is immediately necessary to hazard it all again. A major wrong choice, however, is irrevocable. It has the power to cancel everything.

The Gower Drugstore episode, which occurs early in the film, is worth examining at considerable length as a means of showing the various, almost invisible turns of emphasis and perspective Capra makes in developing a situation toward its peak moment. The section I wish to analyze begins when George Bailey (still a young boy at this point in the narrative) is shoved through the doorway of the drugstore where he works part-time by the group of friends he's been walking with. Even when it is necessary for Capra to open a scene (as in this case) with a formal entrance, he strives to convey the slightly accelerated impression that comes of being in media res; hence, George is literally tossed into the scene by his out-of-view companions in the street, and Capra uses this angled motion to bump the action into life a bit off center.

He then provides George with a small, matter-of-course transaction with a venerable old cigar lighter which, on one level, renders the space intimate by showing it familiarly accommodating itself to the youth and, on another level, reveals George, in the first articulation of his "dreams," trying to project himself out of the space, to imagine a state of affairs in which he could cease "feeling local." George closes his eyes, declares aloud that he wishes he had a million dollars, then presses down on a lever which raises the lighter and sparks a flame. This apparatus is a friendly oracle and always confirms the hopes of its user.

Unnoticed by George during his hurried entry into the store is a small girl sitting on a stool by the counter. Her name is Mary Hatch, and she will one day become George's wife. Capra includes a shot of her, in a reverie of her own, watching George make his public wish. Within a minute or so we will see her leaning over George, as he bends to put away the "explorer's magazine" in which he maps his mental journeys to faraway places, and planting in the hollow of his deaf ear (with the not-to-be-fathomed experimental tenderness of a sensitive child) a whispered vow of greater moment: that she will love George Bailey until the day she dies. Like the miraculous letter in the folktale, patiently coiled up in the hole of a dead tree, it will, at the proper time, find its way into the hands of the one meant to receive it.

For the present, however, I would like to freeze-frame George Bailey (as Capra will do in a later scene), catching him at the instant when his eyes are closed, with one arm half-upraised for luck and the other on the wonder-working lever. This image, in a more ambiguous fashion than may at first suggest itself, illuminates what is to be the central gap in George Bailey's self-understanding throughout the film. Where the needs of others are concerned, he spontaneously achieves a whole-souled comprehension of the present's limiting circumstances, and by the quality of his giving, draws forth from them a restorative element which returns to the present some measure of its possible beauty. In matters involving his own needs, however, he persistently closes his eyes or turns his back on the things in sight or within reach, though from our vantage point, so many figures and forms are casting out rays for him to gather. He only learns to see how he fails the things that his life, in fact, most completely honors—whether it be his wife's love or his father's legacy—and looks to the "moon" to provide him with an image of what he's after, a dream which will expand the soul.

To return to our example, then: the situation of a boy, obliged to work part-time in a drugstore to earn extra money for his family, improvising an Aladdin's lamp for himself out of an old cigar lighter, appears to mark a progression from demoralizing commerce to revitalizing fantasy, but actually the order should be reversed. What we have here is a delightful instance of the exotic "mooreeffoc" quality G. K. Chesterton singles out in Charles Dickens's thrillingly skewed and revitalizing descriptions of ordinary locales. "Mooreeffoc" is "coffee room," in mirrored reflection, not as the latter slippery word is customarily seen, but as it *should* be seen, from a privileged inside angle on the far side of a dingy glass door. With the perspective reversal Capra demands on the image I've chosen to hold, it is actually the store itself that is the softly glowing fantasy—where everything seems "a hint, a handle, a help" to George's happiness—fading into commerce: the conventional aspiration for plenty of "hard cash." For Capra, as this sequence goes on to show, the place where one best fits is "naturally" the place where one is most needed, and it is in the needs others have of us that we often find cunningly disguised fulfillment of our own needs.

George's employer, Mr. Gower, is introduced to us standing near the entrance of the pharmaceutical supply room, largely obscured by a pane of frosted glass. He peers through an opening in the glass upon hearing George, angrily snaps, "You're late," and then quickly steals a drink from the flask he's holding. The shot is designed to provoke a laugh, and it invariably gets one. Interestingly, the reason one laughs is that it seems that the man, through his unsuccessful attempt to conceal the vice that he would no doubt prefer to remain hidden, has given himself away—yet, in fact, that is precisely what he has not done.

Once again, as in the case of George's wish, there is a problem of blocked seeing, and, as before, the problem does not pose itself as a problem until after the block has been removed. Capra's strategy throughout *Wonderful Life* is to ask us to look at things as though he expected us to grasp them immediately, to catch them at a glance, as it were (and we do proceed with that confidence); then, once we have taken the incomplete view as the complete one, Capra "remembers"— with the convincing illusion of afterthought common to master story-tellers—that what we have effortlessly sized up is "not quite all" that we need in order to make a correct judgment. The "forgotten" detail that he delays bringing into play until that point when the viewer supposes that nothing further is required, usually transforms entirely his sense of what is truly the matter at issue. Capra's continuously oblique, "look— now look again" approach to the substance of a scene is comically ad-umbrated during the opening episode of George's story when Clarence proves unable to decipher anything but a blank image where Bedford Falls is supposed to be until his heavenly superior refocuses for him.

In *The Poetry of Necessity*, a brilliant critical study of Thomas Hardy's verse, James Richardson accounts for Hardy's practice of pon-derously weighting certain lines in a stanza in terms that are equally applicable to Capra's surreptitious "misguiding" of our perception. Hardy often deliberately tried for an effect of constriction, say, in the middle of a stanza because "he felt the need for an anchor, a new per-spective, to keep the poem from evaporating into the breezy speed which his lesser contemporaries called 'polish,' but which he apprehended as lack of feeling. Feeling requires effort, and effort is expressed through a change of pace wrought by the thwarting of expectations."[11] Thus, before Mr. Gower's plight can be identified, it must be located in a denser medium than the purely "affective," one that is somehow resistant to facile comprehension.

If Gower were instantly framed for us as a man deserving pity because he had just received word of his son's death, we would have access to him only through the pity which the "loss-of-a-loved-one" situation automatically, and indiscriminately, generates. This type of sentiment floats in a kind of nimbus around the one who suffers rather than making itself known to us emphatically as *this* individual's manner of responding, in a terrible isolation, to *his* pain. In our first contact with Gower, Capra makes certain that we "miss him" altogether while at the same time giving us a standard, "closed image" of the harsh employer— that of an amusing Dickensian grotesque with grizzled hair in frantic disarray, a lean, woebegone look accompanied by a dismal stare—which allows us perceptually to dispose of him. When one is unexpectedly alerted to the fact that there are additional components (foremost among them a consuming sorrow) to be reckoned with, one must somehow work one's way back to his character through the now solidified mask created by one's earlier, summarizing gaze. In the viewer's effort to force this mask into alignment with his newly obtained knowledge, he necessarily slows the rate at which he comes to grasp the reality of Gower's tragedy. This scarcely discernible retarding process is sufficient to impart to Gower's loss the felt "embeddedness" of a thing rooted in life.

George discovers what has happened to the druggist at the same moment we do. The telegram bearing the news of the son's death has been left open by the cash register. Coming, as it does, almost directly after Mary's secret pledge of love, the telegram seems to materialize as a second whispered message, this time directed to George's good ear. George turns to look at Gower and hesitantly enters the back room to inquire if he needs anything. The druggist's anger has momentarily subsided, replaced by a state of unseeing emptiness. His grief looms so immense as to be unapproachable. He exhibits a calm of that deadly sort that looks for any opening to break out of itself; and the wrath that shakes him by fits is the form of relief that beckons most strongly. George's desire to commiserate no sooner arises than it is denied expression in an atmosphere that is silently edged with fear.

Here, as in so many other sequences in the film, a mood that begins to gain ground is checked by a kind of lightning reflex before it has a chance to stretch out full length. Capra's intention is never merely to cut the mood off, however, but to put other elements in its way, in effect setting it behind a temporary restraining wall where it can accumulate pressure as it waits for a later, stronger point of release. (One of the most impressive instances of this is George's genuinely desperate embrace of Mary after the telephone scene which, properly regarded, is not the culmination of his present visit to Mary's home but rather the delayed end-point of the dream-emblazoned walk he had taken with Mary four years ago—that had been broken off by the news of his father's stroke. The entire weight of the intervening years, where the plentiful hopes of that night lie unwoven, is part of what George clasps as he holds Mary.)

65

From within the supply room, George watches Gower stumbling about, in ominous self-detachment, as he attempts to fill a prescription for another child who has fallen ill. The old man accidentally mixes a toxic substance into the pills, an action that eerily imbues his son Robert's death with a ghostly afterimage. It is almost as if the child's death is asking to repeat itself, as a way of being brought nearer. This time the father will not be absent. He will have mixed (and felt) the death with his own hands. George is reasonably certain that he has observed an error in Gower's preparations, but when he begins to question the druggist he is ordered to leave and make his delivery.

There is a perfectly judged cut back to Mary, still seated on her stool, shortly before George departs from the store, and another, following his return, after Gower has begun to slap him. In the latter shot, the imagined pain of the beating she is unable to see is registered on her face. Capra, as we've noted several times already in this sequence, continually rotates the perspective among all the characters whose position he has established in a scene, creating an effect of spaciousness in his handling of even the most closed-in events.

The "natural observation post" of the Italian filmmaker, Vernon Young once stated, "is the family bosom, so to speak . . . and society is simply *famiglia*, writ large. . . . In Italy, to be *private* still has much of the old Roman denotation: to be deprived."[12] Wherever possible, Capra seeks to give the actions he portrays a centrifugal thrust, pushing out from the solitary ego to one or more witness points. Every important occasion is broken into pieces, like a loaf of bread, and distributed to a number of sympathetic beholders who retain not a private but a collective memory of it. In this way its chances of fading out or being altogether lost are lessened a bit. This is a world where essential matters are left pretty much in the open, like Gower's telegram, rather than buried beyond reach within various inner solitudes. Mary's flinching while George is being slapped is also the announcement of that mysterious process by which their souls are gradually brought into synchronization, which is delightfully continued during their much later walk home after the dance when they strive to harmonize their voices on the last line of the "Buffalo Gals" song.

As George attempts to find some pretext to stall before leaving the drugstore, he aimlessly looks up at the wall in front of him and is struck by what seems to be yet another magical directive: a small pipe advertisement carrying the reassuring inscription, "Ask Dad, he knows." Once more, Capra forecasts by a single, seemingly transparent detail, a form of encounter that he has no intention of materializing. One anticipates that George's meeting with his father will resolve his crisis, but instead it places George at a still further remove from security. He is to be given no opportunity, at this juncture, to find out what his father knows, but he will be called upon to demonstrate what it is that he knows about his father.

The porter at the gate of Peter Bailey's office when George arrives there is the boy's Uncle Billy, a perpetually addled man whose ineffectuality has always dwelt side by side with his magnanimity. Capra introduces him with a visual reference to the strings he habitually keeps tied around the fingers of one hand whose function, here and in the future, are to remind him of appointments that he always fails to keep. Billy's strings, that seem at this point a standing joke in which he amiably, if a bit embarrassedly, participates, are the tiny clue—no bigger than Zuzu's petals—to his identity. As we learn in the Pottersville nightmare, the strings he places around his fingers are his fragile holding-action against an ever-threatening mental collapse. Along with the Bailey family's love, they are what precariously tie his world together. Numerous crucial details of this sort are slipped into the narrative by Capra with such rapidity and such a glancing touch that it almost appears as though they were not meant to be recalled; but, of course, they are, and it is gratifying to feel that a whole host of things one casually latched onto in passing prove to be essential pieces of knowledge later on. All of them are eventually called back, just as the entire community is in the film's closing scene, for an emotionalized rediscovery.

George easily manages to get past Uncle Billy and enters his father's office where the latter is engaged in a painful discussion with Henry Potter, the town's leading (and happily conscienceless) businessman. Characteristically, George momentarily loses sight of the distressing purpose that brought him there as he watches Potter grimly bear down on Peter Bailey with accusations that will, in a not too distant time, be turned against himself. Potter identifies the pliability and incapacity for "sharp dealing" that Peter displays in his business as the essence of his nature. His unprofitable altruism flimsily veils a craven willingness to be exploited, and perhaps a hidden hankering for personal failure, nothing more.

It is Potter's chief function in the film to hold a compelling false mirror up to honorable behavior. He expertly identifies not only the absurdity but also (startlingly) the lurking inhuman horror of too much selflessness. Potter's constant attendant in his rites of belittlement is an annulled personality wearing the fastidious, constricting black garb of an undertaker; he never speaks, but his level, passionless gaze serves to confirm, beyond any hope of appeal, that what one sees in Potter's mirror is what one is. George has moved, then, from one area of threat that is at least sharply delimited, to an imagined place of safety where he is confronted by a menace large enough to crush his father.

Though George isn't old enough to understand the precise meaning of Potter's insinuations, or the basis of his attack on his father, his instincts put him in touch with something that Potter has never seen and that his father has only glimpsed fragmentarily, and with much self-doubt—the shape of a life authentically centered on others' needs. It is this understanding, undimmed by any trace of shame or humiliation, that impels George in his short, unbidden defense of his father and simultaneous urge to strike Potter. Ironically, when George eventually reaches the age where he can comprehend Potter's reasoning as it is made to work against himself, he becomes more deeply susceptible to it than his father was, and cannot formulate, privately or publicly, an adequate response to Potter's judgment of him.

Mr. Bailey leads George out of his office after his son has been pulled away from Potter and, by a very brief, weary half-smile as he stands in the doorway saying goodbye to George, measures the moment in which he's been restored to himself. At the same instant, however, George remembers Gower and the undelivered medicine and looks away, maintaining the careful balance we've noted throughout the sequence between delicately transmitted emotional signals and delayed or blocked reception. As the office door closes, George faces the prospect of returning to Gower's back room, and confronting his impenetrable rage alone.

For the climax of the sequence, Capra adopts what is for him a rather unorthodox mode of visual presentation. He places his camera behind a line of angled shelves covered with vials, beakers, and jars in the pharmacy's supply room. It is a vantage point that, first of all, appears to honor the promise of secrecy that George makes to Gower at the very end of the scene. Because Capra's images so seldom give one the sense of being closed off from full participation, whenever he imposes a distance for some length of time it has the effect of a willed exclusion. In this instance, one occupies a position analogous to that not quite invisible place at the family table during a dreadful quarrel that in no way involves you, where you are not meant to be present but somehow find yourself there anyway.

Capra is obviously very concerned that Gower's final breakdown not be illuminated in the wrong way. To be situated directly on top of him, visually speaking, as he is brought to his knees by the realization of what he has almost caused to happen, would be to take unfair advantage of the wretched extremity to which he's been driven. The act of looking, rather, must be chastened by a consciousness that one's presence is partially withheld from the event, and this is achieved by making it necessary to watch Gower in a manner that feels half-turned away. The distance and the interposed barrier clarify the path to an appropriately restrained sharing of the old man's deliverance from a second calamity. (I am reminded of Renoir's handling of Maréchal's first embrace of Elsa in *Grand Illusion*. The two acknowledge their feelings for each other in the middle distance while we are stationed in another room, watching through an open doorway.)

George's return to the drugstore coincides with a concerned telephone call to Gower from the customer who is still waiting for the child's medicine. Considerably drunker than in the earlier scene, Gower fiercely yanks George into the back room as soon as he hangs up, and delivers several harsh slaps to the side of his head. (Is this attack somehow a completion, in a different moral realm, of the boy's thwarted attack on Potter?) The first blow, as I previously mentioned, is "intercepted" by Mary's reacting presence. Her subsequent elimination from the action subtly disengages the crisis from its one stabilizing feature. The viewer is pushed, without any further "holds" or "controls," to the startlingly intense center of the disorder. The situation suddenly acquires a drastically restricted circumference from which everything but pain has been excluded. There is a rapid accumulation of negative weight on a single point, and any sense of deliverance must yield half its share to sorrow in the passage through it.

George pleads with Gower to stop hitting his bad ear that has begun to bleed and cries out his suspicion that the old man had unknowingly "put something wrong in the capsules." Troubled, Gower moves over to the table to check the pills, and after the few moments it takes him to ascertain his error, he begins to tremble; he turns to George and motions to him strangely. Capra suspends George's recognition of Gower's intention for several critical "beats"—that is to say, time intervals containing separate units of meaning. As Gower's hands shakily reach out to clutch at him, George misconstrues the action, for the moment unable to apprehend the difference between two forms of desperation, one born of enraged grief, the other of gratitude. This results in a delicate refinement on the ancient comic mechanism, the double take, elevated here, as it is again in the pivotal bridge scene when George is returned to life, by the fact that it is unexpectedly played for feeling.

In the bridge episode, our awareness that George's plea "to live again" has been granted runs ahead of his own, so that the pressure of our forcibly restrained eagerness to share the good news with him lifts the pendulum of the anticipated mood swing to a higher and higher point. When George finally does "see," a moment that coincides with his recovery of Zuzu's petals, the pendulum descends with an exhilarating rush, and as with the double take, the impact of the reversal is sufficient to knock things off balance. In a Mack Sennett double take, the comic falls backwards when he takes his second, verifying look at a hitherto "unabsorbed" peril, giving physical expression to a collision taking place in the mind. Similarly, on the bridge, George crazily springs into the arms of his friend Bert as the outward manifestation of a whirling emotional turnaround in which he more or less trips over himself midway.

For the drugstore scene to conclude appropriately, it is essential that George be a somewhat confused interpreter of Gower's self-humbling action. As Gower staggers forward to hug him, George is principally conscious of the fact that the extended hands are those that have just struck him. While Gower moans, "No, no, no . . ." in an effort to reassure him, George replies, "Please don't hit my sore ear again." The visibly bleeding ear anchors George's perspective to his own distress, and even in the midst of the reconciliation he cannot be entirely torn away from it. He begins to cry for his own pain, and if, in the process, the pain opens to include another, there is enough personal anguish mingled with the commiseration to make the response deeper than simple pity. The druggist, having now fallen to his knees, embraces the child, but George does not react to the embrace as though it were a gesture of repentance or a request for forgiveness. He is only mindful of the man's terrible air of deprivation, and he strives to say something that will make Gower know that his sorrow has received some small notice. With this chord, which Capra holds for no more than a few seconds, the sequence draws to a close.

Earlier I spoke briefly of Capra's inclination to have us come to know things in their absence, a point I would like to expand upon in the final section of this essay. Donald Willis, writing about *Lost Horizon* in his study *The Films of Frank Capra*, convincingly suggests that Capra is only able to bring his vision of Shangri-la movingly to life in that instant when Conway, pausing in his departure up the mountain, turns to view it for what he believes will be the last time.[13] Against all odds, Capra makes his Utopia fleetingly reverberate at a distance in a manner that it never has when experienced at close range. So too, in *Mr. Deeds Goes to Town* (a far more impressive film), the citizenry of Mandrake Falls is introduced to us at the railway station where we are immediately obliged to take leave of them. This hazy bucolic realm, which until now had only been memorable because of the astonishment and humor that the wised-up city dwellers brought to their perceptions of it, acquires an identity laced with a certain poignancy as it is observed from the rear platform of a fast withdrawing train. Deeds, a lone tuba player lingering on this platform, sounds a few dolorous bass notes from "Auld Lang Syne" as he drifts away from his orchestral fraternity. Or, to cite one further example, the John Doe organization in *Meet John Doe* comes closest to a unified sense of its moral destination as its members stand, a sea of umbrellas under the arc lights and rain in Wrigley Field, awaiting a speech that will spell their ruin. These are merely large-scale instances of an abiding tendency in Capra, which is to have things disclose the properties that make them indispensable only when they are set at a vanishing point. It is with this end in mind that Capra so often tries (especially in *Wonderful Life*) to create the sense of desired conditions or spaces hovering on the margin between presence and absence.

A somewhat analogous ambition, I believe, lies behind the nervous lyricism of Francois Truffaut's *Jules and Jim*. The soft, sun-dappled Impressionist landscapes which form the background for so much of the action in the Truffaut film seem, on the one hand, always to extend an unvarying promise of buoyancy, tranquillity, and replenished youth while the gliding camera rushes on with a carefree abandon of its own, suggesting that it has no more urgent goal in view than a possible picnic on the grass. On the other hand, the steadily mounting disquiet in the characters' relationships asserts itself in the agitated "off-rhythms" of the editing, a kind of stabbing punctuation in an otherwise harmonious flow. One feels this sprung rhythm almost viscerally as a cutting in or shutting off, a sharp reminder of what Carlyle once called "the troublous, dim Time element," similar in effect to the uneven breath of a dying man in slumber, as it tries to break through his strangely serene dreams of home and childhood.

The shimmering countryside and the bright, swirling music of Georges Delerue exude a confidence that in the presence of so much beauty every destructive impulse must evaporate; but Jules, Jim, and Catherine cannot forever live up to the demands of innocence that such an environment seems to make on them, and the editing, by turns abrupt and dislocating, is a means of interrogating the spirit of confidence without fully dispelling it. Opposed forces—the enchanted place and swiftly passing time—unceasingly challenge one another, each proclaiming the other's incapacity to extend its influence any further. It is the peculiar triumph of this film to let this contest remain undecided. Catherine and Jim disappear at last into the dimension of things lost to time, but their world is no less radiant for their passing, and I don't feel that the effect of this radiance is either ironic or sentimental. The landscape that they've traversed has not turned sour, but neither does it appear mindful of their absence. It stands exactly as it stood before, in a state of gracious expectancy, summoning one forth to fresh adventures.

The tiny episode in the film that most perfectly typifies the quality of suspension that Truffaut is aiming for is one that does not depend on editing. Jim and Catherine's child by Jules, Sabine, are rolling down a slope in the meadow, laughing excitedly. Over and over they turn and with each roll their elation grows, but we watch with the knowledge that the marriage that produced this child is, in effect, over, and that the man bringing such happiness to Sabine is destined to take the husband's place. Almost subliminally one is made to feel that it is just such easy motions as this tumbling in the meadow that set the years moving, and that the wind that stirs alike the grass and the child's hair is time-laden.

In *It's a Wonderful Life,* the latent force which holds Bedford Falls on the verge of apparition is Pottersville, which, of course, is itself something of an apparition. Capra has conceived two competing environments for the same space, and in the interstices of one there always forms the shadow of the other. Having felt obliged to read on more than one occasion the decidedly slight Philip Van Doren Stern tale which served as the basis for Capra's film, in an effort to determine what Capra could possibly have seen in it, I've come to believe that he was most deeply struck by the fantasy-premise (clearly linked to the experience of war) that a beloved place could be utterly obliterated, and then magically reestablished. What happens to Bedford Falls is eerily close to the newsreel of the planes delivering their payload of bombs to Dresden in Vonnegut's *Slaughterhouse-Five.* When the newsreel comes to the point where the bombs are released and begin their visible plunge earthward, one has only to throw the projector in reverse to see the same bombs lifted back into the planes and the lethal aircraft disappear.

When preparing *Wonderful Life* for shooting, Capra was obliged to stake out all the essential sites in the narrative twice and to imaginatively superimpose each area upon its negating counterpart. Thus, the long shot of Bailey Park midway through the film, with its loonily tilted pioneer wooden lettering on the archway leading in, functions first as a passageway for an old, wheezing truck piled high with furniture and an equally overloaded car (both filled with voices comically caroling fragments of Italian songs), and then, on its reappearance, also in long shot, as a grimly symmetrical, noiseless cemetery where even the snow conspires to obscure the names on the stones. The point, I must emphasize, lies not in the contrast itself, but rather in the fact that everything in Bedford Falls has been consciously shaped to accommodate its phantom replacements in advance. It is designed, looking-glass fashion, as something to be completed in reverse, and that quality of each place in Bedford Falls which is to be grasped when confronted with its negative image, in effect, lies ahead of itself, contemplating its own end. The half-century that has elapsed since the film's first release have been exceedingly generous to Capra's intentions in this regard. No sooner does Capra reveal Bedford Falls to us—in a hushed sequence of shots of its main streets and buildings on a snowy Christmas Eve—than we are already in the presence of a world that, at least in its external features, we know to be past recapture.

Once in Pottersville, we find everything that had seemed poised to slip away throughout the film actually gone. What is terrifying here, of course, is not simply that a strange city has all at once "heaved up in the center" of George's town and blackened its sky,[14] but that it is filled with shadows of familiar things that have somehow become unknowable. The place that George has always been desperate to leave manages suddenly to leave him, and the surfaces that had given witness to his life flatten out to nothingness. The darkness of Pottersville, however, by virtue of Clarence's abiding presence, is of a sort that everywhere points out of itself toward its own defeat; it is a darkness that identifies as its own only the things that yet stand free of it, that it has no claim on. Conversely, luminous Bedford Falls with its atmosphere of continually impending crisis, seems haunted in advance by the forms that Pottersville will eventually assume.

Pottersville is a cemetery which knows itself to be empty but would convince one otherwise. And yet the grim landscape is also an immediately recognizable version of the postwar urban environment that many GI's discovered on returning home. Paradoxically, this spectral city ultimately defines itself as George's anguished memory of a lost reality he still firmly possesses. All that George has to do, though he does not know it, is turn his back on the clamorous woes of Pottersville and reopen the door of his briefly adjourned life. Then he will have the solace of finding, in confirmation of the greatest of all human longings, that those who were forever gone are still here. This sequence of the film is where the terrible extent of war losses and confusions seems to emerge most forcefully, in a tangled, painfully overwrought set of images. The film invokes presence and absence in multiple registers, and makes us wonder where to seek out our own sense of life—in the terrain marked as dark, all-too-credible mirage or in that earlier Bedford Falls of "thwarted dreams" and captivity, that has suddenly gone missing.

"We are happy," Yeats said in one of his letters, "when for everything inside us there is an equivalent something outside us." This fairly describes the condition George arrives at in the closing scenes of *It's a Wonderful Life*. Yeats went on, however, to add the converse. "It is terrible to desire and not possess, and terrible to possess and not desire. Because of this we long for an age which has the unity which Plato somewhere defined as sorrowing and rejoicing over the same things."[15] George Bailey has passed, in swift, unbearable succession, through both of the dismal soul-states that Yeats alludes to—that of "possessing and not desiring" when he resolves to take his own life, that of "desiring and not possessing" when he enters Pottersville, and discovers that life has cast him out and will have no part of him. From the instant that George emerges safely on the far side of his double tragedy, aptly dramatized on a bridge, the rather awesome "unity" that Yeats yearns for is at hand for George, and, for the ten minutes or so that remain in the film, for us as well.

I can't help regarding Capra's entire career as an arduous apprenticeship for the supreme achievement of this film's conclusion, an apprenticeship in which all the other, sometimes jerry-built "happy endings" he conceived may be rightly understood as preliminary drafts for this one. In *It's a Wonderful Life*, the joy liberated from the depths of sorrow achieves a force that is nothing short of titanic. Capra manages to actualize, just once (and to the best of my knowledge it has only been done once on film) a joy that seems almost without limits, as sharp and intense as any form of grief, and allows it to break, in wave upon wave, during George's lengthy run through the streets of Bedford Falls and through the rooms of his recovered home. Then it gathers itself up for a second outpouring, sweeping through the downstairs with the sudden influx of a crowd of friends. It is a force that seems, for the moment, to be superior to any negative emotion, kept alive, in fact, by the powerful intimation that it has absorbed all of them into itself. This is a joy capable of repairing for a brief spell whatever breach tragedy has opened. With the outlines of Pottersville still fresh in our minds, in which the Bailey house has figured as a gutted ruin (unwarmed by any trace of human presence), we observe one figure after another materializing in the restored space of the richly metaphoric *living* room, as though released from the shadows that had formed over them. They can see George and he can see them, and the ability to see is a blessing they communicate. How much loving, reciprocal awareness, one wonders, can four walls be made to hold?

This room is one more small space into which something immeasurable has been squeezed. And there are spaces within spaces inside this rectangle that contain still other secret fullnesses. The detachable knob on the newel post of the Bailey stairway that had worked in just the opposite way from the cigar lighter in the drugstore, *never* confirming the hopes of the one who grabbed hold of it but serving rather as an agonizing reminder of everything that frustrated George in his "settled" life—this hated object suddenly transforms into the sweet, incontestable proof that George's home has returned to him, in the beautifully imperfect state in which he left it.[16] Uncle Billy, whose failed memory had been responsible for the loss of money that brought George to the brink of bankruptcy, is singled out to carry in the basket of money that Mary had collected from George's friends.[17] The community-wide preparations for George's brother Harry's "hero's welcome" and homecoming (following his acceptance of the Congressional Medal of Honor) are quietly diverted to a celebration of George's spiritual homecoming. The Christmas carol that George and Mary's daughter Jane had nerve-wrackingly played over and over again on the piano in an unintentionally mocking counterpoint to George's profound depression, has found its proper flow in time for her to accompany George's friends as they sing it while assembled about him. Zuzu, whose vanished petals had marked more surely than anything else could have the loss of George's identity and place in the world, straddles her father's back, with her arms securely wrapped around his neck. She is the element of lightness in all the burdens he willingly takes up again. Mary stands next to George, where she has always stood, her face wet with tears. Her constancy effortlessly transfigures George's sense of what it means to be stuck: We may recall the swimming pool that opened up beneath George and Mary when they first danced together. Once they resurface after the shock of falling in, they immediately reconnect in the water and dance on, unfazed, *in place*. Finally, the tinkling of a tiny bell on the Christmas tree carries the joy to the last place in the homemade universe of the film that it has left to go—beyond the walls of this world where a wingless angel enables the enchanted spectators outside the frame to partake in the rebirth of imagination. It is we, rather than Clarence, on whom the "winged state" is most movingly conferred.

3

Thinking about Movie Sentiment: Toward a Reading of *Random Harvest*

> The life of human beings is not passed in the sphere of transitive verbs alone.
> —Martin Buber, *I and Thou*

> The work of someone like Dorothy Wordsworth consists of the effort to melt the hostile knot of self, which is perception in the I-it relationship. When the heart melts, it can itself become the vision, and a reciprocity has been established that goes beyond the transitive view of nature.
> —Irving Massey, *The Gaping Pig*

The sentimental film is a tempting but troublesome place to begin any discussion of the formidable role that emotion plays in the act of movie watching. It is tempting because this type of film so directly solicits feeling and revels in its display. The difficulties arise from the discomforts and uncertainties of speaking about the process of emotional identification in the first person, from a position that is, unavoidably, vulnerable. A familiar alternative strategy, amply explored in current film theory, is for the spectator critic to distance herself from the emotional content of the sentimental narrative. By reconstructing a film's method of positioning an imaginary spectator *within* that content, the critic can demonstrate how she has been coerced, deceived, or otherwise taken over by "mechanisms" of feeling. An arguable weakness of this strategy is that it tries to interpret emotional response from a place too *far* removed from it, as though the flow of feeling, when strongly resisted, is still much the same phenomenon that is encountered by the "immersed" and assenting spectator. To modify some well-known lines from T. S. Eliot's "East Coker": "Because one has only learnt to get the better of

Paula (Greer Garson) trying to see through the eyes of her lover, Smith (Ronald Colman) in *Random Harvest*.

[feelings] / For the thing one no longer has to [feel] or the way in which / One is no longer disposed to [feel] it."[1]

The rhetoric of sensibility, in the impoverished form in which it survives for us as a vehicle for aesthetic and moral inquiry, seems inadequate for the task that confronts us: treating the force of sentiment in film as an actual experience rather than an *object* for theory to act upon. "Sympathy," "passion," "idealization," "powers of spirit," "exaltation" are no longer terms to which we can readily assign values or take for granted as valid components of imaginative expression. There is considerable doubt among literary theorists whether any of these "states" can be pried loose from the delusive hierarchies and exploded assumptions of the religious/cultural systems that gave rise to them. Can we presently speak on behalf of the feelings that sentimental films sometimes make available to us without becoming apologists for old orthodoxies and subtly tyrannical codes of behavior that we do well to leave behind? Perhaps no one would deny that at least some of our emotional identifications with films are beneficial and blameless, but it is possible

Smith (Ronald Colman) about to awaken to a world without Paula after being struck by a car in *Random Harvest*.

to make such concessions without lessening one's skepticism about the rhetoric of sentimental movies. The majority of identification points established for female spectators, say, in the "women's films" of the forties, as Mary Ann Doane, Linda Williams, and others have compellingly argued, create false positions for women to occupy, denying them—through an enticing mirage of victim attitudes—not only a room of their own but also the basic materials of identity. (What happens to the female "gaze" and "voice" and the possibilities for an active, independent life in these narratives?)[2] In the face of such persistent threats of distortion and entrapment, it is reasonable that feminist critics demystify the lure of ennobling tears and reveal the dangers of "natural" responses to powerful rhetoric.

Is it possible, however, to separate the emotional content of film scenes from other ways of knowing what the narrative is "saying" through them? In making such a division do we not lose those aspects of film reality which only emotion can reveal? Sentimental films typically contain one or more significant scenes which do not merely invite our emotional involvement but command it, urgently summoning our swift involuntary surrender to something whose value can only be apprehended if we are *made* to feel it. For those who successfully resist such summons, what appears in place of the intended recognition is a straining apparatus that has failed of its purpose, gesturing toward a hollow space that could only be filled by our answering presence. It is not enough to say that the unmoved spectator has an experience of a different order than the spectator who is "taken in." In moments of sentimental epiphany and transformation, if one does not participate, one is left with nothing *but distance,* an awareness of what one isn't affected by. Because the acute consciousness of distance differs so markedly from the desired "merging" of viewer and image, one not only stands outside the experience of the film but may well feel authorized to repudiate it. Images which stake their entire being on the unrestrained presence of feelings one cannot share have the destitute appearance of something queasily unreal. We have no secondary experience to consult that could help us know the reality we have missed by being absent, excluded. The truth that we seem justified in asserting about our failed connection is that it exposes some deficiency in the narrative mechanism. A fiction has been devised to *extort* a sympathetic response from us, but we have managed to see through it, and thus save ourselves from a response in excess of what the fiction has earned.

But does this narrow escape from sentiment necessarily give us an advantage over the more credulous spectator who has wept rather than turned away? If one is not moved by the endings of Dreyer's *Ordet* or *City Lights,* to cite two instances of films where everything seems to depend on a final catharsis, can one know the most important things these films are capable of showing? Reduced to their ideas, both endings seem crude and extravagantly melodramatic: a woman is raised from the dead because, in part, a child has faith that it is possible; another woman, cured of blindness discovers that her rich benefactor was, in fact, a starving tramp. If the images through which such ideas are communicated lack emotional resonance, what would cause us to attend to them, to believe that there is a substance here that matters? It is too frequently assumed that sentiment depends for its effect on obviousness and that the rhetoric of sentiment is overwhelmingly committed to an almost primitive transparency of intention and to an immediate understanding of the emotional stimulus. In *City Lights* and *Ordet,* quite to the contrary, the unexpected force of one's engagement and emotional release is what awakens us to the presence of something not at all transparent in their final revelations. As is so often the case with art, the first intimation that a film has achieved something difficult and worth understanding may be the depth of our imaginative identification with what we see. And our sense of depth is commonly derived from an investment of feeling larger than the ready-to-hand concepts we might use to contain it. We are provoked by the strength of our response to interrogate the elements that brought it forth, to find out what the images have spoken to inside us that has led us to *believe* in their significance. It is next to impossible to reconstruct accurately an emotional experience after the fact, or to be precise about how the feeling content of our relations to a narrative interacts with other ways of thinking about it. Nevertheless, to simplify or disregard the process by which our feelings have been actuated and have somehow "gotten the better of us" for the sake of greater objectivity and detachment results in a highly misleading account of one's encounter with art. In interpretation, irony seems to provide a more solid foundation for value claims about a narrative than sentiment. Sentiment seems to offer us assurance that we can have the things we most ardently desire. Irony opposes such assurances with reminders of how the world as we know it keeps things out of reach, or how we spoil what we do manage to obtain. "Bare reality: what a crook it sometimes is," Robert Walser writes. "It steals things, and afterwards it has no idea what to do with them."[3] If we imagine a dialogue between irony and sentiment, it is hard to see how irony (with death as its trump card) can be denied the last word. In sentimental films, sentiment is given the last word (or resolving image), but in those that I find most remarkable and likely to excite wonder, irony is not bypassed, curtailed, or forgotten. The conditions for emotional transformation are born in the very midst of irony. Irony might be said to provide the walls that enclose the image, or frame the prison cell in which the imaged desire lies captive. The tension of the sentimental ending is almost always generated by sentiment's need to find some permissible, authentic form of potent expression before irony vanquishes it. I am reminded of the last image of Strindberg's *A Dream Play*, a giant chrysanthemum mysteriously blooming at the top of a burning castle. Sentiment strives to articulate an image of possibility that irony is not equipped to defile or efface. Through the most fragile, easily challenged transitory illuminations of an ideal (which is to be known by seeing rather than having), sentiment seeks an occasion to affirm, bless, and deify existence. But the affirmation—being spiritual—has its life only in the moment (the consecrated act) of being made visible. The sensations of fullness attained as we behold what sentiment has a knowledge of is taken away from us very quickly, almost on the instant. It is as though one had suddenly remembered *completely* what it felt like to be in love with someone one no longer cared about, then lost the feeling again, but retained an impression of what had occurred. The recovered heart, "seeing" what it had long ago gladly relinquished as once more the highest good, the source of all well-being, feels that it has never been away from this awareness. And then this certainty falls away as simply as it came, and one experiences with relief the pleasure and freedom of renunciation. It is better *not* to have that love surrounded by danger and terror, which after all proved itself incapable of lasting. Though I rediscovered the truth of the joy that once defined me, I willingly cast it off a second time. For a few moments, everything became clear again by the light of that forgotten attachment and I was *possessed* by it, but irony intervenes with the reminder that this love no longer belongs to me, if it ever did.

Does a faith in sentiment's revelatory power not rest on some rickety, outworn notions of selfhood? I realize it is unfashionable at present to maintain too unskeptical a faith in the self's existence. Nevertheless, I am not persuaded by even the most ingenious rhetorical demonstrations of the self's "hall of mirrors" illusoriness, for the simple reason that no one has yet shown me what one gains that is socially or personally helpful by assenting to such a position. I cannot, try as I might, rouse the will to believe it. If Hans-Georg Gadamer is right to assert, in *Truth and Method,* that "the self-awareness of the individual is only a flickering in the closed circuits of historical life," I would see that as a strong incentive to be prodigiously attentive to that "flickering" and to do what I can to extend its light and life. Our common task (in criticism and in life) is to find ways of extending what D. W. Winnicott calls the "potential space" of autonomy and sharable culture. It is *less* "helpful," by this logic, to accept the model of a subject entirely subordinated to cultural pressures and social definitions than the model of a self struggling, with some chance of success, to relate inner and outer actualities. The good office of a struggling self is to resist the calculable shape of a dull cultural construct (the latter no easier to specify or prove in its "determined" particulars, surely, than a self such as Keats envisioned, forming and reforming itself in a "vale of soul-making"). Mary Ann Doane and numerous other theorists have offered compelling descriptions of some of the conditions of spectatorship and the feasible "deformities" resulting from unimaginative assimilation of conventional narratives. What they have failed to do is to offer an adequate representation of a *living* spectator.

Is it any less perilous for someone who has no sense of humor to translate the mysteries of comedy into a formal mechanism than it is for someone who refuses participation (or at least the avowal of participation) in "uncontrollable" spectator emotion to say what is psychically involved in the experience? If all issues pertaining to *personal* identity are infinitely problematic, as current theory argues, where do we derive our assurance that we can construct meaningful diagrams of "others"? If the private self is lost to us, by what trick of language or gift of providence have we suddenly acquired a reliable picture of other minds—the mind, as it were, of society? Does even the most sophisticated understanding of how movie conventions operate (at the level of *somebody's* intention) allow us to fashion a spectator who perfectly inhabits, with no area of resistance or supplemental awareness, the fantasy space prepared for her? Ingmar Bergman, in his well-known early essay "Why I Make Movies," argues that the chief difference between our involvement in film experience and in the act of reading is that films (even very ordinary ones) have the power to engage our emotions directly, while literature always requires some effort of will, in conjunction with intellect, to make language into pictures and sensations vivid enough for feeling to assent to. Bergman compares the rhythm of films to the immediate physiological effect of music: "inhalations and exhalations in continuous sequence."[4] He also touches upon the familiar analogy of film and dream. We are seized by the film image, in much the same way that a dream seizes us. The kind of sense that a movie narrative makes is only belatedly rational. Under normal viewing conditions movies enter the psyche as a ceaseless flow; one needs leisure to reflect, which this "flow," by its very nature, refuses to grant. The mystery of the process by which fictional representation earns our acceptance and involvement cannot be solved by saying that images calculated to produce specific emotional effects and to reinforce social norms function in just the way they are meant to, or solely at a collective level.

Most psychoanalytic film criticism at present follows Jacques Lacan in sanctioning a metaphysics of absence in contrast to the increasingly defenseless metaphysics of presence central to so much of Western religion and philosophy. Donald Carveth usefully reminds us that metaphors of presence are intricately involved with the "matriarchal values of union and similarity." He argues that the currently dominant metaphors of absence (and the metaphysics that they imply), far from transcending patriarchal bias, are pervaded by it. Separateness and difference are granted more "reality" (and value) than the concepts of connection and the form of "likeness" that permits nonillusory fusion.

A new form of denial and repression may be required to make lack and radical isolation the privileged terms in our hierarchy of values. Why has it come about that presence, connection, and plenitude are viewed as obstacles to authentic understanding, or as things too visionary or culturally conditioned to hope for in any trustworthy forms? As Carveth suggests:

> On a deeper level, the patriarchal insistence upon the facts of separateness and difference, its emphasis upon boundaries and limits, and upon the gap, space, nothingness or "lack of being" between self and other, subject and object, can be seen as a desperate distancing defense against both the threat and the *temptation* of merger. Whether the defense is mainly against an oedipal desire for incestuous union, a pre-oedipal symbiotic desire for merger with the primary object, or an unconscious need and longing to be the object of the empathic look and adoring smile of the archaic mirroring self object—and presumably all of these meanings can operate simultaneously—the fact remains that the very intensity of these fusional wishes can give rise to a reactive or compensatory insistence upon boundaries, separation and distance.[5]

Metaphors of absence, taken literally and then required to *reify* the experience of emptiness, confirm Freud's sense that the castration complex is our "psychic bedrock." The very idea of presence is devalued in two ways. Presence is either a sign of a persisting religious fantasy of transformation or a regression, toward infancy—the engulfing maternal bond, say, that Ingmar Bergman shows us in the prologue of *Persona* when a male child reaches up to explore a gigantic image of a female face. No good, apparently, can come of our dreams of presence. They must be outgrown.[6]

The fear, amounting to terror, that many spectators feel at the prospect of an emotional surrender to the *presence* of film (a fear that is often instinctively transformed into a more manageable "resentment" at being manipulated) may have a great deal to do with the always existent, always profound, always problematic issue of the "longing for the mother," for the repair or recovery or full recognition of the lost primal bond. I fully concur with Carveth's conclusion that psychic development involves putting oneself continually at risk in the "potential space" *between* such oppositional terms as connection and separation. Film theory, for much of its brief history, has seemed fixated on problems of differentiation (overcoming the dangerous susceptibility to "fusion" with the film image). Too often ignored are the possible psychic benefits of integration: a less guarded way of attending to the visions and voices that film offers us. Integration, as an imaginative experience depending on a willingness to be "seized," a willingness to be wholly vulnerable to something, to be released from the protection that control and distance give us (at a price), may well bring normally isolated areas of the psyche into healing contact with each other. The bridging of inner gaps which the conscious mind does not really know how to accomplish (or perhaps even to ask for) is one of the possible results of a strongly emotional participation in film.

Most current film theory proposes "power" as the crucial term in assessing how popular movies are designed to affect us. Uncritical, undistanced participation in movie narrative (which, when it does occur, rarely lasts for the length of a film) involves an act of submission to the filmmaker's authority. More troubling, in the view of many theorists, is the fact that the spectator also submits to the dominant ideology which the filmmaker either naively or cynically upholds. No one making commercial films, after all, can avoid complicity with the requirements and "values" of the production system. The enlightened spectator, if she is to escape manipulation and the reinforcement of seductive ethical norms, is obliged to challenge and undermine the power of the movie image at every turn, and by every means available to her. She must, first of all, deny the primary emotional force of the image its legitimacy. Emotion, we are told, should be approached as an industrial (as opposed to aesthetic) construct, something engineered, as it were, to bring about a form of automatic assent from the viewer, an assent that she is better off withholding.

How tempting and natural it is, for academics especially, to persuade themselves that the Brechtian vantage point of scrupulous detachment from the turbulence of the dramatic spectacle is the right (and difficult) position to occupy when trying to understand what films *really* communicate. The mysterious enthrallment that each of us who cares for films recalls experiencing when the cinema first took hold of us— and which we still feel intermittently, in spite of ourselves—is antipathetic to the aims of rationality. We must step outside the condition of "dependence" on what the screen offers in order to penetrate cinema's meaning. As though the sensations of being dependent were not perhaps the most vital component of that meaning.

The political education of the film viewer logically entails the suppression of those impulses associated with false persuasion (perhaps all culturally sanctioned persuasion is false), victimization, and the illusions of identification. As we overcome the lures and stratagems of movie narratives, it seems that we are engaged in the healthy process of taking power *away* from the screen image and reclaiming it for ourselves. The stakes in this struggle for a less dependent relation to film images are clearly different for men and women, to say nothing of those minority groups whose status in Hollywood narratives is even more compromised than that of women. But suspicion is not for any spectator the only legitimate response to scenes of sentiment, nor is it always the most instructive. Cynthia Ozick once spoke in an interview of an artist's obligation to "dare to be wounded" in the creative process. And the same injunction might be offered to film viewers. Perhaps we might say of viewers that if they are not at risk, they are not viewing.[7] Ozick's phrase recalls Kafka's celebrated description of art's attempt "to break up the frozen sea within us." The axe of art cutting painfully into the frozen sea is an image that speaks equally to the needs of artist and audience. Surely there is a danger in imagining that the exposure and deconstruction of the liberal humanist "dogmas" underlying, say, De Sica's *Umberto D.* is a more valid and exacting process than exposing *ourselves* to the force of its vision. To do the latter may reduce us to a state of irrational helplessness. What, finally, is there to *say* about loneliness and old age that can rise above or offset the terrible, wrenching clarity of De Sica's images? The film becomes much more manageable if we exchange emotional disarray for "scientific," or knowing, political discourse. Perhaps we could examine *Umberto D.*'s sign systems and generic conventions for evidence of De Sica's vaguely blameworthy capitulation to Christian or bourgeois orthodoxy. Or we could show how the film's despairing fatalism leads the viewer to accept bewildered passivity as a meaningful response to institutional injustice.

The acknowledgment of efficacious tears, in any event, lies outside the domain of any analysis primarily concerned with the political *power* of the medium. Power has lost its positive, aesthetic meaning in most contemporary film theory. In its place is the Foucauldian idea that power is always war, "a war continued by other means," and the Nietzschean corollary that power is inescapable. "This world is the will to power—and nothing besides! And you yourselves are also this will to power—and nothing besides!"[8] What do we sacrifice by imposing a silence about the secret web of our emotional dependence on certain film images and situations—a dependence that cannot be mentioned until one has decided to renounce it? What sort of distortion results in our thinking about ourselves as spectators if we embrace the view that tears necessarily perpetuate the role of powerless victim? Catharsis becomes little more

than a lapse of judgment, whose cure is ironic distance or a more sophisticated political awareness.

An emotional response to sentiment in films often involves more
than a naive surrender to the mass-produced rhetoric of pathos. Such
rhetoric, moreover, is not merely, or exclusively, an act of deception, in
spite of the corporate selling of vast tracts of feeling-based activity in
the form of ad spots on television and in maudlin commercial films.
Making discriminations about the occasions in film where the language
of feeling warrants imaginative or empathic assent is no easier than any
other form of aesthetic judgment. What is easy, and rash, is the conclusion that because spectator emotion not sheathed in irony always involves some sort of blindness to existing power relations, the metaphor
of blindness somehow resolves the problem of feeling.

Is a power-centered discourse incapable of imagining (or craving)
an *end* to its reductive master-slave logic? Might emotional release not
form part of a necessary dialectic in which the mind-set of power occasionally gives way and acknowledges the needs which underlie it—
needs which cannot be addressed in power's own voice? There is
strength to be had in the continual recognition of what one's experience,
or belief system, has led one to deny or leave out of consideration, even
if the reasons for doing so seem obvious. What is obvious is frequently
that which is most in danger of being forgotten, and therefore most in
need of reassertion. Nothing prevents us, of course, from translating
everything we encounter into terms compatible with our beliefs—in this
instance, the ideology of power. But translation risks falsification. Power,
like Christianity, is a narrative in quest of coherent closure. On the other
hand, what do we gain by entrusting ourselves, however briefly, to a
vulnerability (resembling defeat) and the values, potentially delusory,
attached to it?

Let us concede that there are numerous variables in the spectator's
relation to the movie image, and that one of the most significant is the
degree of closeness to—or felt participation in—the image's "life"
(within the narrative). Presence for the movie spectator might be defined
as the sense of being inside the image, a condition of enclosure that is
at once protective and perilous. When full presence is achieved, we are
temporarily unable to control (or even monitor) what is happening
within us. Can we speak accurately of our response to films without
taking account of that part of us which longs to confuse boundaries, to
wake up somewhere else, to be freed from the burden of remembering
our limits? The surrender to tears perhaps beneficially marks the dividing
line between the pressure to escape some aspect of our lives and the

returning realization that we are, indeed, caught—tied to the memory of loss or lack or withheld intimacy that separates us from the fullness (tragic or sentimental) visible on the screen. Tears are inherently self-reflexive; we cannot forget that it is *we* who are crying. Moreover, our emotional submission to the exigencies of the fiction drives us out of it (acutely self-conscious) at the same point where maximum connection has been achieved. It is a falling back to the limits of selfhood from the trancelike height to which our imagination has lifted us. The emotional truth that tears attest to may well have very little to do with the movie narrative, or the world beyond it. It may also be the case, as many critics of sentiment have maintained, that the crying inspired by the plight of fictional figures on screen seldom has much to do with compassion: it is always, to a large extent, self-absorbed—a crying for oneself. But I think it would be wrong to dismiss such displays as a caving in to weakness or self-pity, any more than one would speak in such terms about tears shed in therapy. In both situations, there is often an unsettling lack of knowledge about *where* the tears are coming from and what has caused them to arise. A common form of apology, at movies and in therapy, is: "This is so stupid; I shouldn't be crying like this . . . I don't know why this is happening." The feeling that literally *escapes* is a source of confusion and surprise. All that one can say for certain about movie-generated tears is that something the viewer has beheld has produced an association strong enough so that the impulse to cry is not resisted. And that submission brings the viewer back to himself, by its sudden rupture of the state of passive or rapt concentration. The truth I do not wish to dispose of is that the tears themselves have their foundation in something real, which the movie, by fair or suspect means, has tapped into.

I have not yet dealt adequately with the argument that tears are as readily elicited by the manufacturers of popular entertainment as laughter or fear. There are, beyond question, well-established formulas for each of the basic movie emotions. If tears can be as calculated an element of a movie scenario as a car chase, then where is the mystery? What is it about sentiment that merits special consideration? My tentative reply is that tears signify more suggestively than anything else the ways in which we lose and regain ourselves in the act of watching. I am struck by the need of the spectator (including the one I know best) to yield large areas of unmapped privacy to the power of fiction—a yielding that often surpasses what we are willing to grant to others, in "live" interactions. As Harold Pinter once observed, "to disclose to others the poverty within us is too fearsome a possibility." When I cry at a film, I often find myself remembering, with a measure of surprise, that I *can* cry, and in the act of remembering that capacity forgetting what has occasioned the tears. This is an experience not unlike losing contact with a dream at the moment of waking. (On at least two occasions, my weeping at a film caused me to remember that I was alive. How could such knowledge be mislaid? This critically suspect and barely admissible "fact" is undoubtedly the source of this essay.)

Our "disproportionate response" to moments of sentimental intensity forcibly reminds us that most film experience does not take place in the lighted regions of the mind, where we can rationally come to terms with it, but in the back of the mind, where we regularly lose touch with who we are. It is the place where we do not need to sort out appearances. As Michael Wood has wittily phrased it, appearances never end; we build our sense of the world and our always shifting relation to it "out of all we see and all we don't see." It may be worthwhile then to remystify the act of movie viewing.

I have found that with certain films the catharsis experience is repeatable, at times with lesser intensity, at times with even greater force than was present at a first viewing. The catharsis only recurs, I believe, with films whose core fantasy addresses some wounded area of myself, which is not yet an "open" space, secure enough for full exposure and acknowledgment. Because most sentimental films convey the impression of transparency, of obviousness, we have the misleading sense that the stories they tell are already known to us. We feel that we are having our already sufficient understanding of what they contain confirmed by seeing and hearing them once more. One effect of this confidence (that we can comprehend without effort, without *working* to find meaning) is that we allow the films to "do everything for us." If one is not opposed to this kind of story on principle (which would lead one to quarrel with its lack of "reality" or "emotional excess" every step of the way), the sentimental film can enter one with the swiftness of a dream, and penetrate the space of dreams, the unconscious, to do its work.

Charles Affron has memorably described the "acquisitive strength" of the movie frame when intense feelings are activated in the viewer. Something inside the frame (and inside us), which resists definition, "urges us to fill the voids, the inviting space within its [the frame's] boundaries that are true to the ones that torment us in life." The space we want to fill with ourselves "quickens the rhythm of our desire with its gestures of possession."[9] This passage verges on incoherence, but does so, I think, because of Affron's moving effort to position us dizzyingly in that final phase of enthrallment where we truly don't feel capable of distinguishing the outer image from the inner actuality. We are "tormented," as Affron suggests, by the boundaries of the frame to the extent that we register them, yet at the same time have the impression that the image materialized before us is sustained—as a living presence—by the emotion that it has drawn from us. The image looks back at us in the fullness of all that we have unreflectingly released to it. The frame's reality is, indeed, a narcissistic mirror at each point; like Narcissus we both do and do not know what the reflection is showing us. Tears often form at an impasse between desire and knowledge. They confirm, on the one hand, that we recognize ourselves (or something that we would like to call ours) in what we see. But, on the other hand, they let us know that the sight that overcomes us is not clear enough to be recognized *calmly*. Possibly there is the additional intimation that the image cannot hold us or save us; it is finally uninhabited.

"Only turn aside and you will lose what you love. What you see is but the shadow cast by your reflection; in itself it is nothing. It comes with you, and lasts while you are there; it will go when you go, if go you can." So Ovid sternly reproaches Narcissus by his pool, who unwittingly desires himself and yet "cannot lay hold of himself."[10] Our advantage over Narcissus is that whatever shapes we confuse with our own on the screen are quickly lost to us. Repeated loss is an essential part of our involvement with the images that promise to "fill" us. My own view of the narcissistic transaction with emotionalized screen reflections of the self is that we are seeing not the false, idealized picture of what we imagine ourselves to be (though that, of course, is possible) but rather parts of the self that have been rejected or have withdrawn to a distance and are trying to break through to us.

I can think of no film in which this phenomenon is more impressively the substance of the sentimental epiphany than Frank Capra's *It's a Wonderful Life*. Stanley Cavell has made beautiful metaphoric sense of the *social* dimension of the film's ending.

> The sentiment in the scene is very deep. It has been constructed as cunningly as a Keaton gag; what caps it, finally bursting the dam of tears, is the crowding of this band of goodness (George Bailey's friends and family) into this hero's house, each member testifying individually to his or her affection for him; so that the good of society, the good society at large, is pictured as this man's family (personally sponsored, what's more, by a denizen of heaven). This justice, hence this society, is poetic or nothing.[11]

Perhaps less knowingly "constructed," that is to say, with respect to sentimental intention, is our half-conscious recognition in the Pottersville nightmare of what it means to be wandering in the dark, with all the best parts of ourselves separated from and blind to us: what it means to be in utter desperation weeping over the loss of everything that has formed our ordinary, taken-for-granted self and pleading for our life to be given back to us. Life, in this fantasy, means a "feeling" relation to things. The concluding celebration in George Bailey's living room is, of course, most obviously moving in its imaging of social acceptance, of what it looks like and might feel like to be surrounded by people who love you, and are actively concerned for your well-being. But also envisioned in this living space of "reopened" faces is a return home within the psyche, the unlocking of the doors that have made our spiritual dwelling increasingly small, bare, and uninhabitable.

The surely legitimate terror of being engulfed by all we have closed ourselves off from and denied (in many cases, to insure our survival) enters into our tears at the sight of a room rapidly filling up with a living throng that does *not* annihilate. And we may be angered by the impulse to weep because what we are looking at challenges (so naively) our settled belief that love is never offered without a price, and the price generally exceeds our means. What is freely given and freely accepted has nothing to do with us. Possibly, however, the well-established inner censors of feeling, which Alice Miller calls the "parents' heir" in matters of control, do not prevail over the exquisite poem of looks exchanged between members of the group and George, and between George and the viewer, and the final chorus of "Auld Lang Syne," which binds *everything* in the film's world together. There's coercion here, to be sure, and calculation up to a certain point, though the film taps into a region in many viewers that is deeper than any formulated plan. Capra's ending is an invitation to celebrate the possibility of achieved community; it provides an image of human togetherness that makes potently literal the second great commandment. The ending is just as importantly, however, an invitation to mourn. We grieve over the many faces of our own selfhood that seem forever lost to us—those that have been killed in childhood, those that are still in hiding. Without some occasion to cry over what has been done by others to our capacity for love, and what we have gradually learned to do to ourselves, we have little hope of improving on Narcissus's plan for "laying hold of himself." "The true opposite of depression," Alice Miller reminds us, "is not gaiety or absence of pain but vitality: the freedom to experience spontaneous feelings."[12] Part of what sentiment movies can accomplish is to restore access to our own buried feelings, in however early or infantile a form. Alice Miller is speaking of therapy rather than movies in the following passage, but she conveys my exact sense of our appropriate response to "feeling" situations in films that seem, in some obscure fashion, addressed to us: "The more unrealistic such feelings are and the less they fit present reality, the more clearly they show that they are concerned with unremembered situations from the past that are still to be discovered. If, however, the feeling concerned is not experienced, but reasoned away, the discovery cannot take place, and depression will be triumphant."[13]

> And why, too, on waking up and fully returning to reality, do you feel almost every time, and sometimes with extraordinary intensity, that you have left something unexplained behind with the dream? You laugh at the absurdities of your dream, and at the same time you feel that interwoven with those absurdities some thought lies hidden, and a thought that is real . . . something that exists and has always existed in your heart.
>
> —Dostoevsky, *The Idiot*

All of my recent thinking about the place of emotion in our identification with film experience leads me to believe that there is a crucial connection between movie sentiment and dream work. My argument so far has been that the seemingly transparent emotional incidents in melodrama which may be the triggering mechanism for tears rarely have a direct correlation to what the art of crying actually has reference to or is seeking to "articulate." As I previously noted, the initial surrender to tears is made somewhat easier if we imagine that we can "see through" the familiar movie conventions that affect us. It gives us a measure of control over our emotional participation, keeping us *on the surface* of what promises to be a wholly readable fiction rather than in the more worrisome terrain of our inner life. Wish fulfillment, which according to Freud's famous dictum is the central force of all dreams except those formed by trauma, is far more demonstrably present in the workings of popular film—and most blatantly in films of sentiment. As Thierry Kuntzel and others have suggested, the nature of the wish fulfillment in movies (as in dreams) is likely to be deeply disguised, though not necessarily by the design of the director or the writers or any clearly identifiable human agent. There are certain forms of story that seem to lend themselves "naturally" to a highly emotional film treatment. Invariably they contain structural patterns similar to those we find in ancient ritual and myth. These "found" patterns, I would suggest, become the chief agents of dream work in the narrative.

The work of defining the relationship between movies and dreams has always been hindered by the fact that the spectator does not *produce* the film he is watching. The material of the film does not form itself in response to the spectator's recent experiences, nor does it distort those experiences or re-construct them in ways that would seem useful to interpret. Furthermore, as Stanley Cavell has noted, "most dreams are boring narratives (like most tales of neurotic or physical symptoms); their skimpy surface out of all proportion with their riddle interest and effect on the dreamer."[14] But at the same time films have an uncanny way of interacting and confusing themselves with other films and actual life-memories in our always wandering, half-unconscious consciousness. Cavell speaks of "certain moments from films viewed decades ago (which) nag as vividly as moments from childhood. It is as if you had to remember what happened *before* you slept. Which suggests that film awakens as much as it enfolds you."[15] What sort of unconscious activity do movies convincingly reflect, and is it possible to be at all specific about how the unconscious enters the viewing process?

Movies that are designed with the intention of giving emotional reassurance carry some residual awareness of deep, fundamental anxieties, anxieties which it is the task of the story to block and transform. A narrative that successfully plots an "escape" from a particular fear may well have had its source there. The narrative must, in any event, remain in close touch with the fears it opposes if it is finally to dispose of them in an emotionally persuasive manner. Similarly, the viewer who watches the film fantasy with the hope of finding a brief respite from *real* problems and *real*-life conflict wants the film to supply a hallucination of fullness and cohesiveness strong enough to override his sense of "being in the world" at the present moment. The viewing experience thus involves at least two kinds of deflection. The work itself imposes one type of displacement in order to mask the "unconscious" of the narrative— that is, what the narrative needs to deny to find its desired form. The spectator's participation adds a second layer of repression, through the effort to substitute temporarily the sensory field of the screen for one's own reality sense. The "I," vibrating in darkness, wills both its dissolution and fantasy enlargement through the act of identification with the presences on screen. In sentimental films, participation involves an unusually intense sort of substitution. One cannot say merely that one's real emotions have been put on hold for the duration of the viewing. The self one has half-forgotten is penetrated by the dream self in the outbreak of tears.

Mervyn Le Roy's *Random Harvest* (1942) is a film whose surface story offers a rich emotional fantasy of perfect love and perfect union which cannot, for reasons that are left tantalizingly obscure, be connected to the empty "waking life" of the amnesiac protagonist. The price the hero (played by Ronald Colman) pays for having his memory restored to him midway through the film is the loss of his capacity to feel. By a complex series of exchanges in its extraordinarily ingenious plot, the film establishes a resonant metaphoric equivalence between being unknown to oneself through loss of memory and being unknown to oneself through loss of feeling. That is to say, memory and feeling become *one*, and their final fusion is our invitation to weep—as well we might, since for all we know it is the extent of their separation in our own lives that makes it so difficult to be sure who *we* are. I can think of no movie plot that positions us so firmly throughout its length on the borderline between remembering and forgetting, so that everything that is made visible to us can only be grasped and felt in terms of this central opposition. As with Hitchcock's *Vertigo,* the dreamlike character of events is emphasized from the outset, and the meaning of the story seems available to us only in the language of dreams, or the myth fragments bodied forth in them. Unlike *Vertigo,* however, which is willing to declare itself a nightmare (a nightmare that ultimately denies formal closure to the plot's "mystery" and threatens to replay itself endlessly), *Random Harvest* does not seem to know what sort of dream it is elaborating. It is in that respect naive about its relation to trauma and to authentic, perhaps unassuagable, human pain in ways that the Hitchcock film is not.

The narrative of *Random Harvest* seems to trust that Greer Garson's patient, sacrificial love will be strong enough to efface the haunting emptiness in Ronald Colman's gaze. Our emotional need, as engaged participants in this dream, is to have Colman finally succeed in remembering "everything," so that the gap inside himself that prevents him from truly *seeing* any other person can be closed. It must be closed, our emotions tell us; otherwise, this man's world, and our world to the extent that we recognize ourselves in him, is not sharable. The just barely averted tragedy in *Random Harvest* is strikingly similar to that consummated in *Vertigo.* James Stewart in *Vertigo* is romantically obsessed in a manner that requires nothing short of the obliteration of his beloved's image (and living person) for him to be *saved* from desire. Yet nothing—

literally nothing—awaits him on the far side of his terrible longing. *Random Harvest* replaces overt violence and a frenzied fantasy of possession with stillness. Its hero is a man who could never raise his voice, who aspires everywhere to goodness and honorable behavior. It seems such a tiny distance, such a "small thing" that separates him from the object of his love. And yet the size of the inner gap is deceptive. Sight alone is not enough to rescue him, to carry him across the divide. It is as though he must retrace all the steps of his life in their proper order to find the space of warmth and yielding tenderness that he has lost. Until such time he is the self as movie viewer—one who is not truly there.

Colman, called "John Smith" in the first part of the film, initially appears to us gazing out the window of a mental asylum, yearning—we have heard from the doctor who is treating him—to find his parents, or at least someone with the power to show him where he belongs. His view from the window, which we do not see, preoccupies him without affording him the images he seeks. (Windows are the film's dominant visual motif. Smith, or Charles Rainier as he later comes to be known, is repeatedly positioned by them. On some occasions he sits or lies, visibly disquieted, with his back to a window, suggesting a refusal of the place of vision, or more precisely a forgetting of how to enter such a place and open himself to what he sees.) Smith searching for something at this window invokes further associations with the situation of the movie spectator. He is temporarily out of phase with his life, though unlike the spectator, this fact is profoundly troubling to him. His dislocation seems linked to his horrible stammer in the presence of others, generally reducing him to silent, beseeching looks. The world he discovers himself in is wholly alien to him, and yet, again like the spectator, he craves to find a point of emotional connection so he can have a sense of belonging. He is willing to entrust himself to anyone who will lead him out of his isolation; he is looking for safety in the form of kind companions (or parent surrogates) who will lessen his fear of things by giving him a part to play in their lives.

Smith is outwardly compliant, yet withdrawn. He has been injured on World War I battlefield, but he has no recollection of being wounded, or the place where it happened. The war experience and everything that led up to it have been swept away. War is one of the subjects that the film itself is attempting both to evoke and, at a deeper level, to forget. The very title, *Random Harvest,* offers a sharp, half-hidden metaphor for war that functions equally well, and perhaps more assertively, as an image for the mysterious workings of memory. At the time of the film's release (December 1942), the United States had been involved for a year in World War II; peace (or victory), if attainable at all, seemed a very distant prospect. Apart from a single, highly compressed flashback scene midway through the film, *Random Harvest* contains no direct visual references to battle. Yet the sense of war as a phenomenon to be reckoned with, and, if possible, escaped from, is omnipresent. A 1918 Armistice Day victory celebration in the streets, experienced from Smith's point of view, appears as frenzied and frighteningly chaotic as a nocturnal bombardment. The deafening noise, combined with the hysterical, pressing mass of bodies in the fog, drum against Smith's overtaxed senses with all the force of the war his memory has blanked out.

In the novel on which *Random Harvest* is based, James Hilton describes "the shock of exultation" in the Armistice celebration, then goes on to speak of its aftermath: "The war was over . . . but now what? The dead were still dead: no miracle of human signature could restore limbs and sight and sanity; the grinding hardship of those four years could not be wiped out by a headline. Emotions were numb, were to remain half-numbed for a decade, and relief that could have eased them could come no nearer than a fret to the nerves."[16] Ronald Colman's Smith, in the extremity of his dislocation and "numbness," is England's plight and hope for recovery writ large. Hilton's novel spans the two wars, ending shortly after Hitler's invasion of Poland. LeRoy's film concludes at an indefinite point prior to the *new* war's eruption. It is thus able to consecrate "private feeling" as its highest truth, with no competing claims from the public realm. As I have already suggested, however, the presence of the war, though partially displaced in the film, is felt as a constant enveloping pressure on the film's central fantasy and on the elaborate visual artifice which is its protective enclosure. The War, it was generally understood, had the power to obliterate everything: all civilized values, all sense of continuity with the past. Americans believed that the continual reaffirmation of those values (values which include a commitment to the inner life, the life of the soul) would give proof through the long night of struggle that the past was "still there," surviving intact. The following powerful exhortation from Alfred Kazin's *On Native Grounds* (1942) is infused with this sense of hope in crisis: "Never was it so imperative as it is now not to sacrifice any of the values that give our life meaning; never was it so imperative for men to be equal to the evil that faces them and not submissive to its terrors. The world seems to be waiting, waiting for its new order."[17] Equally pervasive in the period was a "what-if-the-world-should-end-tonight" mood, which would seem to run counter to the emphasis on *preserving* values for the good of an abstract "future society." The often overwrought emotional rhetoric of melodramas released during the war arises perhaps from the attempt to conflate altruism with a total capitulation to the imperatives of private desire. The rhythm of films like *Random Harvest* fluctuates between a fully exposed, dauntingly extreme emotional need and carefully measured gestures of containment. To some extent, this pattern is operative in all romantic melodramas, but in the war films the urge to compensate for terrible loss and a fear of emptiness by a torrential release of feeling is especially great. One also encounters a belief, not yet hardened into a convention, that the lost home of the "heart's desire" and one's threatened home in society can be somehow persuasively fused, at the level of metaphor and vision.

The war dimension of *Random Harvest,* however much it is scaled down from Hilton's novel and denied complete expression, is a part of the story that one can be reasonably certain its writers took fully into account. Less clear is how much attention was given to the implications of parental loss in Smith's quest to regain his memory. The film opens with a camera tracking up a shadowy, desolate, tree-lined walk to the Melbridge County Asylum, at the end of which appears a silhouetted figure (presumably a guard) with his back to us, behind a closed door with a barred window. We are later reminded of this walkway to the asylum when Smith passes through another gate that opens onto a blossom-filled path to an "enchanted cottage." In this "unreal" dwelling he will briefly experience the tranquil, healing love of Paula (Greer Garson) through the period of his convalescence. In what ways, we are invited to consider, are the two opposing paths actually the same?

In the film's first dialogue scene, two elderly parents searching for their son (missing in action and believed dead) are being interviewed by the doctor in whose care Smith has been placed. When Smith is informed that he will be meeting this couple—and that they may prove to be his parents—he stammers out their last name (as if trying to "hear" it in some relation to himself) and then adds, with trembling effort, the questions: "My—My parents? My—father?" Groping for words laden with the full weight of his effaced beginning, he calls himself into being as a character in this act of supplication. A few moments later, we see him waiting in a bare room for his interview. He sits facing a door with a frosted window pane as another silhouette blocks with an extended arm the arrival of the couple who may have the authority to "recognize" him and thus the power to take him away from this place. We hear their muffled voices behind the door. When they do enter in the company of the doctor, Smith stares at them helplessly as they lower their gaze and shake their heads in grieving refusal. The scene dissolves before Smith has uttered a word to confirm his own sense of loss, and we immediately observe him walking in the late evening fog near the asylum's entrance. He is mumbling received phrases of reassurance to himself and trying to work his face into an acceptable social mask ("I'm all right, thank you"; "Coat's very warm; like to walk") when a siren sounds accompanied by church bells and shouts that "the war is over." The asylum guards leave their posts in the general excitement, and Smith, seized by an impulse to escape, slips through the gate with no difficulty.

I have described the opening scenes in some detail, stressing the precise sequence of presentation and the placement of the dissolve in order to make clear my sense that Smith's escape is directly tied to the scene of parental "rejection" and abandonment. When he shortly afterward seeks refuge from the crowd's uproar in a tobacco shop, a woman's voice quietly addresses him from behind. "You're from the asylum, aren't you?" As he, and the spectators, turn to identify her, we see her face framed in a soft, dreamlike close-up: she is apparitional, a face coming toward him out of the mist. This woman seems to be formed out of Smith's immense psychic need for a protector who will guide him to safety. She is there for him just in time to aid his "second escape" (from the tobacco shop owner, who is phoning the asylum to report his flight). Somewhat later, when declaring his love for her, he claims that "my life began with you." He movingly asserts that he's never let her out of his sight since he first saw her in the little shop, and entreats her never to let *him* out of *her* sight; then he concludes, enigmatically, "Never again."

There is no mention of Smith's mother in the movie version of *Random Harvest,* though it is clear when "Charles" reenters his family home immediately after his father's death, that she has died some time earlier. Hilton's novel sheds more light on Smith's/Charles Rainier's childhood relationship with his parents. Speaking of his mother, who died of tuberculosis when he was still a small boy, Rainier says: "I loved her very dearly. She was a delicate, soft-voiced, kind-hearted, sunny-minded, but rather helpless woman—but then most women would have been helpless against my father. *He* loved her, I've no doubt, in his own possessive way. . . . He insisted on taking her for brisk walks over the hills on January days. It was a cherished saying of his that air would blow the cobwebs out of your lungs. It also blew the life out of my mother's lungs" (57). The screenwriters of *Random Harvest* (Claudine West, George Froeschel, Arthur Wimperis) in all likelihood eliminated any discussion of Rainier's childhood from their script because they believed it was inessential to the film's structure, adding nothing but clutter to an already exceedingly complicated plot. My own reading of Hilton's novel would place the lost mother and the hard, unapproachable father at the center of the story: both Rainier's amnesia and his "fantasy" relationship with Paula are an intricate dream displacement and "working through" of early trauma. I would further suggest that the elimination of any overt reference to Rainier's mother in the film and of clear visual links tying her to the whole problem of memory—and its relation to love—does not (and cannot) reduce the importance of the maternal object. If it is, in fact, the psychological core of Hilton's fable, it will find expression somehow in any version of the story that is told. Indeed, the sheer visual (and aural) force of Greer Garson's maternal presence in the first half of *Random Harvest* could be said to give even more persistent emphasis to Oedipal conflict than the text of the novel. The absence in the film of an explanatory framework for her role in Rainier's "recovery of himself" (beyond the simple and unsatisfactory notion of a perfect, abiding love) serves to deepen the effect of the psychic material, giving it the murky slipperiness and duplicity characteristic of all important dream content. In other words, the mother image, instead of being removed from the film, is repressed in the act of being passed over as an interpretive key. It thus enters what I would designate, cautiously, the realm of the film's unconscious.

Kaja Silverman and other feminist/psychoanalytic film critics might wish to characterize what I am doing as a "reauthoring" of the classic Hollywood film. My "discursive resistance" to the thoroughly conventionalized aims of "dominant cinema" could be construed as an attempt to minimize the negative impact of that "dominant cinema," which communicates to the "average" spectator only in terms of culturally binding stereotypes.[18] My reply, similar to that I presented earlier in my comments on Mary Ann Doane's treatment of movie pathos, is that I cannot *know* this average spectator well enough to speak for him or her. To differentiate in any meaningful sense between film fantasies that "bind" and those that help us to envision ourselves (what we have lost, what other than skepticism might be left for us to gain), I think that we need to locate, as accurately as we can, our own identity themes as they manifest themselves in our responses to individual films. (This does not mean that we should attend less carefully to the ways in which the narrative stands separate from those themes. Extending ourselves as far as we are capable to the film in its otherness, is more difficult and rewarding than trimming the text to our own specifications.) I cannot see the point, however, or the theoretical usefulness, of continued reports on what other spectators are supposed to have "seen" in a movie if they are not accompanied by some kind of personal accounting. What have we seen for ourselves, and how has the complex bundle of desires and fears that all our experiences draw from helped to shape what we have seen? The subjectivity of the analyst is always at issue, as every psychologist knows, in the evolving reading of the patient. Surely this is as likely to be true of psychoanalytic theory (feminist, Freudian, Jungian) when applied to films.

"John Smith," largely deprived of his voice at the beginning of *Random Harvest,* and wholly deprived of his place in the world, turns his back on the asylum and the painful isolation it represents, and escapes to a relationship that is absolutely undemanding and nonthreatening. Paula, a music hall entertainer, appears "out of nowhere" to protect and nurture him. After we have watched Smith be terrorized by an unruly mob, we see Paula, in her role as entertainer/impersonator, bring the same crowd to something approaching harmonious order with her singing voice and gestures. She has installed Smith in a special viewer's seat, far above the rest of the audience on a high platform behind a railing. When the crowd—at the end of Paula's song—dissolves the boundary separating performer and audience, and flows into the stage to form a circle of dancers, Paula disappears from view. At this point, director LeRoy introduces a startling cut to Smith's now empty chair and slowly draws the camera back to reveal his unconscious form prostrate beside it. In our next view of him, Smith is lying in bed in Paula's room with blankets drawn up to his chin. Against his halting protests that he is not like the others, that he can't under any circumstances return to the asylum, she assures him that she will not *let* him be taken back. In this scene, as in all of their exchanges prior to the proposal scene, Garson's voice vividly approximates, in its power to soothe and contain, the idealized mother's voice of infantile existence, the voice that Doane has characterized as a "sonorous envelope" which "surrounds, sustains, and cherishes the child."[19] Being always in the beloved's sight and hearing is the core fantasy of the film. Smith is permitted a second birth. In effect, he learns how to speak all over again. He also learns how to feel connected to the world, as if for the first time. The protective enclosure of Paula's room is eventually replaced by an isolated rural cottage, where words never miss their object because the object never varies, never blurs. The maternal object is an utterly receptive, *listening* presence. Paula's chosen task is to reflect Smith back to himself without ever declaring her identity as an other. Instead, the other is offered as a prelapsarian sameness: it is the self restored to oneness, no longer divided from anything in the world.

In spite of Paula's continual protestations that complete emotional security is attainable ("It's the end of the world, lonely and lovely. We'll be safe here"), Smith's dream of unbroken communion with her is scarred from the outset, by moments of Oedipal terror and transgression. When Paula urges him to flee with her from the urban prison of Melbridge (where it always seems to be night) to some "quiet place" of rest, Smith's assigned escape route is blocked by the imposing presence of Paula's employer, Sam. In another jarring use of ellipsis, paralleling Smith's fall to unconsciousness during the music hall performance, we discover—at the same instant Paula does—Smith standing over the body of a man we do not at first recognize as Sam, who appears to be dead. Smith mutters rapidly in a kind of toneless panic: "I pushed him and he fell. I'm no good. Let me alone. We can leave him. . . . I'm no good. I better go back." Paula insists that they abandon this body, which lies directly in front of the doorway that is their only passage to freedom and safety. To cross the threshold, Smith cannot avoid stepping over him, and, following Paula's lead, he does so.

In the cottage that they adopt as their final place of refuge, the fantasy of being a child begins to become confused with that of "playing house"—taking on the role of husband and father. Paula's tutelary function radically diminishes at the point where she brings him his first check for an article he has written. She presents it to him beside a stream, where he feigns sleep resting against a tree—fishing. As a writer, he is no longer merely echoing Paula's words, or producing words that are exclusively their possession as a couple; he is now in the business of making words for others. The presence of the stream, conventional to be sure, accompanies our first glimpse of Smith tranquilly alone. And it is by this stream that the dream configuration associated with the myth of Oedipus begins to give way to the story's dominant mythic paradigm: Echo and Narcissus. The sovereignty of Paula's maternal voice, its power to initiate and validate all significant utterance, its power to enthrall whoever listens to it (recall the captive crowd to whom she sings at the Armistice celebration) comes to an end when Smith openly declares his love for her. Henceforth, her voice will be distinguished chiefly by its capacity to imitate and mirror his. It is fitting, viewed in the light of the Narcissus story, that this power reversal takes place next to "still water." Smith tries to find words that will express his love for Paula and that will *allow* his love an erotic dimension.

One recalls that the nymph, Echo, prior to having her body reduced to a voice (more precisely the shade of a voice, capable only of repeating the last words of the phrases she hears) used to delight the goddess Juno with an endless flow of talk. The purpose of her pleasing discourse in Ovid's version of her story was to allow Jupiter to "lay with the nymphs" on the mountainside without Juno discovering him. "The powers of Echo's tongue" are almost entirely taken away by Juno as a punishment for concealing what one might term her "sexual knowing." Echo's subsequent fate is to become the secret pursuer of Narcissus, whom she fell in love with when she saw him "wandering through the lonely countryside." She is unable to reach him because she cannot speak the words which would make her love, or even her presence, known to him. What must remain hidden, sealed up—though she longs to speak of it—is the fact of her own desire. Her single meeting with Narcissus takes place in a woodland, where she echoes the final word "Here" when he calls out, "Is anybody here?" "Deceived," Ovid tells us, "by what he took to be another's voice," he says, "Come here and let us meet."

> Never again would she reply more willingly to any sound. To make good her words she came out of the wood, and made to throw her arms round the neck she loved; but he fled from her, crying as he did so, "Away with these embraces! I would die before I would have you touch me!" Her only answer was: "I would have you touch me." Thus scorned, she concealed herself in the woods, hiding her shamed face in the shelter of the leaves, and ever since that day, she dwells in lonely caves.[20]

She languishes away, with her love for Narcissus "still firmly rooted in her heart," until at last "her voice is the only part of her that still lives." The echoing voice that is the mark of her imprisonment in the "lonely caves" perfectly rhymes with the sheltered reflecting pool where Narcissus lies captive, gazing "at the shape that was no true shape with eyes that could never have their fill."[21]

Echo's situation seems more tragic than that of Narcissus. Echo is connected, in a manner that is not wholly illusory, to another person, and yet cannot achieve any autonomy in love. She is capable of seeing beyond herself, but she cannot give expression to her feeling without reinforcing her dependency. Feeling for her is all dependence when projected outward, and self-consuming when held within. She withers away into a voice within the hollow spaces to which she has fled. Echo's inability to "consolidate a separate self" resembles the condition of a person who is attempting, through her own empathic mirroring of another, to make clear the very form of feeling response that she most urgently requires herself. "If I can learn to be fully sensitive to someone else's needs, pain, and longing," Echo might be saying, "and to express that sensitivity openly (with no thought of myself), the person I have loved in this way will 'answer me' with the very looks and words *he* has received, and a space in me that has always been empty will be filled. That will be my cure. I will no longer have to echo once someone has, of his own volition, chosen to echo me." If we place this speech in the mouth of a mother, it becomes disturbing. We can clearly recognize the danger of love confusing itself with desperate need, of the mother merging with the child so tightly that the latter becomes *all* mirror, engulfed by the identity lack that has brought the child into being. In the mouth of a lover, the speech seems less disconcerting, more affecting, perhaps because we can envision so easily the means by which the figure so loved can offer resistance, refuse reciprocation, slip away. We are also more likely, in the lover's case, to consider the question: "How else can the void be filled? Is there any solitary route that Echo can take to achieve the desired goal of loving herself?"

As Smith reaches the point of proposing marriage to Paula in *Random Harvest*—the point of perfect reciprocity in the fantasy, when Paula stands ready to "receive"—love becomes a different sort of "all or nothing" arrangement. Heretofore, Paula has satisfied Smith's yearning for unconditional maternal love and total presence—a merger, to quote Donald Carveth once more, "which can tolerate no difference, distance, or separateness." After Paula gently leads him to the place when he can begin to give love to her out of *his own* strength (however much it has been "borrowed"), the father figure inside Smith who until this point has been successfully repressed, intervenes with a piercing psychic message: "Relationship means engulfment." Better to "retreat altogether from relationship" as Narcissus does, into an enclosed space where you can never be reached (the calm pool of self-reflection). Here the soul's sight and love are reserved for invisible things. Though he is transfixed by an *image* of self, what Narcissus seeks is to be found "nowhere"; it has no placement, no substance. Smith's vision of separation is precipitated not during the literal wedding ceremony, though the undoing of his relationship with Paula is prefigured there by the mute presence of a boy behind wooden bars, staring blankly forward in an unsettling close-up. This boy, I would argue, is the "lost child" of Smith's memory attempting to materialize itself, as though in protest of the union of his "grown" self with the forbidden mother. At the same time, he is the child to whom Paula will shortly give birth, who is assigned Smith's own adopted name of John, and who will mysteriously die once Smith abandons Paula. The involuntary desertion follows a *second* loss of memory, which restores Smith's recollection of everything prior to his first breakdown. His primary objective, once he has forgotten Paula and his newborn son, is to return to his childhood home.

The door to the "facts" of his life before Paula can only he opened, in the terms of this fantasy, if the door to his life with her is closed. The psychological factors at work in his leaving of Paula (and his loss of her image) are difficult to present as a unified explanation but are worth juxtaposing. John is now the father of a child; the infant mirrors the part of himself that had been "found" by Paula at the beginning of their relationship and that all of her subsequent love, though she does not know it, has been directed to reviving, restoring to life. Their love has removed, for a dreamlike interval, the necessity of Smith suffering through the wounds of his early life—learning what they have been, and how to mourn for what has been "missed," at what Alice Miller calls "the *crucial time.*" The crucial time is the time of early childhood, which fantasy cannot really give back to us, or make up for. The road to Smith's asylum, so associated in his mind with isolation and suffering, is the road *not taken,* but the road not taken is in this instance perhaps the only road to personal freedom. Smith avoided this road because he managed to find another, more comforting road—to an idyllic cottage presided over by an angel who ministers to him with perfect kindness and who never interrogates. The possibility of the cottage's (and the angel's) continued life depends on Smith's ability to know himself as someone ontologically distinct from the infant son who severs Smith's own maternal bond with Paula and thus usurps his former place. He rejoices at the child's arrival because it is the most emphatic sign imaginable to him that his new existence is more than figurative. It would seem to suggest that he is not merely in flight from things but going forward as well: to become a father, after all, is very different from repeating his life as a son. And yet the *father's* place, however much he craves to occupy it, is not an identity that his total absorption in Paula has prepared him for. He must somehow *remember* the father as a decisively separate category of experience before he can be constituted as a subject in that role.

Significantly, Smith leaves the cottage at just about the time his own father is dying, though Smith is not yet *consciously* aware of his father. He recovers his memory in an accident that nearly kills him. (He is struck by an automobile while attempting to cross a street. This occurs during his first day of separation from Paula.) As a result of this accident, he forgets Paula completely and remembers instead everything that led up to his traumatic shock on the battlefield. The return to "unconscious-ness" after the car accident almost perfectly coincides with his father's disappearance in death. When Smith (now Charles Rainier) travels to his family estate after awakening in the street and receives the news that his father is "gone," he does not lose his self-possession (if one can call it that) for a moment. There is no thought of tears and apparently no need to regret the fact that he has been absent for the entire length of his father's final illness. His return home (at night) is in some sense like a return to the asylum. It has none of the qualities one associates with homecoming—for the simple, or not so simple, reason that "Charles" has not yet discovered what home is. His one explicit acknowledgment of relationship with his father occurs when he stands before an impos-ingly large and severe full-length portrait of his father as "Captain of Industry." The portrait hangs in a high-ceilinged, austerely elegant room with no windows. Charles wonders aloud what his father would have had him do with his life. It is at this moment, still without grieving over his loss, that Charles seems to be choosing belatedly his father's imagined plan for him. As he deliberates on the possible shape of his future, he holds the key to the forgotten cottage in his hands, vainly struggling to recall the door that belongs to it, which the key has the power to open.

The memory problem that the rest of the film openly addresses is how emotional memory relates to identity. The true subject of Charles's story is repression in all its subtle guises. What is it that keeps Charles from remembering his life as John Smith? What mysterious, as yet un-attained strength of his own will enable him to find his way back to the lost cottage door? The brilliance of the plot in this section of the film arises from the remarkable decision to place everything that defined his former life as Smith, including Paula, directly in front of him, to make all of the pieces of the forgotten life but the cottage itself successively visible to his (and our) gaze. Paula is constantly there for him—first, working in his office; later, organizing his political campaign and actually entering into a second, "business" marriage with him, which by his in-sistence includes no physical intimacy. But he is incapable of recovering, in the absence of memory, any of his previous emotional attachments. He can repeatedly *see* her, and *see* the necklace that he once gave her, and *see* the suitcase filled with clothes that he took with him on his final departure from her (as Smith), but still remain utterly detached from them. Paula, like Echo, appears bound not to speak; she cannot reveal herself to him through language, she cannot (will not) tell him the his-tory of their previous shared life. He will either remember who she is by himself, or remain blind to her always. Until Charles is able to re-vision his life *emotionally*, there is no real seeing. No external accom-plishments, no amount of compliance and self-control, no displays of sympathy or generosity offer, by themselves, an adequate basis for re-covery. His capacity for loving and for experiencing his own life lies, as Paula tells us, "buried in a little space of time [he's] forgotten."

The insufficiency of Paula's own previous maternal relationship to Smith is dramatized in reverse through his brief attempt to fall in love with his "half-niece," Kitty. Kitty imagines that she has found in him an ideal replacement for her own lost father. Charles seems perfect to her in his very unapproachability. He has successfully taken on the strong, supremely competent persona that he identifies with (*as*) his own father. He hides behind a masked view of himself, yet barely registers the fact that he *is* hiding, that everything isn't all right with him except at those moments when he distractedly fingers his key. He plays the role of his father—that is, a smoothly functioning emotional absence—until it seems a natural fit. The role, after all, is so well-defined, and it works so completely in terms acceptable to the world "out there." The cost of Charles's consistently good behavior, his unfailing politeness, and careful *command* of his responses in all situations is "depression and a sense of inner emptiness. The true self cannot communicate because it has re-mained unconscious and therefore undeveloped."[22] Kitty finally, intuit-ing that she can offer nothing that will assuage his painful isolation and convinced that she will never, in fact, assume a "true shape" in his con-sciousness, breaks off her engagement with him.

The undismissable insight which enables Kitty to withdraw from the powerful spell of the man she still feels certain she is in love with parallels the difficult growth going on in Paula herself. Deprived of both her fulfilling/constricting former roles in Charles's life (the first purely maternal, the second maternal and sexual), she is forced to some aware-ness of who she might be apart from him. She dwells, though not by choice, in an emotional space that is truly private—that is to say, where she is neither image nor object. Charles has not defined this space for her, nor is he privileged to enter it as the person she has *known*. She remains in close proximity to the man she loves, but in her lonely years of self-imposed silence, she overcomes the compulsion to repeat her own childhood scenario of narcissism, centered on the loss of her own self-objects. It is, in fact, only when she reaches the conclusion that there is nothing more she can say or do for Charles to bring him back to life "as he was," and decides to let him go for an indefinite period while she travels by herself, that the walls enclosing him finally begin to break.

Paula letting go parallels Charles's earlier decision to separate from her for a brief time, which resulted in his accident.

Propitious circumstances lead him to journey (also alone) back to Melbridge, the site of the asylum, and the site of his first meeting with Paula. One by one he revisits each of the places of his initial solitary wandering. He slips back once more into a state of possession which in this film, as in *It's a Wonderful Life*, is a spiritual return to anonymity. As he begins to remember the man he had once been, this counterpart with no name and no emotional tether rises to meet him, as if nothing "real" had ever stood between them. (Where have you been? Why have you kept me waiting?) Suddenly released from a bewildering numbness, he encounters as someone new to his own experiences the places of his torment and redemption. What he appears to have recovered, like a traveler in the underworld, is the ability to see and make contact with his own losses: to finally know what loss is. It is as though Paula awaits him at the end of a landscape where every step he takes opens him up further to his mother's death. Freud, speaking of the maternal body, wittily reminds us that "there is no other place of which one can say with so much certainty that one has already been there."[23] Can all dream-like returns to forgotten places in films be understood as carrying us to the same destination? Is it always the mother who awaits us? I find the idea momentarily tempting, because it promises to cut through the Gordian knot of memory questions posed by the film. But it is a not wholly satisfactory resolution to the journey Smith/Charles Rainier is making, because it is an idea which hardly requires the elaborate complications of this film's full experience to be understood. And yet Charles's reawakening to the Mother as one both lost and found in death surely has something to do with the emotional logic of *Random Harvest*'s conclusion.

How does my relationship to inviting spaces in film (usually rooms, staircases, doorways, landscapes framed by windows) compare with actual living spaces that, for whatever reason, my memory has consecrated? When I return to these real spaces after a period of separation, I feel for a brief interval intensely, pleasurably contained by them, as if it might be possible to repose there always. Then their ability to sustain me—as they have the power to do in memory—abruptly ceases. They begin to enclose without protecting, and because in my imagination I have invested them with the very essence of insideness, when I find myself no longer "taken in" (magically enfolded) I cannot simply return to a normal state of being there. Instead I feel stifled and almost desperate to flee. Still photographs that *remind* me of places I have loved or which make me wish that I could tranquilly surrender myself to the imaged space (both what is visible and what lies *behind* the picture surface) do not fail me in the same way. The longer I stare at them, the more habitable they seem, the more I feel myself narrowing the distance that keeps me hungrily outside. Roland Barthes has noted this paradox of how stillness or "intense immobility" deepens the sensation of lived presence.[24] An active, nonfetishized engagement with a space puts up barriers to seeing it. It is never still enough to be properly absorbed; or rather, it cannot gather itself to a point, and thus gain the strength to absorb me. Perhaps things do not emerge from the distraction of their appearances while we are still able to touch them. Part of us must be excluded to experience the sensations of being truly inside a space.

Why am I so moved by Charles encountering things in Melbridge exactly as they were before? Why is it *right* that he should begin to find Paula, and know how to recognize his attachment to her, only when she is transformed into rooms and streets of a lost time? *Random Harvest* presents the idea of the lover's absence in a very unusual fashion. The second half of the film requires us to think of how one can satisfy *all* the conditions of absence without ever having departed. Paula waits for the return of the man who has not gone away but who is still right there beside her. He does not know how to go away and come back; he is *away* in her presence, even as he returns her gaze. Paula's desire is for the "present" being who has innocently abandoned her. Charles has become the very definition of an image in his apparent solidity: that which promises to contain and fulfill our desire, but from which we are excluded. (As with all benevolent images, it is never his *intention* to exclude.) The ending of *Random Harvest* has no choice but to make *death* part of its solution. Paula enters the world of shades, as it were (the lost past) in order to remember the Charles she loved. The Charles she knows in the "living" present is a ghost in search of his former life, the world he has forgotten. Charles journeys by a different route to the same place. He remembers Melbridge in minutely correct pieces, as the frozen images of the lost time come back to him in their proper sequence. Nothing significant has altered in the time he has been away; it is a world of *images,* pure film in its avowal that things can seemingly be in motion while secretly standing fixed and inalterable. Though he is not known in this place, it seems to have materialized for the sole purpose of giving him a *definiteness* sufficient to reflect his existence back to him.

It is with the calmness of death that he recovers the ground he walks on. He has passed over to what feels like the other side of things, and moves *forward* into what is irrevocably behind, perished inside him.

"His body," in Rilkean terms, is being treated "in some sort like a soul." Though still alive, he is also wholly spirit, "already living elsewhere, [who] sadly enters what has already been gently laid aside, in order to belong once more, though even absent-mindedly, to a world once felt to be so indispensable."[25] He is turned toward objects in the way of one independent of them. Because of this new freedom, objects take on a hypnotic quality; a strange halo emanates from them attempting to conjure Paula's image at the very heart of absence. I look again to Rilke for assistance. The world always stands in the way of that "pure space into which flowers endlessly open." By the time Charles sights Paula, in the closing moments of the film, she is "that pure unseparated element which one breathes without desire and endlessly *knows*."[26] The space of the film opens for him suddenly like a roomful of light. Charles carries the no longer heavy burden of his father's life to the door of a house that belongs to his mother—empty now of everything but the presence of a death that does not deny him. The entire truth of Charles's experience on earth (on film) is gathered together in the eye of memory, all at once, to form a unified image. "Father" and "Mother," untrammeled at last and with nothing further to conceal from us or from each other, cross the divide that separates them and acknowledge each other by name. Having opened the cottage door with the key that is the "clear solution of his heart," he hears Paula call his name behind him. Now he is able to enter an embrace that need not be thrown off, an embrace that "sees all time and itself within all time, forever healed."[27] If we weep at the conclusion of *Random Harvest,* it may be because this pattern is not wholly strange to us; it is the content of our deepest dreams, and we long to be *present* in it.

4

On a Train to the Kingdom of Earth: Watching De Sica's Children

> They drop bombs because they say: I am dropping a bomb; nobody would drop it if he had the patience to say: I am dropping a bomb which will fall on that square yard of that town X and will hit the home of C. and of P., of T . . . and blow three fingers off N.'s hand, shatter P.'s left breast, C.'s neck, the teeth of S. who was saying to M. that R. is etc. There is no patience.
> —Cesare Zavattini

While researching Vittorio De Sica's filmmaking activities during World War II, I encountered an intriguing plot outline of his virtually forgotten 1944 film, *The Gate of Heaven*. The unadorned account of the narrative situation nicely frames many of the elements that give De Sica's work its distinctive form and ethical direction during his neorealist decade. A group of invalids and religious pilgrims are journeying by train to a shrine of the Blessed Virgin Mary at Loreto, on the Adriatic coast. A large number of the passengers are afflicted with some form of paralysis; the sufferers and their companions, nearly all city dwellers, come from every class and age group. Naturally, some of those making the journey lack strong religious convictions and have little hope of a cure but for a variety of reasons have seized the chance to escape briefly from their onerous present circumstances. The film ends at the shrine, where an impassioned ceremony invoking the Blessed Mother's healing powers is in progress. We leave the pilgrims before we have witnessed either their desperately awaited miracles or their disappointed return to outwardly unaltered lives.

I shall quickly identify the structural and thematic features of this tantalizing, unseen film that are central to my reading of De Sica's work. First, we are presented with an open-ended journey that is also a search.

Young Prico (Luciano De Ambrosis) caught between his father (Emilio Cigoli) and mother (Isa Pola) in Vittoria de Sica's *I bambini ci guardano/The Children Are Watching Us.*

Second, children form a crucial segment of the company of pilgrim sufferers. (A frail, paralyzed boy is one of the main figures in the narrative; he is accompanied by a young girl, otherwise alone in the world, who has pledged to assist him.) Third, paralysis, spiritual as well as physical, is a shared condition of those making the journey to the shrine. It is the obvious general term for what is most in need of cure. Fourth, the initially expected transformation of circumstances (miraculous healing) is gradually replaced by less easily identified "openings" for vision. The experience of *waiting* becomes ever more closely linked with the process of meeting and finding one's world (one's fulfillment?). Finally, the search depicted here, as in other De Sica films—whether it be for a literal miracle, an absent parent, a stolen bicycle, a lost dog, or a white horse bearing an estranged friend—eventually leads us to borders between the material and metaphysical realms, borders of "sacred longing" where we (like De Sica's characters) are confronted with what John Stuart Mill has termed "the permanent possibility of experience."

My brief plot summary, coupled with the title, *The Gate of Heaven*, suggests that the viewer's destination in this narrative is the threshold or gate of potentially redemptive vision. As so often with De Sica, the means to a solution of the characters' distress is shown to be out of their hands—beyond their imaginative reach and, to a similar degree, beyond the reach of the filmmaker and implied viewer. Yet we are invited nonetheless, for furtively mystical reasons, to contemplate the physical/emotional environment that the characters are left with in the here and now as something more than an impasse. Love, conceived as a surge of vision entering a human space torn open by enormous, acutely exposed need, is the integrating miracle that nearly every De Sica film of the neo-realist period aspires to. The purging of despair, or what Irving Massey calls "the potential for nothingness in the things that we look at," takes place, if at all, through an act of illumination in which objects and human souls are somehow lifted up and beheld in the light of love.[1] The Austrian writer Hugo von Hofmannsthal describes in his celebrated "Letter of Lord Chandos" a state in which every common experience, however worn by repetition or clouded by pain, "rises toward me with such an abundance, such a presence of love, that my enchanted eye can find nothing in sight void of life. Everything that exists, everything I can remember, everything touched upon by my confused thoughts, has a meaning. Even my own heaviness . . . seems to acquire a meaning; I experience in and around me a . . . never-ending interplay, and among the objects playing against one another there is not one into which I cannot flow."[2]

Needless to say, any fictional effort to make "ordinary" tragedies that seem steeped in hurt and helplessness and loss less terrible through an inexpressible, "deus-ex-machina" love force is one rife with danger and temptations to falsity. The vision that De Sica attempts to make real for us is not spiritually consoling in any familiar sense, nor is it politically consoling. There is no ready-made rhetoric to guide us to a correct response or to a reliable higher authority. What De Sica does repeatedly endeavor to attain (and again I see parallels with Hofmannsthal's ethic of integration) is the greatest possible degree of self-suppression, which might allow "the real" to awaken and begin speaking in the filmmaker's place. Theorists repeatedly point out, with mantralike confidence, that any attempt to document "reality" in film is naive and doomed to failure. And yet, the distinctiveness of De Sica's hold on the vibrant surfaces of *his* reality must still somehow be accounted for. De Sica (together with his most influential collaborator, the screenwriter

Cesare Zavattini) sees the road to knowledge and love leading us toward a *complete* identification with the world and all it contains. The unique properties of the camera as recording instrument allow maximum respect for the ever-fluctuating world-object and ceaseless opportunities to renew the act of identification. The nature of the photographic medium, as De Sica and Zavattini apprehend it, makes the desired harmony of ego and world conceivable, if not in any respect easy to accomplish.

What might De Sica regard as the ideal result, the perfect fulfillment of the camera's encounter with reality? Here is how Hofmannsthal evokes the weaving together of perceptual spirit and the forces of nature and human life in his essay, "Colours":

> I do not want to strengthen anything in myself which would isolate me from mankind. But truly in no moment am I more a human being than when I feel myself living with hundredfold strength, and this happens to me when that which has always lain mute and closed before me and is nothing but massiveness and strangeness, when this opens and, as in a wave of love, entwines me with itself. And am I not then at the inner core of things as much a human being, as much myself, as ever I could be—nameless, alone; not, however, petrified in aloneness, but as if there flowed from me in waves the strength that makes me the chosen mate of those strong, silent powers which sit around me mutely as on thrones? And is this not the spot you always reach on dark paths, when you live active and suffering among the living? Is this not the mysterious heart-kernel of personal experience, of dark deeds, dark sorrows, when you have done what you should not and yet had to do, when you had experienced what you had always divined but never believed, when everything had collapsed around you and the Frightful could nowhere be undone? Did not the embracing wave then wind itself out of the innermost centre of experience and draw you into itself. . . . Why should not silently wooing Nature, who is nothing but life lived and life that wants to be lived again, impatient of the cold glance with which you greet her, draw you into herself at rare hours and show you that she, in her depths, also has secret grottoes wherein you can be one with yourself, you who were estranged from yourself in the outer world?[3]

The mystical fusion so strikingly envisioned here is, we are reminded, the unpredictable beneficence of "rare hours" (or, less optimistically, rare *moments*) when the mood of the so often frustrated seer offers no impediment to a full encounter. In the ordinary course of things, both the observing eye and the waiting world seem veiled—closed in so many ways to the desired effortlessness of presence. Who knows what makes it possible for love to sometimes forge ahead and enter freely into "the open," a relationship with things in which no barriers assert themselves? Hofmannsthal's times of entering-in come about, as a rule, in the kinds of places where nature poets' visions typically arise—in the solitude of a forest, in the silence of a field, garden path, or high mountain, on the deck of a ship in the early morning. When he talks about obstructions to identification, he returns us to the teeming, multifarious ground of the gloomy city, where he lives (or fails to live) "surrounded by faces ravaged by money which they owned or by money which others owned. Their houses . . . their streets were for me [in a moment of disgusted recoil] the thousandfold mirrored grimace of their spookish Non-Existence."[4] For De Sica and Zavattini, by contrast, the experience of world-identification *must* take place in the very midst of such a city, or nowhere. The impoverished, paralyzed, and fear-burdened multitude replaces the isolated natural setting as the realm for purifying encounter. The crowd's mystery must penetrate us as fully as the waves heaving toward one on the lonely deck of a ship. The crowd, as much as anything, is the beckoning whole of our existence, rolling toward us (wave upon human wave) and "foaming up in inexhaustible presence." World identification must reckon with the totality of the city and never seek to exchange the city's true qualities, whether they be scatteredness, greed, starvation, or overt hostility, for ones more amenable to the progress of love. The role of imagination in De Sica's best films adheres scrupulously to Shelley's definition of its chief purpose in *A Defence of Poetry*: imagination enables us to identify with another person's suffering, without the necessity of explaining it, resolving it, or making it exemplary.[5]

In 1944, Zavattini wrote of his conviction that "only in this moment" of the final phase of the war of liberation in Italy do people possess "a power of sincerity that they will lose again very soon. Today a destroyed house is a destroyed house; the odor of the dead lingers; from the North we hear the echoes of the last shellings; in other words our stupor and our fear are whole."[6] If cinema is to document this "moment" of sincerity without the customary level of distortion, it must "abandon its usual narrative methods and adapt its language" to the not-yet-covered-over revelations in the city streets. The camera, Zavattini be-

lieved, would have less difficulty than formerly in finding the truth of
the city's life by attending patiently and with vigilant expectancy to how
everything—right now—appears. The surface of life suddenly seems to
go deeper, thrown open to the camera's power by the rent in the social
fabric brought on by war's still-fresh catastrophes.

The discussions of neorealism that I am familiar with devote too
little attention to this phenomenon of the ravaged city world stepping
out (like a ghost of itself) from its everyday condition of deep concealment. This is what I take to be the substance of the sincerity Zavattini
alludes to. In its stunned efforts to awaken to its unreckoned losses, the
city surrenders all the pride and instinct for deception that might defend
it from the camera's scrutiny. Something previously withheld from view
now reaches out to us for a brief interval and bids us contemplate it—
freely, without the usual preparatory labor required for meaningful discovery. The neorealist opportunity emerges with the realization that in
the hyperexposed present of the war's end, it would require more work
to keep one's eyes closed than fully open. The common sights recompose
themselves in the collective gaze of the populace with a painful intensity
of being that seems natural. Is it not "natural" for Italians to greet the
urban landscape as it is being given back to them—pitted with scars
and burns and corpse-strewn rubble—and to see in it an extension of
their own bodies and consciousness? Aren't the boundaries of what
might still survive for them to know and love so tenuous that they do
not yet need to determine where any one person's "property" leaves off
and another's begins?

Jean Vigo, the director of L'Atalante, once spoke with plaintive
force about the near impossibility of gaining adequate knowledge of
other lives: "About a human being, however much one can love and
want to understand, one must, I believe, renounce ever reaching the
reality of them. . . . What anguish one feels in this race before a maze
of mirrors, which only yield up the image of our own image, always of
our own image."[7] Without being more confident of their capacity to
know others, De Sica and Zavattini turn Vigo's metaphor of the mirror
into a positive potential source of contact with neighboring destinies.
Everything is everywhere, if we can be made to see it. Everything reflects
us, which we remember in the act of waking up. Wherever we find our
own image in the face of another, we are enlarged by the recognition
and possibly less surprised and fearful to consider that our responsibility
dwells here as readily as with the things that stand closest to us.

Another entry from Zavattini's war journal: "De Sica tells me he
saw a woman with a decapitated girl in her arms. What is the difference

116

between De Sica who saw her and me who didn't? Between events known and events seen?" (218). He goes on to express his distrust of seeing as an automatic form of knowing. The decapitated child, as a fragment of a scene, a glimpse of horror without sense or remedy, can do little except entangle us in nothingness. "We tend to make everything definitive," Zavattini observes elsewhere, "but since nothing stops, our stopping is changed continually as it stops" (227). This statement helped clarify for me Zavattini's and De Sica's passionate commitment to the ideal of portraying suffering and other forms of experience "in their actual duration." The flow of things in a time that is not sensationalized by the overemphasis and isolation of shocking particulars is a way for film to keep a sense of the whole operating, and a respect for the sheer quantity of significant relations that persist even at the dead center of what is tragic. An old woman is buried under debris after the collapse of her dwelling; her children arrive and embrace one another desperately, hoping "in desperation that something will change. . . . A short time after the catastrophe a door that gave on the void came open every now and then and somebody looked out." Off to one side, to calm himself, someone eats a cake. Eating a cake "might evade, especially in this moment, the law that all is either good or bad" (215, 216). Where in all of this going-forward action does the tragic event, as a privileged single entity, reside?

Paralysis, in all of its guises and manifestations, serves to express the naturalness, but not the necessity, of our separation (or withdrawal) from experience. Paralysis is the tempting, reasonable halting place before the unknown forces that may destroy or rekindle us. The search, as the logical opposing movement to paralysis and capitulation, somehow puts us in contact with the "far distance" as a vital dimension of our life in the present. In De Sica's hands, the search does not empty out the present in favor of some chimerical future goal but rather enlarges, as in Capra's films, the present's powers of attraction. Returning to the metaphor of the train journey in *The Gate of Heaven*, one seems so often in De Sica's world to be moving at unaccustomed speed toward the far distance, so characters can feel the influence of, and linkage with, a spiritual destination before any literal arrival.

Perhaps the images in De Sica which most fully convey to me the force of distance in its decisive relation to the near-at-hand occur in *Bicycle Thieves*. Ricci, having been separated from his son Bruno after a brief, fatigue-induced quarrel, hears at some remove cries that a child has drowned. As he runs toward the frantic, disjointed activity of defeated rescuers and hovering witnesses, he tries to make out whether the small body being lifted out of the water in the distance is his son. Almost at the moment of Ricci realizing, with trembling relief, that this boy's fate is someone else's tragedy—and just as the need to see his own son alive and well replaces all else as a sign of highest earthly good—the child appears, silhouetted on a flight of steps high above him. Bruno, still mindful of his own hurt and isolation, cannot see that the father crying out to him from below has been shaken and transformed in the short time they have been apart. He moves somewhat tentatively toward the familiar shape summoning him by name, a presence as well known to him as any in the world, but who in the trifling space of a few moments' absence has turned mysterious. All the love and gratitude Ricci has in his possession are now, for a few overwhelming moments, spontaneously released toward his child.

The implicit question raised in this episode—raised perhaps just as we see the image of the boy raised at the top of these *actual* steps, against the sky—is how long the recovered son can be a sufficient good-in-itself to alter the reality represented by the still-lost bicycle. Behind the boy, in other words, if one *must* look past him, is a vanishing point where the struggling worker's entire means of livelihood is still gone, still hopelessly hidden. If Ricci chooses, the boy himself can be reimagined instantly as a bearer of luck in an otherwise frightening world of pure contingency. "Because my boy has come back to me, other valuable things may come back through him. He may be showing me, through his safe return, that I have as much right as anyone to find what has been unjustly taken away. This moment's reunion is a preparatory experience for the *full* joy of going home with my child *and* bicycle." Where one "opening" is revealed to the seeker, others may naturally follow. But the idea of searching in De Sica is always complicated by the suggestion that the small, easy to overlook acts of incidental recovery along the way are the true sum of what will be shown to us. Only this much; is it enough? In Loren Eiseley's suggestive phrase, by way of answer: "Anywhere along the way it could have been different."[8] We need to make our reckoning of gain from returns as ill-sorted and unfitted to our pressing concerns as the oddments that the distant sea continually washes up on the shore. The water, like every other carrier of experience, either seems to live or die at our feet with its enigmatic postings from "far away."

Another episode from De Sica, nearly as resonant as that from *Bicycle Thieves* in its manner of investing remote things with kinship and of unsealing a possible avenue to love, occurs late in *Umberto D.* The old man Umberto is taking an early morning streetcar ride as he prepares himself for suicide. On the almost empty vehicle he is abstract-edly in the company of the beloved dog he must still find an adequate home for and another man, a stranger, whose age, solitude, and air of bereftness are a mirror of his own. Umberto is barely cognizant of either mute, adjoining presence as the streetcar pulls away from the building where he has lived for so many years. In some strange way, the *viewer* feels compelled to fasten onto these overlooked companions in misfortune and make something of them, as the strongest immediate evidence of what "mere existing" consists of. Perhaps it strikes us as a limitation of Umberto here that he cannot see himself in the man beside him, or offer him the slightest passing acknowledgment. As has often been the case, Umberto is so taken up with the immensity of his own privation that he evades contact with any being, other than his dog, that he cannot appeal to for assistance. The film grants us no explanation of the forces that have shaped Umberto, of how he has come to be harsh and self-enclosed, though he does not seem markedly less responsive than the "ordinary others" in his environment. Nor does De Sica encourage us to imagine that a more yielding and compassionate disposition would provide a remedy for his terrible (and common) plight.

What we *are* shown, unexpectedly, is a window: as Umberto stares blankly out his own streetcar window at the passing forms of the apartment buildings on the street where he has lived, we notice high above him a small pocket of intimacy in one of them. Maria, a servant girl he knows, has lingered to watch his departure from an open window. She appears very briefly (the streetcar is in motion and soon leaves her image behind) but the mere fact of her watching is quietly arresting. Her persisting presence somehow intimates the elusive ways that we are connected to the world, in spite of the countless times and places where the world seems to refuse us. De Sica has the good sense to treat this detail as if it were minor; we cannot be sure what value, if any, Umberto assigns to it, or how the act of attending to it might lessen his resolve to end his life. What I do feel justified in saying about this image—like so many ephemeral "noticings" in De Sica scenes—is that something enjoins the viewer to remain in it, and to inquire into its seemingly disproportionate capacity to make a difference.

I am reminded of a streetcar ride in Jiri Weil's novel, *Life with a Star,* in which the narrator, a Jewish ex-bank clerk in Prague during the Nazi occupation, is traveling with a group of fellow Jews (all of them strangers to him) after a lengthy interrogation by Nazi-appointed officials. They are still, nominally, free to go back to their homes. The narrator observes as he listens to snatches of the passengers' conversation that "everyone seemed to be learning something or wanted to learn something. They were excited, as though their lives depended on learning something. I felt left out because I wasn't learning anything and didn't want to learn anything."[9] (This repudiation unconsciously brings him closer to the psychology of those in charge of arranging the Jews' transport to the camps, for whom "it was imperative to forget everything quickly and never see anything."[10]) The dog at Umberto's feet, the old man at his side, and, most expressively, the young woman watching from the distant window are all silent and separate, yet the film threads them together—nearest point connected to the farthest—as though they were part of one injunction: to draw the things you might experience around you, like a coat against the wind, and seek, if possible, to "learn something" from the mere readiness to experience. Umberto, who has as much cause not to wish to take anything more in as Josef Roubicek, the narrator of *Life with a Star*, appears like Josef to be "left out" by his decision to repudiate the flow of meaning. He absents himself from conversation with the particulars of his own existence. In facing facts, he believes he has come to the end of learning, so he turns his face away from possibilities.

Zavattini records the following experience in his war journal: "I met a friend in Via Bertoloni, ciao ciao. He interrupted me; I was counting the paces that separate my house from Piazza Verdi, probable target of airplanes. They miss by no more than five hundred yards, no more, I thought: a thousand and one, a thousand and two, a thousand and three, as the number of paces increased my family became safe and therefore I was scattering dead bodies for a radius of three or four hundred yards" (218). Zavattini carefully measures out, in even steps, the distance separating probable life and safety from death. In imagination he purchases a reprieve for his loved ones, on the tangible edge of projected calamity. But his imagination also pays the price of identification with the faceless pilot-executioner. In the process of counting out his family's precise degree of removal from peril, he seems in his own mind to be sowing the intervening ground with corpses. Part of him glories in such necessary fantasy stratagems for outwitting disaster. He delights in securing a modest space for likely survival (where every detail that persists, even a damp circle on a bedroom ceiling, can be loved because it is clearly his—*saved*, as it were, for him). Another part of Zavattini abhors the idea of distance-as-disconnection-from-other-lives, as though it were all moral crimes in embryo. Notice how even in this short anecdote we begin with an interruption of self-absorption by a chance encounter with a friend. As one endeavors in isolation to chart a protective distance *within*, from a countering real distance *outside*, a figure who is known to you felicitously emerges. He recognizes and approaches, bringing news from another quarter, or perhaps simply the same story he always tells you. There are always interruptions, thank goodness, Zavattini means to remind us. Yet he also knows we must persist in the essential inward labor of fortifying ourselves against interruptions (the wrong kind), of building something apart from others that is strong and large and inviolate. It is a matter of survival, what we posit against the awareness of "how accidental we all are." This withheld force is anything we dare not entrust to the world's keeping, for fear that we will be placed too much at its mercy. Call it, in the broadest sense, our right to say "no." It is what we hold in private, ironically, that enables us to face the world lovingly, that gives us quick, attentive eyes and the urge to seek unity of ego, expression, and world-object. Only from the ongoing tension between self and world springs perceptual strength. This tension is "the very structure of our conscious life and the source of all articulated orderliness."[11]

The commonly demoralized and debilitated figures we encounter in De Sica's films, I would like to suggest, are shown to be suffering from a bewitchment of vision (perhaps identical with our own). It is the nature of this bewitchment that the eyes find it easier to turn away from possible experience than toward it, and to approach life situations chiefly in terms of what is missing from them, what they do not yet contain. To look past the immediate particulars is, of course, the essence of imaginative freedom, as well as the beginning of every attempt at social reform. But the danger always bordering on this freedom is the loss of relation with what is already at hand, always in some simple, baffling sense already ours to claim if we could but know it. (This is George Bailey's dilemma in *It's a Wonderful Life*.) Is it possible (and revivifying) for our vision to go, in effect, on holiday from the pain and misfortune in our lives? Or is vision as bound to the facts of distress as our knowledge is to mood? William James supplied me with this idea of holiday in his philosophical approach to knowledge. "Having reached the limit of its possible competence," knowledge goes on holiday, and there philosophy (for the pragmatist) begins. James is concerned to find in every supposition and belief "what works best in the way of leading us, what fits every part of life best." And where the absence of certain knowledge seems a barrier to belief, we need not look to knowledge to set our limits.[12]

De Sica's recurrent implicit questions in his early films seem to be these: What is it in a given predicament that prevents the world from remaining fully present and connected to those who are involved in it? How does privation not merely keep one hungry or cold or alone but also unseeing? And if feeling-filled sight is restored by some propitious act or by the pressure of circumstances (let us say in the absence of other, more urgently sought relief), what is it that has been gained? The nature of these questions, and the aptness of the term "bewitchment" to characterize the malady of eye and spirit awaiting cure, leads me to describe De Sica's neorealist films as fairy tales, in the highest, most dignified sense of that frequently belittled form of expression. It is the utopian drive toward spiritual transformation and the redemption of "mislaid" vital attributes of the human that I see De Sica suggestively sharing with Nathaniel Hawthorne, Gottfried Keller, Oscar Wilde, Goethe, Theodor Storm, and Hofmannsthal in their socially pointed, often tragic, tales of enchantment. For all of Zavattini's repeatedly expressed scorn for movie artifice and "story," I find a gravitational pull in his scripts for De Sica toward moments of veil parting: a sudden recovery of lost time or world image; a soul reabsorbed by love into the force field of magically amplified, present *being*.

Though only one of the De Sica-Zavattini collaborations, *Miracle in Milan*, contains a prominent magical or supernatural dimension, there is almost always a passage or interlude in the other films that conveys a deep affinity with fairy tale procedure. Think of the fortune teller in *Bicycle Thieves* and the white horse in *Shoeshine*. Moreover, the whole problem of vision in a De Sica film returns us again and again to the mysteries of childhood. The search De Sica typically dramatizes invokes the child's salutary defenselessness before unaccustomed, nameless sensations and longings and also the child's admirable openness of gaze. It might almost be said that the children in De Sica films are called forth to repair and balance that other, reverse image of the murdered child, which Irving Massey has termed "the key to the Holocaust."[13]

"At noon I was in Largo Argentina, in front of walls covered with drawings by children of the village of Nasino . . . who paint suns, not the way Roualt sometimes does to create a luminous nail on which to hang a heavy picture, but whirling or dripping suns over the good and wicked (this phrase recurs often in the simple explanations the schoolchildren give their work on the back of the drawing). Once again I feel the desire to make a film in which the oldest character is seven" (Cesare Zavattini).

We are once again on a train track, this time with a runaway five-year-old boy named Prico in De Sica's 1943 film, *The Children Are Watching Us*. Prico is on his way to Rome to find his father, after chancing upon his mother in the arms of her lover (the fearsome, inescapable "enemy," Roberto) during a vacation at a beach resort. Having been thwarted in his efforts to purchase a train ticket, Prico asks an elderly woman outside the station to point him in the direction of Rome, and with no more knowledge at his disposal than that the tracks will eventually arrive there, he compulsively sets out on the long journey home.

Earlier in the film, we saw Prico with his father as passengers inside a train compartment, bound for the same destination. Prico was ill with a fever throughout the first trip and had slipped into delirium while gazing at his reflection in the train window. The window then transformed into an Expressionist mindscreen on which a nightmare barrage of fever-dream images was projected. This array of terrors culminated with Prico's mother's image darkening and dissolving into a landscape, abandoning the child—in an all-encompassing departure— for the inseparable mysteries of eroticism and death. When finally awakened from his traumatic dreams, Prico found himself in his familiar bed at home, with his mother once again present and gazing at him in a "language" he recognized. Her look and manner conveyed her best intentions to take care of him and stay close. The mere fact of being returned to his room on that prior occasion had been enough to bring his world back to order. Now the child, back on the train tracks, is trying to regain that remembered place of "getting well."

What might we decide is the primary emotional color of Prico's flight? Does the sight of the boy stumbling up the rock bed beside the rails to the smooth, clear path of the wooden ties stretching to the horizon yield more grief or astonishment at the size of the task this tiny figure has taken on? We feel no guarantee of safety in Prico's setting out, no magical dispensation from lasting harm of the sort that surrounds every young child's adventures in the very different country ruled by Disney. In fact, when a train blindly bears down at great speed toward the place where the boy is walking, and he does not immediately react to the danger, I think we can believe equally that he could perish (summarily obliterated from his own narrative, which at this juncture seems not *necessarily* his, for much longer) or leap just in time into the clear. Even without the train tracks, the composition of the shots documenting his journey are reminiscent of Buster Keaton. A vast, impersonal environment fans out into the distance, and a single, small figure balances all the things his surroundings might threaten with his isolated attentiveness and bare will to proceed. In this unpopulated context the child does not, any more than Keaton, appear in the guise of a social being. Rilke has memorably characterized this shedding of ordinary relations as one in which the human form is "placed amongst things like a thing, infinitely alone, and . . . all which is common to them both has withdrawn from things [and child] into the common depth."[14]

Prico is restored to self-consciousness after he is almost killed by the train. A railway worker suddenly appears to yell at him for being where he was not supposed to be (in danger of death), then, as a delayed second part to the same thought, inquires with genuine concern whether he has been hurt. It is perhaps the sole instance in the film where an adult assumes that Prico is capable of considering a specific injury he has received and reporting accurately on how it affects him. The chance encounter comes to nothing. Prico has fallen and scraped himself as he runs from the train track (from which he has just been banished) back to the beach, a setting strongly associated in his mind with both his lost mother and her "betrayal" of the family with her lover. Prico comes to a halt and takes a momentary inventory of the damage to his clothes and general appearance, as if that might furnish him with clues about what his present feelings are. The seat of his short pants is dirty and he also discovers a tear in them, which he probes tentatively and with mounting visible agitation. The rip carries with it, by habit, the anticipated reprimand for carelessness, but now the additional possibility that there will be no more mother to provide the scolding. The damage to Prico's clothes swiftly acquires a potential dimension of permanence, something not to be fixed or put aside for a garment that is whole and washed. The rip that the child probes with his fingers extends to his days, his entire future, which he can picture at this juncture, as something equally ragged, dirty, and beyond notice. De Sica cuts from this pondering of tatters to the seashore at night, glittering under a moon rendered maternal in its fugitive, beautiful pour of reflected light. Prico encounters another version of his torn clothes in a hanging fishing net, and through its window of coarse threads and holes he observes the approach of a blind-drunk elderly sailor. Another flight ensues. This time it appears as though the boy is pursued, as in his fever-dream, by bodies that have turned into shadows.

De Sica recalls the limitless expanse of the train tracks and the moonlit beach at the end of the film when he shows us a mammoth interior space at a Jesuit boarding school, an environment that would work equally well as the hollow marble heart of a Borgia palace. In the magnificent final scene, which contains one of the most complex series of revelations in any De Sica narrative, we are suspended not once, but twice, in the imposing vastness of the Jesuit academy's high-ceilinged reception hall. Prico slowly moves first into the hall (toward the camera) and then, after a brief interval that is dramatically unresolved, turns around and walks with equally measured gravity back to the door through which he first entered. (The camera's perspective is the same for both shots, repeating a setup established in a previous farewell scene when Prico watches his father travel the same course after he delivers his son to the Jesuits' care.) The reception hall functions most obviously as the architectural expression of the father's final parting from his son: the outward shape of abandonment. It is also the swelling-to-infinity experience of emptiness in the wake of the father's actual death. (He commits suicide not long after saying goodbye to his son.) Prico's return to this cold chamber occurs immediately after he has been told by one of the priests that his father has died. When we see Prico's slight form enter through a doorway in the remote depth of the frame and hesitantly make his way toward us, it seems as though each step that he takes is sharpening his realization of what his freshly absorbed loss encompasses. There is so much vacant space for him to traverse before his face is brought into focus, that we have time to recall how his whole manner echoes (and continues) his previous journey on the train tracks. He appears utterly exposed and unaided.

Waiting for him at the other end of the room (in effect, by the viewer's side) are Prico's mother, Nina; the elderly family domestic, Agnese; and the priest in charge of the boarding school. In a film marked by a succession of closed doors imperfectly functioning to keep adult activity out of a child's view and hearing, and by an equal number of waiting areas where Prico is left to distract himself while his parents contend with difficulties they cannot help regarding as more urgent than his own, we are finally brought to a room where it seems that everything lies open to him. It is as if the boy's world has momentarily grown too weak and forgetful to shield itself from his painfully lucid inspection. Nina, his mother, offers no protest when he refuses to embrace her and turns instead, briefly, to the less complicated solace offered by the house servant. Prico is also able to ignore the priest's demand that he observe the etiquette of family tragedy by going to his mother and allow her the right to grieve with him. His face, when we finally see it, contains as much pure sorrow as it could visibly hold, and yet there is no destination for it, no place where it can meet with some relief, at least a partial disburdening. The most surprising feature of his encounter with the group is its brevity and inconclusiveness, given the length and held-breath quality of our wait for his arrival.

There is, of course, nothing ambiguous or muted about his refusal to accept any comfort from his mother, or about the lacerating reproach we feel in his single, sustained look at her. One is strongly tempted to infer that his capacity for trust has been permanently blighted, and that even at the basic level of his ongoing need for maternal love (however imperfect), something irrevocable has occurred. Where ambiguity does appear is in the mother's response to his rejection. On the one hand, she appears to revert to a familiar form of paralysis that both she and her husband have repeatedly manifested in the face of sudden, large demands and tormenting choices. On the other hand, her physical stillness and silence in response to her child's decision, however much they owe to guilt, nevertheless grant her son the right to his rage and his present disowning of their connection. I am struck by a kind of bravery in her willingness to leave the child alone in this excruciating ordeal, to assert no claims on his attention (even though the priest encourages them). I credit her with an awareness that nothing in the immediate situation allows for either pleas for forgiveness or a self-serving explanation of her feelings. To impose herself in any way—even by unobtrusive efforts to move closer to him—would confirm our perhaps too facile judgment that she does not *know* him, that he is not merely estranged from her but, in some ultimate sense, a stranger as well. Instead I think De Sica wishes to emphasize her understanding that a five-year-old can declare himself a separate entity and be believed; he may already be as aware of what separateness means as she is, how it punishes and lies in wait in everything. Prico's face displays to her (and the viewer) a mourning in which, for now, there is no room for her, or for anything she may eventually, with his forbearance, find a means to give.

If Prico were older—let's say closer to the age of Chaplin's tramp—it would be far simpler for us to draw sustenance from his taking on a solitude that is, after all, our common legacy. We might then invoke Rilke's bracing injunction in *Letters to a Young Poet*: "how much better it is to recognize that we are alone; yes, even to begin from this realization. It will, of course, make us dizzy; for all points that our eyes used to rest on are taken away from us, there is no longer anything near us, and everything far away is infinitely far."[15] The second sentence in this quote perfectly captures my sense of how the Expressionist environment works in De Sica's final shot. The "unequalled insecurity" of the child's abject departure is conveyed by the interior architecture's chill breath of worldlessness, a world taken away and placed at such a remote distance from the child that he is presently lost to the very possibility of its beckoning existence. But who would be so rash to presume that Prico, in losing his child's world, based on a faith in being with others and a dependency on these others that is both natural and good, is preparing to enter a better world by becoming a heroic solitary of the Rilkean sort—one who "accepts" *everything* that comes to him, as a confirmation of aloneness.

In 1957, Zavattini recorded some notes for a film scenario about the Chaplin tramp taking refuge on a mountain, where he lives for decades without encountering a single human being. Having become an old man who has grown afraid of people, he is at last drawn out of hiding by the "heart-rending appeals" of a young girl. He reluctantly makes himself known to her but "does not say a word because he has lost the habit of speech." He begins a journey *back* to the city with her: "little by little life comes toward him with its noise and all the rest." Before very long, outfitted in a new overcoat and derby and holding once again the carefree cane of the adventurer, he remembers how to live in the streets: "how he enjoys every little thing, how he savors the pleasure of greeting others and being greeted, of being in the crowd, of looking in shop windows, reading poetry. To recover lost time, greedy for everything, he takes part in everything, he runs from a funeral to a wedding, to a baptism, nothing is alien to him . . . coming upon him, few ask who he is because he is so natural and his companionship seems so spontaneous." The fable breaks off after the tramp, having regained his acceptance of the endlessly surprising world and his old, peripheral place in it, discovers that war once more has broken out. The "invisible threads" by which he "seemed bound to everyone else" seem to dissolve. He is alone again, in a different way.

In Zavattini's lovely myth of Chaplin as the universal, resilient child, we have a picture of Prico's own continually disclosed adaptive skill, freshness of response and eagerness to take part. How impressively he manages to right himself throughout *The Children Are Watching Us* whenever the state of emergency abates. Living so close to a foundering marriage whose daily tensions and upheavals profoundly threaten his stability, he can still find opportunities everywhere for brief truancies from agitation. He finds abundant rewards for his inquisitiveness and tiny free spaces in the general atmosphere of neglect and unhappiness where marvels readily reveal themselves to him. One image that will stand for many is Prico's transfixed state in the presence of a magician at the beach resort who is drawing the usual assortment of birds and swirling fabrics from empty hats. The magician openly expresses annoyance at the boy standing so near to him—as though Prico's rapt concentration posed a "close range" threat to illusion. An interesting tension is established between the man who works spells by rote, as if he were a carpenter hammering nails, and a child who has the audacity to remove all distance between himself and the healing powers of belief. The magician has oddly forgotten that wholehearted credulity is not an obstacle to his performance but its only justification. No one else in his audience is able to muster anything like full attentiveness. Behind Prico's back, as it were, a widening net of betrayal, seduction, and subterfuge of a drably routine sort spreads itself among the adult audience. Facing which direction is there more for the boy to learn? Is Prico less completely a part of his situation than those *grounded* in the reality behind him, who feel "freer" to crudely flash their raw desire when Prico is *not* watching?

When a child is watching in what we take to be the spirit natural to childhood (broadly speaking, whatever we mean by the term "innocence"), he or she is a kind of ideal mirror for a person or event's best intentions. I'm reminded of Prico standing next to his father (Andrea) in a tailor shop late in the film, wearing the pinned-together scraps of a military coat (still missing an arm) and gazing into an actual looking glass with him. Prico has told the tailor that he dislikes the cap that tops off his uniform. He is no doubt anxious at the thought of the school which his finished costume will consign him to. When Prico's father replaces the tailor at Prico's eye level in the mirror frame, going down on his knees to do so, he personalizes the cap by setting it on his own head. ("I used to wear a cap like that.") We see the boy immediately soften as he succeeds in taking on his father's warmly reminiscent attitude. The father not only smiles but chuckles as he looks at himself in the cap—one of his rare concessions to openly shared satisfaction in his son's company. ("I was so happy. . . . Come, wear it.") The child's face is radiant with pleasure and expectancy as he transfers the now treasured object back to his own head. The cap becomes, on the instant, a charm strong enough to instill happiness in his profoundly melancholy, so hard-to-reach parent. Prico's receiving the cap's meaning as it is reflected in Andrea's face, without the slightest intrusion of skepticism, is one of the most perfect renderings on film of a child's original openness to the world, that blessed, unforced fit between vision and the unspoiled offerings rising out of experience. Father, cap, and the intimation of lasting well-being are absorbed in one breath.

Included in the same scene is a shot of a child mannequin resembling Prico, neatly outfitted in a uniform like his, a tailor's forecast of the perfectly correct finished product. Prico's father, Andrea, in the irrationality of his own misery, is trying to build a secure, unchanging image of the son whom he will soon leave behind. If the boy acquiesces in his regimental makeover, he might learn to hold himself together like his contented frozen replica, in a void of steadfast forgetfulness. The father will enter the stasis of suicide; the child will be left in a stasis of priestly care, where he will get a new set of rules that will somehow *manage* his future and bring him repose (as though that were the only surviving goal for either of them).

Images of mannequins in black-and-white films nearly always strike me as a self-conscious admission of the deception and limitation inherent in film's attempts to lay hold of reality. Mannequins evoke the dead-time of the single frame, where the trick of living motion is subtracted. They can remind us that the filmmaker's commitment to process is equally a desire to make things appear this way and no other, once and for all. Images embalm actions in the course of attending, seemingly, to their free unfolding. Black and white, more readily than color, attunes us to this deathly undersong, in part, obviously, because monochrome film sees things we do not see in a manner decisively at odds with ordinary perception. In Paul Coates's interesting formulation, black and white "insists on the existence of a phantom presence within reality, a world we cannot perceive."[16] How effortlessly the well-designed mannequin stands up to the camera's scrutiny, as though it were the ideal film subject, and how smoothly it harmonizes with everything in the black-and-white world that is allied, to the slightest degree, with immobility. It is as if the space of film were suddenly able to confront, in the mannequin's gaze, the specter of its own emptiness, which its noisy, "borrowed" life usually submerges. The mannequin is the "unmasked" death element in the black-and-white film's lordly conjuring of the appearances of life.

Prico's duplication in a resplendent, plastic alter ego hints, of course, at the child's fast-approaching enclosure in the static remoteness of absolute mourning. But I think it is also De Sica's declaration that he has authored the ending, in its potentially ostentatious, even heartless bleakness, and is as responsible as either of Prico's parents for the child's final placement in a space that reflects nothing back to him but loss. Who is the doctor, after all, who has prescribed the wholesale obliteration of an imaginative child's escape routes (the apparent sealing up of his responsive, mobile, capacious gaze) as his necessary "treatment"? If Prico, that quietest of boys, is unaccompanied in the last shot during his long walk toward a distant dark door, it is De Sica who has willed everything ("for the time being" of the ending) out of his reach. How would he have us respond to so much concerted erasure of elements that urge a possible sense of continuation?

I will be returning shortly to the details of the conclusion in order to demonstrate their congruence with what I take to be De Sica's ethics of integral presentness. The first precept of this ethics involves, in Roland Barthes's phrase about Antonioni, "always leaving the path to meaning open."[17] De Sica's images, at their representative best, stress what is emergent and thus undecided in a situation rather than what hastens us toward the desirable *definite*. An especially pertinent example from *The Children Are Watching Us*, which guides me toward my reading of the ending, sets us once more by an open window, just after Andrea has grasped that his wife has left him for the second time. Their marriage has run out of chances to be saved. In preparation for his wife's homecoming, Andrea had purchased curtains for the window, which he "knows" she has wanted. He has just finished hanging them (a carefully planned surprise) before getting a surprise of his own: she will not be coming back. In a point-of-view shot belonging to Andrea we are shown the window containing the curtains. Interestingly, the buildings visible outside the window, warmed in the gentle city light of early evening, are more prominent in the shot than the curtains. We need to make a slight effort to recall the curtains and what they meant to Andrea (since a bit of time has elapsed in the scene after his work with them) in order to *find* them in the shot and identify them as the actual thought motivating Andrea's look. Our own inclination may be to savor the inviting reminder of a world still there outside this problem—awaiting Andrea's willingness to recollect it as well—rather than share his concern with the wasted gesture of his intended gift. (His wife will never see the curtains; he in turn will never regain the state of mind he so easily occupied when putting them up.) Customarily with point-of-view shots the viewer is directed to take on the attitude or mood of the person looking. But De Sica, whenever possible, extends a choice. If your eye rests *here*, it will find an object that proclaims futility, ignominious defeat, the ironic end of one set of hopes. If the eye ventures further, over *there*, or forgets that the curtains are for Andrea the only point of looking, one will see a field of action whose unknown solicitations are at the very least not identical with the moment's searing pain.

The sheer duration of Prico's walking in the final shot: is this not De Sica's nearest approach in the film to the heart of an as yet uncodified neorealist aesthetic? That which cracks open the death-in-life mannequin (*one* symbolically complete version of Prico's ending) is the stubborn persistence of the camera's interest in the fact of the boy's walking—first, all the way forward and then, all the way back. De Sica intuits that a return over the same ground will not merely repeat a meaning but rather, in a manner that resists paraphrase and complete directorial control, will *extend* it. There is, to be sure, the coercively Expressionist architecture—linked with dim, grandiose mausoleums from which God and the warming traces of human fellowship have alike been drained out. In one respect, a child walking into such a "prepared," univocal setting is like a noun receiving the weight of a single, heavy adjective (say, "crushed"). But duration, for those of us who do not need to rest our gaze, paralyzed like Andrea's on the "full stop" of the "window curtains," restores a hunger for details even in the face of resolutely frozen situations. That barely discernible priest, for example, who appears at the door in the far distance, waiting for Prico in the final shot, is he to be understood as another figure cut from the same cloth as the cumbersome Church official we have already met, someone almost unapproachable, thick with mechanical assurances and received ideas? Or should we credit this disagreeable priest's words when he tells Prico's mother that the boy "loves Father Michael," the otherwise purely mysterious presence in the background? It is he, we recall, who had been entrusted with the delicate, wholly unwelcome task of informing Prico of his father's death. As the shot continues, we may attach some modest hope to the reappearance of this stranger who will accompany Prico through the door once he has proven strong enough, in his own small selfhood, to arrive there. And, as I earlier suggested, from the other side of the room (where the mother, Nina, stands offscreen, watching her son choose to "enact" his felt distance from her) I feel a power approximating love is at work, keeping her from moving forward—to thwart his will and impose herself, not for his sake but for her own. There is no way for her flawed but by no means valueless love to reach him, at present, but given the significant reality of the *allowed* open space behind him, she may—if she is fortunate—eventually succeed in narrowing the gap. She may in time partially repair the injury that her weakness and that of her husband have caused. My point then about the empty space revealed in Prico's wake as he walks away from us is that it is not, in spiritual or human terms, purely empty, any more than the space that Zavattini counted off between likely bomb sites and his family's safety were empty of imaginatively authorized corpses. ("As long as the bodies are not those of my loved ones . . .")

Almost exactly contemporaneous with the birth of neorealism in the bombed cities and impoverished countryside of Italy, the style of film noir was devised to express an almost entirely antithetical response to urban malaise in the United States. Noir is all about isolated egos falling out of a clearly lit picture in which traditional social values are seen as reasonably well-aligned with individual needs and aspirations. They pass from a well-illuminated life to a beckoning night world. The darkness and thrill of film noir come from a glamorous desertion of social accountability; the shadows bespeak a potent alternative landscape of the "moral occult" in which normal routes to judgment or self-knowledge are of no use.[18] Neorealism, conversely, is about the peeling back of shadow, as in the aftermath of a detonation or a spray of random gunfire, when those who survive emerge from their places of hiding and take stock. Exactly who and what remains to us?

Elizabeth Bishop once created a lovely concord out of brute, "meaningless" succession with two plain pronouncements: "The world is a mist. And then the world is / minute and vast and clear."[19] The proliferating horrors of senseless carnage and the stealthy, shameful compromises of the Occupation comprise the "world as obscuring mist" phase of Bishop's weather report. Neorealism, the "what comes after" phase, strives to earn the *right* to a postfascist vision by being "minute and vast and clear" in its rendering of the harsh miracle of survival. Out of this jumble of inexplicably spared citizens, dwelling places, and land-marks, we must do our best to discover continuities, revived purpose, some basis for praising the literal, common stuff of dailiness that is not beholden to fascist rhetoric. The beguilingly shrouded city stage sets of noir provide a fascinating visual-metaphysical tension with the Italian streets dreaming of a downpour of clarifying light. "Only those who will be really different will survive," Zavattini rather too hopefully writes in his war journal, "so one death or the other has to take place" (218). And in a memorable rough draft of the theology of "open endings" as he and De Sica will pursue them, Zavattini conceives a nature of God that accords with the full weight of war disasters: "God cannot have created anything of which he has to expect the outcome" (221).

At what point in *The Children Are Watching Us* does the plight of the individual child, Prico, seem to join up with the multitude of others alluded to in De Sica's haunting title? (The 1928 novel from which the film was adapted is merely called *Prico.*) The "children" are unavoidably associated, given the date of the film's release (1943), with the young population formed within the environment of war. The war is never mentioned in the narrative, as though *that* reality were of a different time and place and character, unrelated to the conditions of this private family tragedy. But I would argue that, as in *Random Harvest,* there is a space reserved for the war in the immense, desolate interior which Prico passes through at the end of the film. The lostness of his spiritually orphaned state summons up a ghostly company of others wandering aimlessly through city streets, peering out from the smeared windows of buildings and waste spaces where they forage for any kind of nourishment. The door toward which Prico moves, with the eerie dignity of one carrying the fragile remains of *all* childhood in his own person, opens out on a future larger than his, yet of course every bit as uncertain. It is important to know, in Ethan Canin's words, that "there [are] as many worlds of anguish as there [are] doors."[20] Perhaps the clamor of child inmates in the prison-yard of *Shoeshine* is already faintly audible behind the door that belongs to Prico.

De Sica's customary tactic, in closing his later neorealist films, is visually to disperse the problems of the main characters' stories into the collective life of a crowd. The implicit question—why should *one* arbitrarily chosen individual's experiences be privileged to rise above others and become more worthy of our attention?—is always being posed. Visibility, in a higher, more consequential sense than we normally experience, is the goal in De Sica's films, but the limited narrative time for "making things visible" is always time *besieged* by what is excluded or neglected. De Sica's camera seems under a steady pressure to shift or extend focus, to secure more room, more light for observation on either side of an always too narrow aperture. The chosen center of narrative vision dissolves into this wider field at the end of De Sica's best known films, almost as an act of ritual sacrifice. The beloved particular, however much sympathetic awareness it generates, is never enough to carry us home. "Home" is our world at flood tide, a selfless, deluge totality.

In *Children,* by contrast, the retention of the singular fate of Prico as final focus feels like an attempt to personify the essence of the "periphery," the unnoticed casualty wandering at large, in its mute, intractable *thereness.* The title of the film reminds us that we live surrounded by the appraising witness of somehow overlooked beings, more often than not assigned to the vague outskirts of conflicts which adults (or anyone wielding power) regard as their private property. Again and again throughout this narrative, the camera draws back to reveal the child's presence as the forgotten or lost component of a situation, which, when located, drastically alters our sense of its emotional boundaries. We are shown how experiential meaning is always a radius of possible influences, involving everyone who partakes of an event or its aftershocks, even when the sole connection is a weak thread of distracted or bewildered looking.

And by what dreadful paradox does it happen that those least responsible for a terrible predicament, and perhaps least comprehending of its "facts" (the parts of the drama, in other words, that can be left out of our description of the main action), are elevated to first place in the order of suffering? Indeed, the thing left *up to them,* as if it were their natural portion when the dinner plate was passed, is suffering, pure and simple. The resourceful or agreeably stoic adult embroiled in misery might find solace in the truths of discontinuity and serendipitous contingency, when a brief respite from pain arrives. He might exclaim, like a character in Dostoevsky: "It's funny, isn't it, Karamazov, all this grief and pancakes afterwards."[21] But can the child victim be ministered to by the reliable presence of irony in every serving of sadness? Where does the young sufferer go in the wake of loss large enough to mark the final phase of wonder, when he intuits just how much can be taken away in life for good? Where does the child go, in the act of "displacing the air of childhood"? Into the inconceivable spaces where his unlived life awaits, an existence possibly stripped now of marvels and the spontaneous spirit to embrace them. (Of course, it is the common lot to experience such losses.) What shape of love, De Sica's camera inquires with characteristic patience, might it take to bring the child Prico back from so formidable a space of absence—once so many bombs have dropped? As we wait for the child to leave our sight, it is *our* challenge to inhabit our own gaze more deeply, as if that were the child's best hope of recovering a fit world (De Sica's world) beyond his door.

II

THREE FACES
OF HITCHCOCK

5

"If Thine Eye Offend Thee . . .":
Psycho and the Art of Infection

I took from my waistcoat-pocket a penknife, opened it, grasped
the poor beast by the throat, and deliberately cut one of its eyes
from the socket! I blush, I turn, I shudder, while I pen the
damnable atrocity.

—Edgar Allan Poe, "The Black Cat"

Once all the narrative surprises of Alfred Hitchcock's *Psycho* have been
discovered and its more obvious emotional provocations understood, I
find that the most potent sources of my uneasiness while viewing it are
still unaccounted for. Discomfort with this work is, in my experience,
an endlessly renewable response; it is like a slowly spreading stain in the
memory. The film feels as stifled and stifling as the indecipherable mind
of its protagonist, Norman Bates. Not only does *Psycho* contain no point
of release for the viewer—it also remains unclear what precisely the
viewer expects (or needs) to be released *from*. *Psycho* offers a number of
gestures of release—a snarling tow chain craning a vehicle out of a
swamp, Marion's slowly upraised arm as she sits in the tub after the
shower stabbing—which turn out to be no release at all. In the latter
episode, for example, Hitchcock caresses us, in the dying woman's presence, with a hope of recovery, then immediately crushes it out as Marion
extends her arm beseechingly *to us* (Why don't you *do* something?),
clutches the shower curtain and collapses on the floor. Marion's gesture
to save herself answers our felt need, then instantly turns that need
against us. Part of Hitchcock's complex achievement in the film is
gradually to deprive us of our sense of what "secure space" looks like or
feels like.

Psycho properly belongs in the company of such works as Edgar
Allan Poe's short story "Berenice" and Georges Bataille's *Histoire de l'oeil*.
These narratives, in addition to achieving their respective forms of por-

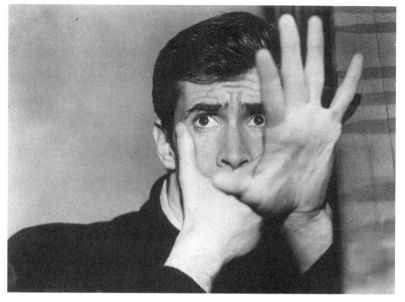

Norman Bates (Anthony Perkins) tries to fend off the enemy within in *Psycho*.

nographic intensity by impersonally rendered shocks, also attach the same obsessive significance to the *eye* as metaphor. Metaphor rather than object: the eye asserts its value and power chiefly through its "migration toward other objects," as Roland Barthes has suggested in his essay on Bataille's *Histoire*.[1] The true content of the narratives has much less to do with the fate of characters than with the fate of an image—the eye—as it undergoes repeated metamorphoses. Perhaps because the eye seems to represent identity simultaneously at its point of fullest concentration and maximum vulnerability, it naturally functions, in works so deeply concerned with aggression, as the principal locus of metaphoric trans-formation and exchange. The eye, after all, is the ultimate goal for any act of violation; it is the luminous outward sign of the private soul one wishes to smudge with depravity. But the eye is also profoundly linked with repression, and here it becomes threatening to the violator as well. Everything from the realm of experience that has proven damaging to the self, that has inflicted psychic wounds, has been channeled through the eye. Inevitably, the eye will be the vehicle of recurrence. The "in-vader," whatever his harsh business, always breaks in through the same eye window.

In Poe's "Berenice," there is an effort to limit the eye's potency by treating it as though it were inexpressive to the point of blankness. "The eyes [of Berenice] were lifeless, and lustreless, and seemingly pupilless, and I shrank involuntarily from the glassy stare to the contemplation of the thin and shrunken lips."[2] The narrator flees from the overwhelmingly oppressive presence of the eye, persuading himself in the process that the eye cannot see whatever it is that the narrator himself is afraid to see, that is, what he is struggling to repress. In his desire to avoid Berenice's gaze, however, he begins to fix his attention on her mouth, which instantly acquires the characteristics of a substitute eye. The mouth becomes an organ of intellection, whose teeth are oddly endowed with the eye's "sensitive and sentient power." As Daniel Hoffman has pointed out, Poe requires us to consider, perhaps for the first time, the ways in which "mouth and eye resemble each other. Each is lubricated by a fluid of its own origin, and each leads inward . . . toward the mysterious interior of the living creature."[3] The eye and mouth also take on the attributes of the opening that most frightens the narrator (and, in all likelihood, the author as well), and that forms the content of his repression: the vaginal orifice. The mind has made the latter unthinkable by confusing its properties with the mouth's. The vagina too is furnished with teeth that demand to be removed ("long, narrow, and excessively white, with the pale lips writhing about them"). In "Berenice" the eye's transformations can be construed entirely as an effort to block the passage of forbidden material to the conscious mind. With the sort of hideously perverse logic that we encounter in Poe's most distressing tales, the eye must turn into the thing it dreads in order to be spared the sight of it.

Georges Bataille's *Histoire de l'oeil* may appear, at first, to offer a less suitable analogue for the workings of *Psycho* than Poe's "Berenice." Hitchcock resembles Poe in his relentless preoccupation with repressed material. The spread of a massive, buried hurt or wound seems, as in Poe, to paralyze Hitchcock's narrative from within, finally rendering all of its wary, questing-for-order surface activity beside the point. Bataille, by contrast, foregrounds his horror, coolly displays it in a naked state, and plays with it at close range, like an intimate. The sordid and vicious so fully define the surface action of *Histoire* that the reader can't easily feel that this surface is potentially a screen for something worse. Bataille's story, nevertheless, strikes me as blocked in much the same way that Poe's and Hitchcock's are. His central overdetermined image—the eye, once again—feels like the only solid thing, the only living variable in a world of copulating phantoms. (The characters dwell in "a world so frail that mere breath might have changed us into light."⁴) Eyes and their metaphoric substitutes—eggs, a saucer of milk, a bull's testicle—are visually "there" for us in a way that nothing else is. Bataille imagines a world in which the eye, divorced from a specific personality and body, can pursue a life of pure objecthood, witnessing with pristine detachment acts of staggering vileness. Even when the eye becomes the focus of these acts (to be caressed, licked, pissed upon, punctured), it somehow always seems to float free in the end, aloof and intact. Bataille's repeated emphasis on the slicing and spilling open of eyes has the quality of a magician's demonstration: however mutilated the ceremonial object appears to be, it is perfectly restored in an instant. Though continually assaulted, the "eye" of the narrative can never go blind.

Punishment inflicted on the eye is not only a means of severing someone's ties with the world (as in the case of Oedipus); it can also be a way of reducing one's consciousness to the status of an object, so that one must learn to deal with consciousness entirely in object terms. The torture of the eye can mark a refusal of inwardness. One can't get past the literal eye, Bataille insists. Nothing stands behind it. Bataille's psychic strategy is to make his inner world so ossified and remote that no living experience, no emotionalized thread of memory can adhere to it. When Bataille addresses us in what we are meant to accept as his own voice, in the final section of *Histoire de l'oeil,* he disturbs us more thoroughly than at any point in his previous litanies of the monstrous. He recounts memories of his childhood—an utterly frozen landscape—as though they belonged to someone else. His hideous family ordeals are assigned the same value, and given precisely the same sheen of obscenity, as the events of the preceding narrative. Bataille's language refuses at every point to possess what it touches; it is truly a dead language. One finds it almost inconceivable that it could have been formed from the inside, that a life could speak through it.

Tonally, Bataille's endeavor to empty himself through indifference approximates (in function and effect) the austere, insulating wit of Hitchcock's *Psycho.* The best account of Bataille's attraction to the possibilities of indifference occurs in a passage from his study of Manet's paintings: "Manet's was *supreme indifference,* effortless and stinging; it scandalized but never deigned to take notice of the shock it produces...."⁵ The stuff indifference is made of—we might say its intensity—is necessarily manifested when it enters actively into play. It often happens that indifference is revealed as a vital force, or the vehicle of a force otherwise held in check, which finds an outlet through indifference. Bataille's *Histoire* aspires to show us the paradoxical vitality of an indifference without limits. This indifference might be said to commence at that hypothetical point in the life of an endless scream when the sound is so customary that it is no longer worthy of notice. Personal pain is generally regarded as the one area of experience to which insensibility cannot extend. If, like Bataille's forever entranced character Marcelle, we were to become so lost to our feelings that we had no way of "telling one situation from another," we would still be alive to the shock of physical torment. It is this last bastion of aliveness that Bataille desires to level out. What *Histoire*'s narrator reports are agonies without personal dimensions, sensations that mimic those of misery but that somehow exist in a flat, becalmed state. By granting pain a significance, by making any form of emotional concession to it, we only increase its power over us. Let us rather do life the appropriate disservice of denying to all of it the force of a lasting impression. Indifference alone rescues us from the humiliation of engagement.

Wit is Hitchcock's less conspicuous means of announcing *his* indifference, his refusal to be engaged or soiled by his transactions with suffering. The persistent presence of wit in *Psycho* should not be mistaken, in the calmness of its operations, as a mitigation of brutality. *Psycho*'s wit is hard and deeply ingrown; it stays well below the surface of action, strangely unavailable (on a first viewing) to characters and audience alike. It is only with Norman's final speech that the director's mode of joking seems to merge with the awareness of a figure within the film's world. When the mysteriously mocking voice of "Mrs. Bates" at last reaches us, we cannot avoid the feeling that in its paradoxically "vacant" depravity it is the one voice we have heard that genuinely expresses the film's tone: "It is sad when a mother has to speak the words that condemn her own son." Bataille once wrote that "decent people have gelded eyes. That's why they fear lewdness." Mrs. Bates, whose sockets are both full and hollow, directly scrutinizes us (the viewers) with the gelded eyes of decency. She speaks quietly to us of a mother's duty to put an end to a bad son while we are confounded by the sight of her effortlessly inhabiting the lost son's body. (Yet another case of a character's gaze turning into the image it is forbidden to see.)

One is not really permitted to go anywhere with this image, or with the speech that accompanies it. Everything about them is sealed in, like the dead eye "soaked with tears of urine" that peers out of Simone's womb near the close of *Histoire*. We are almost beyond the language of "implications" here. Mrs. Bates's speech, imposed on Norman's rigid features, is offered as the impenetrable punch line of the joke that is *Psycho*. In the widest possible sense, we are left in the dark.

For Hitchcock, who is as sedate and comfortable in his chair as Mrs. Bates is in hers, wit always has the right to assert its innocence. It provides the inner life with a means of guarding itself absolutely in the very act of unveiling. Wit opens a place for the self to stand, composed and invulnerable, at a vast remove from any sense of pain that could damage it or spoil its game. Wit allows one to punish to one's heart's content, in the manner of Mrs. Bates, and yet remain blameless. It is the public guarantee that a crime or sin (regardless of appearances) has not quite been committed. The underlying content of art that compulsively seeks out some form of "joke container" for the expression of disorder may be understood as "the holding back from things," a phrase Sanford Schwartz has applied to the early paintings of de Chirico. "The pictures are about waiting, keeping oneself clean and untouched. The undercoating of nightmarish dread in them comes from someone who fears making a certain move."[6]

The fear of making a move is pervasive in Hitchcock's work, but it achieves special prominence in *Psycho,* where neither the characters nor the imagery seem to possess any alternative to immobility. Perhaps it is the complete dissociation of authorial self from an imagery that is struggling to express it that gives to *Psycho,* "Berenice," and *Histoire de l'oeil* their "infected" character. The normal poetic activity of making metaphors becomes precarious in these works because images have somehow lost the capacity for internal growth. An image cannot build beyond itself, provoking new connections with the "world at large" when it is entirely cut off from the impulse, desire, or need that called it into being. Instead of widening its range of associations, it can only replicate itself obsessively, craving the origin that is denied it, futilely attempting to burrow inward. The artist can neither separate himself from his dominant image nor see it plainly enough to penetrate it. Art that lacks all mobility, as this art does, can only fester in the place where it's stuck— and hence communicates by infection, spreading the mess that can't be gotten rid of to whatever it touches. Bataille, Poe, and Hitchcock cannot—in the works we're examining—give their oppressive metaphors any outward, public meaning except that of shock; but they are equally blocked from carrying the "eye" image inside. It is the interior, above all, from which this image is in flight. Like Scottie Ferguson, standing traumatized at the edge of the Mission Bell Tower in the final shot of Hitchcock's *Vertigo,* unable to take a single step forward or back, these narratives can only articulate the hopeless stasis that has engendered them.

Having made some progress in establishing the nature of the metaphor we are concerned with, I will try to show how it operates in the shower murder sequence of *Psycho*. Once more we are confronted with a narrative situation in which a vicious, morally appalling act (murder this time), that would seem to demand our full emotional engagement, is subordinated to an eye's encounter with visual analogues. Why are we encouraged to notice, while Marion Crane is being stabbed, that the shower rose, Marion's screaming mouth, and finally the drain into which her blood flows all correspond, at some level, to the victim's congealed eye? In a culminating extreme closeup, this eye contemplates us with the alert fixity of death, while a false tear, formed by a drop of shower water on Marion's face, announces that emotion (of any kind) has no further part to play here. The tear might as well be a fly: nothing is but what is. Why does Hitchcock linger so long over this image, and why does the match cut between the drain and the corpse's eye seem so conclusively to define the imaginative center of the film?

Oddly enough, Marion does not appear to lose her place in the world of *Psycho* after being brutally slain. Instead, one has the feeling that she has at long last *found* her proper relationship to that world. When Hitchcock's camera seems to emerge from the darkness within the drain *through* Marion's eye, and then eases back further to reveal her twisted head insensibly pressed against the floor, the camera comes as close as it ever will to caressing the object placed in front of it. We are being invited—before we have had any chance to recover our equilibrium—to participate in the camera's eerie calm by looking at things in the ways that the camera instructs us. How *evenly* dead this girl is. How perfectly and compliantly she harmonizes with the other blank surfaces in her environment. Turbulence has surprisingly given way to an order, a settled view, that nothing can put a stop to.

The camera elects to remain in a room that is temporarily deprived of any human presence. Its purpose in doing so is to tranquillize this setting by invoking an aesthetic response to it. The fearful disarrangement of the bathroom space that horror has just visited is not simply curtailed, it is denied. By the time Norman rushes into the motel room, discovers the body, and turns away from it in panicky disbelief, his response is already disproportionate to ours. His anxiety subtly registers as an overreaction. Norman's agitated gestures fly in the face of the hypnotic stillness and order that the gliding camera of the previous scene proposed as normative, reasonable.

For a number of years now, the standard means of justifying the shower murder to viewers who find it repellent has been V. F. Perkins's argument that Hitchcock's skillful montage succeeds in "aestheticizing" its cruelty.[7] After all, we never actually see the knife penetrating Marion's flesh; we are only required to imagine it. Clearly this line of defense needs to be reexamined. There seems to be an underlying assumption that an aesthetic effect automatically acts as a cleansing agent, or as a guarantee of moral discretion in the creative process. But as we have seen in the case of "Berenice" and *Histoire de l'oeil,* even the most unsavory, abhorrent imagery can be made to yield a powerful aesthetic impression.

Before drawing any conclusions about the formal lucidity of Hitchcock's conception of the shower sequence, one would do well to consider the massive weight that this episode achieves within the total narrative structure. In Robert Bloch's potboiler novel, from which *Psycho* was adapted, Marion's death—far from being the central action in the plot—is matter-of-factly reported in a single, terse sentence. If it is appropriate to point out that Bloch made nothing of an event that Hitchcock responded to with astonishing imaginative intensity, it is also appropriate to inquire why Hitchcock made so much of it. Does it seem either dramatically feasible or fitting that a female protagonist whose status in the narrative never rises above that of pitiable victim should be disposed of in so extravagant, prolonged, and visually intoxicating a fashion? Is Marion's shabby, useless death a proper occasion for a virtuoso set piece? Surely an abbreviated, less conspicuously artful presentation would honor the victim more, if the *meaning* (in human terms) of what transpired figured at all in the artist's calculations.

The consequence of Hitchcock's aestheticized rendering is, instead, to enlarge the minutiae, in the manner of a pornographer prowling around flailing torsos, seeking out details to close in on. Hitchcock wants to make the act of slicing wholly *legible,* as opposed to merely averting his gaze. Hitchcock designs the stabbing to be as salaciously riveting as possible. We are meant—in fact, positively encouraged—to *see it all,* both what he shows and what he refrains from showing. The blanks that his editing leaves can only be filled in one way. Marion's degradation is increased immeasurably by our awareness that nothing in the moment-to-moment scrutiny of her ordeal is random or accidental. The entire murder feels densely inhabited by the director himself. What are we to make of his calm determination to extract a kind of classical shapeliness and beauty from this broad, unbeautiful pour of chaos?

It is impossible to understand the vision that *Psycho* as a whole is expressing in any terms other than those used in the shower sequence. But, as I hope to have demonstrated, Marion's murder refuses to accommodate any of the humanized or aesthetically dignified meanings one would be inclined to project onto it. I am sure that Hitchcock was not trying to deceive us when he said that the shower sequence had *no* meaning, as far as he was concerned. He placed it in that strangely aseptic realm of "pure cinema," where images, like poems, should not mean but be. For an image simply "to be," in Hitchcock's terms, it must be acknowledged as something with no depth—the screened image is both literally and ontologically flat. As Garrett Stewart has suggested in his essay on Keaton's *Sherlock, Jr.*, the most formidable illusion of movie space is that we seem to be looking into a frame "past which is recess and perspective."[8] Hitchcock's style is predicated on the belief that the *surface* of a screened image is absolute. It never yields to anything "within." The only interior it has is supplied by the mind of the spectator.

For Hitchcock the passage of material from life to the cinema involves an immediate (and total) subtraction of unmanageable elements. Film is not a medium for introspection. Disordered activity of any sort has no place there. Hitchcock conceives the act of building a patterned sequence of images as a means of asserting control over a "problem" without ever being required to *examine* it. In designing a series of shots, the mind can limit itself to lateral motion. There is no need to "look down," to probe past the image surface. One can always substitute further complications of formal arrangement for the distasteful messiness of analyzing one's position. Joseph Stefano, the screenwriter of *Psycho*, memorably described Hitchcock directing a nude model in the shower sequence. He stood on a platform above the shower in his dark business suit, "a model of rectitude and composure. One sensed that Alfred Hitchcock does not stand in front of naked women, and that he has precisely this feeling about himself, so that for him she was not naked, and that was that."[9]

Arranging a composition for the camera is the way to demonstrate that its content is manageable. And the only level on which this content has to be seen and accounted for is the level of form. It is possible, therefore, for Hitchcock to work in the very midst of his obsessive fears and unacceptable desires, yet not be confronted by them. His negotiations with obsession are never carried on from the inside. He has only to "frame" his anxiety, flatten it into an image, for it to be held in place. Viewers, of course, as he well knows, will very likely "dirty" themselves as they imagine the experience that he has at no point felt obliged to touch. They cannot keep the images at a regulated distance (and thus handle them with the proper delicacy) because they did not control the process that brought them into being. Control, as always for Hitchcock, is to be understood here as the ability not to internalize. However much he may be stirred by his proximity to the extremes of sadism in the shower killing, he is persuaded that the search for visual order is an adequate safeguard against fixation, and that he can endlessly brood upon the separate details of the action while keeping his perceptions chaste. Hitchcock's decision to link the "eye" throughout the shower sequence with as many other ovals as possible derives from his conviction that any painful subject can be stabilized if one locates a point of concentration apart from the "thing itself." There is invariably something distinct from the business of suffering to claim one's attention.

But eyes and eye surrogates, as the examples of Poe and Bataille make clear, are never safe resting places. In fact, the three Hitchcock films that seem to me the purest (and most extreme) embodiments of his imaginative concerns (*Rear Window, Vertigo,* and *Psycho*) make an affliction of the eye their ascendant theme. *Vertigo's* credits present us with a masklike female face in which only the nervously moving eyes betray any distress. The camera then proceeds to move into one of these eyes, passing mysteriously through the pupil and coming out "behind" it—thus marking a path to which Hitchcock will return in *Psycho*. Only in the latter he reverses his direction, as the dark drain "proposes" a withdrawal from an eye that is dead. Interestingly, all of the eyes that matter in *Psycho* are counterparts of this dead eye—cruel, staring, or frozen, they seem to hold only one expression. And eventually we discover that this single, ominous look, forever resurfacing like a figure in a nightmare, has belonged from the outset to Norman Bates.

Earlier I suggested that Norman's voice at the end of *Psycho* is the only authentic voice we hear in the film. He is simultaneously revealed—at that instant when he finally meets the camera's gaze and looks directly at us—as possessing the only acceptable pair of eyes. The man whose stare has become an awful and limitless conjunction of emptiness is *Psycho's* one true seer. The hobby of this seer, one recalls, was taxidermy, which allowed him to conduct studies of birds to find out how eyes "die" (or, as in his mother's case, fail to die—transformed into living wounds that the son must try to heal). The film as a whole is equally concerned with the process by which eyes surrender their identity (or life) to Norman. By a spectacular feat of absorption, Norman ultimately manages to contain the entire world of the film in his pitiless glare.

Psycho's next-to-last image is a dissolve of Norman's face into the mummified features of his mother; for a moment he seems to peer through the empty sockets in which his eyes are now imaginatively sealed. The dissolves could continue almost indefinitely, however, because Hitchcock's key imagery in the film is nearly all constructed on the same principle: Mr. Lowery's accusing glance, which launches Marion's flight by car; the policeman's sunglasses looming gigantically over her as she wakens from sleep; Marion, throughout her nocturnal journey, peering toward us anxiously from behind the wheel of her car as we share her thoughts. (At one point, when imagining Cassidy's threat to replace his stolen money "with her fine, soft flesh," she smiles in close-up, and her expression hauntingly anticipates Norman's final, mocking look.) Following Marion's introduction to Norman, we are shown the silent company of stuffed night birds that "watch" Norman in his parlor, one of whose wings are extended so that the attacker appears forever in passage toward its prey; when Marion has left the parlor, we see Norman's eye, in mammoth close-up, intently fixed upon his hidden peephole—a large, dark, circular gouge in the wall with a single point of light at the center. (The hole-eye linkage clearly prepares us for the comparison of eye and drain.) And as the shower sequence commences, there is a close-up of a toilet bowl flushing down a torn scrap of paper that Marion doesn't wish anyone to see. By this juncture, as we have already observed, the eye is fully available for complex metamorphic exchanges with other objects. The toilet bowl, like the drain, is yet another visual sign for the eye evacuating its contents.

Once Marion is dead, and Norman sets about eliminating all traces of her presence, two additional eye metaphors emerge. Thus Hitchcock completes the series that began with Norman at his peephole by circling back to him and, in effect, showing how Marion's eye has resolved itself into his. There is an overhead close-up of the circular rim and black interior of Norman's pail as first his bloodied cleaning rags and then the mop with which he has cleaned the sides of the tub are thrust into it. Here, and in the more potent image that soon follows—the top of Marion's car forming a ghostly white spot in the middle of an encircling swamp—the hollow eye of the drain is replaced by more clotted and retentive ovals: eyes filling up rather than emptying, but only with unwanted things. Norman contrives to make whatever disturbs him disappear from sight, but instead, like the vehicle suspended in the swamp, the objects of his anxiety look back at him.

Norman relates to his field of vision as though it were somehow interchangeable with the field of consciousness. (In this respect, he resembles Hitchcock.) The successful manipulation of perception is taken to mean that the mind is under equally strict direction. Life, for Norman, has gradually been reduced to an endless tidying up of his barely manageable visual space. He is forever devising fresh hiding places for

147

his mother's (and his own) garbage. Anything that his mother judges depraved (i.e., anything provoking strong desires in Norman—and mother always knows) must be dropped from the perceptual frame. "Out of sight, out of mind" is the chief article of faith in the Bates household. If one thinks about it carefully, one realizes that the dramatic situation in *Psycho* literally dictates that Norman and his "mother" can never see the same things at the same time and never see them in the same way. They are constantly vying for possession of the same visual field; whoever "sees" at a given moment is empowered to make an interpretation, but the meaning of the visual field alters radically as control of it shifts back and forth. The question that I feel is necessary to consider is, Where does Norman's vision go, where do his knowledge and desire hide during those intervals when he is not permitted to absorb what his eyes perceive?

Norman's extreme but eminently logical solution to his impossible filial bind is to learn how to see and do the things that are forbidden to him without actually seeing anything. That is to say, the fact of his presence and involvement in acts that are literally unthinkable for him is "dropped from the frame." As his mother blindly wields the knife, Norman's eyes are somewhere else, trying to stay focussed on what is decent. It is doubly imperative then that he do a thorough cleaning job when "something bad" happens, because he must expunge the event from both public *and* personal view. As Norman desperately suppresses his own powers of vision, he comes to believe that the work of seeing has been taken over by the inert forms that fill his landscape. His closed world has truly become a beast with a thousand eyes, whose sole end is to keep him under surveillance.

Norman's perception is restricted to the order he manages to maintain within his frame. Beyond that increasingly close-at-hand point where order ceases, he encounters a blank wall. But the various "holes" he has filled for the sake of order—the swamp, the fruit cellar, the parlor with its mounted birds, his mother's corpse—have sprouted eyes whose awareness is rooted in that ugly disorder Norman has gone to such pains to eradicate. The blank space where Norman's vision tapers off is the place where theirs begins: "they" can see further because "they" can see into things. And because Norman's carefully limited outer world has become hopelessly confused with his inner world, he experiences any form of looking as a violation. As he tells Marion in his parlor, he knows what it feels like to have "cruel eyes" studying him. His survival, however, depends on his ability to keep the perception of this undifferentiated other split off from his own. He cannot allow himself to imagine, even for a moment, what it is those alien, impenetrable eyes might know about him.

This aspect of Norman's predicament helps to explain the omnipresence of mirrors and reflections in *Psycho*. Beginning with Marion's decision to steal forty thousand dollars, which she arrives at while looking at herself in the mirror, almost every interior scene prominently features a mirror that doubles as a character's image, but that *no one* turns to face. In Marion's case, as James Naremore points out in his valuable *Filmguide to Psycho,* the ability to confront her own image is lost after the theft.[10] This is one of the many ways in which Marion's surrender to her "nameless urge" serves to draw her ineluctably into Norman's frame of reference. After Marion is repeatedly shown attended by reflections of herself that she does not acknowledge (in the bathroom of the used car lot, at the motel registration desk, and in the motel room itself), the pattern is given a sudden, disquieting twist. While Marion is stationed in profile beside the motel's dresser mirror, Norman stands in for the reflection in the following series of shots. In Hitchcock's shot-countershot cutting between Norman and Marion, we notice that the profile views of the two facing figures are perfectly symmetrical. Norman occupies the extreme right-hand side of an imbalanced frame, Marion the extreme left-hand side in alternate shots: mirror images.

Norman's imprisonment in the midst of steadily more ominous reflections is shadowed forth in Marion's situation at the motel. In the world of *Psycho,* whenever one picture of the self cracks or is denied recognition, another, more dangerous image must form in its place. Inside the crack, so to speak. Marion refuses to look at herself, so Norman will look for her. He will reflect her life by making it into a likeness of his own, although he doesn't understand (any more than she does) what this will entail. Once this life mirroring has commenced, it proceeds on a number of levels. Norman seems to stand in for Sam Loomis, Marion's lover, as well as for her (the physical resemblance of the two men has been noted by many critics). The last, frustratingly inconclusive meeting of the two lovers is replayed in a more somber key by Norman and Marion.

Sam Loomis, who is not strong enough to act upon his love (or whose love is not strong enough to require action), gives way to an even weaker Norman, whose emotional energies have been strangled and for whom "falling in love" can only mean what it means to Scottie Ferguson in *Vertigo*: falling into the void at one's center. Norman's eye for beauty is really an incurable appetite for nothingness. And yet strength of a certain kind exists in Norman. He is sufficiently strong to punish a *desire* for love that has no right to assert itself (mother says so) and nowhere to go. Unlike Sam, he will carry things through to an end point; if Marion can only threaten and confuse him as an image of love, she can be made to reflect him some other way that will allow for a completing action.

Marion had stolen the money, as she sees it, because she chose to stake everything on love. She flees by car through the night, driving, she imagines, toward her love, but at some point in her journey passes "through the looking glass" and ends up facing Norman instead, a ghastly inversion of that love. Then Hitchcock, having revealed the things that prevent love from becoming what it wants to be in the world of this film, discloses what is left for it to become. "On the right hand could slide the left glove," as Robert Graves wrote in his poem "The Terraced Valley." "Neat over-under."

Norman's "courtship" of Marion revives, in ghostly fashion, many of the gestures, conversational topics, and objects of attention present in *Psycho*'s opening love scene—whatever filled the intervals between Sam and Marion's dispirited, unsatisfying embraces. The meal that Marion "didn't touch" in the hotel (and that Mrs. Bates wouldn't permit her to touch in the intimate precincts of her household) is finally completed with Norman in the motel parlor. Both Sam and Norman are given a moment where they throw open a window in response to the felt pressure of Marion's presence—Sam, out of discomfort with her talk of marriage; Norman, in his embarrassment at being alone with Marion in her bedroom. (The sudden, rasping sound of the venetian blinds as Sam jerks them up matches the sound and motion of the shower curtain being torn open.) Marion counters Sam's suggestion that they leave the hotel together by pointing out that he hasn't got his shoes on. These are the joking terms of their final separation. Sam remains behind, and we last observe him standing motionless, staring down at his stockinged feet. Just before Norman and Marion get together for their private supper, Norman registers his guilty delight at her acceptance of his invitation by stammering instructions to get herself settled "and—and take off your wet shoes." The removal of her shoes will serve to hold her there in the bedroom until his return—that is to say, in this particular bedroom, the site of all his secret erotic investigations. For Norman, requesting a woman to take off any article of apparel signals a daring advance in intimacy; the mention of shoes is his nervous, shorthand approach to "Why don't you slip into something more comfortable—and revealing?"

Later, in the parlor, Norman picks up the thread of Sam's earlier talk about "traps." Sam had described his life as a confinement within the "tiny back room" of his hardware store. (After Marion's death, Hitchcock provides a long-shot view of Sam at his desk in this room, from a camera positioned in the main doorway of the store. This shot neatly matches the hallway perspective of Norman seated at the kitchen table of the Bates mansion directly before the shower scene. The mammoth interior of this house visually dwarfs him; the only spaces that he feels free to occupy in his own person are "out-of-the-way" rooms behind the main living area.) Sam had also complained to Marion about having constantly to "sweat for people who aren't there." In the parlor scene, Norman vastly extends the scope of Sam's plight. "We scratch and claw, but only at the air, only at each other. And for all of it, we never budge an inch." There is no distinction to be made between "the air" and "each other." We want the world to at least double itself for us when seen through eyes of love, but it remains intractably single (whatever our delusions to the contrary). We are always much "further out" than others think, to paraphrase a famous line of British poet Stevie Smith, "And not waving but drowning."[11] The only movements we make that are truly answered are those we see in our mirrors. And this too is empty space; we are forever thrown back on ourselves, possessors of nothing.

The only fully spontaneous moment Sam and Marion have together—one in which Marion's desperation is as much in evidence as her attachment to her lover—occurs when she runs toward Sam for an extended embrace in front of the large screen of a closed venetian blind. The next time Marion is placed before such a screen, it has become a shower curtain. Now it is Norman who is coming toward *her*, to be joined with Marion in a different kind of embrace. Touching and caressing have, of course, been the subtracted element in Norman's halting variation on Marion's assignation with Sam. He has only managed to touch her nakedness with his eye. At last he presents himself to her without barriers—on her side of the curtain screen—and enacts his "violent feeling" for her in the only way possible for him.

From Marion's standpoint, the shower (prior to the attack) is both a moral cleansing and an act of self-restoration. Afterwards, she will once again be able to meet her own gaze in the mirror. But as we have seen, Norman has replaced the image she turned away from. Having lost sight of herself once, while in the grip of compulsion, she is denied any chance to find her way back. In the course of her journey to Bates's motel, she has had to escape from one distrustful, accusing face after another. "Who are you and what are you doing?" is the unspoken question in every conversation. And Marion could not begin to formulate an answer. Everything conspires to turn her world inside out. In this condition, she at last lights upon the sympathetic image of Norman Bates, someone whose look she is not afraid of. He offers to keep her company in the darkness. As she listens to him divulge the story of his barren life, he becomes more troubling, but at the same time she begins to recognize herself in his tormented presence (or thinks she does). She sees him as the instrument of her salvation: "This could be *my* life; I must not let it be." Having reached this understanding, Marion turns away from Norman, just as she withdrew from the uncomfortable figure regarding her in her mirror at home. But she is forced to confront this dim, hovering reflection one more time in the shower episode.

In Hitchcock's exceptionally demanding metaphoric scheme, where the eye is the faculty for "unseeing" and mirrors are present only so that they can be avoided, the shower murder, as I've previously argued, is the point of greatest metaphoric blockage, and consequently, greatest pressure for release. It is the place where Hitchcock, like Bataille and Poe (but equally like Norman and Marion), can neither separate himself from the image, nor see it plainly enough to penetrate it. Hitchcock goes to such extreme lengths to create the impression that Norman and Marion and Marion and Sam mirror each other because the world of *Psycho* is traumatically fixated; it has no capacity for enlargement. Everything in it seems to be formed at the point of rupture in Norman's vision—the blocked passage between his public self and "lost" private self. This is the point at which *nothing* can ever be seen or taken in. In his brilliant study of metamorphosis in literature, *The Gaping Pig*, Irving Massey suggests that "trauma, like art, develops at the point where imitation replaces action. . . . We mimic what we cannot fight off."[12] The shocks in *Psycho* all seem to erupt from within, as they do in dreams, where characters form and reform under the pressure of a single image, and where all movement leads to the same place. ("And for all of it, we never budge an inch.")

I have already compared the shower curtain to the screen of the venetian blind in the hotel room. (And recall that Hitchcock's camera, anticipating Norman's shadow slowly advancing behind the curtain, introduced itself in *Psycho* by entering like a phantom behind the venetian blind and probing the dark opening of an eyelike window. This first descent into a vacant eye is the action that brings the film's world into focus.) The curtain also invites comparison with a mirror. Norman's dark silhouette serves as a mirror for Marion when she whirls to face it because all the unresolved elements in her experience seem to converge in it with hallucinatory force: the car windshield wiper making "knife strokes" against the rain; the policeman's huge, disembodied head in dark glasses startling her awake that morning; the swooping owl in Norman's parlor; Norman's visible desire for her; his anxious, lonely eyes suddenly turning rigid and glowering as he leans forward in his chair; her fear of being captured and exposed; and ultimately, ending at the place where she (and the film) began, her own body lying motionless (on a bed/bathroom floor), eyes fixed upon a man looming over her: Sam/Norman. Marion's recognition—that this death is meant for her and not anyone else, that all her confused strivings have been directed to this goal, which imitates her life and which she fends off like a traumatic recollection—solves nothing, of course. It simply places her squarely on the hopeless ground she is doomed to occupy: "Now I know where I am." This is more than the viewer can say as the film's action comes to a dreamlike halt with the death of its apparent subject, and then—inexplicably—continues.

When Hitchcock's camera finally relinquishes its hold on Marion, after fully expressing its fascination with her immobility, it moves out of the bathroom and over to Marion's night table, where her stolen money lies wrapped in a newspaper. The camera registers uncertainty about what its subject should now be; it does not appear to know what it's looking for. This is an uncertainty shared by all of *Psycho*'s remaining characters.[13] Once Marion's theft, her guilt, and the money itself have been eliminated as concerns of the film, Hitchcock contrives to keep the subject of *Psycho* physically absent and morally indefinable. It is pushed out of everyone's reach. No one, including Norman, is in possession of what is withheld. To the extent that it can be identified at all, *Psycho*'s "issue" becomes the silhouette behind the curtain—an image poised to shatter at the eye's moment of contact with it, like the double reflection that startles Marion's sister Lila during her search of Mrs. Bates's bedroom. (As Lila turns to accost the woman behind her, what she discovers is her own distraught face in the looking glass.) *Psycho*'s missing subject is perhaps best described as a figure glimpsed but never quite seen; a dim outline in a lighted upstairs window; the spectral imprint of a rigidly coiled form on a mattress. On a first viewing, we chiefly feel it as a threat of recurrence that is under no one's control.

The various subjective filters through which the search for answers is carried forward (Arbogast, Lila, Sam) seem to know less and less about the quality of dread that fills the air. Our only link with these characters is the act of searching, but they are only able to search for things that we know are not there. (Marion rolled up in a curtain; the money rolled up in a newspaper.) They futilely retrace each other's steps and imitate each other's actions, without ever having the sense of what their eyes need to connect with. In effect, they are all the same character, existing only to pass through the rooms of the motel and house, exposing themselves to the disturbing features of a landscape that will never be made clear. This composite searcher belongs to the "inside world" as surely as Norman Bates does. From Norman's side of the mirror, it is the strangers' search which poses the danger of uncontrollable repetition: it is the shadow of *his* trauma that seems to draw nearer with Arbogast's and Lila's furtive movements through his domain. They are closing off his mental exits, sealing him in. The only place for him to hide from the object of his dread is within the object itself: "Hold me, Mother; hold me tight. I'm afraid to go to sleep." As long as Mother is there to protect him, the dark places can't be opened. To quote Massey once again, trauma "may be a thought that has never been killed, that has never been set off from the self."[14] Norman's murders are attempts to eliminate a thought that must not take form. Killing is, paradoxically, the deepest place of forgetting.

It remains to inquire why so many of the films made by Hitchcock in this period place the problems opposing the characters so fully in the realm of mind, but out of the mind's reach. Hitchcock's customary starting point in a film project was a situation in which *outer* circumstances had somehow passed out of one's control. The emphasis shifted decisively in *Vertigo*, where inner circumstances become the unmanageable factor. As anyone who has studied Hitchcock's style is aware, the basic building block in his narrative structures is always the "reacting look" of his characters. Major scenes are typically conceived as an intricate juxtaposition of glances with various objects and figures to which the perceiver has a clearly defined emotional relation. Hitchcock generates suspense by uniting the viewer's gaze with a character who for some reason is prevented from seeing his situation whole. Characters are menaced either by details they've failed to see or by the sheer mass of what they do see. The audience generally has no difficulty in reading a character's look because they know what to make of the objects set before him; they understand why the character finds those things important.

In *Vertigo* Hitchcock is no longer dealing with "transparent" reactions. The precise nature of Scottie Ferguson's relationship to what he sees is in doubt from the beginning. *How* his eye sees becomes vastly more important than the information it is given to process. His perceptions reflect a mounting internal strain and distortion; there has been a poisoning at the source. The camera in *Vertigo* repeatedly performs hypnotic circling movements around its subjects so that everything comes to be seen in the light of Scottie's disorder. Circling also defines Scottie's problematic visual relationship with the objects that seriously engage him: they form a vortex for the eye. He stands helpless under their spell. For example, Scottie discovers that he is in love with Madeleine as he stares himself into a haunted state. Being in love means not being able to look away, being so utterly lost to the properties of one image that no other is in any meaningful sense visually alive. Whatever is associated with the beloved is hyperfetishized—which is to say, rendered static, immutable. If Madeleine would return his love, she can only prove the genuineness of her feeling for him by remaining forever the same, exactly as he first saw her.

Scottie has been immobilized by a profound emotional shock in the film's opening scene (a policeman attempting to rescue him as he hangs suspended from the side of a building loses his balance and plunges to his death). Scottie attempts to free himself from this trauma by exchanging his fear for what he takes to be love, but the only form of love he is open to is one that will reproduce or imitate the conditions of that original shock. He requires a love that will not participate in the dangerous flux of reality—that will stay frozen, suspended, at a fixed distance. The cure for vertigo, he believes, is to make something in his world stand perfectly still. There is no need to question his own immobility in the presence of one who is compelled to share it. Naturally, a love with trauma at its base must eventually find its way back to that trauma. Both of Madeleine's declarations of love to Scottie are quickly followed by the sight of her falling from the tower of the Mission Dolores. Madeleine's plunge to annihilation is at once an absolute barrier to love and its only possible expression. The vision of her descent possesses Scottie completely. The real reasons for Scottie's continual resubjection to the image that blinds and paralyzes him are not those manufactured in the external plot. What numbs the viewer, finally, in *Vertigo* is that all of its mysterious occurrences seem called into being by a terrible inner necessity. To meet the demands of Scottie's love, Madeleine must literally fall through the hole of his gaze. It is only there, where love empties itself and dies, that he is able to see her.

In *The Birds* it might appear that Hitchcock has returned to the realm of purely external aggression, but an examination of its structure reveals that the terms of inquiry are a further elaboration of those in *Vertigo* and *Psycho*. Once again, and in a most daring manner, Hitchcock effects a strange separation between his characters and a subject that resists formulation, perhaps even widening the gap that we feel in *Psycho*. As so many critics complained at the time of *The Birds*' release, the painstakingly elaborated network of psychological relationships that is Hitchcock's primary focus for roughly the first half of the film has only the most tenuous pertinence to the bird invasions that dominate the second half. The latter seem to function more as an interruption than as an extension of the film's thematic concerns. Furthermore, one is not convinced that the birds have any role to play in the elucidation or working through of the characters' difficulties. They appear to be there for their own sake, and Hitchcock consistently baffles our efforts to make anything of them.

I would argue that, like the "dead eye" in *Psycho*, the birds are a metaphor caught in transit—one that can only repeat itself because it has no capacity for growth or conversion. The birds are the "forgotten" image in Hitchcock's world, the shadow behind the curtain ("so vacillating and indistinct an outline") that cannot quite be seen for what it is or truly named. For that reason it is empowered to translate everything (at any moment) into its own dark language. Only once in the course of the film does Hitchcock provide us with direct visual evidence of the worst that the birds can do: in a lake of silence, the camera executes three harrowing jump-cut moves toward the corpse of Dan Fawcett, whose pecked-out eyes have become rings of blood. The "shock that has no end" is the secret quarry of *The Birds*. By the end of the film, each of the surviving principal female characters—Melanie, Lydia, and Cathy—has been steeped in a trauma that she will never be able to decipher. The child, Cathy, is obliged to stand by a window and watch, stunned, as the female protector who had just pushed her to safety behind the door of her own house (a gesture which costs her her own chance of entering) is swiftly mutilated. Lydia, upon her discovery of Dan Fawcett's corpse, rushes from his house in a daze and struggles, for what seems an eternity, to find a word or a scream that can be fitted to what she has beheld. No sound will come forth, and thereafter her main activity in the film is listlessly to survey the contents of her household, waiting for them to resume their former connection to her, or hoping perhaps to stare them back into some form of sense. Melanie, who is subjected to a long, tremendously savage attack near the film's conclusion, offers us, as one of her last gestures, a "clawing of the empty air" in front of her in a desperate attempt to stave off a horror she can still see. *The Birds*, then, is also about the process of being caught in spaces from which there can be no mental advance.

In *Psycho* Hitchcock's camera can never complete its search for "Norman Bates" because from the very outset it is so firmly fused with the object of its quest. The camera eye, in effect, is seeking to uncover itself, recalling once more the moment when Lila is trapped between the two facing mirrors in the Bates mansion. It is in this sense that *Psycho* demands consideration as a *personal* film. Both the proclivities and areas of withdrawal in Norman's mode of vision—in fact, his whole strategy of structured avoidance—faithfully reproduce Hitchcock's own method of screening the world, where exposure is always an act of concealment. The landscape of *Psycho* is one that no one inside the film knows how to look at, and the camera merely reinforces the characters' arrested gaze. In no other Hitchcock film does the camera close in on so many objects that refuse to disclose their significance. The nearest thing to a penetration of the interior is Lila's exploration of the Bates house, but here, as before, whatever the inquiring eye approaches seems instantly to escape what it designates. Moreover, like the front door of the Bates dwelling, which appears to move toward Lila as soon as it looms into view, the space seems sentient, as though a living thought were trying to remember itself through these objects (the bronzed hands; the flower-patterned sink; the imprint of the bed; Norman's dolls and stuffed animals; and the untitled book that Lila prepares to open as the house search ends). Lila's function in this episode is like that of the silent menial at the close of Poe's "Berenice," who merely points at the objects that need to be seen until they are recognized and can "freeze" the eye that knows them. But in *Psycho* there is no final shock of recognition. Everything we have witnessed in the film ultimately appears to have been pulled through the hollow sockets into which Norman's face dissolves in the last scene. In the strikingly simplified visual field of *Psycho*'s conclusion, there is only a rigid form against a blank screen. The psychiatrist's explanation that has just ended has no more to do with what we now see than Marion's money had to do with her as she lay on the bathroom floor, her eye firmly fixed on nothing. All movement has subsided except for that of the steadily advancing camera. When Norman meets its gaze, the camera halts, as though transfixed by its own reflection. The image dissolves to reveal a half-submerged object, coated with filth, rising toward us from the swamp; and here *Psycho* ends.

6

Rear Window as Critical Allegory

> Attention is a task we share, you and I. To keep attention strong
> means to keep it from settling.
> —Anne Carson, _Economy of the Unlost_

The most suggestive early readings of _Rear Window_ focused on two major thematic clusters. The first of these has to do with the relation between Jefferies, the photojournalist protagonist of the film who is temporarily confined to a wheelchair, and the spectator in the cinema. The tenement windows facing Jefferies's own apartment resemble movie screens, and the stylized action they exhibit corresponds to miniature movie narratives, conflating different plots, moods, and genres and offering us illicit voyeuristic pleasures of precisely the sort that typical movie experiences give us. Discussions of this issue stress Hitchcock's complex anatomy of the act of movie watching, dwelling on the odd mixture of passivity, emotional complicity, and the gratification of potent dream-desires that defines our involvement with screen events. The spectator, having chosen a secure, hidden position in the theater, is spatially removed from the experience he or she observes, which frequently encourages the illusion that one is free to participate or remain disengaged. The principal consequence of this illusion is that the spectator sees the film image as under his authority. Because the film presents itself as there for his benefit, "submitting" to his desires while posing no recognizable demands of its own, the imagination assumes, as in a dream, that it is in control of the film's workings. Hitchcock demonstrates how the movie experience is calculated to persuade viewers (Jefferies's surrogates) that the story belongs to them, and that they can manipulate it for their own ends. The more viewers surrender to this fantasy of control, however, the more completely, and unconsciously, they can be manipulated themselves.

The second dominant theme treated by the film's first wave of commentators is the ethics of voyeuristic involvement in other lives. Critics have tried to establish the nature of Jefferies's (and, by exten-

L. B. Jefferies (James Stewart) persuades Lisa Fremont (Grace Kelly) to focus her
attention on murder rather than marriage in *Rear Window*.

sion, the viewers') culpability in the relentless visual probing of Thorwald's privacy. What sort of transgression has taken place in the act of
watching? To what extent is the impurity of Jefferies's motives something to worry about? When the truth (of the limited kind that this
genre attends to) comes out at last and Jefferies's hypothesis is publicly
confirmed off-camera by Thorwald's admission of guilt, is our certain
knowledge that a murder *has* been committed and that Thorwald's
actions have been correctly fitted to the crime (that the crime now
firmly belongs to him) sufficient to decontaminate Jefferies's originally
suspect spying?[1]

Recent Hitchcock criticism encourages us to further enlarge the
optics of suspicion. We are now expected to be attuned not only to what
Jefferies fails to take in from his strangely hermetic observation site—
that is, the possibility that his manner of seeing does not truly edify, or
come home to the self as moral knowledge; we are also urged to interrogate Hitchcock and the conditions of *his* looking. Given Hitchcock's

Jefferies (James Stewart) spies on his neighbor with the tools of his trade in *Rear Window*.

rigorous imposition of formal control, where does his authority over *how* we see his images break down? In the first section of this essay I shall sketch out three partial readings of *Rear Window*, working successively within the frameworks of Marxist, deconstructionist, and feminist critical perspectives. To varying degrees, each of these methodologies is concerned with challenging the self-sufficiency and completeness of the work as it can be imagined under Hitchcock's control, and shifting responsibility for the making of the film's meaning to the *necessarily* insubordinate interpreter. Submitting to Hitchcock's plan for the coercive management of viewer response is conceived (in each case) as a form of naïveté: the naïveté of the enthralled spectator, or the naïveté of the critic who is determined to honor the film's *objective* form (itself an illusion). Viewed less tolerantly, this submission to the work's governing intelligence (its "greater knowledge" of its own structural imperatives) might seem to reinforce habits of mind that keep us subject to the oppressive orthodoxies of our language and culture. The overthrow of the "completed text," by contrast, is an expression of imaginative freedom. Or if that too is a naive supposition, one's refusal of the text's authority strengthens the conviction that authentic freedom is possible and *true* somewhere. Having concluded my three readings, I shall, in the second section of the essay, attempt to reposition myself *within* the film—that is to say, within *my* understanding of what Hitchcock understands to be the case in *Rear Window*—and formulate a reply to this many-sided challenge.

A Marxist critic would presumably want to demonstrate that the apartment complex Jefferies observes is a microcosm of the capitalist life-world, where nothing exists in supportive relation, but rather as mere senseless juxtaposition. The rear windows are like the randomly assembled, emotionally de-natured human interest items in a tabloid newspaper. This critic might wish to argue that what neither Jefferies nor Hitchcock comprehends about the film's general setting is the degree to which the possibility of murder works as a paradoxically reassuring vehicle of integration. It introduces coherence and a methodical, if hidden, plot into a panorama that initially contained no activity that was not sterilely repetitive and disconnected from everything else. Jefferies and the audience are given the impetus (as well as the detective's familiar procedure) to logically order a portion of this distressingly fragmented environment. At the same time we are encouraged in the belief that the connective process is not arbitrary or limited in its effect—that it somehow naturally inheres in this space. A potentially limitless number of similar subtle joinings might be achieved if only we had the time to collect more facts, more evidence of how things related. The quest for love in the rear window flats would be a plausible, secondary integrating theme for Jefferies to contemplate.

Murder, however, proves the most satisfyingly dimensionalized and intense instrument of linkage, because it suggests that the real connections (the connections that *make* things real) must be sought behind the screen of the visible. Though the view from one's window may offer a daily scene that is at most points unvarying, even slight discrepancies warrant careful scrutiny. The troubling detail, properly apprehended, yields an entire world to make sense of. The coordinates of this world are never revealed by appearances, though the latter are richly evocative "clues." Thus, murder opens the possibility of establishing a play of vital difference within the cellblock of leisure where the tenants continually reenact the same handful of defining gestures. Experience under capitalism is so devalued that Hitchcock can present a series of wholly reified behavior formulas as a convincing embodiment of urban diversity. The comedy of recognizing cozily eccentric types performing domestic routines, by turns familiar and mildly exotic, in imagined privacy is Hitchcock's strategy for transforming a pervasive condition of estrangement and lonely automatism into something that *feels* intimate: an almost comforting mirror for the audience.

At the same time, the Marxist could propose that Hitchcock unconsciously prescribes a rhythm of action for his window dwellers that is virtually identical to the rhythm of office and factory labor. The pleasurable hum of daily life in the courtyard is thus made ironically continuous with the master-ritual of commodity production and consumption. In addition to Jefferies's visual encroachment of his neighbors' world, there is a more insidious form of technological encroachment that seems to have emptied out in advance the significant privacy to which Jefferies seeks access. The tenants' "characters" are products of manufacture. Like Chaplin's tramp in *Modern Times,* whose work gesture has been so completely internalized that his mind and body alike are twitchingly enslaved to it, Jefferies's neighbors present their single, overdetermined traits (dancing, composing, making love) too emphatically. It is, in fact, all that keeps them noticeable. Without an eccentric practice that can be read at a distance, they visually fade into the anonymity of the crowd. The apartment block *has* to become the scene of a crime before the mechanism of surface variety is exposed in the act of wearing out. Nothing short of violence will prevent the attractions of this setting from turning unreal, or its cumulative liveliness from disintegrating into a strangely blank nervousness. Jefferies's observation *must* discover evidence of something that resists the pressure to duplicate (or mass produce) itself. The sudden disruption of Thorwald's act (the ongoing quarrels with his wife) satisfies Jefferies's craving for an experience that will reactivate his environment. It is an experience that promises to go somewhere—not immediately return on itself and become yet another version of Jefferies's own immobility.

The principal objective of the Marxist critique is to undermine our sense of cohesion, order, and a solid social space in *Rear Window*— and to replace it with a heightened awareness that violence, far from being an aberration in the generally tranquil cityscape, is the only conceivable instrument of change. Indeed, it appears to be a secret collective wish. (Jefferies, Lisa, and Stella quickly exchange their initial pose of shock at the possible tragedy that has occurred for a passionately eager affirmation of the crime's existence.) Thorwald's dismemberment of his wife can be regarded as horrible literalization of the mode of city perception T. S. Eliot identifies in "The Preludes" and "Morning at the Window": where hands (divorced from bodies) raise identical "dingy shades in a thousand furnished rooms," where short, square fingers stuff pipes, where "twisted faces from the bottom of the street" are "tossed up" by the waves of fog.[2] Physical dismemberment is a correlative for visual fragmentation: strangers' lives pieced together from fugitive glimpses of inconclusive segments of action. A dog lowered from a window in a basket, a body sunning itself, another one vacuuming, the head of a woman apparently taking a shower: Thorwald's crime has an almost Orphic power in this context. The scattered remnants issuing from his murderous rage might be said to *reconstitute* the life of the building. The concealed crime has a contagious power. The absence that Thorwald has created somehow manages to evoke everything left intact in the surrounding apartments. His transgression opens cracks through which all the reasonableness and easy containment of the *Rear Window* theater threaten to disappear. Rage provides a hidden agenda for all the aimless energy exhibited by the isolated members of this noncommunity. The effort to project one's life outward in such a place results only in one's facing a public void (recall the outcry of the woman whose dog was killed); the move to inwardness, on the other hand, is consistently portrayed as a kind of anxious invalidism. The theater of the private self is macabre and hallucinatory, as the behavior of Miss Lonelyhearts, the Thorwalds, and Jefferies himself attests.

Locating and defining the nature of the hole or gap that desperation has carved out of the center of this bourgeois idyll obviously serves the ends of Marxist interpretation. The gap is what focuses and steadies Jefferies's perceptions for most of the film, though it is his conviction that by concentrating on the gap the apparent disorder can be rationally plucked out and the original harmonious social arrangement restored. Political readings would contend that the gap cannot be closed. The image of absence that Thorwald has gropingly brought into being is the true image of the general life around him. The order posited after Thorwald's capture feels utterly contrived. The painters who materialize in Thorwald's room (during Hitchcock's ironic coda) to eliminate the last traces of his occupancy are part of a final pattern of absolute, neatly interlocking symmetries and closure. The composer plays his finished song (entitled "Lisa") to a rapturously grateful Miss Lonelyhearts; Miss Torso's husband returns from the service; the childless couple have a new dog; Jefferies is once again (as he first appeared to us) sleeping, with Lisa watching over him from an easy chair, deftly combining his world with her own in her choice of reading matter. However, as Philip Fisher has noted, commenting on resolutions in a Dickens novel: "Too many connections call connection itself into doubt in a final way that is more threatening than the early isolation, always pregnant with hints and possibilities of connection."[3]

A deconstructionist's critical task would converge with the Marxist's in the contemplation of *Rear Window's* unclosable gap. The shift in emphasis would chiefly be in the attempt to dissolve whatever appears stable in the system of narrative representation, rather than dissolving the claims to legitimacy of the social order that holds the narrative's values in place. A Derridean poststructuralist interpretation would inevitably fasten on the elusive origin of Jefferies's knowledge about what Thorwald has done. This critic, like the Marxist, would be reading against the text's authority, erasing any secure basis for rhetorical knowledge and autonomous form. What Jefferies actually sees, according to the deconstructionist, becomes progressively more displaced from what he imagines he is seeing, from the impressions he uses to form judgments. Vision grounds itself on the vagaries of desire, on the hypnotic appeal of continuously projecting something onto the visual field beyond what is manifestly there.

Equally significant is the discovery that the greater part of the film's conversation (its discourse) is formed in response to a troubling absence. The film becomes a commentary on the threatened or degraded status of immediate events: temporal experience conceived as presence. What is present to Jefferies is blurred and directionless, both inside his room, with Lisa's constantly thwarted efforts to achieve intimacy, and in the world outside his window, where things that can be openly observed function as little more than time-killing distraction. No matter how much promise of an illuminated present Lisa brings with her (she turns on several lights as she announces her name), she never really loses the quality of a shadow or phantom that is Jefferies's first and most compelling image of her. It is only when Lisa crosses the border into Jefferies's fantasy space and acquires the magical dispensation of an agent in a dream to violate Thorwald's inner sanctum that she acquires an aura whose appeal he passionately acknowledges. Absence rather than presence provides an impetus for the mind to rouse itself. Creative perception essentially gravitates to the hole that denies presence, whose structure is not authorized, where instead of possession, in the words of Paul Fry, "we have a phantom of possession that is always in retreat from one site to another."[4] As Lisa and Jefferies persistently test this gap—the indeterminate center of their visual and rhetorical sense of things—and feed increasingly elaborate speculations into it, the differences in their characters that have early in the film been postulated as clear and binding identity themes mysteriously disband. The differences become a product of a rhetoric whose terms will not stay solid. And as our awareness of statable difference between Jefferies and Lisa erodes, so too does our security about how Thorwald stands distinct from the man whose business it has become to watch him day and night.

Thorwald's final confrontation with Jefferies in Jefferies's own room, and his asking of a question for which, surprisingly, there can be no adequate reply ("What is it you want from me?"), leads to an assault on Jefferies by a cornered predator who, in some sense Jefferies has willed into being. One is startled by Thorwald's enormous bulk at close range—having become accustomed to viewing him from what I would like to call a story distance—and one feels Jefferies's silence following Thorwald's speech as something that only violence has the capacity to fill. If we regard Jefferies's main action in the film as an extended oral commentary on his own imaginative creation, he becomes the author of Thorwald. Thorwald's murder can be taken, in William Gass's phrase, as "an act of narratology" that Jefferies has "committed."[5] It is thus the barely averted death of Hitchcock's surrogate author—by analogy, the destruction of the initiating voice, the erasure of the story's point of origin—that is signified by Thorwald's quiet, "camera-blinded" attack on Jefferies's darkened form.

The feminist critic's point of entry in the film might well be through yet another expression of absence: the comically conceived female artist's one visible finished work. It is a spherical sculpture, with a hollow center, entitled (no doubt, jokingly) *Hunger*. This artist is arguably, though by default, the most independent, self-directed female presence in the narrative; yet it is strongly hinted from the outset that both her spinsterhood and "hobby" are a consequence of her appearance, not a matter of meaningful ambition or discerning choice. Her sculpture reveals a preoccupation with signs of gender conceived as an emptiness rather than a fullness. Implicitly, it is the function of the unattainable male partner to fill the hole that has never been filled. Lacking that union (to which nearly all of the film's women attach fetishistic importance) the sculpture remains an "O"—the cipher that her veiled self-portrait inscribes. I am thinking here of the spinster's meditation in J. M. Coetzee's *In the Heart of the Country:* "If I am an 'O,' I am sometimes persuaded it must be because I am a woman."[6] The females in both apartment buildings (with the possible exception of Stella) are designated and chiefly differentiated by their capacity to hold—or repel—the male gaze. There is no decisive residual effort on Hitchcock's part to align the spectator's sensibility (or Jefferies's) with other possible sources of value.

Miss Torso (her nickname, of course, disturbingly linking her to Thorwald's crime) defines one extreme of desirability, while Miss Lonelyhearts affords us a symmetrically negative counterpart. Miss Lonelyhearts's desires (presumably resembling those of the female sculptor) are played out in a mime with phantom male dinner guests, a performance whose grotesquerie is not appreciably reduced by the inherent pathos of her situation. Miss Torso, like the more elegant, genteelly erotic Lisa, is imaged throughout as a consumable. Her function in the narrative code is of the same order as the gleaming dinner from "21" that Lisa delivers with herself when she enters the film, to enhance the gift of her presence. Miss Lonelyhearts's highest aspiration is to achieve similar edible status. But the proffered banquet of the female form quickly turns to surfeit, as the predicament of the newlywed husband in another of the apartments reveals. His now endlessly available wife, clamoring in the background for the marital fulfillment that he *owes* her has already been transformed into a second meaningless job. The pleasurable image advertised during courtship becomes a standardized product whose mystique has evaporated. The husband's periodic escapes to the apartment window are like a factory worker's cigarette break: a harried "coming up for air." One of the magazine ads John Berger includes in his highly influential lecture series, *Ways of Seeing,* shows a "delicious" model pouring Haig scotch into a large tumbler. Her lips are parted and her look is provocatively inviting. The picture is captioned "Say when."[7] The nightmare of marital confinement in *Rear Window* is predicated on a pouring that never stops. The female usurps the right to "say when" and the moment doesn't arrive until all feeling is dead. The "tender trap" of marriage, engineered (the song tells us) by females, proves to the man inside it a heartless bondage. Married "love" is a constant waiting on the alien machinery of the wife's personality. The wife's point of view, significantly, is not judged worthy of interest. She exists for us chiefly as a supplicating offscreen voice, whose tone would be the same whether the request was for sex or taking out the garbage.

The organization of audience attention with respect to the female image is everywhere problematic in *Rear Window*. Feminist critics have referred to the appropriation of the female form for fantasy dispersals of our sense of human wholeness as the movement from "being" to "being looked at." "Being looked-atness" (or camera appeal) is one of cinema's principal luring mechanisms, perhaps the most potent means of establishing viewer involvement, but the body-image as locus of plea-sure is often the beginning *and* end point of spectator connection with the female. The favorable reception of the male body-image heightens our engagement with a sequence of activities. Somehow it is coded in such a way that it can dissolve into that activity, to become one with it. The female body-image, on the other hand, even in the midst of its involvement in plotted action, keeps returning (as if for validation) to its primary condition as a desire-fixated *appearance*. Miss Torso's spon-taneous, seemingly unself-conscious dance rehearsals in her apartment have been designed by Hitchcock to divert the aesthetic qualities of her performance into a purely erotic channel. Hitchcock tantalizes us with the ambiguity of her intention. Her possible unawareness of being watched (if she is considered as a character) has to be conjoined with the *actress's* awareness that the principal function of her dance is to make herself into a creature of fantasy for James Stewart.

Perhaps the film's most arresting metaphor for the primacy of ap-pearance-manipulation in the female order—that is, *instinctive* prefer-ence for the authority of the enticing pose over alternative male-domain possibilities for heroism and challenge—is *Rear Window*'s concluding joke. Grace Kelly, "enticingly posed" in a chair, like a dream guardian (mother/mistress/wife-to-be) for sleeping Jefferies, exchanges the book of Himalayan adventure she is apparently absorbed in for another text (*Harper's Bazaar*) that claims her real allegiance. Her involvement in the life of danger and risk taking is finally exposed, if further exposure were needed, as a socialite's stunt, similar in kind to the escapades of other spoiled rich girls in screwball comedies. Her objective in breaking into Thorwald's apartment—the strongest motivating action she is given—is, not surprisingly, to retrieve Mrs. Thorwald's wedding ring. And no sooner does she have it in her possession than she places it on her own finger and impulsively flaunts it in Jefferies's direction. Her bravery is as coyly seductive as her petite overnight bag. She uses the latter to perform a metaphoric "striptease" for Jefferies. The goal of both of these emblems is to hold Jefferies's gaze in thrall, and the shift from one strategy to another implies no interior development.

168

If I have not distorted the concerns of the three critical methods I have chosen to employ in my efforts to demystify *Rear Window*, perhaps I have earned the right to suggest that what each of them appears to lack is an operative *sense* of lack in their separate quests for authority over the narrative. Critical expectations are derived from systems whose core assumptions seem less available for questioning, testing, and possible revision in the interpretive process than the assumptions of the work under scrutiny. These expectations too strongly and too readily structure what the interpreter sees. This is hardly a novel insight, but it has special relevance to the case of *Rear Window*, whose protagonist, in addition to being a voyeur and a prototype of the moviegoer, is also a critic of sorts. Returning to the question with which this paper began, the ethical question of the precise nature of Jefferies's transgression, one might reasonably argue that as a critic Jefferies is guilty, at the very least, of arriving at judgment without understanding. At no point does he feel the pressure to arrive at a more difficult self-knowledge. Nor does he come to an acknowledgment of how deviously self-ratifying most experiential knowledge is. Such knowledge becomes "firm" by the repression of contradictions and by the soliciting force of an ingrained disposition.

From the beginning of Jefferies's effort to explicate the pattern of Thorwald's story, he effectively distances his own discourse on the subject (so that his language stands at the same remove from Thorwald's life as his physical observation is). Jefferies is always moving his speech away from a consideration of his own motives, from the meaning of his intensifying need to entrap Thorwald in a binding configuration of guilt. Why does Jefferies's hermeneutics of suspicion and exposure so easily drive all competing schemes of value from the field? Moreover, why do so many viewers conclude that Jefferies's method of seeking edification, given the stakes and the possibility of Mrs. Thorwald's murder, is "natural"? It is a mode of inquiry that is endlessly resourceful in preventing challenges to its procedures from taking hold. No space for reflection is created in which the mesmerizing labor of the negative reveals its potential for *infecting* the knowledge and claims of social justice or truth-seeking that are its putative higher ends. In other words, Jefferies's (or anyone's) capacity to envision the ideal, to act credibly in the name of a truth better than the radically imperfect "givens" of the present can be subtly deformed by a consistent reliance on a terminology obsessed with negation and hidden tyranny. One recognizes how Jefferies's investigation finds justification in the fact of its own momentum, in the cumulative weight of confirming instances and particulars. How can Jefferies, as it were, change the subject (or the terms in which he conceives the subject) once his system has begun to think by itself? *Rear Window* shows us how tempting it is for us not to change subject or terms once they have been established, at the risk of confusion or the risk of exposing our own slippery, irresolute ground.

Miles Coverdale, the narrator of Nathaniel Hawthorne's *The Blithedale Romance* and the preeminent voyeuristic interpreter in nineteenth-century American fiction, is much more conscious than Hitchcock's Jefferies of the perils attendant on building systems out of our distracted, always selfishly slanted perceptions of other lives. He is equally skeptical of all attempts to "solve" or answer for the enigmas of human conduct by reference to those systems: "We thereby insulate [the person we examine] from many of his true relations, magnify his peculiarities, inevitably tear him into parts, and of course patch him very clumsily together again. What wonder, then, should we be frightened at the aspect of a monster, which, after all—though we can point to every feature of his deformity in the real personage—may be said to have been created mainly by ourselves!"[8] Coverdale later declares that persistence in wasting one's sympathies and judgment on affairs which are ultimately "none of mine" result in "attenuating one's own life of much of its proper substance."[9] "Diffused among so many alien interests," one's imaginative will to engage positive values is demoralized.

The central moment in *Rear Window*, it seems to me, is that in which Thorwald catches sight of Jefferies looking at him, and Jefferies attempts to hide from his gaze in the shadows. Too much contemporary criticism which insists that interpretation takes precedence over the text uses this assumption as a rationale for hiding from the "eye" of the work, for denying that the work has the power (or even the right) to meet the interpreter's gaze. The most comfortable position for beholding art is obviously from above, rather than from a bewildered and vulnerable eye level. If we are to part company with Jefferies's complacent critical vision, we must grant the work an occasion to look back and take our measure. *Rear Window*'s continuing power over many of us lies, I am convinced, in its profound intuition of the self-deceiving uses vision rationally proposes for itself. The film's form carries this knowledge—about whose implications interpreters can never pose too many questions. If one wants to disentangle some portion of this issue, the only place to begin is with our blurred images of self. One must be willing to reexamine the suspect ways in which the self constantly exchanges its confusions for fantasies of settled order and out of this order contrives a limited world to inhabit. If our language is not to grow tyrannous in its manipulation of what we perceive, our theoretical persuasions, with their growing vested interests, must initiate challenges from within to their own authority. The practiced ease of any method is the greatest threat to its continued ability to say things that matter. It is precisely this ease that we need to oppose. No system exists to rescue us from tentativeness in our engagement with art and what it knows (about itself and about us). I am reminded of the poet Byron's provocative comment on our shared Jefferies complex: "when a man talks of systems, his case is hopeless."

And yet, having offered what amounts to safe, corrective counsel to the always assailable "extremist" critics who claim authority over a work under protection of a self-sustaining method, I have not shown what my own reading of *Rear Window* would reveal in the film that other approaches neglect or falsify. Is it possible for me to speak on behalf of Hitchcock without soon taking refuge in some form of methodology? And would the process of self-questioning continue to be an integral part of my analysis, once I have finished demonstrating that Jefferies— cast in the role of critic—does not examine his own motives and assumptions sufficiently?

It is worth noting here that the three partial readings I have proposed do not stand apart from my experience of the film; they "belong" to that experience, and have clarified for me many plausible implications of the film's visual rhetoric. If I have been skeptical in my employment of three somewhat distinct, though frequently overlapping modes of discourse, it was with the intention of discovering what portions of the *Rear Window* text it would be convenient for me to lose sight of (suppress, if you like) so that the "objects" of my Marxist or feminist or deconstructionist suspicion might achieve dominance and centrality. I also found myself arguing internally with each of my "readers," trying to learn how I might enter unself-consciously into the spirit of their inquiry without resorting to parody. The only way in which I was able to escape the Jefferies trap of "viewing from above" was to treat issues in each reading that genuinely engaged me and to formulate them in language that sounded like my own. It was necessary for me not to conceive this shifting of perspectives as a game, without risks or consequences. I regarded my objective rather as equivalent to the Jamesian endeavor to honor, as completely as possible, the assumptions and disposition that mysteriously comprise a "point of view." I became more mindful than usual of the ways in which I experience "being on the inside" of character in fiction (whether as author or reader). The critic characters I was choosing to play had to be located somehow within me before I could speak for them, or allow them to speak *through* me. It was at once a kind of pretending from which I maintained a certain degree of detachment—though my sense of how I was detached was interestingly blurred—and a willingness to be possessed. The experience of possession intensified as my imagination permitted me to forget where the critic's ideas were coming from, and how they could be used in staking out my final position. I grew curious about how this activity differed from my identification with Jefferies in my early viewings of *Rear Window.*

The aspect of the film which none of my partial readings of the film more than fleetingly acknowledged is its double existence as conventional murder mystery (a structure of action whose plot, in Peter Brooks's phrase, is "a closed and legible whole") and as commentary on the process of viewing and making a film.[10] What is most striking about the commentary in its implied relationship to the mystery is its deliberate unassertiveness. The murder mystery never requires the spectator to move beyond its own carefully delimited boundaries. Its progress is only for brief moments interrupted so that the viewer can be "lightly" reminded of the presence—and authority—of the director.

In Antonioni's *Blowup,* a film which is often compared with *Rear Window,* character and conventional mystery pattern are postulated only so that they can be broken down and finally dissolved altogether. The viewer is obliged, if he is to stay involved with the film at all, to think about the metaphysical status of appearances (of what it means for things to be present and absent, known and unknown). In *Blowup,* the deconstructionist's project of revealing the "abyss" of indeterminacy under the landscape of signifying forms is carried as far as camera narration can conceivably go, without abandoning visible phenomena completely. *Rear Window* anticipates the deconstructionist in a quite different and, I am tempted to say, more radical way. The film presents us with a narrative structure that is serenely intact, yet at the same time authorizes endless rupture. The rupturing process begins when the spectator recognizes that the perfect order of the film's surface story is a "blind" for another story in which the camera's point of view is at variance with that of the characters. The same images that make it seem reasonable to view *Rear Window* as a self-sufficient, "naive" genre film also invite us, without compelling us, to see *through* the devices that hold us captive to the story. A mystery whose solution has seemed to depend on the gathering of external data conceals, but also discloses (to those moved to attend it) a more basic mystery of perception: how our window on the world "out there" ceaselessly transforms into a mirror of our desires and perceptual habits.

In a provocative essay entitled "The Wilderness of Mirrors," Albert Cook speculates on the self-referential functions of mirrors and windows in Renaissance art, reminding us that both entered Western Painting about the same time:

> The completed painting is a mirror too, since it gives back the world and arrests the viewer into a social set (the functions of painting in his society), and perhaps also into contemplation. In a painting, though, the mirror-like image is already fixed; it doubles the work but not the face of the viewer, except by the implication that a doubled object *means* only what the "face" of the viewer can bring to it while standing in the absence of what the doubling frame, the mirror, can usually give him, a direct representation of his own face. The window, by contrast, gives on part of the wide world beyond, or stains some of it out in the stained glass window, or curtains off much of what a private world within has organized, if the window is seen from inside.[11]

Images of windows and mirrors, finally, are alike self-referential (referring us back to the painting) insofar as both afford views of an order congruent with that of the scene framed by the painting.

Rear Window begins with an image of window blinds being raised by an invisible presence (by implication, Hitchcock) in a manner that reminds us of curtains being raised in a theater. The idea of a frame being artificially opened to give the spectator the semblance of an outside view—in contrast, say, with a character inside the narrative raising blinds or opening a window—could hardly be more self-consciously linked to questions of performance, to the "staging" of the frame's contents, and the spectator's relation to the image. The camera then proceeds to pass through the window and conduct a "casual" survey of the courtyard, the apartment dwellings opposite, and their tenants, returning twice in a kind of circling motion to James Stewart, the sleeping occupant of the room whose windows were the starting point for this guided tour. Hitchcock's camera actively asserts its independence from a character's point of view in this prologue, insisting on not only its separation from but its superiority to the perceiving consciousness of any figure contained in his film's "world in a frame." The camera makes itself felt as an intruder in Jefferies's apartment, studying his dozing form with its prominent plaster cast, then stealthily taking in his photographic equipment and framed examples of his work as a photojournalist. Hitchcock ends the prologue with the camera's movement from a large photographic negative to a developed version of its initially cryptic image on the cover of *Life* magazine. The progression then, in the opening of *Rear Window*, is from inside to outside space, with a double return to inside. Hitchcock neatly establishes the central window of the apartment (and, by extension, the film frame) as two way. The window serves as the camera's pivot point, in addition to being the dividing line between inner and outer, so that we are acutely aware of when the line is being crossed.

The arresting strangeness of the camera's way of positioning itself in relation to this environment, its manner of taking possession (proving mastery) of what it calls into being, is the "mirroring" dimension of Hitchcock's narrative. It is the second realm of the film's existence, what I would like to describe as the realm of allegory. In Hitchcock, the allegorical space is that which "enters the picture" when the camera disengages most conspicuously from the subjects of the movie story and makes the power of its presence felt at least as strongly as the narrative information contained in the images. One of the things that the opening segment of *Rear Window* unveils for us is the process whereby the camera simulates our occupation of film space. We are also made to concentrate, as part of the same thought, as it were, on Jefferies/James Stewart's status as a sleeper, a *watched* sleeper. How are we united to the film's world before this character awakens to it, before he establishes by his active involvement in it that it is *his* world rather than the camera's that we are to be chiefly concerned with? Invariably, as Leo Steinberg notes in his essay "Picasso's Sleepwatchers," "the encounter with sleep implies opportunity," and "the one caught napping, victim or beneficiary, is the butt of the action. Sleep is the opportunity of the intruder."[12] Hitchcock's camera shows us, here and throughout the film, that to see someone not seeing automatically heightens, and thus leads one to view more intensely, whatever that person does not see. The sleeping figure maximizes the tension of looking covertly in film (the primary movie response)—attending to what is "for our eyes only." Stewart/Jefferies is blind to the camera's intrusion in his room, as, of course, Lars Thorwald will later prove blind to the probing of Jefferies's telephoto lens. The camera moves in intimate proximity to the sleeper without disturbing him, all the while "posing wakeful questions" to his—or, by a logical substitution, the spectators'—"dream life."[13]

The indefinite dream space "materialized" by the camera as its separate domain, sealed off from the much more precisely defined life of the characters and space of their story, is, in allegorical terms, our picture of the invisible. Hitchcock, like the medieval allegorist, begins with an immaterial fact (in this case, the camera as self-aware, creative force) and then invents a visible action whose highest purpose is to reveal the camera's nature—in effect, giving the camera reflexively back to itself as the "power behind all things." While Jefferies sleeps, the camera conducts a preliminary search for its own image, exchanging the view from the window (where the unfolding dramatic action seems to be given primacy) for a glance in the mirror. The photo negative and its "awakened" counterpart (the smiling model on the *Life* cover) serve as such a mirror, asking us to consider, if only for a moment, the process by which images of the sort we have been looking at are generated. Hitchcock emblematizes the "other world" behind the plane of projected appearances that the camera as recording mechanism is always in touch with. It is a place where light values are reversed, and where the illuminated object seems to decompose, returning to a condition of specular disembodiment. The "mirror" emblem (the negative vs. the shadowless glamour portrait) is reintroduced and further complicated at a later point in the film, when Jefferies, dozing for a second time, is approached and enveloped by a shadow. As he opens his eyes, the shadow transforms for him and for us into the radiantly beautiful image of Grace Kelly/Lisa. Hitchcock prolongs Lisa's moment of metamorphosis from phantom shadow to "living" presence by displaying her advance to kiss Jefferies in a stop-action, dreamlike slow motion. Here again the camera finds a way to mirror its fabrication of the face which fills the screen, interposing itself between the silhouette and the character that is coming to life out of this "negative." The camera is the source of the image, and as Lisa, in extreme close-up, *sees* the camera and leans into it, as if in yielding her face to be kissed, she acknowledges the entity that gives her life, and, in a mysterious but real sense, *is* her being.

When Jefferies sleeps for the third time in the film, the camera discovers yet another dream image of the female—a figure, clad in black and leaving Thorwald's apartment with him, who is at too great a distance from the camera to achieve a clear visual identity. This woman, whose precise relation to Thorwald (wife? mistress?) has a crucial bearing on our reading of *Rear Window*'s plot, disappears from the film entirely once the camera, spying autonomously, has beheld her. The camera announces its presence and authority here by breaking what is, by this stage of the narrative, a firmly established convention of presenting all our rear window observation from the point of view of one or more of the film's major characters.

Hitchcock's overt "mirroring" gestures (when he most clearly alerts us that, indeed, there is no "outside" space in *Rear Window*, that everything in the frame is addressed to the camera, and that what the viewer "discovers" looking out Jefferies's window has been seen first by the camera, and exists nowhere outside of its gaze) occur only at great intervals. Hitchcock veils his allegorical scheme for much the same reason that the allegorical poet does. "In Horatian terms, [the poet] gave profit to the few and pleasure to the many."[14] A viewer/reader, as Michael Murrin suggests in *The Veil of Allegory*, must be prepared to "recognize in allegory a specialized form of discourse, something which demanded of him an unusual mode of thought. Otherwise, despite what natural qualifications he might have, he will react to a poem with limited comprehension of its analogical truth."[15] The nonrecognition of allegory, however, in no way prevents the viewer/reader from taking delight in the work, or from feeling that she understands it perfectly in her own terms. If Hitchcock sanctions a division in his audience, it is not a division designed to exclude anyone. It is effected "silently, painlessly" so that the veiled narrative never disrupts the popular narrative for more than a few moments at a time, and never in a manner to provoke bewilderment. Hitchcock no doubt understood that the potential power of a revelation is not reduced—on the contrary, it may well be deepened—when it dwells beyond the casual spectator's concerns, and is conceived as something inessential to his experience of the film. ("The poet covers the sun with clouds, through which people may see its light, though they cannot tell its exact position.")[16] Hitchcock also understood that the revelation, however much it runs counter to what the casual spectator seeks from the story, should never be assigned more importance, in the planning of the film's structure, than this spectator's interests. The extraordinary imaginative resonance of a Hitchcock film derives, I think, from his matchless ability to hide things in plain sight— to create "open" stories that are entirely taken up with subtle acts of concealment. A Hitchcock text perfectly fulfills Paul de Man's conditions for "the essence of the literary": it is a text that has no "blind spots," that "implicitly or explicitly signifies its own rhetorical mode and prefigures its own misunderstanding as the correlative of its rhetorical nature."[17] Thus, we have Hitchcock almost wholly submerging his camera "mirror" from the end of the film's prologue until the point when the woman in black leaves with Thorwald, when we become conscious that the camera in Jefferies's window is sole witness. The smooth advance of the naive genre film has been a calculated "misunderstanding" of the prologue.

In exactly similar fashion, the voyeurism issue, central to nearly every critical study of *Rear Window,* is submerged as a charged moral issue in the second half of the film. At the risk of oversimplifying the way in which audiences respond to moral problems in traditional genre films, I will suggest that they generally take their cues from the characters in the story whom they regard as contextually normative: characters who are at once "in the know" about things and sympathetic in their behavior. Stella and Lisa each take on the role of reliable moral arbiter in the early scenes of *Rear Window.* They express concern about "rear window" ethics and inquire into Jefferies's reasons for spying, urging him to be less preoccupied with the secrets of his neighbors' lives. Gradually, however, both women become eager accomplices in Jefferies's spying on Thorwald, having been convinced (along with the viewer), that Thorwald has committed a murder. Their alliance with Jefferies creates a consensus within the film's world about the appropriateness, perhaps even the necessity, of spying under *these* circumstances. Voyeurism as a problem to have lingering qualms about is effectively dissolved by the imperatives of the mystery form itself. Everything is comfortably marshaled into the service of the audience's "natural desire" to see and know more. Voyeurism ceases to be central to the audience's understanding of the story if we are confident that Jefferies's "watchfulness" has uncovered a crime that would otherwise have escaped notice.

Does Hitchcock then actually offer a sustained critique of voyeurism in *Rear Window*? Surely, Hitchcock *knows* that the voyeuristic drive is always and inescapably present in the art of watching movie narratives. Moreover, both in his choice of subjects and his method of constructing film stories, he consistently displays his own fascination with every form of illicit gratification of the prying gaze. Finally, and perhaps most problematically, are narrative films ever, in any meaningful sense, *against* the inclinations that they arouse and satisfy?[18] Can a thematic intention, if it is at odds with the visceral and subliminal content of a film's images, undo or equal in effect the "play" of those images in the viewer's imagination? What we actually feel about what we see on the screen seldom coincides with the moral positions staked out in dialogue by a film's characters, though we may often be convinced that what characters are telling each other directly is the message of the work that we are absorbing.

The famous production still from *Rear Window* showing James Stewart holding a telephoto lens seems to communicate the voyeurism theme more starkly and ominously than any scene in the film, since it

177

fixes the voyeur as an emblem to be contemplated, and presents Stewart himself as a more disturbing presence than he ever appears to be in the actual narrative. *Rear Window*'s dominant strategy for luring the viewer into the story is, of course, to align his or her "looking" with Stewart's, so that we share his perspective and find ourselves gazing along with him rather than gazing at him. To the extent that this continually reinforced identification process holds for the viewer, the film "disperses" rather than concentrates the power residing in the production still. The purpose of the camera mirroring moments that we have been discussing, to return to a point I made earlier, is to introduce a *potential* break or rupture within the otherwise seamless pattern of our involvement in "Jefferies's narrative." Finding the camera and questioning its purpose in declaring itself is equivalent to being briefly released from the spell of James Stewart's seductively benign (or, at worst, stubborn and overzealous) presence. It is an opportunity to reverse the film's light values (as in the processing of the negative in the prologue) and to realize that Stewart's face is neither an adequate "window" to use in discovering the meaning of the events across the courtyard nor a fit "mirror" for a morally responsive spectator.

Let me try to sharpen this distinction between "mirror" and "window." If we become aware (as we watch the movie) that the Stewart persona has been chiefly designed as a mirror for our position as spectator within the film story and that this mirror not only anticipates but seeks to control our sense of what we are perceiving, we are free to reject the Stewart/Jefferies mirror as the key to the spectacle framed by the window. If we agree that such a rejection is part of the work that Hitchcock has given the ideal reader of his allegory to do, it will become clear how the critique of voyeurism can be suspended on one level and yet continue, far less accessibly but in a form that might lead to true rather than spurious instruction, on another. As long as the Stewart/Jefferies mirror fixes our role, *Rear Window* is open to the charge of being a clever but inconsequential exchange of prurient fantasies: the fantasy of the artist arousing a debased version of the same fantasy in the viewer. A quite different experience results from watching ourselves watch Jefferies, while repeatedly posing Thorwald's question to him—"What is it you want from me?" Continually interrogating our relationship to the voyeur can arguably help us to understand something *real:* the nature of our investment in fantasies of this sort.

In one of her contemporary Platonic dialogues, Iris Murdoch has Plato say that "there are dark low levels [of the human mind] where we are hardly individual people at all . . . Eros is there. This darkness is sex, power, desire, inspiration, *energy* for good or evil. Many people live their whole lives in that sort of darkness, seeing nothing but flickering shadows and illusion, like images thrown on a screen [Murdoch invokes here the familiar analogy of Plato's cave as movie theater]—and the only energy they ever have comes from egoism and dreams."[19]

Out of boredom and a hungry self-absorption, according to Murdoch's Plato, we cling to rear window images. We justify our immobility by finding incriminating patterns that place others in the "darkness" we are loathe to identify as our own. The Stewart/Jefferies "mirror" encourages us in the assumption that our imprisonment, like his, is natural, that we are convalescents seeking innocent distraction while our "fractures" mend. We only spend our time spying because we are temporarily less than whole. Given our situation, this is the best we can be expected to do, or be. Rear window images penetrate the consciousness only as empty palliatives or as suspicion. (Something may be *wrong* out there, so one is well-advised to remain hidden in the shadows and look further, until one can be sure.)

At the climax of *Rear Window,* when the "real world," in the form of Thorwald, enters Jefferies's "cave" and asks him, in effect, to make his investment in Thorwald's life clear, Jefferies's response is to cover his eyes and attempt to freeze Thorwald in place by blinding him with the light of flashbulbs. In this final violent conjunction of the camera mechanism with the hidden eye games that constitute the life of the film's protagonist, camera and subject alike empty themselves out. Now that the object being looked at knows it is being looked at and traces the surveillance "mechanism" to its source, the camera responds with a paroxysm of flash exposures that yields light but no picture, an illumination that obscures. Thorwald and Jefferies confront each other in a mutual blindness, culminating in Jefferies dropping out of the window (the rigorously controlled frame of the film's world) and Thorwald disappearing into the darkness inside. Jefferies's fall, in allegorical terms, is the final severance of the idea of the privileged, justified spectator from the "window"; the film decisively shows the window as something not belonging to him, something whose capacity to reveal is *not* predicated on his presence behind it.

I would like to think that Hitchcock is also acknowledging here the drastic limits of the *camera's* power to image truth. Significantly, it is the camera that Jefferies instinctively seizes as the protective barrier between himself and Thorwald's "reality." If I am right in assigning this intention to Hitchcock, what he may be doing is denying melodrama's fitness to offer visible signs of the ethical. Such a denial is comparable to (though formally less explicit than) the splitting and burning of the image of Alma's face in Bergman's *Persona*. In *Persona*, Bergman attempts to mark the point past which the camera cannot go in imaging authentic suffering.[20] In *Rear Window*, Hitchcock marks the point where a genuine ethical question threatens to undo what de Man describes as "the intelligibility and the seductiveness" of the logic that has "animated the development of the narrative."[21] The naive genre film must find a way to turn the ethical problem immediately back into familiar spectacle or break apart in the effort to absorb it. The point has been reached when the allegory is about to converge with the action of the film's literal plot. This would be tantamount to a full unveiling. The camera must either side with Thorwald in opposing the figure that claims to stand for the camera's authority or relinquish its implied status as a source of higher revelation. Hitchcock chooses the latter course. If the camera can no longer withhold itself from view, it will proclaim itself part of the "empty" fiction rather than attempt to *show* what is real. Hitchcock may be suggesting that the camera's truth *always* resides in what, at the last instant, eludes capture, never in what can be made literally visible. The action of *Rear Window* never appears more "unreal" than when it depicts Jefferies's struggle at the window ledge and his plummeting to the courtyard; his fall is a fall into value-renouncing artifice. The only depth that the camera makes visible, as its own response to Thorwald's *demand* for depth, is transparently a conjurer's trick. In the film's final scene, the artifice of the fall is extended to everything on screen. The camera reinstates itself in the narrative as an instrument of closure. It offers a series of neatly ironic images that give a "proper" final distance to the story. At the same time it declares *Rear Window*'s world of appearances a fantasy—and eases our way out of this world, since nothing that is mere fantasy "matters."

Returning to the question of how the spectator is meant to see this film once she has broken the "mirror" identification with Stewart/Jefferies, I should stress that Hitchcock provides no solution to the problem. If the Stewart persona's enacted desire does not *have* to dictate the desires of the spectator, it certainly is of no help in determining what kind of viewer response is more legitimate. The decision to place ourselves in opposition to Stewart's character, once made, proves very difficult to honor in practice. In order to do so, one needs to go well beyond mere denial, and try to become conscious of the impulses that successfully "bind us" to film spectacle. How are we to keep those impulses we would designate as "higher" (in terms of moral responsiveness) from secretly allying with or transforming into those we regard as "lower?" It is not enough, and surely not interesting, to keep repeating as we watch the voyeur in action, "This is not right." One should also be prepared to say, as far as one's knowledge permits, "This is what I want from the story; my inclinations, often to my surprise, lead me here rather than there." Frequently, perhaps, the Jefferies "mirror" response will not be experienced as coercive. It may, in fact, precisely anticipate and match our own, with no directorial duplicity required to ensure identification. Finding oneself in agreement, however, is by no means synonymous with finding Jefferies or oneself morally validated. Whether we are comfortably contained in the mirror of Jefferies's gaze or remain steadfastly outside it, the difficulty of ascertaining where we are, really, as watchers of this film—and why—is formidable.

The deconstructive critic must contend with the possibility that the film is so multifariously self-aware that it has no "blind spots." *Rear Window* has not only deconstructed itself but by separating, through allegory, the deconstructive process from the naive narrative has left the latter artificially self-enclosed and extraordinarily resistant to meaningful interference from the viewer "suspicious" of unified texts. Its conscious "unknowing" is the basis of its continuity and achieved wholeness. Similarly, *Rear Window* thwarts the efforts of feminists and Marxists to expose the system of patriarchal, bourgeois values that it "covertly" rests upon, and presumably affirms. Such critics must first account for the ways in which the doubling of windows as movie screens *places* the contents of these frames as calculatedly two-dimensional "genre pantomimes."[22] It is impossible to fix the point where intended visual irony ends and unexamined cultural irony begins. The greater the distance of the neighbors' window/screen from the camera, the more the occupants must take on the flatness of stock images in order to be fully readable by the viewer. Hitchcock equates readability in movies with the loss of human dimension. Flat figures, moreover, will always suit the moviegoer's purposes; one can so easily project things onto them. All of the tenants initially resemble animated cutouts from consumer ads of the early fifties. Gradually, however, they acquire a certain pathos and an aura of mystery by virtue of the fact that Hitchcock makes distance a constant in our relation to them. Even though the behavior of the tenants remains stylized throughout, an *effect* of solitude and isolation (that is to say, a reality effect) is imparted to their ritual "performances"; this results from the camera's violation of the narrative convention that all figures who are to exist as "characters" in a film will be brought near to us. Moreover, windows arranged in symmetrical rows, whose occupants seem to be living out a *fantasy* of privacy in enforced silence, cannot help achieving the appearance of prison cells. No one knows better than Hitchcock how to orchestrate complex perceptions by staging objects and segmented actions for the camera. Surely, for example, the film visually comprehends the irony of the apartment block as a female hierarchy, with the unloved and unattractive consigned to the lowest level, the "free" sunbathing bohemians on the roof, and the more ambiguously trapped and restless married women placed in between.

The method I have employed to "save" *Rear Window* as a film authored and controlled by Hitchcock from critics who underestimate its own powers of suspicion and ironic self-awareness requires me, I believe, to end with some questions. I would ask, with Charles Altieri, how, given critics' recent preponderant emphasis on entrapment and the immovable objects of linguistic and cultural determinism, we are to find sanction for articulating forms "that free us to see who we can become" as lovers of the available real?[23] A critic who conceives the artist either as an oppressor or as a depersonalized transmitter of cultural codes already in place can only grant imaginative authority to texts as armored in skepticism as the perspectives he or she brings to them. If openness of any sort is always an incitement to suspicion, how can openness (surely, our best hope of freedom) survive as a value?

7

Mother Calls the Shots: Hitchcock's Female Gaze

And I, my mind in turmoil, how I longed
to embrace my mother's spirit, dead as she was.
Three times I rushed toward her, desperate to hold her,
three times she fluttered through my fingers, sifting away like a
shadow, dissolving like a dream, and each time
the grief cut to the heart . . .

—Homer, *The Odyssey*

Even when he [Cézanne] wants to show us the body's interminable shifting and reconstruction in the space of desire, he wants the space to be literalized and the body's states to be individually solid as a rock.

—T. J. Clark, on Cézanne's *The Large Bathers*

It may seem late in the day to consider, yet again, the problem of Hitchcock and his quintessentially male camera eye. Ever since Laura Mulvey settled upon Hitchcock as Exhibit A in her endlessly cited essay, "Visual Pleasure and Narrative Cinema," it has been exceedingly difficult for admirers of Hitchcock's work to evade or decisively answer the charge that there is something wrong—pervasively wrong and violating— about Hitchcock's way of representing women on screen.[1] To use a term that Mulvey and other gaze theorists would hesitate to sanction, but that the Jesuit-trained Hitchcock was intimately acquainted with, he is "sinfully" preoccupied with certain images of the female which overdetermine his attempts to imagine them and decide how they should be looked at. Equally sinful, in consequence, are the identities and narrative positions he assigns to women in his progressively more misogynistic cinema fantasies, and his canny manipulations of the spectator whom he hopes to ensnare in these fantasies. Hitchcock's narratives, it has often been argued, systematically deprive female characters of their

The second Mrs. de Winter (Joan Fontaine) studies the mark of her predecessor in *Rebecca*.

power, their human agency, and do so from the director's initial decisions about how women are "appropriately" framed by the camera. The woman typically enters the world of Hitchcock's films as the preordained object of looking, and henceforth dwells always under the punitive regime of the male gaze.

The intensely moralistic force of the discredited word "sinful" helps us perhaps to account for the hidden surplus of culpability and contagion seemingly attached to Hitchcock's continual abuse of his authority. It is somehow not enough to say that his films present too limited a range of options for female characters or that the films' themes and attitudes, if uncritically accepted, might—like most other movies— reinforce longstanding prejudice and social inequities. Hitchcock's "murderous gaze" has become emblematic (and symptomatic) of all the optical crimes against women, conscious and unconscious, that have been perpetrated since the beginning of narrative cinema. In the mythology of gaze theory, he has been assigned the role that Eve played in Genesis. He is the one who must remain guilty if the "original sin" of the male camera gaze is to preserve its coherence, credibility, and explanatory power. No one has ever suggested, of course, that Hitchcock was the first director to determine what the motion picture camera could destructively accomplish as the secret conductor of the male gaze. But, like the officer in Kafka's "In the Penal Colony" who keeps the torture machine working, in perfect obedience to the wishes of its original designer, Hitchcock is an expert "keeper of the faith."[2]

No attribution of intention or discovery is necessary to assign Hitchcock the symbolic office of Warden in the prison house of cinematic looking. Centuries of painting conventions have bequeathed to him their ample work of pathologizing woman's status as visual object. Hitchcock is not obliged to understand or interrogate the inheritance that he ceaselessly draws upon. In a theoretical system which repudiates the existence of a too knowing, too integrated subject identity, it makes strategic sense to designate Hitchcock as the gathering place for forces which shape and govern his practice without his "active" knowledge or choosing. However aggressively his camera may exercise its voyeuristic male authority, Hitchcock can most usefully be described (for theory's sake) as the passive functionary of a film apparatus whose meaning and expressive resources precede him. He is culturally determined in his handling of film form, since the camera gaze will impose its maleness in any case, even if Hitchcock were striving to resist it. The gaze system, at the same time, exalts Hitchcock's role as the ideal transmitter of an infection that has always been latent in the visual process of cinema. Given his proclivity to make the gaze *conspicuous* and imperiously central to every story situation in his films, the infection naturally finds in him its perfect breeding ground.

Hitchcock diagrams the camera's ongoing alliance with the male gaze in a manner that makes it suddenly intelligible to spectators who had previously been hypnotized by the normal rhetoric of looking and being looked at in movie narratives. In Hitchcock narratives, it is now commonly understood, the male gaze typically extends its dominion at the expense of the female object, who is denied the power of looking back, except on those occasions when she is at the mercy of a violent assailant—or so vulnerable that an assailant's presence is implied. The lure of the female and the camera's entranced acknowledgment of the lure ignite a double desire in the spectator whose terms are eventually revealed as synonymous. The desire for the woman is the desire for a crime. The more sinuously insistent the camera gaze, as it tracks the woman's movements and "private" behavior, the more frustration it invites at the distance still separating it from the never *fully* absorbed/ consumed/possessed female image. Violence is the only gesture strong enough to penetrate the female's impassive mask and her sly, teasing reluctance to be "found out." Finally exposed to violence (and exposed *through* it), she is resolved by being at one with her objecthood. At last she will lie still, and the camera gaze can be satisfied that there is no more to her than this ultimate passivity. The reduction of the female image to stasis is the logical fulfillment of the camera's quest.

This is my composite version of the myth of the Gaze, as laid bare in the supremely fetishized "romantic mysteries" of Hitchcock (especially the American Hitchcock films). The necessarily brief summary of how Hitchcock's camera frames, pursues, and entraps the female object does not, obviously, coincide precisely with any one commentator's analysis. Nevertheless, I am claiming that the negative case against Hitchcock's depiction of women and his bondage to a camera system that everywhere privileges the male as "bearer of the look" rests on assumptions very similar to these. If I am guilty of caricaturing what the gaze has come to signify to a number of film and art theorists, or of misunderstanding why Hitchcock is so central to their arguments, then my present counterreading will serve no purpose. I am fully aware that both Laura Mulvey and Raymond Bellour, as well as the many critics who have been influenced by their work on Hitchcock and the gaze, have intelligently queried and modified the position set forth in Mulvey's "Visual Pleasure and Narrative Cinema." Lacan, Kristeva, Foucault, and other architects of gaze-haunted systems have been regularly invoked to shed supplementary light on the problems of "seeing" in Hitchcock.

Two core ideas (or idea clusters) in Laura Mulvey's article, however, have proven strong enough to survive repeated challenges by skeptics. These two ideas, which I see as interlocked, undoubtedly help to explain why so many readers (including myself) keep returning to the essay, and why it still seems provocative—stubbornly alive. First, the patriarchal codes governing looking and desiring, which are deeply embedded in the history of Western art, inevitably extend their sovereignty to the "new" medium of film. Since the art gaze and the social gaze (which infuses and dictates the normative vision of art) are traditionally male, the camera gaze, to the extent that it obeys the laws of culture, will mirror the maleness of the sign systems that are in place. Second, in order to see how the gaze generally operates in narrative cinema, we could find no clearer example than a Hitchcock movie, where the camera is persistently allied with the gaze of male characters, and where females, however much they may know, or are given to do, are relegated to an almost preordained position as "spectacle." They are *made* to be images, and thus victims. The privileges that come from controlling the gaze are steadily denied to them. The simple question which initiated my essay is this—how much does the first idea cluster depend for its plausibility on the demonstrable truth of the claims about Hitchcock? The more I think about Hitchcock's films, the more I become convinced that the real power in them, positive as well as negative, belongs to the female. For Hitchcock, woman, not man, holds the key to the gaze and its mysterious authority. The camera's power to search things out, to look deeply, is a power "borrowed" from the Mother, whose gaze is omniscient and whose law is nearly unchallengeable. Further, the possibility of wresting power away from the Mother and finding less autocratic uses for it rests almost entirely with Hitchcock's female surrogates in his narratives. Perhaps the act of depriving Hitchcock of his accustomed role as "monstrous father" in the story of the Gaze would be comparable to eliminating Eve's part in the fall from the story of lost paradise. If that overstates Hitchcock's importance to gaze theory, one can still legitimately ask, who else might so capably "take the fall" for the sins of male looking in cinema?

As William Rothman has convincingly argued in his many readings of individual Hitchcock films, the gaze is not only a central device but a dominant theme at every stage of Hitchcock's filmmaking career.[3] If one grants the director *any* individual consciousness in his art at all— no more, let us say, than a theorist must possess in order to write about him—it is impossible to deny that Hitchcock is highly self-conscious *at all times* about how the camera gaze works and how it implicates the spectator. Sexual spying, the viewing trance, and the confusion of romantic longing and the longing for death are some of the issues, of course, that *Psycho* and *Vertigo* set out to explore. Whatever Hitchcock may fail to understand about the aberrations of Norman Bates and Scottie Ferguson, he clearly depicts their manner of looking as transgressive and pathological. Hitchcock endeavors to build viewer identification with these figures in order to convert the initial bait of pleasure into something deeply troubling. The destination of the spectator, in both narratives, is a place of fear and unknowing. The spectator's initial confidence as an interpreter of events, her security in putting things together, is replaced, through the simple act of "seeing with" certain characters, by an abyss. Norman and Scottie's gaze, far from being stable power positions, are, almost from the moment these figures enter their narratives, marked by an obscure ailment that threatens to recur. Their seeing disorders, when they "erupt," have the capacity to unman them, quite literally in Norman's case.

It would be a mistake to maintain that Hitchcock's thinking about vision in film—as a means of entrapment, as a means of spreading stains in the viewer's mind—exhibits the "right" degree of self-awareness, whatever that would be, to silence the objections of those who find his depiction of women repugnant. Hitchcock's command of the language of film does not mean that this language never succeeds in using *him*. He does not arrive at that utopian point Roland Barthes has described in relation to writing, where "a total language [is at one's service], in which nothing is obligatory."[4] It would also be a mistake, however, to claim—as the logic of gaze theory requires—that Hitchcock is ever wholly unconscious of what the male gaze is up to in his films. He would need to be unreflective, to some degree, in order to supply evidence that there is a gaze system already in place which determines "gendered looking" in cinema. He must emphatically not be seen as one who oversees, with complete freedom of choice, the operations of the gaze in his narratives. But how are we to determine those occasions when his sense of things is preordained, or when our skepticism moves ahead of his?

Let us reconsider a canonical moment of menacing male looking in *Psycho*, one that is closely conjoined with an act of violence against a female. Here, as in the many other scenes and moments I shall examine, I intend to move from the image of the eye (or the fact of looking) to the internal space behind it that Hitchcock allows me to recover and dwell on. The full effect of the gaze can only be understood when it is attached to the character consciousness whose purposes it serves. Though the spectator forms a relationship to the images of a film that is distinct from that of the characters, it doesn't seem sensible to me ever to disregard the tension of the character's predicament in our consideration of what we see. The character's stake in the action, at any point of crisis, is a significant component of our viewing experience.

Norman Bates, having concluded his brief visit with Marion Crane in the stuffed bird sanctuary behind his office, removes a print of a classical "rape" painting, *Susannah and the Elders,* from the wall adjoining Marion's motel room. Behind the print is a "wounded" wall space. Plaster has been broken and torn away to form a dark oval, allowing Norman peephole access to Marion. The small hole of light at the center of the larger oval appears to be the pupil of an inanimate, "constructed" eye—ominously shadowed—that fixes Norman with its own gaze as he moves his head toward the wall cavity. Norman's head must enter this massive eye before he can glimpse anything himself. When we share his perspective on the motel room, we discover Marion Crane in the process of undressing. Our sense of *her* (and our own) vulnerability here is heightened by the fact that until this crucial juncture in the narrative, Marion's point-of-view has been consistently dominant and normative.

The world of *Psycho* has unfolded for us chiefly as Marion's agitated reception of it. The transfer of the point-of-view from Marion to Norman occurs almost immediately after Marion "comes to her senses" about her theft and her futile attempts to escape detection. In effect, by seeing herself dimly reflected in the mirror of Norman's trapped circumstances, Marion regains sufficient composure and self-awareness to make a firm resolution. She will return the money she stole from her employer in a fit of blind desperation, and accept the no doubt painful consequences. Her behavior from the moment she watched herself taking the money now appears to her not only reckless but demented: a protest against a condition of entrapment that merely enlarged her trap. The attainment of a properly measured knowledge of what one is "guilty" of and how one can go about making restitution for it is extremely rare in Hitchcock's films, for either men or women. Perhaps because free-floating dread of exposure is so thick and ubiquitous in the Hitchcock atmosphere, guilt avoidance is a highly cultivated skill among his protagonists. The prospect of facing up (without coercion), either in public or private, to what one may have *done* is almost inconceivable for them. Repression and scapegoating (sometimes legally sanctioned) are the usual means by which Hitchcock characters conduct their moral business. Possibly this is owing to the director's root conviction that life is mainly *about* fear, more precisely what Jenny Diski has called "'nowhere to go' fear," endlessly regurgitated from childhood.[5] Hitchcock is almost incapable of imagining any source of forgiveness or clemency equal to the demands of this fear, or the guilt it is always struggling to ward off.

Marion's face and gaze register calm and relief for what seem to be the first time as she thanks Norman for what he has helped her come to terms with, and then, as she leaves the room, parts company with both him and us. We are left behind with Norman. The logic of the point-of-view shift is that Marion's gaze is now lifting free of the anxiety that is *Psycho*'s only available language. As in a relay, Marion passes control of the gaze to one who is not simply her match but her superior in the expression of inner turmoil. Norman promptly converts her honorable resolution to make amends into grounds for paranoid suspicion. Marion's decision to come out of hiding and reclaim her actual name is taken by Norman to mean that she has been lying to him from the moment she signed a false name into his motel register. Norman, who arguably resembles gaze theorists a little in his preference for fiercely binary thinking, concludes that the act of lying puts Marion in league with *whores*, and justifies his desire to spy on her. Whores, he believes, have no right to protest a man's furtive sexual curiosity, since they eagerly accept money for much worse.

After the spectator-as-Norman observes Marion through the peephole, half-undressed, Hitchcock gives us the celebrated shot of an immense, disembodied, voyeuristic eye absorbing its shameful pleasure. I question whether this eye, aurally accompanied by Bernard Herrmann's creepily ominous, drifting, and coiling orchestration for strings, is a comfortable sight for any viewer. To begin with the most obvious source of unease, the shot forcibly breaks the trance of "innocent" spectatorship. It declares our presence in the scene problematic. Movie conventions instruct us to accept the illusion that whatever action is shown to us in framed images is ours for the taking; we are intended to be the carefree proprietors of all the sensation-inducing pictures we have paid to see. Norman's eye interrupts the *game* of participation, and asks us to assess what the act of looking, our looking, signifies at this moment. I risk belaboring a familiar point because this shot in *Psycho* represents, in my moviegoing life, the beginning of self-consciousness about watching movies. For the first time I was caught, if you like, watching myself watching, and the effect was immediately unnerving. Confronted with an eye that has temporarily supplanted all other human functions, that has *become* the world in the frame; confronted with it at a charged 1960 site of forbidden pleasure (impending nakedness) I and the audience I imagine myself belonging to became queasy *sharers* with Norman of this peculiar urge to see something scandalous, while remaining safely unseen in the darkness. How do we measure the distance between this eye's rapacious appetite and our own hunger to see, well, everything, but from a protected vantage point?

This is an old question, which gaze theorists, following Mulvey, claim to have boldly recast, reminding us that the camera view here is male and that "he" derives his imagined power, typically, at the expense of a female object who is fetishized and fragmented (as always) so she can become the appropriate grail for the male viewing quest. The cosmeticized, passive feminine is the very essence of spectacle; "she" is what the anxious but still culturally determined male camera seeks out to prop up its power, and thus hold the remnants of the endangered phallic regime together. What power, one might ask in reply, attaches to this eye in the act of having its need to work in secret exposed? How is the eye *less* vulnerable when rendered an object for scrutiny than the image of Marion Crane it fastens upon? In place of the anticipated unveiling of the female body, we are given a surrogate eye looking (on our behalf) at the "thing" that is denied us. When a countershot of Marion arrives, she has already put on a robe. The eye has, at least for now, covered her escape from "our" prurient interest in her.

The eye—in narrative terms—is jointly owned. It belongs partly to Norman, partly to the spectator, and partly to Norman's absent mother. The Norman part has nothing to do with strength, and, as we learn from his wholesale misreading of Marion's behavior and character, nothing to do with knowledge. A weak, wrongfully suspicious, utterly controlled, fearful, and possibly mad Norman succumbs to the impulse—the sordid impulse—to watch a woman undress. This woman has served, to as full a degree as any identification figure could, as our sole interpreter and reference point for virtually all the previous events in the film. And now that she has finally broken free from her earlier disorientation and panic, she can readily be allied with our hope that we too might be able to transform ourselves positively, and regain perspective in the midst of crisis. Marion has been generous and tactful in her dealings with Norman. She has understood enough about what has led him to his current impasse and senses enough about his isolation and helplessness not to dismiss him or judge him harshly. Her evening meal with him has yielded the first substantial, mutually open and risk-taking conversation in the movie. This much we know: Norman lags well behind us both in sympathy for Marion and in situational understanding. He has repaid Marion's considerate treatment of him with a shoddy betrayal. Even if we assume that certain viewers are delighted by Norman's disclosure of his peephole and his determination to use it, the prospect of sharing an eye with him—of becoming Norman's eye so explicitly—is a rather grim bargain. The shockingly disproportionate scale of the eye image can only take us by surprise, and derail any chance of linking up with its so-called "power" by normal editing conventions. The image emerges for us as a provocative rupture—signaling, as I've noted, an unwelcome outbreak of self-reflexiveness.

Finally, of course, there is Norman's mother, the eye's third owner. Mrs. Bates is the psychic space that Norman, even at the best of times, half-occupies. His destination as a character proves to be an evacuation site for all that can be conceived as "not mother." What do we do with the fact that Norman's gaze is in no respect directed or governed by the law of the father? The law of the mother is the only law he has ever encountered or complied with. It has remained absolute for him even after he kills her. The literal death has merely extended her sovereignty:

she is now metaphorically present in every object Norman attends to. The tiniest assertion of a male prerogative to stare where he chooses is promptly checked, in Norman's case, by the unappeasable Puritan matriarch built into his gaze. "So, you enjoy looking at this whore; well, I have already caught you at it, and will see to it later that you are appropriately punished. Unless, of course, you would prefer me to punish *her*, instead. It is what she *is*, after all, that made you look." The trail of the gaze in *Psycho* ends, bafflingly, at the empty eye sockets of Mrs. Bates's skull, subliminally superimposed on Norman's intensely watchful, grinning face. "Norman" is watching us; he is persuaded that the extremity of his alertness, combined with his ability to foresee and defeat the enemy viewer's agenda with respect to his cleverly disguised person, allows him to control the gaze that "polices" him. And the viewer, looking back, although knowing that Norman is lost to himself and replaced by a defiant, cunning, and surprisingly cohesive mother persona, somehow feels more controlled than in control of what she witnesses. One's fleeting, unsavory impression of being held captive by a gaze that is itself governed by forces it cannot name or sort out may suggest a compelling alternative to the model of an "essentialist" male gaze that guards, like a dragon, the terrain of consequential action for itself, while consigning the "remaindered" female to eternal passivity.

Recall that it is Mrs. Bates's *voice* that defines the last image of Norman and what his gaze imparts to us. Without the voice to cue us, the blanket-shrouded figure sitting motionless in a bare room is adrift in a terrible, lonely sea of madness. The voice confers purpose, focus, and access to what is otherwise a closed category. It also genders the gaze as female, effectively overriding the strong visual presence of Norman Bates, as well as the presence of Anthony Perkins. The gaze speaks to us clearly because there is an audible female intelligence behind it.

It sometimes seems as though feminist gaze theorists, and their frequent Lacanian allies, conceive of film as still a predominantly visual medium. The role of the soundtrack in positioning the spectator and making meaning available to her is acknowledged fitfully, but as a kind of awkward afterthought. Kaja Silverman's *The Acoustic Mirror*, while purportedly a book-length study of the "female voice in psychoanalysis and cinema," seems reluctant to use its Lacanian trope of the voice as mirror to illuminate, even by negative example, how sound functions or what it specifically communicates in classical Hollywood cinema.[6] In other words, Silverman can talk about how Joan Crawford's character in *Possessed* (1947) is controlled, in her storytelling, by a doctor who delights in giving her injections but is not interested in considering what sort of voice Crawford the actress "possesses," and what difference it might make that she, rather than another actor, is doing the narration. Silverman and other theorists have not sufficiently attended to the ways in which voice, however it has been formed in infancy, or later deformed, suppressed, and appropriated by male tyrants, leads us back to the unwelcome notion of an individuated presence: an aural unfolding that complements the visual unfolding of something we might call, in the case of *Possessed,* a Crawford character. The word "Crawford" surely deserves to be weighted equally with the word "character." Character and player, in much current theorizing, occupy the unfortunate status that Terry Eagleton confidently assigns to Shakespeare's Hamlet, with or without a specific performer "attached": "Hamlet has no 'essence' of being whatsoeer, no inner sanctum to be safeguarded: he is pure deferral and diffusion, a hollow void which offers nothing determinate to be known."[7] Putting aside for now the question of how this void has managed to keep alive the curiosity and emotional interest of theatregoers, readers, and critical commentators for four centuries, I think it becomes clear why such an approach to character has no room for the voice as a means of self-revelation, self-questioning, and self-concealment. We are always referred back to some version of the Linguistic Deferral shuttle service. In its Lacanian branch line, more or less interchangeable phantoms are driven back and forth between three well-charted and conceptually "frozen" destinations: the Imaginary, the Symbolic, and the Real. The notoriously impossible-to-fulfill Lacanian desire appears to be fulfilled well enough by the reliable presence and predictable operations of these once obscure sites. At present, in Lacan's version of the unconscious, the trains run on time.[8]

The voice in cinema not only has the power to dislodge or render equivocal the authority of the camera gaze and character gaze, as in the example from *Psycho*; it also serves to bend the image earthward, making it feel more material and inhabited, less ghostly. Buster Keaton's gaze, for example, encountered in silence, is an enticing, startlingly fecund enigma. Buster Keaton speaking, in contrast, appears to be a man with almost no secrets. He becomes a heavier, more settled presence, more conventionally social. He seems more approachable when speaking, but arguably at the cost of a deeper viewer intimacy. It is strange how little gaze theory attends to the way that the measured flow of speech, in any dramatic situation, is a thing of consequence, which provides, as much as music does, a compass for gauging a look's meaning, and charting its shifts of feeling and expressive force. Quite unintentionally, Mulvey lends support to the old, punitive, "masculine" distinction between mere words and heroic deeds. Roping a steer and leading men into battle, apparently, convey meanings that *count* to the camera eye. Whereas women no sooner enter the realm of the gaze than they are reduced to the status of erotic lure, of a creature striking poses. As a result, what they have to say for themselves and how they make themselves known to us through utterance and gesture barely register as definition, much less significant human value. Could it be that in the implied metaphysics of the camera gaze, the activities of Zane Grey cowboys are more *real* than the conversational risks in Jean Renoir? Is a Jack London seafarer a more visible maker of meaning than Olive Higgins Prouty's Charlotte Vale in *Now, Voyager*?

I wonder if the current routinization of action hero and working professional gestures for women characters has resulted in a sense of female complexity in cinema that demonstrably exceeds that attained by Lillian Gish characters in the 1920s or Barbara Stanwyck characters in the 1930s and 1940s. When Hollywood formula dictates that a woman must throw a good punch and have a thriving professional career, is there any evidence that women's experience is automatically better known, more fully reflected on, more eloquently rendered than in the classical studio period? Surely the new formulas, like any earlier formulas, can emptily substitute for exploration. By themselves, they furnish little to engage an adult mind, much like the standard repertoire of male action gestures in previous decades. Terms like "active" and "passive," as the diverse examples of Dietrich, Garbo, Gandhi, Jim Carrey, and Marie Dressler remind us, are wholly dependent for their moral and emotional intelligibility on the contexts in which they operate. We can only do justice to "passivity" in film by thinking about it, moment by moment, in relation to specific intentions and obstacles. The "passivity" of Mme. DeFarge knitting in *A Tale of Two Cities* is not that of Jayne Mansfield carrying in the milk bottles in *The Girl Can't Help It*, and even Jayne Mansfield is not always identical with the ways in which her cartoon voluptuousness is typically manipulated.

Making pleasurable varieties of difficulty and asserting difference are, of course, what the details in art are for. Cinema meaning, like meaning in any narrative, requires *time* to unfold. It is in the nature of detail to be somewhat vagrant and capricious, to resist totalization. Theory, while knowing this, is nevertheless forever tempted by totalization, with its false promise of things "coming to rest"—in a system that manages to be impressively radical, yet stable at the same time. It is hard to see, for example, how gaze theorists or Lacanians can justify responding to the *demands* of characterization, or arguing for the "telling" idiosyncrasies of individual performers. Can gaze theory, even at its most gen-erously inclusive, accommodate our wish or need to take the distance separating Doris Day (as voice and visual presence) in a Hitchcock film from Tippi Hedren into account? Lacanians, for their part, are all but committed to declaring the apparent lively assortment of human adven-tures on the currents of desire illusory, embedded (appearances not-withstanding) in sameness. Narrative trajectories never serve to confirm abundance but instead only expose the *lack* and impossibility which were initially concealed by misleading signs of a world being there for us. Which brings us back to Norman Bates and the tantalizing suggestion at the end of *Psycho* that the male gaze disappears, becomes pure lack—despite the appearance of undiminished malevolence—from the instant a soft female voice tiptoes in behind it and begins speaking on its behalf. Does the power of the direct male gaze collapse as readily as this, when an anonymous female voice calls it into question?

A more positive version of this gaze displacement by the voice occurs in Hitchcock's 1955 remake of his own earlier film, *The Man Who Knew Too Much*. Once again at issue, as in *Psycho*, is a mother's determination to retrieve her lost son. Jo MacKenna (Doris Day) has discovered that her kidnapped child is being held prisoner somewhere in the foreign embassy where she is about to entertain an audience of distinguished guests with her singing. She elects to "spoil" her perfor-mance of the song—rendering it shrill and overbearing—in the hope that her voice will somehow prove loud enough to reach her son in his place of concealment. (There is an arresting sacrifice in this choice. She has given up her singing career for the sake of her family, at her hus-band's request, and the opportunity to sing again in public carries with it the idea of a return to public scrutiny. In short, is she still capable of singing professionally?) If her son can receive the auditory message she sends out to him, he may yet be saved from death. The song that she sings is *their* song, which tells of a mother referring all of her child's questions about the future to the serenely impersonal loom of fate and contingency: whatever will be, will be. Hitchcock's camera tracks the movement of the voice through space—pursuing its course as it passes through the public chamber where her immediate, judging audience is gathered, through corridors, and then "climbs" the always hazardous Hitchcock staircase. As the voice moves higher, it steadily loses volume and force. The suspense dynamic here is built on the voice's capacity to preserve its character and audibility as it strives to penetrate the enclo-sure where her son sits, beyond the reach of her gaze. Will there be enough of it left to pierce the oblivious child's consciousness, his "sleeping memory," and thus bring the two together?

The idea for this episode has a lovely mythic dimension. It also reminds me of the no less potent and soul-stirring landscape of Margaret Wise Brown's nursery tale, *The Runaway Bunny.* (Bear with me.) In Brown's lost-and-found scenario, a baby rabbit announces to his mother all the various getaway plans he has dreamed up to escape from her protection. Most involve some form of metamorphosis, which require his mother not only to discover an unusual hiding place and to recognize him in altered form, but also to change herself into something different (corresponding to the change he has wished for in himself). The result of the mother's willingness to follow the child's lead is, in each instance, reunion. The story is in the form of a dialogue. It is—apart from the picture-book illustrations of the child's fantasies—the mother's voice that proves calmly equal to each of the child's increasingly ingenious challenges. Her answers teasingly "catch" him while at the same time encouraging him to "run away" some more. The melodic line of their duet is established by the child; the mother does not anticipate where he will go next, making her arrival at each new hiding place an act of harmonizing. She comes into the space that his voice, through a renewed declaration of independence, has made its own, and then takes over the space so agreeably that he is led to seek out another.

Separation for the child here is analogous to the way in which spectators of a painting delight, in the words of Jed Perl, in making "our own way through a composition, so that we find our own kind of freedom within the artist's sense of order." The order does not limit the choice of direction, or deny the pleasure of repeatedly turning away from security. Patiently following escape routes one has not anticipated in *The Runaway Bunny* is how mother love expresses its infinite adaptability. Mother love has eyes (and a voice) that reach everywhere and will manage to meet the child in any extremity within his power to imagine. "Be as adventurous and unmindful of me as you like; my love is up to it. Go as far as you like, hide yourself to the point of invisibility, you will not be out of love's reach." The story's depth derives from the fact that it glances, for just the right length of time, in the direction of one of the most legitimate anxieties of family life—the dread of never being able to find the right distance (or to escape at all) from home and loved ones. Brown's simple vocal pattern of hiding and being found (on one's own new terms, however strange) convincingly affirms a mother's trust and acceptance of a child's ongoing need to be other and elsewhere. Surely this has something to do with the balance one seeks, not only in one's family but in one's relation to art, with its so often resisted authority and power.

Suppose one were to say that the spirit of the mother's implied gaze in the Brown story—a gaze equipped with a "mirroring" voice— is *one* way to characterize the spirit of the camera gaze as female. Though Mulvey's male camera gaze is never assigned a specific characterization, I think I can propose two strongly implied character models for Mulvey's male gaze that would humanly ground some of its worrisome properties and intentions, and lead us, albeit circuitously, in the direction of what is often taken to be Hitchcock's "character." I would then like to compare these models, briefly, with Brown's less regimented vision of control, and see whether Hitchcock can be productively approached within this alternative scheme.

The first character model for the patriarchal gaze is drawn from the portrait of the narrator's father in Turgenev's novel, *First Love.* In this representation we can find most of the attributes traditionally felt to buttress unreflectingly confident masculine authority. Any child would be likely to quail under the "imagined" force of this man's scrutiny, and at the same time desperately seek confirmation from him:

> My father had a curious influence on me, and our relations were curious too . . . he displayed—if one can put it that way—a certain courtesy toward me; only he never let me at all close to him. . . . God knows how passionately attached I should have been if I had not felt constantly the presence of his restraining hand. Yet he could, whenever he wished, with a single word, a single gesture, instantly make me feel complete trust in him. My soul would open; I chattered to him as to a wise friend, an indulgent mentor . . . and then, just as suddenly, he would abandon me, his hand would again push me aside. . . . He loved all violent physical exercise. . . . Once, and only once, he caressed me with such tenderness that I nearly cried . . . then his gaiety and tenderness vanished without a trace. But when this happened it never seemed to give me any hope for the future—I seemed to have seen it all in a dream. At times I would watch his clear, handsome, clever face . . . my heart would tremble, my entire being would yearn toward him . . . then, as if he casually sensed what was going on within me he would casually pat my cheek—and would either leave me, or start doing some-

thing, or else would suddenly freeze as only he knew how. Instantly I would shrink into myself, and grow cold. His rare fits of affability towards me were never in answer to my own unspoken but obvious entreaties. They always came unexpectedly. When, later, I used to think about my father's character, I came to the conclusion that he cared nothing for me nor for family life; it was something very different he loved.[9]

It is worth noting that this cold master of the patriarchal gesture, this mesmerizing possessor of inescapable authority, is delineated with such emotional acuteness by a deprived *son*. It is the son who feels the punishing weight and equally punishing absence of his lordly being, who struggles, as a matter of life and death, to deconstruct the father's gaze and somehow move beyond it.

My second character model for the male camera gaze comes from the Weimar Republic phase of the work of the right-wing German intellectual Ernst Junger. Junger believed that the act of taking photographs is an attempt to move outside the realm of sentiment and to substitute the task of documenting horror to the earlier humanistic demand of responding to it. The photographer's work parallels the growth, during World War I, of a new, *desirably* disengaged form of human consciousness. The warrior-eye born out of ceaseless exposure to the technology of modern combat is "indicated by the ever more marked ability to see oneself as an object." As an appropriate response to the "growing incursion of danger into human life," one should strive to emulate the shock-photograph's cruelty, invulnerability, imperviousness.[10] We gain strength and essential survival skills by ousting the "feeling reflex" and all its weak offshoots from our engagement with the hard data of sense experience. Gaze theorists seem to argue that the aggressive approach to image surfaces which Junger advocates for still photography, in order to contain and colonize image data, is the basic drive in motion picture representation. Though movement and sound have crucially been added to the still photographer's obligatory vocabulary of silent, mute arrest, the motion picture camera has not fundamentally altered the combat photographer's goal of pinning things in place, of "finishing them off." Gaze theorists are not much concerned with the camera's uncommon gift for registering transitions or the surprising progress of actions. They appear to be haunted by the "truth" of the frozen still underlying the seductive illusions of image fluidity.

Another implication of Junger's impervious photograph as the ideal emblem of modern consciousness is that the camera comes to stand, without apology, for the "mechanized inner life" of the male Watcher, one who is fully at home behind the surveillance lens. Junger embraces unreservedly the life-denying potential of the film apparatus. Rather than be fearful of the camera's objectifying power, he counsels us to push its capacity for disengagement to its uncompromised limit and seek our fulfillment there.

Do these icy embodiments of male authority from Turgenev and Junger have greater title to the movie camera's field of vision and provide more clues of how moving images work than the female construct of Margaret Wise Brown's nursery tale? It would seem to me that the mother figure that I've selected is far more credibly attuned than these fathers to the camera's potential for sustained attentiveness and its capacity for following figures (with sympathetic interest) as they endeavor to transform themselves, in large and small ways, over time. Brown's mother figure allows her child to don fresh disguises, in his continued efforts to conceal himself. She then mirrors and magnifies those disguises in the act of penetrating his place of concealment. Is this not akin to the process whereby film actors adopt character personae while retaining a personality continuous with other roles? The camera can honor both dimensions (visible actor and compelling disguise) without being caught in the divide. Finally, the kind of dance in which one is pleasurably uncertain whether the camera or the characters is "leading" or "following" is equally present in the mother's "hide and seek" and in the magical present tense of cinema, where freedom and determinism so beguilingly unite.

With which model of authority are Hitchcock's camera gaze and authorial voice most often allied—the self-absorbed, controlling, detached parent (of either gender) or the parent who makes a game of control because something larger and more valuable, for the child-viewer's edification, is at stake? It's a complicated question, and I would hasten to stress that the phrase "most often allied" acknowledges that the motive for looking is not fixed. Without a changing perspective and a spacious, unpredictable authorial purpose, there is little chance of interesting narrative development. As far as gendered looking is concerned, Hitchcock comes closest to the Junger absolute—the fully impervious gaze, perfectly detached and unapproachable—when the imagined "eye" is female.

Let us construct yet another character to stand behind the camera and assume responsibility for its "sight." This one bears some physical and psychological resemblance to the Hitchcock that biographies have speculatively assembled, but I shall assume we have no way of knowing, conclusively, this figure's sexual identity. H knows *this* much from "its" negotiations thus far with the gaze and judgments of the world. H is taken to be ugly, grotesquely fat, and by any conventional index, an unlikely candidate for the rewards of romantic love. H stands at an equal remove from the beautiful icons, male and female, who populate "her" storytelling and the theater world "he" loves. H devises a fastidiously formal comic persona that grants "him" a means of entering the social arena comfortably, and gaining a measure of acceptance and a small ration of power there. The comedy of "her" performance depends on a steady deflection of feeling, and an active discouragement of any feeling-based inquiry. H elicits laughter by appearing to be unflappable in the face of outward horrors; H is genially above *any* public loss of control, any display of temperament, though "she" is delighted to gossip about others excesses and misfortunes. H has an unusually great need for order and the consolations of tightly woven patterns, both in "her" work habits and "his" art. H believes that guilt is an inescapable strand in every pattern. "She" might concur with Maria Flook that guilt "can be a strengthening fiber woven into the big fabric, or it can weaken its seams until the garment falls apart."[11] Control of the pattern is H's safety— "his" most effective protection against the swarm of fears which descend on "him" whenever "he's" not immersed in orderly problem solving.

H is well aware that the obsession with control is a problem, a personal weakness. Too much in "her" is stifled, there is not enough occasion for openness and for genuine (as opposed to ironic) self-expression. In the stories "he" is drawn to, control—and with it, safety—are continually taken away from those who need it and have come to rely on it. Those who manage to retain control in these stories are almost certain to abuse it. The human cost of preserving control is frequently shown to be a rigid, sinister, implacable personality, though these qualities are often masked (Cary Grant style) by charm. H longs for the release of *vulnerability* and enters, through the art of storytelling, into secret complicity with those who are openly, even abjectly, emotional and who do not hide their misery behind an iron mask. Vulnerability, however, is closely linked in H's mind with the fear of betrayal and rejection. When vulnerability is most intensely avowed, there is an immediate, strong counterpressure (call it paranoia) to bring betrayal into the picture. The two modes of expression—intimate sympathy and extreme, fearful suspicion—have a Siamese twin kinship for H.

H exalts beauty, with the childlike awe of a Quasimodo who feels it has nothing to do with "himself." H can look at it, from a distance that is both yearning and envious, but "she" has no right to touch it, and no chance of possessing it directly. Beauty is Other, and there is no consolation to be had from dwelling on the chaste gardens of inner beauty. That fantasy plays no part in H's sense of "herself." (In this respect, H is a sister to Balzac's Cousin Bette.) Sometimes the punishment visited on beauty in H's stories has to do with lessening the felt distance between the realm of the immaculate image and the realm of ugly distortions which H sees "himself" inhabiting. The stripping away of beauty's resources and defenses is, in a negative sense, the perverse misuse of H's control, and "she" is arguably well-aware of this. If there is a positive dimension to this often violent attack on beauty, one might think of it as H struggling to humanize the inaccessible image, to question its power, to bring it closer to "herself" as a troubling assertion of kinship. To cite a minor but telling instance of this kinship from the 1941 comedy *Mr. and Mrs. Smith*, Carole Lombard, as Ann Smith, resurrects a dress that she wore several years ago on her first date with her future husband. She has grown too large for the dress and a seam splits when she attempts to force her body into it. In a later scene, H shows us an inadequately pinned skirt with the "penned up flesh" disquietingly finding ways to gape through, exposing Ann not so much to humiliation in the eyes of her husband, but to self-humiliation. H has the feeling of inhabiting "his" images most intensely when something in them is in the process of breaking down. "She" is both the one, for example, who orchestrates the bird attacks on Melanie Daniels and also (masochistically, if you like) "she" who gives herself over to the sensations of being pecked savagely by embodied fears.

When H imagines what will be visible and audible in the camera frame—and it is worth recalling that "he" never looks through the eyepiece of the camera in the course of shooting—the nexus of forces I have arbitrarily brought together in this composite portrait of H are a part of what constitutes "his" *inner* eye and ear. Once we have determined (if that were possible) how the entity called Hitchcock expresses the culture(s) which formed him, we are left with a bundle of surplus particulars from an individual life history. Do the boundaries of gender hold for such a bundle? It is now a critical commonplace that the boundaries of a distinctive self do not hold. What stabilizing agent then could keep the flow of images in cinema moving firmly, ascertainably in a male channel? When the camera eye, for example, searches *for* mother, or searches *as if it were* mother, to whom does it belong? Are we not continually thrown back to the unmapped psychic territory of our earliest images and confusions?

Speaking to Francois Truffaut about the James M. Barrie "spirit" play, *Mary Rose*, which he contemplated adapting to film for a great many years, Hitchcock detailed his plans for presenting the main character, a female ghost: "Whenever she moved, there would be no shadow on the wall, only a blue light. You'd have to create the impression of photographing a presence rather than a body. At times she would appear very small in the image, at times very big. She wouldn't be a solid lump, you see, but rather like a sensation. In this way you lose the feeling of real space and time. You should be feeling that you are in the presence of an ephemeral thing, you see."[12] Hitchcock's comments here nicely bring together his association of shape-shifting powers with the female presence and his interest in making manifest the camera's powers of ghostly intervention and haunting. Frequently in Hitchcock films, when the camera gaze breaks the point-of-view chain either to track toward a distant, coveted object or to occupy a godlike vantage point high above the action, it implicitly makes contact with a spirit realm. Similarly, when a large amount of action is concentrated in a particular dwelling, and it becomes important to "animate" the setting so that it will function as a character, Hitchcock's camera finds ways to haunt the interior space: surveying its elements as though it were a ghost longing to repossess them.

In Hitchcock's first American film, *Rebecca*, the camera gaze— once the narrative introduces us to Manderley—gradually becomes fused with that of the estate's deceased, "rightful" proprietor, Rebecca herself. Though Hitchcock adheres very closely to the structure and details of the Daphne DuMaurier novel he is adapting, *Rebecca*'s family romance (wreathed in Gothicism) still carries us deep into Hitchcock territory. A nameless child-woman is invited by a lonely, distracted, casually brutal father figure to fill the empty place left by the sudden death of his first wife, Rebecca. In spite of Rebecca's physical absence from her former home, the entire world of Manderley feels like a temple consecrated to her worship. All the textures and furnishings, even the quality of light in the rooms, seem to be imbued with her spirit. Her former housekeeper, confidante, and possible lover, Mrs. Danvers, serves as the high priestess in the Manderley shrine, striving with the exactitude of a true fetishist to preserve all the material elements of her mistress's life in their proper position and arrangement. It is as though Rebecca has merely stepped out for a brief errand and will expect, on her return, to find everything undisturbed, just as she left it.

The second Mrs. DeWinter (she has no residual identity) finds it impossible to convey or preserve any sense of herself in this environment. She is so little able to establish herself in the house which it is her duty to oversee that no part of it will convincingly "receive" her or allow her to leave the slightest positive trace. She is remarkably undefined—an unlikely guest brought in by mistake, and feebly sketched into a formidable design that is complete without her. At Manderley, every meaningful decision has already been made by her supremely accomplished predecessor. In her nominal absence, Rebecca has attained a matchless and inviolate perfection in every sphere of human endeavor that might possess value. She has been loved and admired with such single-minded intensity that no aftermath to her emotional presence seems conceivable. Long before her small, orphaned successor has even begun to think of herself, vaguely, as a person, Rebecca has staked out an irrevocable claim to whatever forms of power and knowledge the Manderley world deems legitimate. Replacing or learning to imitate Rebecca are out of the question. There is also little chance of coexisting with the ever more resplendent memories of Rebecca that her entire social circle carries. The second Mrs. DeWinter has no wifely occupation then but to be repeatedly humiliated and effaced. She can only attract notice in the act of making blunders. Like Carroll's Alice, she grows tinier and more crushably a child "nobody" in relation to the outsized, sentient chambers and hallways of the estate.

In the film's mist-shrouded opening scene, the second Mrs. DeWinter addresses us in voice-over, telling how on the previous night— a time that comes very near to her waking present tense—she dreamed of Manderley "again." As she speaks, the camera tracks forward through the gates and winding entryway, approaching the darkened ruin that was (and still is) Rebecca's domain. Though the voice we hear speaks composedly, on her own behalf, as though entitled to launch its own story, the visual accompaniment is not about her leading but rather being led back somewhere, involuntarily. If the images convey the substance of Mrs. DeWinter's dream, the camera becomes the compulsion that carries the dreamer helplessly through scenes that arise, unbidden. From the film's opening shot, then, the camera gaze is secretly in league with Rebecca's vigilant, rival-resistant will. The camera is "born" as Rebecca's surrogate eyes and will be the means by which Hitchcock will make her a surfeit of presence in her apparent absence. She is both the film's most powerful character and its undeclared but inescapable central point of view.

The film ends inside Rebecca's bedroom, while Manderley is burning. Mrs. Danvers, who has set the fire that will prevent the house from ever serving another's ends, has just been killed by a falling timber. No living characters remain inside to witness the action that is taking place. Rebecca declares herself, through the moving camera, most decisively at this juncture. She closes the narrative—spectrally—in a manner not unlike Mrs. Bates's final emergence as the voice and author of Norman's seeing. We advance with a camera ghost into the midst of a conflagration that has ceased to pose any danger and come to rest, intimately, on Rebecca's monogrammed pillow. Unlike its burning cousin, Charles Foster Kane's "Rosebud," the monogrammed pillow seems to transcend the destructive fury of the flames—in fact, to be at one with it. The camera does not seek out the "R" in order to extinguish it, but rather to trace out its indelible signature. Neither the voice-over nor the inquiring look of the surviving Mrs. DeWinter manage to follow us here; Rebecca grants us a private audience, revealing herself, if we are still in doubt, as the story's true teller.

Rebecca contains a made-to-order patriarch in Maxim DeWinter, one whose brusque authority and withheld love seem, for much of the film, to be the main obstructions hindering the timid protagonist's growth. We are carefully misdirected to regard him as the person who holds the key to his new wife's self-definition. Though he bears all the marks of a man in the grip of mourning, we can easily attribute to him an underlying strength and firmness. These traits, we assume, will resurface once his grief subsides to the point where he can again see things clearly. Interestingly, in the episode where "Rebecca's" camera reenacts the sequence of movements leading to her death while DeWinter confesses both his guilt and hatred of Rebecca to his second wife, Maxim is wholly stripped of his previous mystique and authority. He seems hollowed out in the process of revealing himself; he surrenders his stature in the act of surrendering his secret. Perhaps in our relief at discovering that Rebecca had enslaved DeWinter not through passion but through a vengeance-fueled hatred, we do not readily notice how much of his "identity" depended (from the outset) on our fascinated consideration of how he remained *filled* with her.

The most urgent story question prior to this scene has to do with whether the neglected, endlessly disappointing child-bride can seduce her besotted, groggy "father" away from the sorceress "mother," and thus break the mother's relentless grip on the child's desolate inner world. But when the father is shown convincingly purged of love for this superhuman adversary, he sacrifices his earlier morbidly thrilling association with Rebecca's still living, still palpable power. DeWinter collapses into weakness; he becomes, almost immediately, a spent force, a scared, pitiable man in hiding from past actions he cannot even be said to have willed. Echoing the scene of his frightened second wife concealing the fragments of a shattered heirloom in the back of a drawer, DeWinter recounts, with hand-wringing anguish, how in a kind of trance he stowed away his wife's lifeless body in a ship and guiltily managed to sink it. He has trembled ever since at the prospect of being found out. He imagines Rebecca having extended her dominion from his vast but bounded family estate to the boundless sea. One after another, Rebecca claims ownership of the four elements: earth, air (in the form of gathering mists and, in their absence, suffocating rooms), water, and fire. DeWinter seems incapable, after his confession, of making a meaningfully assertive demonstration of love for his long-languishing "second choice." The gaze that he has intermittently directed toward her throughout the film is, in an instant, deprived of its mastery, of its right to make judgments of his wife that truly signify. What he requires above all is a shoulder to lean on. He turns to his wife at last as to someone who *may* possess enough real strength and conviction to hold him together through the crisis of the coroner's inquest. The camera gaze virtually eradicates DeWinter as a presence in his own right at the precise moment when he imagines himself *free* to acknowledge the love that he has for so long rebuffed and made negligible.

Perhaps the most frequently cited occasion for directorial self-reflexiveness in *Rebecca* is the film-within-a-film, disguised as a home movie of the second Mrs. DeWinter's pallid honeymoon. In a darkened chamber at Manderley, Maxim and his wife miserably watch the fugitive glimpses of unforced happiness their amateur camera has captured. The timing of the screening couldn't be worse. Mrs. Danvers, with Maxim's distractedly brutal collaboration, has just finished humiliating the would-be second wife about her senseless, childish act of hiding the heirloom she accidentally broke. The projector threatens to damage the film after DeWinter has clumsily threaded it, but at last the poignantly irrelevant imagery of their nervous, stiffly self-conscious newlywed "happiness" is available for them to contemplate. In the final bit of stage managed footage, DeWinter leaves his position behind the camera while it is still running so that it will "automatically" record a view of his bride and himself together, smiling. Though there is no one at the controls, the camera somehow advances on the couple for a tighter, more incriminating framing. It is customary to argue that this is a moment where Hitchcock intervenes to remind us of *his* controlling gaze and authorship of the cruel proceedings. I think that the film supplies sufficient evidence for a different (if complementary) hypothesis. Rebecca's powers of surveillance—in the darkened screening room at Manderley—take over the film and rewrite its solitary glimpse of marital contentment as an epitaph. The melancholy hints of a gathering crisis blot out what the image aspires to make persuasively visible.

One of the most unsettling surprises in Wilkie Collins's splendid Victorian novel, *The Woman in White*, occurs when Marion Halcombe's narration of her journal breaks off in mid-entry because she is too delirious and physically weak from illness to continue. Without warning, another narrator's voice (or pen) intrudes, belonging to Count Fosco, the cunning plotter whom Marion has identified as her most formidable enemy. The journal has related Marion's gradual discovery of Fosco's intricate, possibly murderous, intentions toward herself and her desperately unhappy married sister. Marion's journal *is* her privacy, the only remaining safe precinct for unguarded expression. Everything in the journal must be kept secret from Count Fosco. If he comes into possession of her "full knowledge," which the journal represents, then she and her sister are entirely at his mercy. Thus, when Fosco successfully invades the seemingly untouchable space of the journal and begins to write in it himself (after absorbing its contents), it is as though *he* becomes the journal's true author. He places a frame around all the troubling events that Marion has observed and painstakingly documented which invalidates their existence as useful knowledge. Once we imagine Fosco "breaking into the temple" and defiling its contents with his sportively salacious reading, nothing in it can serve as a weapon or defense against him. His sardonic critique of Marion's findings and his ambiguous tribute to her displays of feeling become, startlingly and irrevocably, the journal's meaning. Narratively speaking, Marion's arduous prior speculations, as something "determined to make a difference," dissolve. What matters "now" is the fact that Fosco has seized possession of Marion's writing and overtaken (or surpassed) its authority. It is not what she has known but what he makes of her knowing that counts in the narrative future. An entire imaginative edifice is laid waste by his mischievous footnote. Reverse the gender field in *Rebecca* and one can readily see how Rebecca's original and vengefully revived authorial gaze ultimately renders inconsequential all competing sources of meaning and mastery in Hitchcock's film.

In *Rope* (1948), the ghosting effect of the camera's passage through the narrative is more pronounced than in any other Hitchcock work. The reason for this hyperbolic emphasis on the camera's apparitional properties is, at one level, easily accounted for. Hitchcock has voluntarily surrendered the most important formal tool for his characteristic method of film construction: that is, montage, or to be strictly accurate, seamless cutting. (It is seldom noted that Hitchcock's way of using his newfound freedom from David Selznick, after the expiration of his long-term contract with the legendarily controlling producer, is to build for himself an even tighter box than Selznick, at his most tyrannically ingenious, could have devised for him.) What are we to make of *Rope*'s still demanding style—the tensely mobile camera gaze that generates what Raymond Durgnat has aptly termed a "serpentine mood . . . of softly excessive attentiveness"?[13] How is it designed to serve and explicate the narrative's material? What sort of consciousness is the camera imbued with, and what dominant concerns direct and regulate the process of seeing? A number of clues, I think, are provided by the film's title, even though the title is derived from the Patrick Hamilton play which Hitchcock is adapting. The gaze in this film is a "rope" which ties all of the characters and their single interior environment together. Cutting, although it can function exceptionally well as an instrument of viewer control and a means of making firm, lucid connections, at the same time warrants a freedom to disconnect from any perspective whenever it is dramatically expedient to do so.

I shall deal with the perplexing case of *Rope* at greater length than any other film considered in this chapter. I am well aware that it is a by no means obvious choice of a narrative in which the female gaze figures prominently. To begin with, there is no female character (or female presence) with which the camera is explicitly allied. All three of the women featured in *Rope*—an officious, disgruntled housekeeper; an elderly, garrulous "actress"; and a young, romantically uncommitted "friend" of the murder victim—exist at a curious remove from the film's knowledge flow and its emotional flow. Furthermore, none of them manages to establish a position for herself in the course of the action that makes a meaningful difference or affects the outcome of the plot, whether the plot considered is an abortive romance or a foiled attempt to conceal a murder. Instead of being given, as we are in *Rebecca*, a persistent impression of an omniscient, implacable female force overseeing the proceedings, we find that in *Rope* the measurable, palpable influence of the female world is reduced almost to nothing. The most potentially disruptive female action in the narrative is the housekeeper's apparently unobserved removal of all the objects covering the chest in which David's corpse is concealed. Mrs. Wilson claims the camera's entire attention during her slow back and forth trips between the chest and the kitchen down the hall. The viewer waits for the moment when she will lift the lid of the chest to store a number of books that belong there. At the conclusion of this long, tense movement toward a female act of discovery, Brandon—her guilty employer—composedly intervenes and prevents her from opening the chest with a few firm words. He does so in a manner that does not excite her suspicion. Her elaborate scene comes to nothing, as far as her point of view is concerned. (This remarkably complete turning away from female energy, attraction, knowledge, and danger is almost without precedent in Hitchcock's work.)

If *Rope* outwardly appears to create a world, like Herman Melville's "paradise of bachelors," in which women, if not actually banished, have become a forgotten or negligible presence, then how does this suspended force contrive to establish covert points of entry into the narrative dynamic? I have already characterized the camera style of *Rope* as ghostly, but there is no immediate or cumulative sense that the camera presence or narrator is gendered. (If any ghost stalks Brandon and Phillip's penthouse, it would most logically be David's, since his murder precipitates the dramatic action.) If one wishes to think about who is doing the camera's most important objective surveillance work, it would be simple and reasonable to call the floating observer Hitchcock. I have no argument with the view that Hitchcock is directing attention, as so often, back to himself in *Rope*'s highly self-conscious narration. I would, however, suggest that the destabilizing features of *Rope*'s chosen method invoke, with varying degrees of pressure and intimacy, the sorts of authority and purpose that Hitchcock, in other films, assigns to his women.

The unusual rejection of the lure of the female psyche in *Rope* makes me inquisitive about how—as with Rebecca and Mrs. Bates—the fact of literal absence might carry with it the power to haunt the premises. In time, the haunting absence might even reclaim the premises as "her" own. Given the lack of adequate character surrogates to establish a decisive female presence, it seems worth inquiring whether the "missing" female may somehow be relocated in the film's style. More specifically, we might think about "missing presence" in terms of the "excessive attentiveness" Durgnat identifies as the prevailing camera mood in *Rope*. What the ever-adjusting mobile frame of the film attests to is the two-pronged anxiety of something always being either "left over" or "left out." The first anxiety refers to uncomfortable surplus, the second to thwarted search. The surplus has to do with our ongoing impression that the style is catching more in its net than the specific narrative concerns of any given scene justify. The conspicuous phenomenon of a camera marking its transitions, hovering and waiting for openings, creates a feeling of overload, of environmental static interfering with clear, efficient narrative progress. The idea of thwarted search comes from the camera's obligatory ceaseless patrol of its very limited domain. It is difficult to avoid the feeling that something of consequence regularly escapes what the camera at any given moment manages to frame. In this severe-to-the-point-of-being-stifling, interior film, our attention is always pressing us outside the terrain designated to accommodate us, and not merely because the penthouse apartment contains a vast, arching window opening onto a densely layered, Manhattan skyline. Most of the time, we are edgily anticipating the camera's next destination rather than "settling in" to consider strictly what is placed before us *now*. (For a director like Jean Renoir, of course, who glories in the open frame, there is no anxiety about what can't be balanced or fitted in. But Renoir is not Hitchcock.)

Our inability to disconnect from the restless camera and to find visual relief creates, arguably, a stylistic climate that *prolongs* the film's opening encounter with a strangulation in progress. Just as the entire narrative of *Vertigo* remains suspended, dizzily distraught, with Scottie Ferguson as he contemplates the abyss into which he might fall, *Rope* contrives to transform "seeing" into a "loss of breath." I would also suggest that the strangling rope itself gradually becomes the most compelling sign of the female in the narrative, especially in its struggle to achieve definition and authority through its very powers of metamorphosis. The rope captures a central place in the film, in other words, through its adeptness at eluding capture.

Rope is hardly a film which will enable me to "clinch" my argument about how the female (and, more specifically, the maternal) gazes operate in Hitchcock's cinema. I have chosen to make *Rope* the center of my discussion precisely because it offers the greatest possible resistance to my thesis. It promises to thwart my arrival at the critical destination to which my desire for satisfying closure might naturally lead me. Far from firmly delineating a nascent theory of the female gaze, *Rope* is more likely to return the theory to that "waiting room" set aside for gossamer half-truths. Nevertheless, I've always found that the most inviting points in a theory's elaboration are those when it deliberately courts the maximum degree of skepticism and comes closest to willing its own defeat. In this respect, I think my reading of *Rope* mirrors the borderline absurd, easily avoidable risks that Hitchcock (as director) is creating for himself in adopting such a hermetic, dauntingly error-prone style for his film. Theory, at least where movies are concerned, might be characterized as a set of initially intriguing intuitions continually in danger of ossifying as we try to apply them systematically. The best cure for a bewitching assertion is the positing of a more spacious question.

Rope is a film about a secret crime which its primary perpetrator longs equally to cover up and proudly lay claim to. Strict adherence to the passage of time from the moment the crime is committed until it is discovered and broadcast to the world "outside" is the logic for the film's all-in-one-shot construction. The absence of visible cuts expresses a worry about losing so much as a single moment of "real time" in the narrative's progression from original transgression to final, guilty exposure. I am reminded of a statement Hitchcock once made when discussing his routine of recounting his day's activities at the foot of his mother Emma's bed, a routine that persisted even after he became a man with a full-time job. "It was a ritual. I always remember the evening confession." As Hitchcock rendered his pleasurable or tedious or deceptive "full" account of his workday to his mother, the unvarying elements were the *duration* of the telling and the confined, intimate space in which his recitation was staged. One moves straight through the domestic "confession"—gauging its effect on the listener whose gaze is unwaveringly fixed on the son charged to speak. Here is one way of imagining the maternal presence already established in the airless chamber of *Rope,* avidly absorbing whatever the son—who moves the camera nervously/seamlessly from end to end of his enclosed story—elects to show her. Precisely this kind of watcher presence would be the ideal spectator for *Rope,* since "she" naturally channels the storyteller's energy back and forth between the two complementary desires that drive the narrative: to successfully hide something and to be found out in one's clever duplicity.

The rope, as object, has an unusual itinerary in the film. Once David's two friends have finished choking him with it—the action which thrusts the spectator inside the penthouse setting and then obliges her to remain "tied" there—the rope becomes for a time an overlooked detail. That is to say, the murderers are so taken up with the corpse of their slain "friend" that they briefly lose sight of it, forget that it is still lying out in the open. Their neglect, of course, only serves to make the rope a locus for heightened viewer anxiety. The rope becomes the inordinately obtrusive remnant of the crime, the flimsy bit of telling evidence that will give the murderers away if not recalled in time and properly hidden. But full hiddenness is not, in fact, what Brandon, the organizer of both the slaying and the dinner party scheduled to begin within minutes after David's death, has in mind. The elimination of David has been, from the first, conceived by its perpetrators as a purely gratuitous exercise. Brandon lacks the customary fearful resolve of the lawbreaker to keep potentially ruinous signs of his guilt out of sight. The rope expresses the oscillating desire I have already identified: to be, on the one hand, successful in preserving the secret of his monstrous deed and, on the other, found out by the enormously cunning male professor with whom he happens, in some fittingly Byzantine manner, to be in love. Eventually, the rope will be "dangled" before the professor's eyes when Brandon offers it to the victim's father as a kindly aid in making his load of books easier to carry. Later still, the rope turns up in the professor's pocket, reaching its appropriate destination perhaps as he is obliged to discover how he himself is intimately bound to the evil he uncovers. The intermediate function of book "strap" creates a kinship not only between the slain son and the father who is left with a palpable burden of dread to carry away from the party, but also between the professor's book-derived radical skepticism and the death-dealing rope which rubs up against it.

So far the rope seems to function within a purely male exchange system of death and slyly deflected homoerotic desire. I shall now offer an argument for assigning the rope itself a female identity. One of my students, Katie Johns, drew my attention to the oddity of Hitchcock's choice of the color red for the film's printed title—*Rope*—given the fact that the film's one murder is a pointedly bloodless one. She further noted that the most prominent use of red in the film's overall color scheme is in the elegant party dress worn by Janet, the stranded-in-limbo beloved of the murder victim. Janet is thus strangely paired with the rope, and carries in her own person the unreleased color of the crime. In the course of the film, red's only other significant point of entry in Hitchcock's image system is in the evening sky steadily discernible from the lengthy curved window backing the penthouse. As night descends, the redness imperceptibly deepens, gradually staining the entire skyline with the color of Janet's dress and the rope of the title. I regard this triumvirate of crimson clues as a directive to link up the rope with the dispersed and debilitated forces of overt female presence in the film. (Female presence gravitates toward ghostliness as it invites us to think in terms of displacements—a title of the wrong color; a dress that carries more knowledge of the killing than the woman wearing it, and that harmonizes with the blood-suffused air beyond the penthouse window.) As the narrative proceeds, claustrophobia and hysteria braid together to generate a *visible* "red" condition on screen, as in *Marnie*. The coloring of the sky intensifies as the interior setting grows more stifling, for characters and audience alike. The viewer also becomes aware of a pulsing or flashing red light on one of the background buildings. It is small but prominent. Red keeps returning us to the sensations of the film's first physical action—the rope tightening around David's neck, the cutting off of his air supply. Janet, as I've noted, is covered in the redness but is never required to *see* it. What of the other two female characters? Mrs. Atwater, a theatrical lady obsessed with acting, is kept *completely* in the dark about all the theatrical games in progress. Mrs. Wilson, the housekeeper, never manages to discover the dreadful "mess" her employers have made that needs cleaning up. There is a fourth female figure in *Rope,* who is repeatedly alluded to though never seen. This is David's mother, who was invited to Brandon's party, but at the last moment decides not to attend because she isn't feeling well. She and David share the status of missing party guests. Early in the film it is observed that she is unwilling to allow David to "grow up" and become independent. She phones during the party to inquire anxiously about David's whereabouts. She conveys (even as an offscreen presence) the impression of being totally preoccupied with her son's activities. But given her separation from the film's setting, neither her fears nor her desire to know what is going on can gain any purchase.

Hitchcock has an intriguing habit of carrying forward an overloaded element or motif from one film to the next, and in his second meditation on its implications endowing it with a more complex centrality. One thinks immediately of the "release" of Norman's stuffed birds in *Psycho* into the swarming atmosphere of *The Birds,* or of Tippi Hedren's unseeing stare and paralysis near the end of *The Birds* being attached to the trauma-based red of *Marnie.* Equally often Hitchcock will reenact a pivotal or traumatic episode in a later narrative with its outcome and significance reversed. In *The Man Who Knew Too Much* (1955), as I previously noted, a mother's voice carries far enough to reach her kidnapped child—furthering his rescue in part by piercing the defenses of a dark mother counterpart who holds him captive. In the same film, the mother's instinctive scream at the Albert Hall presentation of a choral work by Arthur Benjamin—playing both on her frustration as a retired professional singer and her knowledge that any sound she makes will increase her missing son's jeopardy—spoils the perfect aim of an assassin. This episode, in turn, is echoed in *Vertigo* where Madeleine, clad in a gray suit that strongly resembles the gray suit worn by Jo, the mother in *The Man Who Knew Too Much,* has her scream cut off "midway" by Gavin Ellster, who covers her mouth with his hand, just after he drops his wife's body from the mission bell tower.[14] Ellster's hand over Madeleine's mouth comes to stand for all the suppressed utterance in the film—the many lost or too late voices that cannot make their way (in time) to a beloved object. Perhaps the mad Carlotta—the ghostly mother figure in *Vertigo* who periodically usurps Madeleine's identity, in a variation of *Rebecca,* and drives her toward death—the Carlotta who provides the maternal gaze *behind* Madeleine's gaze, best addresses this issue of sound that will not reach far enough. "Where's my child?" she worriedly inquires of passing strangers as she wanders the streets. She cannot bring herself to remember that her child is already dead. Let us imagine Norman Bates as one of the strangers she passes, attempting to elude his mother with the same hopeless fervor that Carlotta displays in searching for her lost "little one." Finally, as Elise Moore has suggestively observed, Roger Thornhill's seemingly impossible rescue of Eve in *North by Northwest,* as she is on the verge of falling from Mt. Rushmore, makes appropriately dreamlike restitution for the senseless loss of Judy-Madeleine in *Vertigo,* released the year before.

What the length of rope may hearken back to is the hair of Anna Paradine in *The Paradine Case* (1947). In that film, Hitchcock excitedly fastens on the moment when a prison matron uncoils Anna's hair and runs her hand through it in search of concealed objects, or a possible weapon. A woman's hair as voluminous growth, where desire and death twine together, also achieves prominence in *Under Capricorn* (1949), the film that directly follows *Rope.* Arguably the most memorable image in *Under Capricorn* is the dark shrunken head of a woman surreptitiously placed by the housekeeper Milly on the white sheet of her mistress's bed to terrorize her. The wizened face makes a dreadful contrast with the prodigious spread of hair, which seems to have taken on a life of its own after death. It is like someone momentarily giving you the mirror image of yourself that most fully conforms to their hatred and grim knowledge of you. "Your hair," Milly would have her mistress see, "is the tangled growth of the secret crimes you've committed against your brother and husband, and it stains the marriage bed you've stolen from me as deeply as blood." Ingrid Bergman's Lady Henrietta, her own hair unfastened and plentiful, stares at the totem in a state of voluptuous alarm. But it is only the image of a moment. When she later attempts to confirm its existence, it has disappeared. Milly's preferred medium of retribution against her mistress is poison rather than strangling; it is only in the brief scene with the shrunken head that we catch intimations of Robert Browning's "Porphyria," throttled with her own rain-dampened tresses, which she has just loosened to give herself completely to the wrong lover. ("and all her hair / In one long yellow string I wound / Three times her little throat around, / And strangled her.")[15] Consider the prison matron's search through Anna Paradine's hair—a search that reveals *noth-*

ing—as Hitchcock's nascent recognition that the hair itself might be regarded as the concealed weapon. Only braid it, detach it, and fetishize it as a separate entity, and you have fashioned a weapon with a most unusual aura. The hair's original allure tightens until it becomes a potentially lethal threat.

The aura of the innocently murderous rope, in my judgment, quietly and obliquely presages Hitchcock's later full-blown fixation on women's hair. (*Vertigo*, *The Birds*, and *Marnie* mark the highest flowering of this interest.) Perhaps the most remarkable example of an equally mysterious hair analogy I have discovered in Hitchcock's work, apart from the vertiginous spiral of the coiled hair in *Vertigo*'s portrait of Carlotta, occurs in a 1959 television episode of *Alfred Hitchcock Presents* entitled "The Crystal Trench." (Hitchcock directed this episode.) In one scene, a young woman, Mrs. Ballister (Patricia Owens), stands on a balcony staring off at a mountain after receiving word that her husband of six months has perished in a climbing accident. As she looks into the snowy darkness, the camera approaches her head from behind, and we contemplate at some length her carefully arranged hair. As we study her coiffure at close range, waiting for her to turn and give vent to her grief, the sound of the mountain wind rises. An unnervingly swift subliminal transfer of the glacially cold mountain where the husband has been lost to the fetishized upland of women's hair occurs, accomplished by the augmented wind sound. It is as though the hair briefly doubles for the icy "crystal trench" where the husband (as we later discover) lies frozen, but perfectly preserved for decades in his youthful appearance. Much emphasis is placed in this brief story on the taut and slack ropes that give evidence of the climber's whereabouts during his fatal venture.

To further substantiate my impression that there is a plausible, buried (and interesting because buried) linkage for Hitchcock between the rope and the female, I shall briefly allude to a 1945 film about strangling which he had certainly seen (in advance of making *Rope*) and which, like the latter, was adapted from a Patrick Hamilton source. *Hangover Square*, directed by John Brahm, has a pianist/composer as its protagonist. Loud, discordant noises trigger fits of homicidal rage in him which he later is incapable of remembering. During his bouts of sleepwalking frenzy, he strangles two women he is devoted to, employing a makeshift rope. I say makeshift since the rope is actually the tie-back cord for a window drape in his flat. The hidden murder weapon, in its unobtrusive life as a piece of decor, is as invisible to the unconscious strangler as to those seeking evidence of his guilt. The aftermath of the composer's first murder attempt on a close female friend includes a lengthy scene of the woman (who didn't recognize her assailant) running her hands around her neck and wincing as she reaches the spot where the "thuggee knot" made in the cord had pressed against her windpipe. The second murder attempt, which results in a death, takes place in the victim's bedroom, as she sits at her vanity table readying herself for sleep. The first (surviving) victim's hair is neatly pinned up. The second victim, killed at her dressing table, has luxuriant hair that overflows its fastenings. (I should note in passing that the romantically schizophrenic score for *Hangover Square* was composed by Bernard Herrmann.)[16]

In *Rope*, the unassuming, sexually anonymous piece of rope allies itself with everything that is shape-shifting and indefinite, beginning perhaps with the motives of the two young men who use it for killing. It directly participates in the narrative's back-and-forth slide between clammy fear and the macabre pleasure of being utterly exposed. The rope's unambiguous opposite in the film is Brandon's melodramatically forthright revolver. The revolver belongs with the forces of conventional order in the narrative, which strive to make indecently changeable, cryptic actions and intentions into something clear-cut. When the gun appears, late in the film, it provides the almost giddy relief of conveying an instantly intelligible purpose. We understand that Brandon is prepared to use it against Rupert, his former professor, whom he now regards, unequivocally, as his adversary. Shortly thereafter, Rupert and Phillip physically struggle for possession of this weapon, after Brandon has theatrically tossed it aside, claiming (unpersuasively) that he had no thought of using it. The professor succeeds in vanquishing weak, frantic Phillip. The camera focuses here on the two men's hands, which are tensely joined in a manner reminiscent of Phillip and Brandon's joint strangling of David. It is implied that the triumphant, morally vindicated Rupert, who has belatedly become a man of action rather than "mere" ideas, will be in a position to set the terms by which all the film's previous enigmatic conflicts can be understood. Indeed, Rupert rises to the rhetorical occasion once he secures the revolver, making a speech in which he sternly explains to the murderers that he and they occupy wholly distinct moral categories. After rendering a judgment which he is confident will *hold*, he points the gun out of the penthouse window—open for the first time in the film—and fires it. The harsh noise penetrates the collective consciousness of the social throng passing on the street below. Though we do not see the inquisitive crowd, its general voice (the normative, for too long dangerously denied voice of the ordinary social world outside) can literally be felt to rise toward the previously sealed off penthouse interior, and seep into it.

The rope disrupts, and in my view ultimately slips free of, the reductive linear logic of the revolver. Though it begins its life in the film as a murder weapon, it is quickly separated from David's body, from the two killers' awareness, and, most crucially, from its own visual status as a menacing object. It effortlessly recovers the appearance of a nondescript household item—as ordinary in the object sphere as, say, hair is. The object is destined to return repeatedly to hyperprominence, like a fetish, but unlike a fetish its meaning is not frozen or inexorable. It achieves the dynamism of a metaphor as it forms fresh linkages and also the self-effacing character of an article indisposed to carry any weight of attachment for long. It is a disquieting vestige of a horrible crime, to be sure, and an intermittently forceful reminder of it. Yet in its pliability, its modest, domestic demeanor, its implied diversity of uses, it seems ready (and fit) to resume harmless duties. It is an object designed for random glimpses rather than a prolonged stare, which seems demanded somehow by the sharp outline of a handgun. Hitchcock prepares an intensified experience of rope glimpsing for us when the swinging door that stands between the spectator and the kitchen opens just long enough to grant us a peek of Brandon casually dropping the rope into an open drawer. Within a second, we can imagine it perfectly assimilated in the company of odds and ends. I hope to show that the rope not only collaborates with Hitchcock's accident-prone, mobile "female" camera gaze, but also conspires with it to discredit the rhetorically overstated revolver. The revolver works to enforce a stability of meaning by declaring the availability (and moral dependability) of firmly bounded categories. The penthouse apartment is the first model the film proposes of a unified field where everything is laid out, managed, tightly contained, wittily self-referential. The rope furtively insinuates connections between things that aspire, for the sake of locking meaning in place, to stay separate. It honors the integrity of the visual playing field in a different fashion than the gun, by seeking connections everywhere and never calling a halt to the process of making them. The firing of the revolver is, in effect, a repudiation of the slippery penthouse gameboard, and a calling in of outside forces to reaffirm the operations of law and common sense. It demands relief from too much fluidity.

The murder itself and the victim's identity participate in the rope's unspecified character. The killing fails, among other things, to *plot* a relationship between the perpetrators and David. The murder is not a response to anything that David has done, or to anything that his "friends" suppose he has done or might do to thwart their purposes. At one end of the capricious "rope" of causality leading up to David's planned execution is an unsatisfactory meeting between the victim and his girlfriend, where (we are eventually told) he received hints of his changed status as a suitor. (Hitchcock actually filmed David's tepid romantic meeting with Janet on a park bench in his "red herring" theatrical trailer for *Rope*. There was never any intention, of course, of joining this exiled scene to the body of the narrative. It posits a future where there is no future, narratively speaking.) At the other end of the causal "rope" is a visit to a pair of mildly irritating pseudo-friends, who have planned a party that David must go through the motions of enjoying; it is only politeness and a sense of social obligation that bring him to the penthouse. David, like Marion Crane, is cut off at an edgy, unresolved transition point in his story, though the place where he has arrived is much more weakly focused than Marion's final act of cleansing in the shower. The rope slaying establishes a symbiotic link between Brandon and Phillip, as a couple who perform the murder together, at the expense of their connection with David. One human connection is violently strengthened, in other words, in the act of denying another any substance.

The rope's initial method of purchasing connection seems to open up a dramatic space where everything, including the fact of David's death, enters a realm of provisionality and indefiniteness, where eerie gaps appear between characters' ostensible desires and the acts which issue from them. It is as though the twisting rope had, through its utterly senseless summoning of lethal pressure, caused a "break" or leak in the reliable dailiness of daily life. That break steadily widens as the film proceeds, until the characters have difficulty holding on to anything of themselves but the bad performances of their poorly synchronized social roles. *Rope* is a theatrical movie in which theatricality is what people need to be saved from, without there being any way out of it. The human connections that continue to be active and urgent in the film (whether through efforts to pull away or to overcome separateness) mostly have to do with reinforcements of self-as-theater. David's father is the one figure who successfully resists absorption into masquerade. His love for his son and fear for his absence keep him tragically isolated, immune to the solace of staged gestures. But Brandon, as if in recognition of the fact that the father stands too far apart from the others, makes sure that he innocently grabs hold of the murder rope before he leaves. His arranged exit thus combines tragic dignity with an insolent dash of burlesque.

Brandon and Phillip organize a party around the amusing premise that one of the invited guests will appear to be missing, when in fact whatever is left of him lies indifferently in their very midst—turning cold beneath the buffet. David's whereabouts is the party's main topic of conversation—its reliable point of shared interest—while the *film's* main interest is in what it means for the missing element to be *here,* but kept out of play. Hitchcock imitates Brandon, the director of the party, by preparing an utterly controlled environment where the effort of control is always working against itself. Superfluous areas of unaccountable tension are continually being generated which cause the whole fragile enterprise (the party and its overelaborate formal presentation) to feel on the verge of collapse. The strained atmosphere brought on by the requirements of party guest busyness, of feigned cordiality with barely a trace of genuine ease or spontaneous connection, keeps pointing us back to the "director" and the failure of his social arrangements to meld comfortably. There is no disguising the mechanism and strenuously willed artifice of the director's performance, nor the cumulative anxiety of maintaining (with Brandon) a sang-froid pose. The nervously mobile camera, at one level, objectifies the storyteller host, Hitchcock-Brandon, not merely announcing but also *betraying* his presence: his too conspicuous watching, his inability to dissolve at will into his plot. I will be arguing that the tension which works to "undo" our sense of adequate authorial control of the performance in *Rope* is the "female" component of Hitchcock's gaze throughout the narrative. In *Rebecca,* the ubiquitous woman's gaze marks an absolute of power, though the power is destructive of everything but itself. Here the ropelike female gaze more positively infiltrates and calls into question the various masculine disguises designed to convey the secure possession of power. Where, we are repeatedly led to wonder, does power attach credibly to moral awareness and sexual identity in *Rope?*

Hitchcock's elaborate maneuvers to hide the film's few cuts (so that the interior narrative will seem to consist of but one continuous shot) draw as much attention to the act of editing as Brandon draws to David's corpse, with his overingenious ploys for concealing the body out in the open. Hitchcock's editing has never seemed more exposed, more dissociated from the natural flow of events than in *Rope.* The spectator repeatedly catches Hitchcock in the act of searching out "unobtrusive" places to secretly break off his shots; one watches for his staged breaks as involuntary acknowledgments of authorial frailty, as though Hitchcock were forced to declare his presence rather than choosing to do so. Editing, in other words, becomes a form of incrimination. The camera work, like the editing, strangely partakes of the condition of entrapment. The extreme tension of attempting a "flawless" execution of Hitchcock's insidiously complicated visual choreography is strikingly attested to by the film's soundtrack, where Phillip repeatedly performs Poulenc's "Perpetual Movement No. 1" on the piano. The piece seems to embody the fretful, slithering, "choker" quality of the camera's gaze—as it oppressively stalks the characters. Phillip strives to regain a sense of calm and control by retreating to the piano and the security of a composition he knows well. But his music achieves an effect exactly the reverse of what he hopes for once he begins playing. It seems to spill his agitation everywhere. As Poulenc's title suggests, the piece is structured on a ceaselessly repeating pattern. Its destination seems always to be a return to the beginning, to thematic material already well traversed, which fosters a chafing impatience in the ear of a listener awaiting signs of resolution or closure. The more self-possessed Phillip longs to appear as he works his way through the music, the more the rhythm of his playing "gets away" from him. Rupert collaborates in forcing Phillip's rhythm out of control by his manipulation of a "too fast" metronome. Thus, the art realm where Phillip is most sure of himself progressively informs against him, mocking his efforts of controlling a pattern he has confidently memorized. Moving camera, editing calculations, music—all seem to me metaphorically linked to the amorphous rope, which will not stay fastened to anything that might confirm mastery, within the characters' or director's performance of their assigned roles.

The sly, malleable rope is also a discreet emblem for the film's stealthy, never finalized sexual declarations. In *Rope's* opening embrace, as a "female" cord is pulled tight by excited male hands, David yields his weakly normative place in the film's sexual economy to a pair of not quite declared male lovers. (The movie production code, which no doubt contributes to the mystification of sexual identities and objectives in *Rope,* intriguingly parallels the equally oblique homosexual code. In the latter, intentions, looks and "innocent" phrases not readily intelligible to outsiders carry enormous import for anyone attuned to the proper signals. Both codes work within contexts where many forms of openness are forbidden. Both, inventively employed, heighten our sense of the many avenues available to those who have something "inadmissible" to declare.) One strand of Brandon's Nietzchean superman experiment is the assertion of a sublime indifference to a *heterosexual* logic of law and the notions of obedience it circulates to keep its outlaw deviants "out of sight"—in permanent steerage, as it were. Brandon, arguably, has committed his crime in part as a radical means of declaring his feelings to Rupert, his former teacher and housemaster. If the "unexamined love," in Michael Wood's witty formulation, is not worth having, Brandon is giving Rupert the chance to examine his love for him in the form of a murder performed expressly for his intellectual approval. As I have already noted, Brandon's fantasy of disclosure, of showing Rupert what he has done, is as much a spur to his lavish plotting as the more familiar desire to escape detection. He may well imagine Rupert grasping, with a delicious shudder, that David's body is a love gift, placed before him with the same carnivore delicacy that a cat reveals when laying a fresh kill at his master's doorstep. (Hitchcock repeats this pattern much more explicitly in *Strangers on a Train*, when Bruno plans, as his crowning move in the seduction of Guy, the revelation that he has "made good" on his offer to kill Guy's ex-wife.) Rupert's initial shock, in the logic of Brandon's fantasy, will give way to an awed realization of spiritual kinship. After all, the urge to be scandalized is only a reflex of Rupert's still unvanquished conventionality. By giving substance to Rupert's most easily misunderstood longings, by creating an environment where violent deeds are an acceptable expression of intimacy, Brandon hopes to win Rupert's heart.

In Brandon's penthouse "little theater," David's agreeably pointless death strives to confirm, among other things, the weightlessness of the heterosexual moral scheme. "What are we to do with an ethical framework that denies us the right to pursue (or publicly acknowledge) almost everything our appetites fiercely crave and that our unfettered imaginations propose to us?" For Brandon, this is the heart of the matter. The rules that oblige us to deny what our eyes tell us, to look down and away from the truth of our brutal or socially unlicensed impulses, are as empty as our responsibility to a party guest who happens to be "missing." Can the viewer easily evade some preliminary identification with Brandon's jubilantly amoral point of view, whatever her judgments of him, if Brandon is both director of the evening's entertainment and the one who knows most about what has transpired? The camera does what it can to enforce this early identification, becoming intimately aligned, for the most part, with Brandon's knowing gaze: his tightly confident sense of things.

Because of the discomfort attending Brandon's repellently self-enamored and (largely) unfathomable behavior, however, the viewer is undoubtedly anxious to find another character who can more appropriately "monitor" her experience. James Stewart's Rupert might at first seem to afford a safer and more congenial viewer surrogate, were it not for the fact that his role as detective is creepily intermixed with his roles as love object and sleek apologist for permissible atrocities. He is a fastidious bachelor, sequestered from mundane traffic with ordinary feelings in precisely the fashion that Brandon hopes to emulate. His preferred style of morbidly witty disengagement slides us repeatedly back to Brandon's playacting and depraved narcissism. What might stabilize and center the action, one feels, is a recognition by Rupert of Brandon's nervously rapacious awareness of him. Rupert refuses to pick up on any cues that the whole occasion is aimed at him, like a sexual variant of the third act revolver. The party is an extravagantly public form of seduction, with David's body only one of the items secreted in Brandon's veiled glances. Resolutely unresponsive to communication on this plane, Rupert turns every flash of erotic energy into a signifier for a different kind of mystery. Interestingly, after making a great show of departing with the other guests, he adopts the venerable amorous pretext of returning to the penthouse to retrieve something that he left behind. Before declaring what he thinks he knows to the murderers, he allows the camera (and hence the viewer) a private glimpse of the rope that is now transferred to his own person. The rope lies, intimately, in his pocket, an intimacy that is heightened when he furtively runs his fingers over it and pulls it tight, as if to make sure of its meaning.

In all of Hitchcock's best films there comes a moment of charged seeing when a character recognizes something crucial, while failing to grasp something implied by the new discovery that, with respect to self-knowledge, is even more crucial. What the tested character immediately apprehends has to do with the narrative's external plot; what is suppressed or bypassed has to do with the observing character's own part in the incriminating design. Perhaps the most celebrated instance of this split knowledge occurs in the final dressing scene of *Vertigo*, when Scottie gazes in the mirror while fastening Judy's necklace, at her request, and suddenly knows what the jewelry signifies (another rope, of sorts). Scottie all at once holds, in his head and hands, the evidence that Judy and Madeleine are the same person; he understands that he has been the victim of a complicated criminal deception. What eludes his grasp is the full import of Judy's current presence in this room, in this shared mirror. *Why* is she here? Why has Scottie compelled her to dress, in every last particular, as the deceased Madeleine? Why could he only make love to her when the resemblance to Madeleine was perfect? Why could he only begin to acknowledge her as a visible and real person when she agreed to eliminate every tainted trace of Judy? Why has Judy forgotten that the necklace will give her away? Is she not, like a sleepwalker, making herself an even more daunting replica of Madeleine than the fiercely exacting Scottie has known how to request, thus surpassing his demands in the "game" of self-obliteration? Scottie spends the rest of his life as a character in *Vertigo* holding all of these questions at a distance. The self-awareness and "better" knowledge of Judy that a confrontation with such questions might, however painfully, yield are denied in favor of the simpler knowledge of how *he* has been used and betrayed.

Rupert in *Rope* (James Stewart again) works equally hard to repudiate any stain of kinship with his former students, and certainly any suggestion that he has jointly authored (ghostwritten, if you like) their ugly, literal crime. Intellectual seduction must be accorded no weight, no Tar Baby sticking power, in the moral scheme of things. Rupert hastily sketches out an explanatory picture of a Manichean realm in which "from the very start [the moment of psychic formation?] there must have been something deep inside you . . . that let you do this thing. But there has always been something deep inside me that would never let me do it." I detect a bright thread of sexual terror in Rupert's panicked flight to ethical seriousness and certitude. His well-fortified "true nature" apparently lives in a separate country from his earlier, more lubricous exposition of his ideas. Rupert ties his clinching knowledge knot by implying that an inborn sexual twistedness is the hatching ground for all of Brandon and Phillip's susceptibility to vile deeds. How "deep inside" Brandon must one reach in order to find the lethal rope that is now tucked away in Rupert's own pocket? Deeper than Brandon's attraction to his guileful, hard-to-read professor, whose ideas (he learns too late) are as misleadingly "veiled" and in need of decoding as his feelings? Deeper than Brandon's awed sense that his own most savage and immoderate impulses are magically given expression and a lucid, dignified framework in another man's eloquent defense of them? Or, abandoning Brandon for the moment, how deep must one reach into the silence of recently returned World War II veterans who have been schooled in all the nuances of permissible torture and extermination for a four-year period? Rupert, recall, has a visible limp, the result perhaps of his own acquaintance with the terrors of the battlefield.

The ghostly style of *Rope*, by forever failing to close the circuit of seeing, in the way that montage effortlessly allows, also fails to close the circuit of knowing. The shot-without-end strategy mimics the point-of-view congestion of a late Henry James novel, where so many snags and worrisome gaps stand between the perceiver and his intended object. Consider how the soundscape in the final minute of *Rope* shifts the site of knowledge outward, past the bounds of the penthouse frame where the viewer's eyes and ears can't successfully reach. A strong sense of division is signaled between the unnatural, controlled emptiness of the soundscape inside the penthouse after Rupert's summation and gunshot, and the soundscape of the city street struggling to make itself distinct in the absence of further performance noise. A medley of ordinary citizen voices rises, with a confusion that feels both exhilarating and eerie, to challenge the singular voice account of things that has just concluded. Theatricality powerfully resurfaces in the spectacle of three men forced to wait for an indefinite interval, just as Rupert has finished banishing all dangerous "playacting" from his moral sight. Never has Rupert seemed more like a stranded creature of the stage than in the final moments of the film, when he has nothing further to say and no further gestures to perform except to make his way wearily to a chair (Brandon, by contrast, reclaims some of his lost authority by expertly mixing a drink for himself.) The camera cannot quite find a way to justify breaking off its prowling surveillance and declare an end to the performance, apart from acknowledging that the exterior world, which the camera is denied access to apart from a fixed, ever-darkening picture-window perspective, has become more important to attend to than what is happening inside the apartment.

The father's law in *Rope* is not "at one" with the camera gaze in anything like the triumphant fashion that Rebecca's law is in *Rebecca*. The margin of difference, I would suggest, has to do with the female rope which Rupert procures without really possessing. He must exchange it for a revolver before he can stop feeling ominously adrift. The rope can be tied to many things and depends for its "shape" and significance on what it's momentarily linked with and on whomever happens to be making the linkage. The rope, in my sense of it, has, as I argued earlier, its source in fetish: it begins its journey through the film as an object drawn too tight, tight enough to "choke the life out of you." But there is something left over—a surplus value, if you like—once its destructive power as fetish has been avowed, unleashed, and fully displayed. One might call what is left over the enigma of one's attachment to the fetish. (It is worth reminding ourselves that we would not be nearly so confident attributing fetishes to Hitchcock and Luis Buñuel if they did not elaborately point them out to us, and underscore their significance. It is they who confess their vulnerability to the fetish's power whenever it "enters the picture.") No sooner does the camera gaze lose its initial, perfect position for regarding the rope fetishistically (in close-up, at the climax of a sexualized murder), than the rope is promptly demystified and mingles aimlessly for a time with the life of other ordinary things. However, the camera repeatedly seeks to reawaken the rope's troubling mystique. One compulsively returns to something precisely because it is not yet fathomable. The fetish, here and elsewhere in Hitchcock, is connected to everything that he knows he does *not* know, does not yet see clearly enough. He submits himself to the hallowed object as if it were itself endowed with a gaze. Circling back to it is not an assertion of strength, but an admission of weakness. Quite literally, the rope "takes one's breath away." Before it one is exposed as still a child: debilitated, controlled, and, as Norman Bates would have it, "clawing at the air" of one's private trap. (Perhaps even one's trap is not "private"; it belongs, in Norman's case, to his mother.)

Confronting the fetish is to recognize how much distance remains between whatever authority we presumptuously lay claim to and Real Authority. If Hitchcock declares himself to us (partially) through Brandon, he is showing us how dreadfully one can be controlled by the need to control. One is certain that at a certain point the game of control must always break down, that it can never extend far enough to make one feel safe. So Hitchcock-Brandon compulsively engineers his own surrender and breakdown—via the incriminating rope—in order to achieve some control over the unbearable/pleasurable necessity of losing control. Rupert, who never really sees what the rope embodies, defines control as a rationality one need never lose faith in. He is the version of Hitchcock who manages to win through a willful blindness. Rupert is the man who convincingly pretends to know too much, or at least enough to maintain a complacent equilibrium. He makes control disreputable by his fervent belief that it can be kept simple and consistent: murder, like an excessive show of feeling, is about losing control; philosophy (as he practices it), like detective work and a sturdy revolver, is about regaining control, and finding ways to safeguard it.

I have been arguing throughout this discussion that the visual style of *Rope* is on Brandon's side of the control issue rather than Rupert's; it is control driven to undo itself. The camera regularly arrives at what appear to be conventional Hitchcock setups, but the transitions between these setups—the endless maneuvering required to get into and then out of the exactly desirable framing position—makes for a persistent palpable tension. Think of it as a tug-of-war between a female ghosting force, akin to Rebecca, and a male investigator committed to firm definition. The effect of the camera movement privileges the feel of disruption and in-betweenness. It is as though Hitchcock is repeatedly required to relinquish framing control to a stronger, prior force (Norman Bates fighting with his mother for the right to gaze for himself). Power is given back to "her" in small incremental units that attain a cumulative suffocating weight. This disruptive force seems to be in touch with everything that is kept absent, out of sight, inconspicuous—David's body, the initials hidden inside the hat he "left behind," the unassuming rope.

Like the repressed object continually about to return, the invisible female guest goads the space for points of reentry.

A common argument offered by those who find Hitchcock's movies "light" or disappointingly conventional in their "thinking" is that his endings so often serve to put us back "safely within the domain of the patriarchal."[17] It astonishes me that so many critics conversant with (and sympathetic to) the most radical implications of poststructuralist and postmodernist theory continue to regard the ending (and often, even more narrowly, the verbalized ending) of a film narrative as a reliable, "X marks the spot" arbiter of its meaning. Whatever turbulent energy and troublesome questions a film has released or contended with in the course of its unfolding, we can count on the ending to provide a sufficiently firm container for them. My own experience of closure in Hitchcock is that it almost invariably emphasizes the thinness, arbitrariness, and inadequacy of whatever resolving gestures it nominally affirms. Patriarchal consolidation typically amounts to a weakly joined romantic couple being marooned in a conspicuously tiny, unreflective, and morally valueless comfort zone. The comfort on offer depends on something akin to Rupert's willed blindness. The couple, usually at the male's directive, settles for the easier sort of available knowledge, refusing any recollection of the critical juncture earlier in the narrative when the *viewer's* sense of what authentic knowing actually costs or demands startlingly emerged. (The male who best illustrates this repudiation through a gesture is Devlin at the end of *Notorious,* locking Sebastian out of the getaway car. "No room, Sebastian," he curtly declares: his final words on any subject.) To subscribe to the genial or ironic flatness of so many of Hitchcock's final episodes as the best expression of what a Hitchcock movie cumulatively is *for* is simply to join Devlin and Scottie and Rupert in their self-limiting traps. One can always refuse to enter, or even to notice, a Hitchcock film's alternative realm of truly vertiginous interpretive freedom. "To look long," in Jed Perl's arresting phrase, "is to feel free." But a long look is also the hallmark of blighting obsession.

The women in Hitchcock's films often suffer more egregiously than the men, but one explanation of this disproportion is that they *live* with the knowledge that the "rope's" attachment to anything is momentary, never binding. What seems attached will soon not be. They are more likely than their male counterparts—whatever their social masks say to the contrary—to accept the fact that every role and meaning is unstable and subject to abrupt transformation. In Malcolm Bowie's words, "one fabrication must be dismantled and cleared away to make room for another."[18] There is never enough time to adjust and prepare for the lightning-swift collapse of one's reliable circumstances. Like the chameleon objects with which their fate is so often linked, Hitchcock's women derive much of their authority and interest from their talent for internal metamorphosis. Whatever their relationships with men ultimately lead them to, they seem remarkably adroit at seeming to be in transition, launching or at least actively imagining journeys *away* from their current, temporary address. Hitchcock's "wrong man," by contrast, typically assumes that the preposterous mixup that has caused him either to lose his proper place or to be confused with a guilty stranger will be straightened out in due course. He depends on outward conditions shifting eventually in his favor so that he can work his way back to the "waiting" identity he has accidentally and *unfairly* been deprived of. With a restored identity will come a restored sense of control. Hitchcock's women seldom believe they possess a right or fixed identity, or that there is such a thing to be had. Sometimes their male partners would have them think otherwise, with predictably unpleasant results. One can regard this state of affairs (women without access to stable identity) as either wrongful deprivation or a risk-filled opportunity to overstep artificially imposed boundaries.

A woman in possession of a fluid or unsettled identity seems to be the strongest magnet for Hitchcock's dramatic interest in her. He seeks out female surrogates who are ambiguously in passage toward an unmapped "elsewhere"; if they are to get there, they must prove resourceful, but also somewhat reckless, impersonators. A recurrent secret goal of the woman's transfiguring journey is to track the adamant Law of the Mother to its lair. This goal is arguably as difficult to recognize as it is to reach. For Hitchcock, only a female quester might conceivably discover what the mother's strange, incontestable power consists of, and in so doing begin to break the Law's hold. She must first capture, in a metaphor borrowed from *Notorious,* all of the mother's keys, and try them in every lock of the great night kingdom.

Read in the light of a secret but urgent quest to escape maternal law, young Charlie Newton's real struggle in *Shadow of a Doubt* is less with her deranged, homicidal uncle than with his sister, Emma—the woman that all of his victims resemble but who is herself mysteriously exempted from his rage and retribution. In his mind, she is the one surviving remnant of an all-but-vanished world of female gentility, delicacy, innocence. Emma is, of course, Charlie's mother, and one of the daughter's most daunting tasks is somehow to force her uncle out of her home without her mother learning anything about who he has become or what he has done since his "change." She is certain, as is her uncle, that such knowledge would kill Emma. The film concludes with Charlie taking the darkness of her own unavoidable killing of her uncle inside herself so that her mother can be permanently spared (protected from) any further "truth." In *Rear Window,* Lisa Fremont's most important adversary is arguably not Lars Thorwald but his mysteriously disappearing and reappearing invalid wife, Anna. Anna seems, in her shapeshifting way, to double as shrewish wife and ailing parent in the *Rear Window* cosmos, and, of course, her invalid status uncannily mirrors that of the wheelchair-bound L. B. Jefferies. The scene in which Lisa breaks into the Thorwald apartment to verify that she is dead rather than merely "vanished" involves a hazardous (almost necromantic) decision to insert the lost woman's wedding ring on her own finger. Lisa must somehow displace, from a distance, the haunting figure of Anna Thorwald from Jefferies's mindscreen. She accomplishes this by briefly taking over her space and adopting one of her most intimate, defining attributes: her ring. Perhaps the hidden, fairy-tale plot of *Rear Window* can best be understood as involving a man who must be rescued, by a patient and spirited woman, from an evil spell. He has looked too long at a figure who has the power to poison his thoughts, and to make every married or marriageable woman he encounters somehow bear her likeness. (Anyone he marries will surely prove to be an Anna, he sourly concludes.) Jefferies and Anna's shared paralysis is a mark of their secret fellowship, and when she disappears she makes her new living quarters, Rebecca and Mrs. Bates-style, inside him. The lady always vanishes in Hitchcock so that she can reappear again, in ghostly fashion, in another's place. It is Lisa's task to exorcise this maternal demon, who also happens to be a monstrously dismembered wifely victim. Though Thorwald has succeeded in murdering Anna, burying her is beyond his powers.

If the fetish *intact* in Hitchcock can be regarded as the woman's hair perfectly coiled, done up, the act of loosening the hair, uncoiling it, might be taken to signify the breaking of the enchanted male's trance, the disruption of the longing for immobility and for the prolonged infantile pleasure of rapt contemplation. Let us consider the "uncoiling" as the metaphoric move or wish which sets the female in circulation through Hitchcock's imagined worlds. It is "she" who must face all the most harrowing obstacles—she who sets the birds in motion, if you like—because it is only she who is protean enough to meet the equally uncoiled mother force in all *her* cunning guises. She must overthrow or productively merge with the mother force who has seemingly limitless stratagems for captivating the child and holding "him" captive.

In my reading of Hitchcock, *Marnie* is the appropriate culmination of the director's long Odyssean wandering. Marnie *fully* arrives home, in a film that seems to grow directly out of the final images of *The Birds*. (At the end of *The Birds*, a somehow suspect, becalmed mother and traumatized "almost" daughter effect a dazed, reconciling embrace as the vehicle which contains them slowly moves through a bird-covered, spectral landscape, all of whose alien, winged creatures are for the moment subdued, and yet poised for renewed, furious assault.) Shape-shifting Marnie Edgar then, successor and double of the woman torn by birds, is gradually revealed to us as one whose every gesture is an effort to placate her mother and to win a persuasive, spontaneous embrace from her. Marnie can only offer desperately inadequate, bribe gifts to her mother, gifts purchased with money she has stolen from others and denied to herself. The conclusion of her story, entirely without precedent in Hitchcock, reveals her curled up at her mother's feet after having, at long last, encountered this deeply elusive parent as a human whole. Who is Bernice Edgar—apart from a being with a Poe-like name that is both male and female—when she is finally unveiled for us? Wonderfully, she is a host of unresolved contradictions. She is a staunch Puritan and a former prostitute; she is a young girl who, like her daughter, was abused and dreadfully exploited at an early age; she is a frighteningly cold woman and also a warm woman who generously lavishes attention on another mother's neglected child; she is a woman who regrets that she didn't love her daughter better but who believes she has loved well enough, just the same; she is a pathological liar and a teller of harsh truths; she is a self-sufficient pillar of strength and a lonely, crippled shut-in, who is continually in pain. If any character can be said to have gained complete possession of Hitchcock's camera gaze, it is Marnie in her brave, terrifying last meeting with Bernice. The visit ends with a measure of acceptance, understanding and forgiveness, but no real reconciliation. Moreover, Marnie, in the very same encounter, must recall herself as a child, holding a blood-soaked weapon and standing over the man she has just murdered. She is finally able to let herself see that her lifelong nightmare is literally true: as a child, she was guilty of a horrible crime, no less horrible for having been performed innocently, as the result of "mistaken" perception.[19]

Rope's significance as an experiment en route to *Marnie*'s more capacious personal mystery has to do with the restriction of female power in the film's sexual economy to an unimposing trifle of an object, which nevertheless seems vitally linked to the camera's own difficulty in conducting a properly controlled investigation. *Rope* oscillates between the two extremes of Hitchcock's view of his authority, relative to the spectator and to himself. These "extremes" turn, as we have seen, on the question of whether it is preferable to stay hidden or be found out.

The most skeptical way of reading Hitchcock's authority in *Rope* would be to proceed on the assumption that he has callously overinvested in Brandon's "duty-free" perspective. In this view, Hitchcock joins his surrogate director in organizing a merciless entertainment for his own disdainfully decadent amusement. Here the rope as fetish is merely one more element in the game to play with. Instead of addressing (or getting entangled in) its movement from place to place, and function to function—most movingly, for example, when the victim's father is given the rope to make it simpler for him to carry his load—Brandon-Hitchcock denies that the rope has any ability to touch him. He neutralizes it, brings it under control by treating it as an empty marker for the young men's gratuitous sadism. It ratifies the viewer's potential role as a fellow connoisseur of cruelty: the less consequential and less ethically barbed the representation of this cruelty, the better.

In a more edifying scenario, the rope circulates (potently "unattached") as a masked female sign of what is left open and left over when all of Rupert's conventional, ready-made moral knowledge has been declared. It is like Miriam's glasses in *Strangers on a Train,* separated from her person at the moment she is attacked, and bearing independent witness to the crime against her. The object allows the death neither to be lost sight of nor to become mere grist for a detective's eventual tidy solution. Through the medium of the recurring object, the crime itself seems to become imbued with a private knowledge, which the killer has no access to. Because of this unreleased knowledge, belonging to no one, and for that very reason perhaps, undismissable, the object seems charged with the power to see, to look back at the guilty and to draw others into the network of guilt. Hitchcock was one of the first film directors to understand not only how to endow an object with character life on-screen but also how to make it express the whole psychological force field within the frame. The rope or other central object becomes everything that neither the murderer nor the rational investigator can quite get a grip on. Though not explicitly associated with a female presence, the rope is closely connected to the female issue of boundary disruption: the need to know more, the need to acknowledge (like the camera narrator throughout *Rope*) that the thing one seeks is never at one with what is at this moment caught inside the frame. The rope is also linked to the female by way of fetish. The aura of fetish surrounding an object, as opposed to the object itself, is precisely what can't be marked for visual seizure or mapped for rational control. It always gets away and always reveals a strength superior to one's own. Here is where Hitchcock's true authority—which values most what slips free of its imprisoning order—manifests itself. Hitchcock's camera reaches furthest when it becomes an aspiring Mary Rose, a ghost with a female name.

III

CRUEL PLEASURES AND THE LIMITS OF IRONY

8

This May Hurt a Little:
The Art of Humiliation in Film

I asked, how many times, is this the truth of the earth?
How can laments and curses be turned into hymns?
—Czeslaw Milosz, "A Mirrored Gallery"

Andre Bazin's noble dream of cinema was of a window ("the widest possible") opening onto the world. The greatest justification of film, in his view, is its capacity to give the world, which is already ours, back to us in its openness, beauty, and continually forgotten presentness. Bazin's redemptive vision rests on a belief that the camera's natural tendency is to honor those appearances that are exposed to it. If film artists trust the sufficiency of things-as-they-are and the camera's gift for making an accurate, truthful record, cinema will be a place of momentous discovery and ongoing revelation rather than literature's hard-up neighbor. The requirements of narrative, of course, offer continual temptations to forget cinema's privilege of contemplating images for their own sake, as self-contained entities. As director Wim Wenders notes in "Impossible Stories," filmed images "don't necessarily lead to anything else." Narrative inescapably involves "forcing the images in some way."

> Sometimes this manipulation becomes narrative art, but not necessarily. Often enough, the result is only abused pictures.
>
> I dislike the manipulation that's necessary to press all the images of a film into one story; it's very harmful for the images because it tends to drain them of their "life." In the relationship between story and image, I see the story as a kind of vampire trying to suck all the blood from an image. Images are acutely sensitive; like snails they shrink back when you touch their horns. They don't have it in them to be carthorses: carrying and transporting

233

The disgraced Professor Rath (Emil Jannings) prepares for his ritual humiliation in *The Blue Angel*.

messages or significance or intention or a moral. But that's precisely what a story wants from them.[1]

The phrase "abused pictures" is extremely suggestive (like Wenders's reference to the "poison ivy" images of American TV), but it is a provocation as well. Wenders clearly shares Bazin's reverence for images in their "unfallen" state, ascribing to them, without evident strain, the innocence and tender delicacy of uncorrupted souls. Images, in this "story," easily fall prey to manipulative violence of all sorts—from the indiscriminate acquisitiveness of a camera reduced to pure mechanism to the enslaving demands of a plot, which in its speed and falsity, allows no room for genuine contemplation. For Bazin and Wenders, the moving picture camera was created for holy interventions in reality, preserving the truth of moments by being alive to the multitude of large and small relations inscribed there. The camera's high mission is to be a God of love, unreservedly embracing reality in all of its rushing, adamant particularity. It will accept every creature, every unfavored, neglected fragment of even the most dismal urban "wailing wall" as long as no disguise, no face-saving improvements are contrived as preparations for the camera's act of beholding. Ideally employed, the camera eye will show us the dispensability of hierarchical arrangements. Within the stargate of the emergent visible, everything attains an equal worthiness to be looked at, without the clothing of story or moral, and will be judged good insofar as images can *reveal* and make restitution.

As the camera, in Eric Rohmer's words, "keeps tightening its hold on reality," its "natural" impetus is to draw us nearer to what it exposes to light.[2] But does image captivity not also lead, with equal naturalness, to repudiation, to a diminished responsiveness to both the original photographic subject and its continually depreciated representations? The word "expose" houses a range of negative meanings and associations which all seem to tell part of the truth about filmed images: to put out; to deprive of shelter; to leave without defense or covering; to lay open to danger, ridicule, censure; to place in the way of something that would be better avoided. Kafka is reported to have once challenged the description of the camera apparatus as a mechanical "Know thyself." He countered with the phrase "Mistake thyself," arguing that the camera "obscures the hidden life which glimmers through the outlines of things like a play of light and shade."[3]

Photography oscillates excitingly between the possibilities of a saving disclosure and a humiliating betrayal. Why should we trust photography's ability to trace out the spiritual presence or release the aura dwelling in the ordinary shapes of baskets, fences, the human face? If we are not quickened by the force of beauty in our daily contact with "raw" appearance, how does the camera mechanism (or the artists who serve it) "know" how to filter out in their image making the atmosphere of distraction and settled dullness which defines the world for us in so many of our moods? If the filmmaker self-consciously seeks painterly beauty in her images, and imitates the conventions of painters' art in order to heighten the effect of what is photographed, is this artificial "buildup" of surfaces not a confession that the ordinary world is not enough? Must objects be burnished, back-lit, and movingly composed before we can see them again as natural poetry? And does our need to cast a net of beauty, however capaciously, over the face of nature serve the interests of truth-telling?

Nietzsche has posed a characteristically absolute challenge to the conflation of beauty and truth, in one of his intractably severe aphorisms: "To experience a thing as beautiful means: to experience it necessarily wrongly."[4] I would paraphrase, at the risk of distortion, Nietzsche's rejection of beauty to mean that the compulsion to aestheticize (or the habit of it) involves a forsaking of the coarse, tangled-up "many-sidedness" of experience in favor of distillations. The "essence" that beauty extracts is never the whole, though often confused with the idea or sensation of wholeness, and what is left behind, after beauty's comforting sleight-of-hand, is everything too harsh and graceless to yield soul-gratifying patterns. The pursuit of beauty encourages a "will to appearance, to simplification, to the mask, to the cloak, in short to the superficial." Nietzsche is also taking aim against the "ancient false finery" of Greece and what one might call the Greeks' own vision of the photograph: figures seen always against a background of splendor, "complete in themselves as though scissored from the sky by cosmic shears and thrust out into a light" that eternally dazzles (Roberto Calasso, *The Marriage of Cadmus and Harmony*).[5] But if a life lived for beauty is a lie, what is to be gained by denying the sensations of beauty when they arise or assail? Is less harm done, or the cause of truth better served, by trying to suppress our appetite for beauty?

The difference between a "good" and a "bad" photographic image has a lot to do with our sense of whether a revelation has taken place, whether the camera has "surprised" its object and thus our own relation to it, so that we share in the surprise. When an image doesn't work, it often appears that the subject has been reduced to inexpressiveness. A great many of us believe that we are generally not good camera subjects, that we need to be protected from the kind of painful exposure that is the camera's habitual way with us. One often devises a safe camera expression, which if not convincingly natural, is at least less risky than others; the outcome is more or less predictable, and one can live with it. A good photographer is one who lessens the shock of our encounter with ourselves as images, who finds a light or frame for us that spares us in our own gaze, or on rare occasions, finds something in our social being that appears intriguingly private—a fleeting confirmation of a wish that we might actually be seen this way in unguarded moments. Movie actors who do not age in a fashion that the camera can be made to honor know more acutely than anyone else the brutal potential of images to humiliate, to strip of protective covering, and to lay open to the dangers of a terrible collective judgment. To expose what is better left hidden is the ever-present threat in the camera's doubtful promise of truth. I am reminded of Bette Davis's self-loathing masquerade in *Whatever Happened to Baby Jane?* a dismayingly overwrought attempt to outwit the camera's tyrannous, mocking probe of the aging "star" face. Davis adopts a Laughton-like gargoyle makeup that is her own worst nightmare of what the camera will eventually divulge, without her collaboration, to the public gaze. She contrives a form of nakedness that will leave room for subterranean maneuver and ironic "acting" commentary: "If I am brave enough to revel in this hideous disguise, in cruel proximity to a becomingly mature Joan Crawford who not only delights in my mortification but is made beautiful by it, I will rob the camera of its power to persecute me. I have turned myself into a spectacle more repellent than any the camera could tear from me unawares, and since I control (once again) the impression my appearance makes on those who pay to look at me, I have in effect survived my own death as a viable image." Davis's Baby Jane endures the visual equivalent of chemotherapy, choosing to undergo trauma and disfigurement in the hope that a spectral "remission" awaits her on the other side.

The prototype for this kind of humiliation is Gloria Swanson's Norma Desmond in *Sunset Boulevard*, who covets her lost place in front of the camera so fervently that life inside the image becomes her only surviving value. Norma does not know that the "truth" of a close-up will only shame her, that the longed-for shower of cinematic light, far from being a Bazinian God of love, will spear her like arrows. She will be caught in a gigantic frame whose Gorgon stare casts all of her imperfections into a permanence deeper than stone's. *Sunset Boulevard* is about a luminosity that kills rather than redeems: "When we have our naked Frailties hid / That suffer in exposure." Being open to the light of film is ordinarily understood to mean a comfortable insulation in glamour. Outside commercial cinema's repertoire of conventionalized safe reflections (which entice without wounding, but also without deepening one's view) lie the extremes of what camera images can powerfully avow: on the one hand, an increased humility about our common status as visual objects, and the freedom that comes from finding ourselves mysteriously yoked to everything we see; on the other hand, a humiliation which strips its object of privacy, forcing it into a space where no solidarity or shelter is available.

Narrative films abound in humiliation scenes. Their structure commonly traces a movement from a scalding exposure (that seems to mark a point of no return) to a partial replenishment of dignity. The hole that has burned open in a character's self-image is usually closed up by a surge of spectator sympathy/identification that has been orchestrated by the director. The camera takes us to the edge of what we can bear to witness of another's writhing in shame, then answers our need for a reprieve, providing some sort of image protection or veiling which we are tempted to regard as our own doing. It is as though our compassion proved the antidote to a character's misery and reclaimed her humanity by warming it in the light of our own. Transparency is terrifying when one is rendered "obvious" to others in the wrong way. Filmed images are able to register, with the force of a drill, this kind of transparency, born of the childhood anxiety that nothing is sufficiently yours to keep hidden from a strong, adult gaze. Film regularly restages moments when someone is effectively reduced to a stammer, to dirty, guilt-stained hands, or to a spreading, visible wetness on one's pants or dress. At such times there appears to be no way to stave off any form of censorious scrutiny. Anyone with eyes can see to the bottom of one's soul, and it is a bottom lined with sores, immutably abject.

How far is it from this sort of transparency effect to that which Bazin celebrates in his essays on the films of De Sica, where characters are said to be palpably "lit from within" by the director's love for them?[6] Does an image which enfolds some living creature in the security of a generous acceptance depend more heavily on hiddenness (the untransparent) than an image which flays? What, in other words, lies concealed in an image's act of *embracing* a subject, as De Sica's do—without apparent coercion, and allowing room for the subject's separateness, its lonely integrity? And when images are excruciating to watch, is it because things are more out in the open, or is this openness itself a narrowing of range, covering over a field of life-giving connections so that *disconnected* perceptual shocks acquire the force of an absolute? Wim Wenders's notion of "abused pictures" seems linked to a refusal of moderation. Camera vision for him is conceivably more virtuous as well as more inclusive when it is tactful, not "demanding" a response but still respectfully affiliated with what it sees. When the camera seems to lose its conscience and go too far in, say, the invasion of privacy, is it reasonable to assume that it is seeing, in its willful excess, less of a situation rather than more? What, if anything, must the camera gaze suppress or put out of focus in order to lead the viewer to a terrible extremity of "exposure" and strand him there? Extremities might be described, in this context, as places from which there is no clear path back to composure and fellow feeling. Is it possible that camera images are most true when they refuse solidarity with us, when they proclaim distance and difference above everything that might foster the illusion of our finding ourselves in them?

Susan Sontag has suggested that

> photographic images tend to subtract feeling from something we experience at first hand and the feelings they do

arouse are, largely, not those we have in real life. Often
something disturbs us more in photographed form than
it does when we actually experience it. . . . One is vulnerable to disturbing events in the form of photographic
images in a way that one is not to the real thing. That
vulnerability is part of the distinctive passivity of someone
who is a spectator twice over, spectator of events already
shaped, first by the participants and second by the image
maker.[7]

Yet surely the opposite is also true—that photographic representations
of certain kinds of horror stylize and distance in a manner that frees us
from the necessity of disturbed involvement. We are confident that we
would be more intensely shaken by an event floating loose in the world,
whose immediacy rubs against us or sweeps us, unprepared, into the
midst of danger and suffering. Our passivity before film images is typically anchored to familiar forms of emotional investment. We know
approximately how much will be asked from us, and the likely ways in
which we will make our customary payments (of fear, laughter, sentiment). But Sontag's claim that photographs tend to subtract feeling from
experience is worth thinking about. If it is true that spectator involvement in film narrative almost always lives off a current of emotion, and
perishes in its absence, the subtraction of one kind of experience-derived
feeling must be accompanied by the creation of other modes of feeling.
(And where would these surrogate emotions come from, if not from
experience?)

Perhaps the rhythm of film reality is the alternation of feelings
being "subtracted" from pictures, then "added" back to them in a different grouping. As a camera closes in on the action of a scene, for
example, the effect is generally to intensify concentration, to increase
the emotional weight of individual words, expressions, points of realization. When the camera reverses direction or reestablishes distance,
there is as a rule a felt subtraction of urgency. We are permitted, however
briefly, to exchange the accelerated perceptual involvement born of
tightening identification or thrilling trespass for a more abstract, arguably freer, activity of contemplation. Contemplation widens the field of
vision, restores a sense of larger context, and releases the spectator from
the moment-to-moment push of keyed-up, hyperbolized details. This
standing back from the artificial environment of drama is, in Wenders's
version of the ideal film, the place where narrative can give way to the
separate authority of images. The intervals in which long shots (views

from a distance) predominate achieve their truth claims by a cleansing return to less regimented perception, reminding us of the "multitudinous" dimension of appearances, all that is not confined to the exigencies of protagonist viewpoint and dramatic spectacle.

Long shots are, of course, *isolated* views of a setting in the same way that close-ups are. Any sense of internal harmony in a photograph is owing to an arrangement of scenery in which the "isolated" prospect's relation to its surroundings is deformed. And yet the crossing over from a landscape in which the camera is an anxious magnifying glass, prying out secrets from "vulnerable" faces and "exposed" actions, to a landscape where appearances regain the natural mystery of simply "being there," highlights meaningful differences in representation. The camera is as adept at robbing things of secrets as it is in giving secrets back to them. It ravages surfaces until it seems they cry out for protection or a mantle of darkness. And it honors surfaces by often appearing not to ask anything of them, rendering them with a strength of detachment that the human eye is seldom equal to.

I would like to look at a number of film scenes involving humiliation (and barely averted humiliation) of suddenly unshielded characters to illustrate more concretely my sense of how the camera continually crosses and recrosses the line between brutalizing proximity and a restorative distance. Clearly this tension depends on far more than mere camera placement. Sometimes a long shot can seem to tear away every outward support that a character pins his faith on. At the most basic level, distance can convey utter abandonment (a highest pitch of aloneness), placing characters even beyond the spectator's reach. Our desire to join with a figure on-screen as an invisible, hovering partner in grief can be defeated by the swift, cold insertion of a spatial gap, a remoteness we are powerless to lessen. A camera may also, at any point and from any distance, become a collaborator in torture, adopting the perspective of one who is justified in being merciless, or caging a too exposed victim—with no notion of what might be a permissible limit for drinking in details. A close view, conversely, can seem not to violate or bear down on a character at all, but to reveal qualities (to the beholder's protective gaze) that no one else in the world of the film is privy to, or can be made to see with the requisite intimacy of understanding. (I think immediately of Falconetti's face in Dreyer's *The Passion of Joan of Arc*.) Proximity and distance then, in the humiliation scenes I am examining, will be approached as psychic conditions, staged by the camera in strikingly diverse ways.

The Best Years of Our Lives (1946), a film Andre Bazin extolled for its "democratic" use of deep focus, contains a scene in which Homer Parrish, a sailor whose hands have been amputated as a result of a war injury, invites his girl friend, Wilma, to watch him prepare for bed. The episode is noteworthy for its preoccupation with an impending (and voluntary) humiliation that the spectator is certain cannot come to pass. The scene instructs us in all the ways the camera can save a character who pushes himself to the brink of self-abasement. Homer's motive, unambiguously specified, is to show Wilma how grotesque and helpless he will appear to her once he removes his prosthetic hooks. Having seen him so pitiably reduced, Wilma must, in his view, share his realization that they have no future together as a couple. His wholly honorable purpose is to frighten her with the magnitude of the emotional adjustment she would have to make to his irrevocably diminished person. Once she has been obliged to look at his shortened limbs at close range, in full light, her protective sympathy will not be enough—he reasonably fears—to keep her from turning away from him. Her devotion as a friend, her unfailingly good intentions, her memory-suffused attachment to his prewar condition, are not of themselves an adequate basis for a marriage. He undresses himself, hardly daring to consult her eyes, in which something as final as a death sentence on her romantic feeling for him might, quite understandably, be reflected.

What further complicates this episode of valorous self-shaming is the spectator's knowledge that the actor playing Homer, Harold Russell, is also an amputee, bearing an authentic physical loss from his own experience in World War II. If the character, Homer, then, suffers genuine humiliation in Wilma's (and the camera's) sight, we cannot take refuge in the assumption that Harold Russell is not personally at risk in what he displays to us. The scene's potential pathos is enormously enhanced by our awareness that within the framework of fiction we are taking part in a real unmasking. If the camera does not find a means to validate Homer that is distinct from the contrivances of melodrama, if his wounds, in other words, fail to secure a significance beyond their power to elicit our momentary tears, then a second level of shaming (this one unintentional) emerges. At the same time, the inescapability of Harold Russell's real disfigurement, in this episode and throughout the film, limits the narrative's capacity to add a demanding internal burden to the damage the veteran "wears" outwardly. This disquietingly literal victim can be shown (as a character) contending with his family's and friends' awkwardness and discomfort as they painfully adapt to his new appearance and altered prospects, since scenes of this kind stress other people's attitudes and "misguided" behavior as the major source of his problems. But the strength of his own resolve to make a meaningful life for himself, at whatever cost, must never be seriously in doubt. Otherwise, fiction would seem to be conspiring sadistically against the future hopes of one who has suffered a devastating loss in wartime service.

The hyperreality of the images of Homer's hooks automatically confer an exemplary status on this character and his fate. He can hardly escape the task of representing the countless other maimed veterans who are similarly engaged in finding their way back into the alien weave of family and community: a new enemy territory. The film aspires to be perfectly convincing in its surface depiction of Homer's dilemma, while offering every conceivable assurance that the long ordeal of homecoming will ultimately give "lost" soldiers the fulfillment they seek.

The humiliation scene, therefore, must have precisely and unequivocally the opposite effect from that which Homer anticipates. Neither Wilma nor the camera can be permitted to join for an instant in Homer's plan to punishingly expose himself. A visual climate needs to be established that will reveal Homer's "deformities," first, as wholly amenable to dispassionate rational inquiry and, second, as allowing an immediate acknowledgment of unconditional love. The psychic regions in the spectator which might lead him, in other contexts, to savor the lurid evidence of grotesque or aberrant appearance; to be excited by a monster's afflictions or amused by his seeking vengeance; to gather at fires or collisions in the irrational grip of a desire to see strangers suffering—all of these suspect appetites must be rigorously held in check if Homer is to be safe in the spectator's presence. Wilma's manner of watching him as he removes his shirt and hooks—calm, unsurprised, ready to intervene when he requires assistance, unwavering in her preparedness to love whatever she sees (because what she sees is Homer)—is presented as synonymous with the camera's own method of absorbing what shame uncovers. The audience is meant to become Wilma as we are tutored by her healing gaze; there is, in fact, a palpable pressure to emulate this gaze and thus become worthier of such unequivocal feelings ourselves.

Still, there are peculiarities in the staging of the episode. Wilma following Homer upstairs to his bedroom moves with the measured solemnity of a priestess in a formalized rite. It is as though the action she is about to witness is somehow already completed and possessed, by foreknowledge. She enters this ritual space with no hint of trepidation; she appears as prepared for her task as a madonna receiving for the thousandth time, in the dolorous peace of a late medieval tableau, the burden of her crucified son's body. William Wyler, the film's director, is a specialist in the high drama of minute shifts of expression in close-up. Perhaps his most famous scene is Herbert Marshall's death by heart attack in *The Little Foxes,* which we see reflected in the terrifyingly still, clenched face of his implacable wife (Bette Davis). As he staggers behind her, trying to climb the stairs to reach his medicine, she stares forward, willing his collapse and destruction, yet visibly stunned by the totality of her surrender to cold-bloodedness. In its agonizing, held-breath duration, this close-up gives us the impression we are attending to something unspeakable, which is nonetheless rooted in impulses that are not in the least foreign to us. Davis's fixity of expression is deceptive. We are actually allowed to see a tight mask grow tighter, more rigid still, as she tries to be at once wholly focused and wholly removed from what she is doing. And our share in the process is to pretend to resist the lure of her charismatic malevolence, to simplify our response to an appropriately *full* revulsion. The few close-ups of Wilma in the *Best Years of Our Lives* bedroom scene carry no suggestion of feelings in transition. They are the reverse of the steadily complicating Davis close-up in *The Little Foxes;* here we are concerned with feelings that prove their worth by holding fast. Any capitulation to doubt, on Wilma's part, however fleeting, might break Homer further, might push him more dangerously out in the open, where the threat of unregulated perception of his wounds would allow shame a real point of entry. Wyler, a master of humiliation scenes throughout his career as a director, is attempting here to design an antihumiliation scene, where the dreaded self-exposure "miscarries," and every suggestion of abasement is met and dissolved by love.

Lurking about the edges of this dramatic situation is the inadmissible pleasure, so often exploited in other movie narratives, of watching nasty or ignorant strength prey upon a too naked weakness. The removal of a victim's last line of defense, which confirms their (and possibly our) worst fear of lying helpless in an attack, is part of the general atmosphere of war which Wyler must consistently oppose in this film, however often he has savored cruelty, in all its guises, elsewhere. Homer's security within his bedroom must be absolutely walled off from the perils of combat. The remedy for war's ghastly surprises and unending eruptions of chance misfortune is a realm in which nothing whatever is left to chance. No discordant gesture, word, or look will leap out at us during Homer's disrobing, so that our perspective on the event will be even lightly menaced by uncertainty. Voices throughout are as quietly contained as Wilma's perfectly calm, unflinching concentration. And although Homer is implicitly asking Wilma whether she will be able to regard him, unpityingly, as an acceptable sexual partner, there seems to be no way that the unpredictable force of sexual tension can be brought for so much as an instant into play. Wilma, like all of the good women associated with veterans in *Best Years,* enfolds her psychically fragile charge in a selfless embrace of mother love. Before kissing him good night, she radiantly tucks him in, as though there could be no deeper satisfaction. Visible passion, like visible doubt, might increase the like-lihood of Homer's humiliation by the camera. Excess of every sort must be purged from view so that the camera's skill at entrapping objects in the wrong kind of light cannot be exercised.

The impression of camera reverence for what it sees may depend in general (as it does here) on a restriction of the mobility of perspectives, especially volatile perspectives which switch, without warning, from one set of feelings to another. Wyler's respectful standing back from a dra-matic situation through a restrained visual treatment evokes the idea of a potentially comprehensible world beyond the distorting optics of in-dividual moods (ever-fluctuating, extravagant). But this contemplative view is purchased at the expense of everything that resists containment, that veers away from the settled state. Homer's self-exposure to Wilma takes place in a climate that is wholly amenable to patient, rational inquiry. The bedroom's seeming rightness as a field for true vision emerges only after all that is dangerous, forbidden, or extreme is un-obtrusively disposed of as "unnatural." If we were to break the spell by asserting our immoderate difference from Wilma (say, our greater ca-pacity for shock or discomfort or nervous laughter), we challenge the authority of the camera to specify what is really there, and take on the humiliation that Homer is spared (visually, dramatically) as our own. Is our freedom to make such a counterstatement worth anything, the scene, in its near-unearthly composure, *rationally* asks us.

In Roman Polanski's *The Tenant* (1976), by contrast, an apparently tiny humiliation episode expands to gigantic dimensions without the first-time viewer being allowed to see (or in any direct fashion, know) how this is happening. The purpose of the scene is secretly to generate a discomfort out of all proportion to the mildly embarrassing "facts" of the situation, so that we can't identify a specific worry or source of fear and secure a familiar relation to it. Trelkovsky (played by Polanski) wakes up the morning after a "housewarming" party that he has hosted in his newly acquired Paris apartment for a group of disagreeable fellow office workers, and discovers that the floor of his bedroom is strewn with bits of spilled food. We next see him carrying two large bags and a plastic pail of collected party waste down the main staircase of his building and encountering his landlord, who wants to "know the meaning" of the previous night's celebration, whose noise level had interfered with his sleep. After demanding that the heavily-encumbered Trelkovsky offer an immediate explanation for his inconsiderateness, the landlord (Msr. Zy) makes a great show of not listening to it, consulting his watch and frowning as Trelkovsky, staggering under his load, tries to assure him of his good intentions, his reasonableness, and his resolve to be a model of caution in the future. Barely placated, Msr. Zy tells him, as he turns away to begin a slow descent of the stairs, that he had been strongly tempted to "take steps" to cancel his lease for this first breach of faith. Good apartments, he warns, are difficult to find. One of Trelkovsky's bags has been on the point of leaking garbage throughout this exchange. The words that the two men speak, in fact, register far less strongly to the viewer than the widening wet stain on the almost dropped, filled-to-bursting paper bag. Trelkovsky's painfully conspicuous predicament is one to which Msr. Zy remains steadfastly oblivious. He neither hears his tenant's justification nor takes in the sight of the unmanageable refuse. No aspect of Trelkovsky's presence that might humanize him seems strong enough to penetrate Msr. Zy's awareness.

When the landlord's departing form is separated from Trelkovsky by a full flight of stairs, a piece of fruit escapes from the finally ruptured sack, audibly hitting the step that Msr. Zy has just passed. Fortunately, he fails to notice the fruit's arrival, and the possible stain it has made on his venerable, immaculate, and expensive-looking stair carpeting. No sooner has he disappeared, however, than this advance piece of offensive matter is followed by many others, each of them slipping uncontrollably through a soggy rent so large and lengthening that Trelkovsky cannot cover it or stem the flow. Each fresh chunk released onto the carpet during Trelkovsky's ignominious retreat from the building has an identical aggressive tactility, on the order of spilled coffee grounds. Everything is moist and clammy—unappetizing to look at, demeaning to scoop up, almost certain to leave a stain or accusing residue. When Trelkovsky at last reaches the courtyard garbage cans and disposes what is left of his load, the discovery of his little crime by one or more sour fellow tenants, so far avoided, seems to loom in the scowling face of the concierge who observes him from her window.

The dramatic question arising at this point in the scene is naturally, will he be able to clean up his mess before he is found out? (The odds appear to be against him.) And further, perhaps because we have no wish to watch him collect his bits of discharge, or even be obliged to regard it at closer range, there is a competing pressure at work in the scene to have him flee the evidence of his transgression, and face the unpleasant consequences later. What one is given no time or prompting to expect is that Trelkovsky's garbage problem will be magically taken care of. We are meant to share his astonishment as he returns to the staircase, clearly within moments of ridding himself of the bags, and beholds a carpet entirely free of his waste. He slowly climbs the steps in an effort to determine whether the garbage had, contrary to recollection, stopped falling at a higher flight, and also to search out the stranger who has inexplicably undertaken this filthy task. The stairs stretch out, before his and our gaze, empty and spotless. As we begin to search Trelkovsky's expression for a possible clue as to what is going on and how to interpret it, the scene abruptly ends, cut off—as it were—in mid-sentence (or mid-air), with the mysterious cleansing of one source of anxiety the very thing which produces a second level of anxiety. The carpet would seem to have repressed its own befouling, so that its final neatness is visually superimposed on a "dirt" that is still there somehow, waiting for a chance to resurface.

The basic situation in this strange episode resembles a silent comedy routine. If it were Chaplin overloaded with trash bags, haplessly seeking to escape his landlord while trying to keep a recalcitrant sack from ripping and causing further damage, the action would be uncomplicatedly amusing. The garbage would have no visceral impact or independent presence; nor would it insinuate itself into a festering, undismissable kinship with the clown's inner life. In Polanski's version, the routine is performed by a figure whose forebears might be the shit-and-vomit-soaked inhabitants of a Celine novel. Polanski has cunningly introduced a small, easily overlooked triggering mechanism for our "held between mental fingers" intimacy with the scene's griminess. The director's planting of an exactly suitable contagious detail is an example of what the painter Pierre Bonnard refers to as composition at the second degree: "bringing back certain elements which lie outside the rectangle [frame]." Polanski breaks the frame of the comic scene by forcing it to assimilate something that went before, something that is too extreme in its sensory claims on us to lie still and let familiar jokes play over it. Its nasty excess functions in the manner of a possibly cancerous lump one's fingers have nervously detected, for the first time, on one's neck. One's entire body and its fate are suddenly reduced to the size of this lump, and live only in terms of its significance.

The triggering mechanism in the Polanski scene occurs at the beginning: Trelkovsky accidentally steps on a bit of wet, discolored vegetable matter as his feet shift from the bed to the floor, just after he awakens. As Trelkovsky peels the scrap of food from the sole of his foot, we are meant to feel a sympathetic memory shudder of unsavory, leech-like stickiness on our own momentarily "exposed" skin. The viewer's sense of touch is activated here with the same tingling precision as it is in the scene from *The Night of the Iguana* when Richard Burton's Reverend Shannon walks barefoot over shards of broken glass in a fit of sexual agitation so deep as to keep him from feeling the cuts. We suffer the twinges on his behalf, as it were, along with a mounting dread that if he does not swiftly get clear of this mutilating ground his feet will be so gashed that they will have *too many* places to bleed from. A host of little wounds multiplies the sensations of out-of-controlness, unstopp-ability in a most upsetting way. In *The Tenant*, our fingers seem uncomfortably joined with Trelkovsky's as he removes the distasteful food-worm from its clinging place. Thus, our touch involvement extends from the point of his recoiling at the sight of the object he has stepped on until it has been pulled off. There is something transmitted to our fingers as well in Trelkovsky's gesture of wiping his own soiled fingertips on the leg of his pajamas. The queasiness aroused by this need to rid oneself of taint *immediately* while at the same time holding onto it (moving the dirt to another part of one's person) is vastly compounded in the stairway scene, which we jump into just as Trelkovsky completes his wiping motion. His hands are now clutching a great deal more of the slippery remains of his dinner party that he has not yet *finished* dealing with in the galling singular. Because we have already been made to handle one piece of garbage with him, and perhaps carry its moist imprint on our own foot, where we felt it sticking, all subsequent appearances of discharge from the soggy bag are overdetermined in their effect. Polanski counts on the viewer involuntarily responding, at her fingertips, to each additional unsavory lump dropping on the carpet. We imagine (with our bodies) having to pick up all the defiling muck that belongs to us and put it out of sight. And the task gradually expands past our best capacity for coping with it. The multiplier here is very much like the field of shattered glass in *The Night of the Iguana*: too many puncture points translates into leakage beyond remedy (or more precisely, leakage beyond the power of our feelings, at that moment, to contain).

Trelkovsky's encounter with his unyielding landlord is a drama of appeasement played out with all the victim's unsayable retorts to ill treatment gathered in his arms. The bulging garbage bags threatening to give way correspond exactly with Trelkovsky's filled-to-bursting inner state. Trelkovsky's strained meekness as his unlistened-to apology stretches out to ever more cumbersome and pointless length is a barely controlled enactment of composure. He strives to dissociate himself from his seething resentment at having to coddle a tyrant, but the tilting bag with its widening stain overrides the willed blandness of face and voice. If the bag were to empty itself on Msr. Zy, it would be a diffident man's innocent revenge: "I held on as long as I could. I was helpless to stop things once the bag broke. The rubbish had a mind of its own." But the garbage has as much difficulty releasing itself in the landlord's presence as Trelkovsky has releasing his rage.

Our identification prior to this stage of the narrative has been with the well-mannered Trelkovsky, more or less by default. Thus far he has been nearly the sole alternative in the world of the film to a crude, unappealingly loud and narrow-minded aggression that is established as the "mechanical" norm of human exchanges. Trelkovsky has attained a frail but meaningful edge of superiority in the majority of his interactions by being civil and courteous, and by refusing, sometimes slyly, the repeatedly offered bait of rudeness. Too much submissiveness, of course, brings about a strong desire for at least an occasional escape of unfairly bottled-up instincts. Spectators typically ally themselves with long-suffering, passive protagonists in the expectation (and hope) that they will eventually be pushed to their breaking point and earn a just, violent reprieve from "goodness." In *The Tenant,* all the "unharnessed" retribution will turn out to be self-directed, as Trelkovsky is slowly revealed to the viewer as someone lost, unreclaimably, in madness. His apparently justified paranoia at the ghastly belligerence and ceaseless provocations of those with whom he has social dealings has been the deceptive basis of our initial participation in his experience. Without warning, his perspective becomes radically untrustworthy, and the spectator has no choice but to divorce herself from her earlier friendly attachment. Yet the emotional threats that Trelkovsky faces are so vivid and suffocatingly immediate that it is almost impossible not to keep crossing back over the line into unwanted merger with his way of seeing things. Neither the certainty that he is frighteningly deranged nor the desire to keep one's distance from his steadily more repellent and self-destructive behavior are adequate safeguards, in my experience, against renewed identification with him. Polanski constructs his scenes so adroitly that one is continually maneuvered into readopting Trelkovsky's point of view (like an old habit) without conscious consent, and then feeling entrapped by it and struggling to disentangle oneself from him while at the same time drinking in the fear of his predicament.

In the stairway scene, the camera appears to alternate between an "open," objective view of what is taking place and a natural, tightening identification with Trelkovsky as he contends with the landlord and then, in isolation, with the dripping garbage. Underlying these legible, convention-defined camera strategies is a covert attempt to transfer ownership of the visual field to the unforgiving Msr. Zy by, in effect, internalizing his stare and the fathomless depth of its potential condemnation. While the landlord is still physically present, one is led to wonder why he does not register the splitting garbage bag as a presence, if only to upbraid Trelkovsky for not packing it more carefully. It is possible for us to hold such a question in combination with a desire that the unheeded threat may erupt on him, an outcome that would "serve him right." But as I have already noted, the secret quarry of Polanski's camera here, and essential preparation for what follows, is still another recognition—that Trelkovsky's being is somehow expressed or contained by the bags he holds. The objects are a more direct and emphatic assertion of his state of mind than his spare, politely withholding manner. It is useful to recall that the two-dimensional plane of the screened image can easily be made to privilege objects over people, granting the former instant centrality and greater emotional weight. When the first and only intact piece of fruit slips free of the bag and rolls over the landing to *almost* strike Msr. Zy, it is an amusing instance of the garbage bag's capacity to act as Trelkovsky's surrogate in mild aggression. The mobile object is like a muttered insult carried almost within earshot of one's enemy. And because the intended offense doesn't reach its destination, it mutely reverts to Trelkovsky (as something not gotten rid of, which must be covered up). He seems characteristically to have launched an ineffectual protest. The final status of this teasingly defiant, advance scout object is that of an "act" which escaped detection, an innocently insulting gesture which can be safely returned "inside" Trelkovsky. This momentary escape from the landlord's stare is the means by which the staircase is redefined visually in terms of that stare. We are reminded that everything in the building comes under his surveillance, and that nothing shameful or discrediting will escape it for very long. And within this realm of vigilant scrutiny, Trelkovsky's insides begin to give way, leaving excremental deposits (or "bad" thoughts that cannot be kept in place) too numerous, too adhesively stuck for him ever to regain control of. It is as though his inner life has migrated to the carpet, objectified as a repeating spasm of foulness, and in this more solid, credible form seeks to expose its former possessor by living nakedly in the other's gaze.

The camera does not soften Trelkovsky's descent to the inanimate, nor does it protect him from the consequences of this breakdown of boundaries. What the image "knows" as it amplifies the significance of this mess is what Trelkovsky's landlord would know, as though the camera had turned informant rather than share the tenant's secret. "I've found you out. You are the culprit," it declares. "Look at what you've done. You'd better leave each and every smeared carpet step as clean as you found it." Meanwhile, the spectator's hands, against his will, are repeating the touching gesture that was "instilled" in the prior bedroom scene; his fingers approach the moist leavings, one after another. As the sprinkling of Trelkovsky's innards threatens to become a downpour, the task of retrieval and concealment becomes so repellently vast that the viewer self-protectively breaks contact with the suddenly too infectious victim. Almost literally, we wash our hands of him. The simplest way to effect this break is to occupy the camera-as-landlord perspective that has been set up in anticipation of our arrival. The discomfort the viewer experiences at a form of sensory overload she has no time to rationally evaluate can transform, defensively, into anger at Trelkovsky for not having spared her such unpleasantness.

Thus we begin by claiming the mess as our own through our prickly identification with Trelkovsky, and end by shifting our loyalty to the carpet, whose fastidiousness, like ours, has been excessively violated. Trelkovsky teeters under his ugly load on the stairs, more isolated and shrunken than ever by the double draining of the bag-as-self and the viewer's sympathy. When Trelkovsky returns to the stairway after ridding himself of the bags it is as someone who, oddly and inscrutably (like Joseph K. in *The Trial*) merits punishment for a murky crime: a crime that is as manifest as oozing footprints leading back to his door and as elusive as a fleeting evil thought. Trelkovsky is humiliated by thoughts which have turned visible and tactile, challenging the notion that the mind's furtive workings are inaccessible to the camera's gaze. As the tenant returns to the shameful trail he has left, and fails to find it, he (and we) share an anxious bewilderment at its vanishing.

The spectator recovers a close to full involvement with Trelkovsky's point of view at the moment the camera asserts the absence of any trace of an experience that had seemed, throughout its unfolding, inescapably *material*. Instead of relief that the apparatus of humiliation has been eliminated with a cat-in-the-hat thoroughness, Polanski posits a threat of excessive cleanliness dwelling on the reverse side of excessive soiling. It is as though our own prior wish that the foulness go away has been fulfilled at the cost of all perceptual stability. A small child watches as

its feces swirl down the toilet hole, then is filled with fear at its disappearance. "I must have it back again. It is part of me. Without it I am
less, maybe nothing. Mother/'me' might wash away just as easily. Where
did 'I'/it go, in separating from the rest of me?" Trelkovsky is left suspended with his unanswerable thoughts, which may themselves be the
place where his filth (and ours as well) is hiding. The camera restores
the clean carpet to us in the form of a surface to which nothing adheres.
Where, if not here, is Trelkovsky to go looking for himself? The meager
personal life has retreated to the point where it can leave no marks upon
the world. Even Trelkovsky's shame does not belong to him.

The next form of humiliation scene I wish to consider is perhaps
the most familiar from our dream life. A large audience or crowd is
made an essential component of the process. The camera can assume
the outlook of a lynch mob, of course, when there are only one or two
characters present, and rob any action of its claims to privacy. Paradoxically, the necessity of private space for guarding all that is most
vulnerable and inexpressible in the human is nowhere more powerfully
realized in film than in scenes where crowds anonymously enclose or
angrily assail the individual. One of the earliest and most enduring
conventions of movie narrative is the idea of waiting for a crowd to
part like a curtain so that a single point of interest will be disclosed at
the heart of it. In general, the meaning of crowds in film images is
something that stands, however inattentively, against the personal. The
personal continually requires visual rescue from the mass, or needs to
become its sympathetic center of focus if it is not to be dangerously
diluted.

The young boy and his father, with their backs to us, who dissolve
into the throng filling the city street in the final shot of *Bicycle Thieves*
(1948), do not, as might seem to be the case, become one with them.
The shot, in my view, enjoins us to challenge the film's authority to take
this intensely particularized pair away from us. The camera, in the act
of relinquishing them to a multitude that would have no reason to single
them out or value the significance of what they have been through together, generates a need in us to turn them around in memory so that
they continue to face us. If the spectator manages to hold onto them,
against the pull of the crowd, and brings to a kind of memory-stasis the
emotions illuminated in their last actions (thereby protecting them from
the further humiliation of oblivion: tragedy too shapeless and unmarked
to count for anything), then they are not lost. Vittorio De Sica, the
film's director, would, of course, not have us leave the crowd out of
account. The mass, he wishes us to understand, is composed of cease-

lessly multiplying instances, wherever we care to enter crowds and observe closely, of the things we have learned to honor in our experience of an "ordinary" father and son. Ricci and Bruno, in other words, are reflected everywhere in the hidden life of the crowd. Nonetheless, our crucial, just completed empathic act leads us to protest, at least momentarily, the abrupt disappearance into the mass of the two figures that we have come to know. If we feel no pressure to retrieve their separateness, and keep the precise form of their private experience intact, then what leads us to imagine (or think ourselves answerable for) the fate of the chaotic, unencompassable whole?

A brilliantly bizarre scene in the melodrama *Humoresque* (1946) involves the humiliation of a secondary character (Gina, played by Joan Chandler) while she sits concealed in a large concert audience listening to her beloved Paul Boray (John Garfield) play the violin. Gina gradually becomes aware that he is not only addressing his impassioned musical performance to another woman (Joan Crawford), who sits high above her in an opera box, but that the current of music is received so completely by this majestic rival that she is telepathically making love to him. It is not merely the case then of a character discovering, while trapped in the heedless company of others, that someone else has secured the love that she hoped for. The music issuing from Garfield's violin is a secret conduit for actual caresses and whispered intimacies, and is driving its elected object to an exquisite rapture, framed in mammoth, shimmering close-ups. Gina finds herself a frozen witness to a sex scene, as surely as if she had inadvertently opened the door of an occupied bedroom. She is initially caught in the net of Garfield's autocratic harmonies, whose spirit she is so attuned to that she knows the music utterly excludes her. She alone, in this vast audience, can find no point of entry to the performance. The import of the melody is not to remember her, by so much as a distant echo. Gina is then caught in a chain of looks from which she cannot free herself: intensifying close-up communication between Crawford and Garfield's entranced playing in which the romantic stakes are raised higher and higher. The large audience's blindness to this exchange, and the lovers' innocent unmindfulness of everything but their own happiness, exacerbates the force and pain of Gina's isolated seeing. Eventually, as the musically deified couple move toward some transcendent climax, the completely dissolved, disposable witness (whose suffering, even for the spectator, matters far less than the couple's unearthly mingling) flees the concert hall. But her humiliation seems widened and deepened by her flight. Not only does Garfield's still audible music pursue her into the night like an avenging Fury, but she is also obliged to pass, in a heavy rain, poster after poster of Garfield, violin regally in hand, stretching endlessly across the front of the hall.

The whole episode has something of the impersonal terror one associates with ancient mythology. The camera, cruelly complicit in enforcing god vs. human distinctions, depicts a young woman venturing into an arena reserved for more titanic presences (equal in scale to the music), then crushing her for her pitiable mortal's weakness. In Ovid, her being discovered where she does not belong would result in her shedding her human form in the attempt to escape. Her destiny would be translation into some tumultuous reflection of sightless fleeing: a rushing stream, perhaps, whose only thought is "away, away, away from here."

In the justly famous, public humiliation scene from Josef von Sternberg's *The Blue Angel* (1930), an Ovidean release from the captivity of "disgrace without limits" is literally enacted. Professor Immanuel Rath (Emil Jannings) has returned to the town where he once held a relatively distinguished position as teacher to perform as a clown in a cabaret act for the entertainment of his appalled former colleagues, his once hated, now vengeful former students, and a horde of others who have caught a premonitory whiff of blood in the air. As Rath submits to having a knife plunged into his hat to demonstrate his empty-headedness and to having eggs broken upon his head to roars of murderous audience laughter, he becomes aware that the woman for whom he sacrificed his position and self-respect is embracing a new lover in the wings. Urged by the magician who has organized the performance to crow like a rooster in reply to the egg breaking, Rath disappears into a terrifyingly demented impersonation of a rooster, making shrill birdlike noises with the abandonment of one who has shredded his last few ties with the human realm.

The magic act is designed to show Rath blankly assenting to torture that the assembled audience can have faith in as legitimate and "unstaged." The once stern and pedantic language teacher has been poured, as in a conjuring trick, from one rigid container (the costume of authority) into another (a benumbed clown's head, with a disease-fattened nose and a right eye ferociously slit by a greasepaint razor scar). And if the crowd is not to grow sated and weary with the static spectacle—as in the restlessness following a decapitation: what *more* is there to see?—the magician must contrive an even narrower container for his pathetic slave to occupy. The relief Rath finds in his demonic crowing comes from the fact that the sounds he makes at last seem to give full expression to whatever is left inside him. The crowing becomes a command which silences and renders impossible the disciplinary force of the social world. And the film's soundtrack, in its creaking, "dawn of talkies" antiquity, seems to awaken to this new command (in its piercing, repetitive exorbitance) as it has to no other. The bird shriek rises above the foggy ambience of the crowd's reaction and swiftly obliterates it altogether. Moreover, after Rath's eruption there are no more views of the theater audience, as though Rath's cries have dissolved not only its power over him but its very existence. Seldom if ever has castration been so exultantly seized as an answer to prayer. The public skewering of his barely surviving manhood frees Rath, ironically, of the burdens of servility. His crowing may prevail over the crowd's insupportable derision by becoming one with it, as in the schizophrenic fantasy of being joined to a great throng even when alone, and taking one's freedom to move and launch attacks from the collective noise pressing up from within. In Elias Canetti's metaphor, the borrowed strength of countless neighboring voices is like the thrill of slipping out of the house undetected to join a gathering mob in the darkened streets, leaving one's slave mentality and its fears "piled in the cellar."[8]

Prior to Rath's entrance as the clown in the magic act, we see him hiding behind glistening gauze curtains, which clearly afford inadequate protection from the audience's hungry scanning of the stage. At various points in his subsequent ordeal, he vaguely retreats to the white-curtain screen in the hope that it might furnish an escape route, and more than once nearly wraps himself up in it. It is reasonable to think of this curtain as a surrogate movie screen and Rath—as stranded as Buster Keaton before the dreamed movie screen in *Sherlock, Jr.*—appealing to the camera which has laid bare all its devices for negative exposure to spare him the last extremities of indignity. Arguably to an even greater extent than Polanski in *The Tenant*, director von Sternberg is, throughout *The Blue Angel*, an accomplice in Professor Rath's persecution. He refuses to explore the downfall of this miserably isolated, passion-blinded martinet of a schoolteacher from the "inside," and does not readily regard his final condition as worthy of tragic sympathy. Against the apparent logic of the story, von Sternberg seems to collude with the glitteringly amoral conduct of the temptress figure, Lola-Lola (Marlene Dietrich). Her harsh playfulness and coolly self-absorbed survivor tenacity so intensely engage him that they become the film's real, if sometimes covert, center of value.

It would be wrong, however, to claim that the camera finds common cause with the jeering audience and Lola in the final humiliation scene. Rath's harrowing clown face is so eloquently expressive that it attains unchallengeable image authority. Yet there is a sense that the camera does not wish to save him or shield him from any moment of what he is forced to endure. It does not seek out his privacy or bracket off a visual space in which he can deliver himself to us in different terms than his hideous exhibition to the crowd allows. His clown make-up, in its masklike fixity, stands between us and Rath, issuing, to be sure, an anguished bulletin from the dark interior, but not in a personalized form. We could not begin to answer the question of what possesses Rath to agree to this stage appearance, when the outcome is so certain. Rath's relation with himself in the concluding phases of his descent matters much less to von Sternberg than his arrival at some awesome absolute of degradation, where the human becomes so unknowable, so sabotaged in its will to privacy that it has to erupt as something else. The camera embraces completely Rath's emergence as the mad, screeching bird, granting at last the acknowledgment it has withheld for as long as he resisted, with any show of self-awareness, his fate. I am reminded of the rapturous cock-crow in Herman Melville's story "Cock-a-Doodle-Doo!" which instantly robs those who hear it of any sense of human woe, however hopeless their plight.[9] The mere sound of the bird imparts a monstrous animation and giddiness to all the broken spirits it reaches. The crowing enters them like a contagion, so even if one is witnessing the death of one's child, the parent has no choice but to exult.

The reverse of this depersonalizing effect of camera humiliation is achieved in my concluding example, from James Ivory's *Mr. and Mrs. Bridge* (1990). Douglas Bridge (Robert Sean Leonard) stands with a hundred or more young men in a municipal auditorium to receive, like them, his Eagle Scout badge. The awarding ceremony has been arranged to include a tribute to the Eagle Scouts' mothers, without whose "help, love, and encouragement" the coveted highest rank in scouting could not have been achieved. The mothers, all wearing an honorary red rose pinned to their breasts, are proudly seated beside their sons, who stand with military formality while a senior scout official declares that the moment has come for the Eagle-elects to say, "each in the way *she* likes best, 'Thank you, mother.' " Douglas's mother, India (Joanne Wood-ward) sits expectantly as the assembly of sons turn on cue to bend and kiss their mothers, while whispering assurances of gratitude and devotion. She suddenly realizes, with heart-shrivelling impact, that her son alone has remained standing and facing forward. Though the "thank yous" take but a few seconds to complete, she appears to be cast into an eternity of "exposure," as one publicly shunned by a child who cannot perform a simple gesture of filial respect.

At the same time, we see Douglas's acute discomfort at finding himself immobilized. It is not that he is deliberately punishing her in this dreadful fashion. He is, in the language of scouting, "unprepared," having no history of emotional ease with her to draw upon. The prospect of initiating physical contact with her is more alarming to him than the alternative danger of judgment by the assembled onlookers. He trembles with shock at the enormity of his affront, then goes rigid with the effort to put it out of mind. He executes an "about face" with the other scouts, and is greeted with everyone's applause, including his mother's. He finally joins the entire audience in singing "America the Beautiful," carefully avoiding looking at his mother or anything else as he tries not to let any part of what he is feeling "touch" him. One recalls that in the scene immediately before this one he repeatedly flinched and recoiled as his mother attempted to fuss with his uniform and bullyingly pamper him. Now his body and face seem to be fending off the invisible supplicating hands of a prostrate victim.

India Bridge, for her part, is immolated on the altar of propriety. She has dedicated her entire married life to maintaining appearances and "good manners," without a single, significant deviation from the prescribed norms of her privileged class. She is always on the verge of discovering that she doesn't believe in the value of any of the forms she fearfully follows to the letter. It is not only then her accomplishments as a mother, which she has seldom dared to dwell on, that are nullified at the Eagle Scout ceremony, but her whole life as a *purely* appearance-defined being. She sits trapped in the midst of row after row of nicely regimented good citizens in the making. She has no choice but to compose herself (for the sake of what others might think) and find the strength to sing "America the Beautiful" along with everyone else. No soldier about to enter combat has more inner disturbance to subdue than India Bridge as she tries to locate her breath, remember the words to the song, and obliterate consciousness, like her son, in the "drowning pool" of this communal act. Her body reverts, awkwardly, to her prepared script for the evening, and she stands exactly as she would as if she had every reason to be swelling with maternal pride.

At some distance from India sits her husband, Walter (Paul Newman) who witnesses her suffering with discomfort and a slow-footed partial awareness of its magnitude. What he cannot grasp from his "viewing distance" is that Douglas's stiffness and incapacity to give his mother "normal" expressions of affection are modeled closely on his own behavior toward her. Later in the evening he will try to make it up to her in their bedroom, while she gazes in despair at her rose. His version of consolation is, not surprisingly, sexual, the only sort of physical contact he can allow himself, and, as it happens, the kind of attention that means least to her.

There is nothing cold in director James Ivory's quality of detachment from this "minor" incident, and no obstacles to a spectator's desire for wide vision: the fullest possible seeing of what's there. The characters' wounds are amply rendered, but the camera gains its power of discernment in part by seeming to have no specific emotional demands to make on us. We are entrusted to complete the spectacle for ourselves by deciding where, and with what degree of intensity, to place the emphasis. The camera eye, on this occasion, is not synonymous with the crowd's, nor is it that of a greedy spy, devouring whatever better-left-private scraps are set before it. I feel compelled to reinvoke Bazin's metaphor of figures "lit from within," as though the camera's so frequently defeated quest for divinity had once again been rewarded. The sad plight of these characters is accepted with the composure that may be the camera's best equivalent of love. The scale of the action is resolutely, and appropriately, modest. Any visual declaration that we are in the presence of a "big scene" would be ruinous to the overall effect, which depends on a scrupulous avoidance of virtuosity in style. We lack any sense that the telling moments are pushed forward—pressed to the camera grindstone, as it were, for an extra flurry of sparks.

Significance is reserved for the implications of mutually incomprehensible wrongdoing. How *easily* this particular son's offense might have been avoided, and yet the Bridges' habitual practice of communication through numbness (where distance is as indispensable as a heartbeat) made it "unthinkable" for Douglas to act otherwise. Douglas fully intends to do what is expected of him, but a bewildering tightness overtakes him, and he misses the moment when he might save his mother from an all-encompassing shame. In the smallness of the gap between an almost sufficient intention and a lost deed, we are meant to see (hardly for the first time) how things become what they already are, in the stark intervals of human inadequacy. The scene is composed entirely of things being withheld, under terrific strain; and yet every feeling, failing to find its proper outlet, stays miraculously within reach of the camera.

Custom lies upon the Bridges, in Wordsworth's phrase, "with a weight / Heavy as frost, and deep almost as life." Director Ivory so unobtrusively, so *lightly* tunnels through this heaviness, finally touching its quivering roots, that the effect is transfiguring. By requiring us to hold at one time so many separate and contrary shares in the making of an event, the scene gains its impact from something more than sheer force of pathos. Our urge to sympathize, denied a single resting place, overspreads the whole, mingling with the thwarted desire that someone (but who?) be made accountable for all this pain. Perhaps once we have acknowledged our secret kinship with the camera's incitements to cruelty in this and similarly powerful scenes of humiliation, our relationship to the camera's balancing moments of clemency and restitution will be more authentic. By participating with equal force in both, we may appropriately elect *ourselves* to bear the burden of answerability.

9

Obvious Mysteries in *Fargo*

> How do you mean all this—truthfully or ironically?
> —Diderot, *Rameau's Nephew*

The Coen brothers' film *Fargo* (1996) begins with two riddles—the first, a verbal riddle about truth telling in cinema, the second, an image riddle about whiteness. Both of them are worth considering at some length, I think, especially as they pertain to the film's late-arriving hero, Marge Gunderson. She offers an implicit challenge to the ironic solution of the first riddle and a compelling alternative to the nihilistic drift of the second. My Marge-centered examination of the riddles will prepare the ground for an argument about the status of irony in relation to different kinds of visibility. I shall be chiefly concerned throughout this essay with *Fargo*'s rhetorical procedures, and their implications. Questions about how the film situates itself in popular culture, especially in relation to established movie genres, will be touched on only in passing.

The verbal riddle that precedes the opening credits takes the form of a printed text, which, if read cursorily—simply to gain information— might be viewed in the same light as the conventional tag line for countless movies loosely derived from "real events." "This is a true story," the first sentence declares, with no apparent difficulty. "The events depicted in this film took place in Minnesota in 1987." The identification of time and setting seems a sturdy follow-up to the initial avowal of truth, promptly supplying what anyone waiting for facts might reasonably expect to get hold of early on. How pleasant it feels to be able to disregard all the years in the chaotic procession of history but one, and to pin that year to the crisp outline of a northern state, Minnesota, that we may remember from the multicolored maps that greeted us from the walls and geography books of our elementary school classrooms. Surely no item in our early learning environments is likely to have contributed more to our self-confident sense of placement as Americans than the guileless map, with its sea-to-shining-sea demonstration of our neatly

259

Marge Gunderson (Frances McDormand) examines the body of a slain officer in *Fargo*.

compartmented holdings. "Out of many, one," the picture of the "original" forty-eight states effortlessly demonstrates. Thus, whichever state one elects to dwell in for storytelling purposes allows one to be both local and general simultaneously. Any state will no doubt turn out to be a story site linked in essential ways to everything else that we unthinkingly designate American. Are we meant to register the "disparity" (to use a word that one of the characters in *Fargo* will fasten on, self-consciously, when attempting to express worry about a gap) between the state mentioned in the text as the story setting and the city, Fargo, which belongs to an adjoining state, North Dakota, but nevertheless rather grandly gives the film its title? If we are invited to notice this split, it hardly seems enough to excite reader skepticism, or worry.

The Coen brothers' text becomes slightly less manageable with its third sentence, where we learn that "At the request of the survivors, the names have been changed." "Survivors" tells us that the narrative may be devoting considerable space to those who did not survive. The nature of the request the survivors have made would indicate that there are elements in the story to be told which they would prefer not to be affiliated with too directly or openly. There is something unspoken lurking behind this terse acknowledgment which teases us by remaining elusive and sets us, ever so mildly, adrift. The survivors of some misfortune, to which dishonor may be attached, have been in touch with the filmmaker who will soon, they fear, be "rampaging" in the history of other people's sorrows. They have managed to secure one concession from him—that all the names of those involved in the sordid incidents, the guilty as well as the innocent, will be altered. The survivors perhaps recall the narrator's imperious voice on the old television series, *Dragnet,* which assured the audience every week that "only the names have been changed to protect the innocent." How much protection, one wonders, will this scrambling of names confer, when the time and setting of the still recent tragedy are no secret? In the few moments we are given to make sense of this piece of the text, we might consider, not very precisely, how important or unimportant actual names are when telling a true story; where we ourselves stand these days in relation to our own names (it used to be commonly said that one stood behind one's name if one wanted that name to stand for character); and how it once seemed to *Othello*'s "honest" Iago that the stealing of one's "good name" could leave a person utterly destitute. We might also reflect that discretion is an endangered, old-fashioned virtue, as we smile at the naïveté of those survivors thinking they might prevent a hailstorm of publicity for their lost loved ones through the bogus guarantee of anonymity.

In the fourth and final sentence of the preliminary text, all pretense of clarity and straightforwardness dissolves, unless the viewer contrives a pretense of his own that he can still follow the writer's logic. I would guess that the Coen brothers count on our desire to avoid making work for ourselves this early, so that we will docilely accept a nonsensical statement as though it somehow keeps faith with the more or less reasonable ones leading up to it. "Out of respect for the dead, the rest has been told exactly as it occurred." Once the necessary bargain over name changes has been struck with the anxious survivors, the filmmaker firmly resolves to give no further quarter to dramatic license. He will resist all temptations to distort or in any way embellish the facts of the story he is telling, "out of respect for the dead." The dead, after all, can make no requests on their own behalf (unlike the survivors, with their perhaps pardonable inclination to cloak and alter). Therefore, if one is to respect their too easily forgotten rights, and give them what they are entitled to, one must not forgo a single detail in the "exact" retelling of the disaster that befell them.

The filmmakers want to make sure that we grasp how fully they honor the obligations that come with the claim, "This is a true story." Fiction, with its caprices, showy eloquence, and artful economy, is simply not right for the job. As everyone knows, fiction is notoriously *inexact* and lacking in a sober regard for reality's weighty integrity. How can it be expected to give a just, properly full accounting to the dead, who can only be helped now by facts? The phrasing of the Coens' final sentence neatly balances the idea of mourners' etiquette (paying all due respect) with the suggestion of a stirring pledge to take up the cause of the dead as if it were one's own. The Coens shoulder, without complaint, the burden of a faithful reconstruction. If imagination has no role to play in the presentation of this narrative, the viewer will have little reason to bemoan its absence.

At the end of Ethan Coen's introduction to the published screenplay of *Fargo,* he informs the reader that the story the movie tells "aims to be both homey and exotic, and pretends to be true."[1] This announcement is planned, with a good yarn spinner's cunning, as the surprise ending to a vivid anecdotal account of the Coens' grandmother's way of misremembering and innocently reinventing the circumstances of her harsh, already improbable experiences in New York City, as an exile from Russia. Coen's entire introduction can be viewed as a gloss on the four-sentence lie that is our first contact with the world of *Fargo.* The sharp-witted tone he adopts for debunking, yet again, ordinary notions of truth reminds me of several lines from Czeslaw Milosz's poem, "Ars Poetica?"

> and so you think that I am only joking
> or that I've devised just one more means
> of praising Art with the help of irony.[2]

Maybe we derive too automatic a comfort and consolation in this period of round-the-clock irony from Art's irony-fortified retreat from truth telling. The stories that filmmakers, novelists, and other inspired counterfeiters invent can, beyond question, vastly exceed in interest and expressive force the gray, habit-choked, ponderous "daily doings" that Ordinary Citizens persist in maintaining are superior simply by virtue of having really happened. But *Fargo's* unrevoked assertion that it is a "true story" gains some advantage from its appeal to the public record. The director's professed determination to do justice to the victims' experience puts some salutary pressure on our response to the movie's strong preoccupation with the intimate textures of torture and bloodletting, and to its arguably uncharitable comic perspective on a world populated almost exclusively by "funny-looking" people speaking in funny regional accents. Moreover, the spectator will perhaps be more hesitant than usual about dismissing outrageous character behavior or crazy swerves in the plot as mere contrivance. After all, who wants to be the bumpkin, in an after-the-movie argument about plausibility, confronted with someone else's newspaper evidence that the very scene one refused to take seriously in a story was the one that adhered most scrupulously to eyewitness testimony? ("Oh, dear. Then *my* conception of reality was too narrowly conventional!")

What I find most intriguing about *Fargo*'s initial visit to the playground of the postmodern lie is that it is so completely at odds with the mind-set and value system of the film's wholly admirable hero—the seven-months-pregnant police chief, Marge Gunderson. Spurious truth claims designed to mislead credulous moviegoers would almost certainly fail to amuse her, gain her approval, or finally make any sense to her. While Marge is not portrayed as a humorless character (she tells at least one clever joke to her assistant, Lou, and suggests, at various points, that she is aware of a comic element in situations that it would be impolite to react to openly), she does seem devoid of any sense of irony. The absence of irony seems the necessary trade-off to allow the quaint, anachronistic virtues she so conspicuously possesses their arguably unironic triumph in the film. The positive attributes that are central to her characterization are unself-conscious naturalness, consistent sincerity, and good manners. For Marge, manners do not function as a veneer or as some form of artificial, programmed behavior, suppressing a more authentic self-expression she has not had the daring to try out. Instead, manners are—in her way of living through them—a crucial, moving illumination of what Edith Wharton has termed "that vast noiseless labor of the spirit going on everywhere beneath the social surface."[3] While they are not always a reliable indicator of character (Marge, as a police investigator, is well acquainted with suspects' need to dissemble), the breakdown or abuse of manners testifies to a degree of human carelessness that generally warrants attention and, on rare occasions, censure. Recall that Marge's first powerful intimation of Jerry Lundegaard's guilt occurs, Jane Austen-style, when he suddenly surrenders all pretense of civility.

There is a paradox, which eighteenth-century writers delighted in exploring, in the fact that good manners can coexist so easily with naturalness, a condition, of course, that derives from some other source than one's instruction in courtesy and social forms. One of my students declared Marge Gunderson the most natural character she had ever encountered, and while we could have spent time interrogating her assumptions about what that slippery word "natural" consists of, no one in the class, including myself, had any immediate urge to come up with rival candidates for this accolade. Marge's refreshingly unabashed pleasure in her nonstop eating, her thriving pregnancy, her deep, untroubled sleep, and her comfortable sorties into the unpromising, frozen Minnesota landscape suggest an almost magical integration of self and world. Her way of inhabiting her physical and social environment seems based on an acceptance of certain things as *given,* and simultaneously an acceptance that a number of choices she has made are settled matters. She has no urge to quarrel with the boundaries imposed (from without and within) on her life experience. The *need* for irony in the world of this film, by contrast, almost certifies a bad fit with one's given and chosen relationships. Out of disappointment with past defeats and too limited visible prospects, one resorts to withholding some vital part of oneself not only from social spaces but private ones. It is as though one were in flight from openness generally. One comes to disbelieve in a language that can be easily held in common with others and that is able, in a beautifully full sense of the word, to *accommodate* them.

Marge is not opposed to irony, since that would imply a comprehension of the mental condition that calls it forth—as refuge, say, or antidote. She is immune to irony as someone who has never felt deeply betrayed by plain speaking, and who hasn't, from an early age, largely feigned interest in other people's lives. She is nowhere near the state of solipsistic restlessness where conversation means simply waiting for your turn. Though she is not insecure about having her own view of things challenged, and is perfectly willing to declare her opinions on any subject, she has no craving for argument. Argument, as Hannah Arendt once noted, can be a potent "substitute for thought," and, of course, for the demands of listening. Marge Gunderson reminds me of the young child in Penelope Fitzgerald's novel, *The Blue Flower,* "whose experience of life must so far have been favorable, since he smiled at anything in human form."[4] Marge's smiles are not often literal (her face generally wears the stoic expression of someone raised to meet the challenges of a punishing climate) but she consistently greets people with such an authentic air of welcome that it has the affirming effect of a child's easy, trusting acceptance. Individuals have not yet reduced themselves to drearily familiar types in her mind. And their common topics of talk have not grown stale from overuse. When she converses, it is an active exchange, where whatever is on offer is earnestly regarded as a thing of renewable interest rather than impatiently probed for some show of novelty. The ongoing availability of basic human fellowship, with its chance of news or equally agreeable assurance that known patterns are holding steady, is more than enough to keep her involvement alive. Marge finds social occasions, with their accustomed musical rhythm that all by itself "ameliorates the affections," a rich complement to her married relationship to Norm. With her husband, conversation invariably moves at a slower pace and can regularly lapse into silence, with no sense on either side that communication or understanding has abated.

For Marge, making a game of truth (as the Coens do in their introductory text) is the business of liars and used car salesmen. She would imagine that such deceivers eventually trip themselves up or give themselves away. And why would anyone go to the trouble of naming something true that wasn't when there was no advantage to be gained from it? Even if no harm was done, what's the point? Bad habits, like bad manners, will in time become legible—like footprints in the snow. And one can know where such practices lead without wasting a lot of mental energy trying to figure out what gave rise to them. Marge has had enough direct exposure to the varieties of criminal deviousness, large and small, to cure herself of any fascination with them. And although she apparently watches quite a bit of television, she hasn't been infected by that medium's lubricating ironies and pervasive mood of instant knowingness. Literally, she can find no earthly use for irony or any kindred way of thinking which advocates the suspension of plain dealing and the disparagement of ordinary social virtues.

Why are the Coen brothers, whose previous films have been steadfastly ironic (and too often, I fear, smugly so) keeping company with such a hero, one who would have no access to their preferred tone and not even a faint willingness to enter into the spirit of their "hard" comedy? Whatever she finally comes to represent in the film, it does not include being in on the joke. When she first turns up in *Fargo*, it seems reasonable to assume that, in spite of her level of competence in police work, she is being established as someone we will frequently be able to laugh at. Her take on things, compared to ours, seems divertingly unsophisticated. We do not know, or perhaps much care, whether she will prove equal to the murderers she is tracking. What makes the solution of the crimes relatively unimportant is the fact that we begin so far ahead of her in our knowledge of what has happened and why. She arrives in the movie unusually late for a main character. We are encouraged to believe that she is almost a mock representative of the law, one who may eventually stumble onto the truth, but will provide a very restricted perspective on the world she so uncritically inhabits. Marge will not, it would appear, afford us a means of obtaining a more inclusive vision of human desperation and destructiveness than we already have at our disposal.

The fact that she lacks any of the author ironist's tools for crafty readings of the movie's action suggests that her moral growth in the course of the narrative *must* be of the rite-of-passage variety. She will move from a state of countrified insularity to a level of awareness more closely approximating the spectator's own cynicism-nurtured, weather-beaten maturity. In the absence of such development, she will have minimal mobility on the film's complexly layered playing field. It is as though Andy Griffith accidentally drove his Mayberry police cruiser into the landscape of *In Cold Blood* and determined that Mayberry rules would be adequate to the demands of whatever nastiness confronted him there.

Our preliminary expectations about Marge are borne out in one vital but ultimately misleading respect. She remains throughout the film a character available to comic response. When we are invited to laugh at her, it is generally because of some perceived inequality between her sense of what is going on and ours. We might flatter ourselves that there is some advantage, amounting perhaps to superiority, in our being able to see things about Marge that she is not able to see, in the same light, for herself. (And she is, of course, best left ignorant of what we notice and take affectionate comic pleasure in.) As the narrative proceeds, the comedy imperceptibly grows more protective of Marge, stopping short of pushing its observation of her over the cruelty threshold. The Coens bring her closer to us by regularly emphasizing her skill and overall decency. Still, our first impression of her as ingenuous is allowed to persist, in part because she does not undergo any significant transformation of attitude. Even her final confrontation with a sample of stomach-churning evil—Grimsrud feeding his partner's body through a woodchipper—does not bring about a change in her values or basic mind-set. We might well feel disposed to say that she is someone with permanently blinkered vision, whose world, while a source of contentment to her and a "homey, exotic" place for us to visit *briefly,* is necessarily smaller than ours. Marge's sense of how things presently stand in our culture is no match for our more "evolved" awareness.

I think that the Coens intend for us to come only belatedly (if at all) to an alternative conclusion: that she possibly, just possibly, sees things that are beyond us and that our perspective on our own situation is less adequate than we had supposed. What the Coens have accomplished in this "hazardous" film, is something akin to what Richard

Poirier has found going on in numerous Robert Frost poems. Poirier convincingly demonstrates how Frost's "greatness depends . . . in large part on his actually seeking out opportunities for being in untenable positions."[5] In *Fargo*, the untenable position might be described in the following terms. An ironist, who has by no means grown weary of irony's pleasures and is not free to exchange them in any case for some other way of contriving fictions, stumbles upon a protagonist who, taken seriously, might pose an interesting challenge to his value system. This challenge is not the result of a rational argument against irony or a direct confrontation with it. It quietly emerges rather from a set of imagined conditions in which irony is simply invisible to a figure who knows something not instantly dismissable about living in a state of integration—call it a "full, ready and exact" relation to her own experiences.[6] What might it mean for irony's taken-for-granted centrality in any serious approach to life if a person who has fairly estimated her chances for being contented and useful in this dark time, who meets her world daily in a spirit of openness and who knows how to stay grounded, has no need of irony?

It could be objected here that Marge is no more than a fictional construct, tactically introduced as a contrast to other forces and attitudes, and that her interest for us lies chiefly—and properly—in her relation to other figures within the invented structure we think of as *Fargo*. If the Coens had supplied us with a quantity of Marges in the film, without the regular *relief* of monstrous carnage and tribulation, she would doubtless lose her hold on the viewer's ethical imagination. She would appear less worthy of attention and curiosity because she was deprived of her singularity. A whole community of Marges would make the spectator hungry for more reckless, eccentric ways of being. Marge in another context could seem a state of mind too easily attained and one which, if allowed to dominate by force of numbers and bland consensus, would conceivably be a weight oppressively bearing down on other kinds of human aspiration. For the Coens to calculate how the felicitous endowments of *one* Marge Gunderson might serve their narrative purposes on this one occasion and bring a tricky comic story to an emotionally gratifying (because life-affirming) conclusion is saying something quite different than that the Coens have fomented a crisis of faith in their authority as ironists. Clearly in art one can happily occupy all sorts of temporarily amenable mind-sets without feeling logically bound to their terms or consequences. Seeking out the untenable, as Frost and Poirier propose it, has to be understood metaphorically. How then has the ironist made any serious trouble for himself by growing fond of a pregnant police chief?

In reply to this many-sided challenge, I would begin by emphasizing a truth about art that is too often brushed aside or left out of consideration. Just as other forms of life experience leave room for the decisive encounter, the moment of surrender, the wrestling with knowledge or grief or illness that moves you from one state of being to another, so too the act of creating something is commonly launched by the hope, and the attendant risks, of going beyond oneself. The argument against the likelihood of Marge becoming something more than the Coen brothers' customary approach to characterization is equipped to deal with depends, I think, on an overvaluing of those aspects of the creative process directed by reason, will, and well-formulated intentions.

It is easy to consider any satisfying, finished piece of work, after the fact, as the result of an obvious, more or less orderly set of associations and connections. Facing a poem or a painting or a song from the outside, we are apt to be struck—if the work pleases us—by the elements that give evidence of the artist's control: of her craft, discipline, formal decisions, and calculations. Less conspicuous, especially at a cultural moment when so many of the tenets of Romanticism are under suspicion, are the signs of how a work *possessed* its maker, created difficulties and real psychic dangers for her, and led her far astray from some insufficient preliminary plan. It is never obvious to the beholder how something that might have remained mechanical, formulaic, or well-crafted but inert (in short, unmemorable for whatever reason) has been tricked into full-bodied life. Any art that *works* can so readily exhibit the luster of the self-evident. It feels inevitable, rather than an improbable victory over a vastly superior adversary. On occasion, to be sure, the "confident craftsman" dimension of the artist is in control of the creative process from start to finish. She knows, like a good carpenter, what needs to be done from the outset, can see her way to the end of her task without impediment, and supplies what's fitting and delightful *on demand*. Nonetheless, the mystery of so much of the art that holds us captive—that makes us want to come back to it and turn it around in our minds—is a haunting awareness that something has become powerfully visible without anyone quite knowing how, under a particular, unrepeatable set of conditions. We require just *these* words, *these* images, *that* melody, *that* form to secure our enduring, gratefully mystified attachment.

My feeling about Marge in *Fargo* is that she becomes a figure of genuine moral stature and a wondrous source of equilibrium precisely by not meaning to, by not having pedagogic designs on us. I think she takes the spectator by surprise in a manner that echoes the way in which she took her writers by surprise. For both parties (spectator and writer) she only gradually becomes clear, like a figure emerging from a blizzard, where a certain amount of confusion and waiting are an essential prelude to positive identification. I will be arguing that a character (like the narrative that contains her) can be born under the sign of irony, with a prescribed, limited function, but that in order to do her work credibly in such an inhospitable atmosphere, she must generate a different kind of light for herself, which irony can neither regulate nor see by. As I noted earlier, it seems remarkable to me that Marge never comes to see irony as a force to reckon with, something alien that interferes with or challenges her freedom and sense of truth. It stays invisible to her, and, perhaps as a necessary corollary, she becomes invisible to it, insofar as she guides us to a dependable moral shape of things in *Fargo*'s world. (Mere lack of irony, or insulation from it, is by itself, of course, no guarantee of goodness and insight. Jerry Lundegaard, for example, is arguably as unmindful of irony as Marge Gunderson, and it avails him naught. Irony might, in fact, be precisely the medicine he needs to enter, maybe for the first time, the realm of self-awareness.)

Let me say a bit more about how Marge and what she comes to embody may remain somewhat hidden, and unwanted, *even* for the Coens themselves. *Fargo* owes much of its effect of tonal density to the fact that it is not only the viewer but the writers and director who are made somewhat uncomfortable by her demands, and resist the idea of using her, in a consistent or predictable fashion, as a moral touchstone. Ordinarily, in film, it is a matter of no great difficulty for a director to declare and sustain his allegiance to a thoroughly principled protagonist—to make *her* cause his own, for the sake of the story. But I think the Coens initially approach Marge's square sense of honor and uprightness with marked hesitation, and an almost defensive wariness. Old-fashioned virtues, too plainly sanctioned, might well place undue restraint on their robust fascination with cruelty, and their unquenchable urge to revel in unfairness. It is instructive to remember that the camera movement which introduces us to Marge, for the first time, in her bedroom, begins with a survey of her husband Norm's art materials and paintings, including his work-in-progress, a meticulously realistic oil painting of a gray mallard. Norm and his wife are fully at home in the company of art such as this. It seems reasonable to suggest that neither of them has thought much about art which has a fundamentally different, necessarily more oblique and self-conscious relation to its materials.

The Coens do not ask us to view Norm's art realm disrespectfully, but they implicitly declare that they cannot align themselves with his earnest, literalist perspective. His picture of nature, however sensitively observant and skillfully executed, cannot be theirs. And Marge, similarly, can be of no help in determining what their kind of art is for.

On numerous occasions in *Fargo,* the Coens deliberately underscore their complicity with those characters who either take pride in feeling nothing or who are so far gone in breezy callousness that they scarcely notice what's missing. The moments I refer to exacerbate moral tension by refusing to grant us an authorial vantage point clearly at odds with the cold-blooded "skewering" on view. I think immediately of the father-son bedroom scene in which Jerry, who has engineered his wife's abduction, adopts a consoling, worried demeanor with his weeping child, Scotty, in order to insure that the boy will lie about his mother's disappearance to anyone who asks about her. Scotty is effectively cut off, by this request, from those relatives and friends who might care about him and in whom he might confide. We notice during the father-son exchange that an accordion is present on Scotty's bed, and it is likely that Scotty has been attempting to distract himself by practicing his laughably anachronistic instrument before Jerry pays him his brief visit. As Jerry leaves, he pulls the door to Scotty's room shut behind him, at which point we are obliged to examine, in enormous close-up, a poster celebrating the Accordion King, a grotesquely jovial, "Lawrence Welkish" virtuoso in an Alpine setting. The Coens declare a mystifying time-out from our consideration of Scotty's awful predicament in order to elicit a thin laugh at the boy's bad taste in music and bedroom decoration.

Elsewhere, a similarly disconnected mood of hollow derisiveness settles on the Coens' sharp highlighting of crooked teeth, lavish homeliness, and dumb-as-a-brick, automaton cheeriness as the defining features of various cashiers, clerks, and, perhaps most notably, prostitute witnesses in the area around Brainerd. The Coens appear to engage a little too knowingly and aggressively in the humiliation of certain minor characters. They alternate between giving "ordinariness" its due and twisting it for the sake of a rude, caricature vividness. Possibly because they don't wish to be seen genuflecting at the altar of small-town mediocrity, the Coens periodically indulge in wilfully mean "quick sketches." They run the risk with such a tactic of confusing the undeniable pleasures of comically off-center observation with a mere facile smirking at crudely overstressed incidentals of appearance and manner.

As I've already noted, the Coens are reluctant to commit themselves too early or too unreservedly to Marge's ethical stance, or her
easygoing altruism. In at least one scene, Marge's nearly affectless first
encounter with the corpses of a fellow officer and two young victims,
the Coens come close to losing sight of who she is and of what they
ultimately intend to do with her. They may be playing against the grain
of the viewer's expectations that a female officer will be more openly
upset than her "stoic wiseacre" male counterparts in television cop shows,
but the comic surprise is worrisomely offset by an insufficiently layered
presentation of the brute facts. The undependability of moral perspective
in *Fargo,* even at times when Marge is present, leads to interesting confusions and collisions at those many significant junctures where a difficult, emotionally subtle awareness is required of us. At whatever risk
to narrative cohesiveness, the Coens are determined that the *feeling* op-
tion should never be a simple component of a narrative situation. After
all, accepting an unmistakable invitation to be solicitous can be like
treating oneself to a doughnut. As Osip Mandelstam wittily comments
in his "Fourth Prose," once one has finished eating it, "the hole remains."[7]

The opening shot of *Fargo* confronts us, as I mentioned at the
beginning of the chapter, with an image riddle of whiteness. We gaze
at a completely white frame, unable to ascertain whether we are looking
at the blank envelope of the movie screen itself or an ivory background
for the credits to be printed on. There is no evidence that a moving
picture image is already in progress. We are obliged to stay with this
unyielding veil for quite a few moments until we can make out the signs
of windswept snowfall. The white blindness becomes all at once a *natural* phenomenon, what a weather reporter would describe as exceedingly poor visibility. An apparent nothing has converted before our eyes
into a dense, swirling, undifferentiated force that could just as easily be
rising up from the invisible ground as descending from an indecipherable
sky. All that one can plainly discern is that the snow is happening, and
there is no getting past it to some more stable resting point. A single
vehicle emerges, welcomely, from the curtain of snow, with its headlights
on. This object supplies us not only with the sense of a living soul
making progress in trying circumstances (who surely has a better idea
than we have of where we are), but also with the fact of a road, which
will lead us somewhere. "Somewhere" is the eternal promise of movie
narrative, the movement from a blank screen to one lit from within by
our belief in (hunger for) magical revelations. While the car stays small
and far-off, it feels like a benefactor, hinting that its mission might be

to locate us in our state of total disorientation, and perform a rescue. It is escorted at this stage of its journey by a barely noticeable bird in flight. This creature seems not much more than a speck of black in the whiteness, making lateral, random sweeps not too high above the road, as though less confident of its destination than the car. The presence of the bird seems to draw the car somewhat closer to the landscape, as though the storm created a kinship between whatever is caught up and lost in it—an equivalence among wayfarers. There is something movingly instructive in the creaturely search for safe haven. When we have had time to accumulate such impressions, the car disappears for an interval, obscured by a hill. When eventually it returns to view. it has undergone a disturbing metamorphosis. As it draws near to us, it ceases to be good company in the storm. We can see now that it is a car equipped with a hitch towing another vehicle, but this additional bit of information matters less than something newly brutal and looming about the car and its felt relation to us. It bears down ominously, like a slow-moving Juggernaut, and the music that accompanies its advance is heavy and unnerving. (Later in the film, a similar effect will be achieved when the camera slowly reveals to us the Paul Bunyan statue in Brainerd after nightfall. A strong protector is transformed by a trick of light and shift of angle into our worst fear. He is suddenly invested with all the lurking demonic impulses associated with darkness.) We are not granted a close view of the car's driver, so it can easily seem that the mechanism is operated by forces that somehow go beyond a mere individual's will. The car and the extra burden it carries acquire the appearance of something darkly fated, inexorable.

Let us return to the riddle of whiteness and think about the route we have taken in the film's opening. A white silence proposes itself as an appropriate empty space for us to wait in until the story begins. We are in transition; we are given a few moments to clear our minds of anything likely to interfere with our enjoyment of this movie. As long as it doesn't go on too long, whiteness can be a tranquil metaphor for unwanted things fading out. It's interesting how this mental activity of fade-out and clearing away as we wait for something to happen coincides with the breaking awareness that the image is already full and that our eyes must adjust to its dazzling turbulence. There is an undeniable pleasure in such deception. Our ability to take notice is suddenly called upon in a manner that makes us reflect on it. It is like remembering a talent we'd forgotten we possessed. Working our way out of perceptual confusion makes us more than usually attentive to the play of appearances, to how one sort of appearance delightfully masks another. And indeed as we grasp the snowstorm as a reality we have not only seen but imagined for ourselves it strikes us *first* as a thing of beauty. Our eyes have retrieved it from an apparent emptiness, and thus briefly it figures as our own creation. Very quickly, and unreluctantly, we will give up that sense of the snow in favor of a more pragmatic, driver's assessment. The weather is nasty. It is nearly impossible to see where one is going and it would be awful to get stuck in the midst of so threatening a squall. The satisfaction we found as viewers in looking at the snow as something powerfully manifesting its own visibility is fleeting. But our contact with the sheer mystery of snow is worth stressing. We have undergone an awakening, a jubilant awakening to the fact that snow is presently *there* to contemplate. And for the time spent catching the drift of whiteness, it is like we are being let in on a wonderful secret.

Close to the end of *Fargo,* Marge is attempting to learn from the adamantly silent murderer, Grimsrud, what could possibly have led him to take five people's lives. Her last words to him follow her question about what it was all for. Is it possible he really doesn't *know* that "there's more to life than a little money?" "And here you are," she continues, as though it were still not too late to turn even that fact to good account, "and it's a beautiful day." We are then given a view of the road outside her police cruiser which reveals a snowfall no more inviting than that which opened the film. (The Coens absolutely refuse the chance to soften this rough weather with some obvious visual poetry.) I think the challenge that is offered us in this late scene is how to take Marge's words unironically, to consider how there may be beauty in this blizzardy day which one need not delude oneself to casually acknowledge. The casualness is the surprise, proceeding from Marge's assurance that she is saying something self-evident. We are not dealing here with a stern northern resolve to accept the weather's meager benefits without complaint. Neither is it a matter of *willing* into existence all-but-invisible consolations in dire circumstances. Rather, Marge turns her not easily disappointed gaze toward the objects before her in an unusually open fashion. We have experienced exactly Marge's response to snowstorm beauty ourselves, in the film's first shot, whether we've retained the memory or not. We are enjoined perhaps to make the trip back to first things, so the snow will be for us the kind of "first snow" that Mary Oliver lights upon in the remarkable poem of that title:

The snow
began here
this morning, and all day continued, its white
rhetoric everywhere
calling us back to *why, how, whence* such beauty and *what*
the meaning; such an oracular fever! flowing
past windows, an energy it seemed
would never ebb, never settle
less than lovely! and only now,
deep into night,
it has finally ended.[8]

Of course, we are free to look out the police cruiser window with Grimsrud's dead stare, and merely shake our heads. If he had a sense of humor, we could share a laugh with him over the misery-confirming nothingness of the godforsaken place he is leaving behind. Grimsrud is one of two close-mouthed characters in *Fargo*, the other being the garage mechanic and ex-convict, Shep Proudfoot, who "vouches" for Grimsrud's character when asked to recommend someone reliable for the job of kidnapper. Silence is often taken to be a measure of one's degree of at-homeness in nature. The man who is not struggling with his environment or seeking to complicate his strong, simple relation to it is almost expected to forgo language, as if by doing so he has moved beyond it to a deeper, more elemental life. Silence suggests, without much call for demonstration, that one has arrived at a better way of knowing, one less reliant on game-playing, falsity, manipulation of all sorts. Silence can seem like a place of healing as well, from the sickness of too much needless, self-justifying talk, and therefore feels closely allied to wisdom.

Grimsrud might pass as the human embodiment of the Minnesota terrain, in its unmerciful, indifferent stillness. He directs us to a nihilistic reading of the "monumental white shroud that wraps all the prospect around him."[9] The image is Herman Melville's, from the famous catalogue of the terrors of whiteness in "The Whiteness of the Whale" chapter of *Moby-Dick*. Grimsrud's retreat to a realm where language can barely penetrate and his zombielike immersion in the predator's bloody work can be seen as a response to some ultimate blankness figured in "the desolate shiftings of the windrowed snows of prairies."[10] Like Melville's Albino whale, one "sees naught in that brute but the deadliest ill." His senseless killings create a momentum toward Senselessness writ large, as if the only persuasive attribute of the human were expendability. He is what that car seems to be bringing toward us in the storm at the beginning of *Fargo,* after it turns hostile. Instead of rescue or reconnection with what we understand, the car seems to bear tidings of "heartless voids and immensities."[11] Though its lights are on, it is a "blind" rather than a seeing force. The vehicle has adapted itself to prevailing conditions, as it were. It appears to derive a malevolent strength from taking on the *snow's* blindness to any appeal in its path.

In the course of *Fargo's* opening montage, the car (with its tow-hitch burden) is presented to us from a variety of angles and distances, in some of which it appears engaged in normal human business. In one sustained long shot, it is completely dwarfed by the boundless prairie flatness. The car's ability to hold on to its menacing power proves as limited as the viewer's ability to retain her first delighted sense of the snow's mysterious loveliness. One impression of truth gives way to another, and then another. The effect of the entire sequence of shots is a trying out of multiple perspectives on this "undecided" environment— in search of proportions that give the best overall fit to what is being revealed to us. Our shifting judgment of how the car journey makes sense of the landscape, and vice versa, mirrors the mental state of the thoroughly disoriented man who is doing the driving, Jerry Lundegaard. Jerry is en route to Fargo to complete arrangements for his wife Jean's kidnapping. Somehow he has determined that the "deal" he is planning to close with an unknown pair of thugs willing to do all the dirty work is the best way to clear up his financial woes and put his life back in order. The immediate goal of his journey is a first meeting with Grimsrud and his freshly recruited partner, Carl. In order to come up with his kidnapping plan, Jerry must have lost any sense of his wife as a separate, or even a real, person. He has forgotten that what he is doing will result, at the very least, in immense suffering for her, just as he later forgets that he has a son, Scott, who is grieving because she is gone. Both wife and son are confused with elements of a plot he's made up to get himself out of difficulties. He is, in his carefree handling of the lives entrusted to him, a postmodernist of sorts, for whom no story and no attachment to others is truer than the worthless Trucoat sealant he attempts to foist on his customers at the auto dealership. Does his inability to think his way through his assumptions make the consequences of the permanent game he is playing different?

Once again the issue is one of visibility—how a character sees or fails to see what is in front of him. The Coens devise a striking recurrent metaphor for the insidious blur that creeps into our associations with others, even those "ties" which are nominally our closest ones. At various points in the film, we are obliged to look at television screens where the image is lost or partially obscured because of reception difficulties. This is another form of "snow"—one that afflicts frustrated viewers indoors. Jerry's family has turned invisible to him in his solipsistic distraction. They have slipped out of emotional focus without his even noticing he has lost contact. By contrast, when Carl Showalter, one of the kidnappers, discovers that he is stranded in a cabin with no access to a clear television image, he pounds and beseeches the set as though his life and sanity depended on his getting a signal that remained steady. When Jerry returns to his home after Jean's kidnapping, the television show she has been watching has decomposed into snow. The hiss of the set is the only sound left to mark the fact of her recent presence here. It links us to her by a suggestion of abrupt severing and lingering fade out, as if the room itself has not quite had time to move forward; it is somehow still processing and faintly echoing her disappearance. Is this barely audible interior snowfall—accompanied by the slow sift of actual snow through a shattered window—a reinforcement of Grimsrud's empty silence (that is to say, a silence that empties things out)? Or is it better understood as a restorative silence, the kind that solicits us to fill things up?

Grimsrud's silence is contrasted with silences of different character and import throughout *Fargo,* and it is by noting what the changes in silence express that we can finally place Grimsrud's where it belongs, at the lowest level. His silence does not connect him with the natural world. He is as cut off from nature as he is from other people. All that lives inside his failure to speak is a rage of disappointment. Grimsrud has denied himself every state of mind but one; he is addicted to feeling put upon, and finds pleasure only in not giving others what they always unfairly try to get from him: a response. As the territory inside Grimsrud continues to shrink because of his steadfast refusal to see anything of value that might be added to him "from outside," he can only man the barricades with an ever-more combative silence, and violently protect what is his from those who dare to make any demands. He has *not* moved beyond language. He is simply stuck at one of the language learner's first words—an unreflecting "no." His fixity and perceptual poverty are a cancer of the social, not a breakthrough into a more authentic realm.

Since *The Silence of the Lambs,* it has become fashionable in movies to present murderers as cunning philosophers, whose intricate viciousness is a powerful (and maybe legitimate) expression of their well-thought-out radical skepticism. *Fargo* returns the murderer to a condition of muddle and ignorance. Murder in this narrative has nothing to do with lucidity or a coming to fuller awareness. It means entering the snowfield of a television screen as deeply as Grimsrud does when he is finally alone in the cabin after killing Jean for making noise. Grimsrud dazedly watches two actors in a soap opera through a thick, grating haze. The actors trade words like "big" and "small" as they try to organize their responses to someone's pregnancy. The words will not make meaning that can be felt or released. There is too much "interference" to see either actor's expression clearly, and the exaggerated performances lack any conviction to begin with. This is the world that Grimsrud, eerily happy for the only time in the film, comes home to after his crimes. The *truth* of the image for him lies in the fact that nothing whatever needs to come clear, that any distinctions—between the haze and the drama, between speaker and listener, between his own life in the room and the spectral patterns on the tiny screen—are appropriately *lost*.

Let us return now to the silence in the Gunderson home after Jerry discovers that Jean has, in actual fact, been kidnapped. This is a silence that moves us past emptiness to a state of active involvement. We are called upon to pay close attention here and make something significant out of what we see. At first it seems we are attached to Jerry Lundegaard's point of view as he returns home with two bags of groceries and discovers that his crackpot scheme has turned real and sprouted ugly consequences he had not foreseen in his rapt fixation on his own troubles. The purpose of the scene, as it gets under way, might simply be described thus. Jerry is recalled to a sense of his wife's humanity. By concentrating on the mute evidence remaining from her near-fatal struggle with her captors, Jerry will be obliged to dwell seriously on just what it is he has done to her. How can he avoid imagining the ordeal she has been through, and the possibility that she is already dead? The camera quietly reviews the details of the conflict we have earlier witnessed while it unfolded. We see the shower curtain that Jean was covered by as she fled in panic from the bathroom before plunging down a flight of stairs and receiving the head injury that left her unconscious. We see the crowbar that has smashed through a sliding glass door in the living room and pried open the bathroom door behind which she cowered in terror. It now lies on the bathroom floor, close to a bent window frame and a severed phone cord. The shower curtain hooks, still on the rod, are presented in close-up, revealing small remnants of plastic, that remind me, at least, of bits of torn flesh.

Very shortly we will discover that Jerry has come to no fresh realization of the enormity of his wrongdoing. The expression of bassett-hound mournfulness he wears as he lingers outside the bathroom door comes to his face automatically, in case anyone might be watching. One may recall the ease with which he slips into this expression when confronted by customers he's lied to during his car sales. If we assume then that we and Jerry have looked at the same things in the disordered rooms with a roughly equivalent sense of what they mean, we assume incorrectly. It seems to matter quite a bit (to the judging spectator) that he feel the crime in its aftermath, once it is too late to put anything right. When Jerry fails to feel what we decide it is natural and right for him to feel, when he avoids taking in any of the silently eloquent details of the crime, where do we come out, as viewers? Do we decide that we have been tricked into a mistaken reading of Jerry's potential for remorse, and leave it at that? Do we perhaps relish the chance to laugh at the latest proof of Jerry's heartlessness: an extended rehearsal of his phone call to his father-in-law breaking the dreadful news? (Jerry tries out various phrases and sounds that might plausibly convey grief, and since we *hear* his voice before we are shown that he is merely drilling himself with dry runs, we are possibly caught holding an emotion that we have been foolishly conned into sharing.) Is the result of our emotional investment in this silent review of the kidnapping mainly further instruction in irony's superiority to the facile ooze of empathy?

I believe there are more interesting possibilities to consider. Clearly it is not only Jerry whose perspective on Jean's suffering has been narrow and coldly superficial. Do not most spectators respond to the kidnapping proper as though it were a scene of exhilaratingly cruel farce? I do not mean to deny that there are ample cues for a comic enjoyment of the abduction. Nor are we misguided to seize upon these cues as a director-sanctioned release from the sober conventions of typical movie melodrama. The spikily comic surface seems to offer a pleasurably dangerous invitation to take our "fun" too far, past all reasonable limits, and only later, if at all, will we worry about the victim.

What are our recognitions during the early part of the kidnapping scene which launch our giddy slide toward moral chaos? First perhaps there is the banal television morning show which Jean watches while doing her knitting. Her way of watching instantly appears less knowing than ours; she is too credulous, perhaps, too eager to take the show's mock-hospitality and flattery that she is a valued part of things at face value. She is not *alert* in the fashion that a viewer with a cultivated sense of irony would be. Her lack of alertness seems to extend (or carry over) to her take on the black-hooded figure with a crowbar appearing outside the window on her deck. She reacts initially with bewilderment rather than fear. The intruder looks less efficient, less smooth in the accomplishment of his purposes than the felons in television movies do. When he leans forward to peer through the glass in order to ascertain whether anyone is at home, he could be performing a bizarre routine for *Candid Camera* or *America's Funniest Home Videos*. Jean's perplexity and delayed response to the threat are quite possibly owing to her overreliance on television images for her reality sense. Viewers searching for reasons to stay detached from her—or even to judge her blameworthy—might find something culpable in her confusion of television with the messy form of "real events." Jean's high-pitched voice, countrified accent, unflattering pink outfit, and slightly peculiar appearance (like everyone else in *Fargo*, she might be described as "funny-looking") have previously established her as a potentially burlesque figure, one whose credentials as a full-fledged victim are vaguely suspect. Moreover, the time we have spent thus far in the company of her attackers might well cause us to doubt whether they are competent or intelligent enough to carry out the projected crime.

This assortment of intuitions and reflex-judgments can be taken to authorize our detachment from Jean's distress for the duration of the scene. Though we are quite certain when we are briefly trapped in the bathroom with her that she is paralyzed with fright, it is not a requirement for us to enter her point of view so fully that we share her fear directly. We can almost borrow some of the sinister authority of her assailants because we have a fuller sense of them (as characters) than we do of her. Grimsrud's peevish search for "unguent" and the absurd spectacle of Jean flailing within the shower curtain before she topples downstairs confirm our impression that as ironists we gain the most inclusive mastery of the episode's content and procedures. When we return to the scene of the crime in silence, however, we must reckon with the fact that we have missed something crucial in our previous decision about how to experience it. In Jean's palpable absence we may belatedly find some preliminary awareness of Jean's actual suffering—and possibly as well a sense of how bereft she has been of emotional support when we were there with her. In order to hold onto our irony and the satisfactions it provided, we were obliged to freeze out Jean's moment-by-moment experience as a sentient victim.

The freedom to laugh at extremes of pain is usually won by increasing not only our emotional distance but our security that we have the right to that distance under *these* circumstances. We satisfy ourselves that the depiction of suffering is sufficiently unreal or exaggerated that we are not obliged to take it seriously, to believe in it—any more than we would foolishly worry over characters being maimed in a cartoon or slapstick comedy. We credit these latter habitual unfortunates with magical resilience and elasticity. Within moments they will spring back into action, with neither visible scars nor memories of what has just happened to them. If the appearance of reality is not so obviously faked or suspended (as in *Fargo*), one might make one's rationale for distance and laughter the claim that one is not meant to be responsible for one's feelings (or lack of them) toward a character who does not automatically engage them. Why should one pretend to feel in the absence of feeling, especially in fictional situations? There is so much pressure to act the role of a feeling person in one's daily life—why shouldn't fiction confer a complete exemption from any undesirable entanglements? Isn't that one of its chief enticements and pleasures as a medium of escape? Notice how such reasoning depends on our shifting to an unironic insistence that we generally possess the ability to distinguish what is real from what is fictional. (At other times we derive benefit from claiming that such distinctions are naive, that we can never sort these matters out.)

What if a "naive" viewer were to attempt to convince us of our *responsibility* by falling back on the film's straight-faced claim that it is a "true story"? When a work of fiction's close resemblance to a real-life tragedy is insisted upon, are we expected to be more apologetic, or slightly more nervous about our careless disregard of Jean Lundegaard's harrowing ordeal? Or can the responsibility for an inappropriate response promptly be directed back to the filmmakers, who themselves must take the rap for any empathy shortfall? I think we would do well to be less complacent about our freedom (while we are spectators) from the moral and emotional strains that accompany our ordinary, "nonfictional" experience. I believe it is fair to say that one of fiction's many powers is a power deriving from heartlessness—and that spectators likewise have the capacity to turn heartless in the presence of certain "imagined situations" for much the same reasons that such a turn might be made in the normal course of a day.

A suspension of emotion typically occurs because we temporarily *forget* something that we may keenly, vividly know (be in touch with) on other occasions. Another way of putting this, which is perhaps more in line with the themes of *Fargo* that concern me, is that we are unable to see enough of what is presently going on. Not enough of what is there is visible to us, and the choices we make on what to focus on can naturally act as a "blind" for equally obvious, possibly more significant things. To connect strongly with Jean's agony in the very midst of our laughter is to suddenly remember how she is *present*—both to herself and to her crisis. Whatever help irony can be in showing us how to hold more than one attitude or idea at a time, it can find itself helpless when faced with the task of containing an immoderate surge of fellow feeling. It is good for irony to feel chastened and chased by a force that it cannot comfortably integrate. When irony acknowledges its insufficiency, it is not a case of it being vanquished; it is more a matter of irony being temporarily relieved of its duties. A spectator making unexpected contact with Jean—fully seeing her—may have the sense of "letting more life in" to a situation whose too far advanced freedom from the normal range of sympathies is getting stifling.

Sometimes the laughter with the greatest power to reveal and cleanse is the laughter we wish to repudiate. We discover what is *missing* (or denied) by the response of laughter and try to bring it into play, just moments too late for our new awareness to *save* the situation. Laughter that ties us to the mess characters are making gives us a guilty share in the business of making things *worse* than they need to be. That is, we become "secret sharers" in heartless behavior. The fact of our laughter seems to drive the transgressor further, giving him permission to take that final ugly step. And then we see where the final step has brought us, and we inwardly draw back from it. (I shall return to this topic in my discussion of the comedy in Guy Maddin films.)

So much that we call irony is a complex compromise with the exorbitant demands to *feel* that life makes on us. One of the limitations of being human is that it is impossible to feel consistently what we should be feeling, or to easily widen the territory of our feeling to include all of the worthy new sufferers that come to our attention. Irony is a place to go for some *necessary* relief from the unceasing evidence of our deficient responsiveness. It can make hollowness bearable by *knowing* it is there and providing a *free* space to comment on it, from the position of an outside observer, as it were. The danger (and temptation) of irony comes when one imagines that the outside position it offers is superior to the internal one that one has been forced to vacate. Irony can convince itself that hollowness has somehow been transcended in favor of something large and difficult and beautifully self-sufficient. Frequently hollowness has simply donned an elaborate mask and fallen in love with it; one is inclined to forget that the mask is a simpler, more manageable burden than an acknowledged dearth of feeling. Irony judges those who seem to spend more time *inside* their actions and responses unsophisticated, by virtue of that fact. A person like Marge who takes her "rootedness" or ongoing relationships with others for granted must be less knowledgeable than the ironist about how tenuous her relation to world and self really is. Irony can become so expert in its management of its tough-minded responses that it requires no reflection—or testing of its limits—at all. There is not, perhaps, much of a gap between the ironist's nominal freedom to play within any complex situation—trying out all the available attitudes—and Jerry Lundegaard trying out the various accents of grief before phoning his father-in-law.

A parallel scene later in the film shows Mike Yanagita attempting to cajole Marge to sleep with him "for old times' sake" by trying out various emotional poses. When flattery and mild boasting fail to lead her beyond good-humored politeness, he invents a wife who has died of cancer. He tells Marge how much he has always cared for her (Marge), while weeping openly, and embarrassedly, over his recent loss. One has the impression that he believes the tears he is shedding whether the death has happened or not. The obvious truth he inwardly appeals to as a cover for the expedient lie he is presently driven to tell is that he is a man who *has* suffered, and that he deserves more compassion and sexual consolation than he has ever managed to get in his difficult life. He is willing to run the risk of exposing his fake—and, at some other level, genuine—weakness to her, whatever the outcome. Is he far enough away from his feelings and a belief in his own position to count as an ironist? Marge is later informed by a friend that Mike has been struggling with "psychiatric problems."

The laughter that we endorse and participate in during the kidnapping scene is part of what wraps Jean in the shower curtain, so that she is no longer visible. For the rest of the film, in fact, she will either be covered by a blanket or wearing a dark hood without eyeholes that doesn't allow us to connect with anything beyond her body in agitated motion and the sounds that her fear presses out of her. When Jean is finally permitted to get out of her captors' car when they arrive at their cabin outpost, she responds to her slight increase in mobility by making a blind, panicked run for freedom, much like a frightened animal suddenly released from a cage. As she forges through the snow, her hands tied behind her back, she stumbles and falls repeatedly. Each time that I have viewed the film with a sizable audience, a certain number of spectators have reacted to Jean's staggers and stumbles with laughter—as if taking it on faith that the comedy of the kidnapping scene were still in progress. How would we go about demonstrating that laughter here is somehow more heartless—further removed from the desired degree of human awareness—than the laughter that greeted Jean's hysteria in the bathroom? The outline of something resembling other comic situations we have innocently taken pleasure in is certainly present here, and our laughter is one way of filling the outline in. Humans reduced to mechanisms, as Henri Bergson long ago pointed out, are close to the essence of the comic and how we ordinarily recognize it. When the Coens bring us back to Jean's kidnapper Carl's point of view, however, and have him relish this mechanical element by saying "Whoops" and then chuckling, they establish a painful equivalence between the sources of *his* laughter and ours. Could we be laughing at Jean for a different, better reason than he exhibits, and if so, what might it be?

Playfulness runs no risks if it operates in a medium where the lines between appropriate and inappropriate forms of response are securely drawn. The Coens realize that there is a laugh for someone's taking in Jean's clumsy footwork and fear-stricken lurching toward a nonexistent escape route. They pointedly assign the laugh to Carl but tactically delay the beginning of his overt amusement to see whether there are others in the audience who will seize the bait. The scene is constructed as a potential *hood* for the viewer, to induce a temporary blindness akin to Jean's. That is, we might replicate Jean's condition by stumbling into a pit of laughter we neither understand nor fully assent to. Like her we have lost sight of where we are. And we are out of control. If we have forgotten, for the moment, the nature of what we are looking at, comedy can readily take up the slack. It supplies a simple, immediate answer when we are unsure about what is expected of us. As we have noted elsewhere, defamiliarization (the process of making the familiar strange that underlies so many of the discoveries of art) repeatedly works against us in *Fargo*. Our desire to be on the side of cleverness rather than gauche naïveté lures us into making choices (of allegiance and moral attitude) that we may soon after come to regret and repudiate. Cleverness seems, at one level, exactly what is required of us if we are to be on the film-makers' wavelength. This is emphatically *not* the push-button uplift world of *Forrest Gump*. And yet to get ahead of the characters in the way that cleverness sanctions is not finally to see our way clear in *Fargo*, to make connection with what is most impressively offered to us. For that connection to be achieved, we must learn to prefer waiting to arriving, and come to trust small feats of attentiveness (which demand patience, above all) more than the ironist's swift overview.

Carl Showalter and Jerry Lundegaard are not, in all likelihood, a match for most spectators in cleverness and cunning, and yet it is nonetheless true that they both place their complete faith in these attributes. They trust their ability to manipulate others and their knowledge of how to simulate attitudes that will work for them. They regard the notion of feeling anything directly as superfluous and debilitating. Leave that for the victims of their schemes. What happens when feeling manages, against the odds, to break through their defenses? When Carl's partner, Grimsrud, without any advance warning commits the first murder in *Fargo*, and the blasted head of a policeman slides past Carl's stunned face after leaving a slight spray of blood there, Carl takes a deep breath before softly saying: "Whoa . . . whoa, Daddy." For a few instants Carl surrenders any pretense that he is equal to what is going on. He has no ready-made response that is adequate for the extremity of Grimsrud's action—that can either contain it or render it intelligible to him. This is one death that he is obliged to see. It penetrates him, and reduces him for a small, but telling interval to a humane, vulnerable silence. The voice of self-interest—which must calculate how the killing will complicate his chances of staying clear of the law—has not yet had time to focus the situation. Carl is for now simply a man looking at a terrible act, and *naively* taking it in.

In the published screenplay of *Fargo* (though not in the finished film), the Coens indicate that the dead trooper's hat falls in Carl's lap, before his body is thrown backward to the ground. Grimsrud quickly seizes the hat and throws it out the car window after him.[12] The hat's presence on Carl's person—its fugitive contact with him—nicely measures the time of his real knowing: his full openness to an experience he has no name for. How far away is Carl's "Whoa" from his later "Whoops" after Jean's collapse in the snow by the cabin? In the second instance Carl feels in a much more secure position. He would possibly describe his state of mind as controlled and on top of things. He feels free enough to indulge himself in a bit of merriment at Jean's expense. After all, what harm does it do? How does his laughter *change* anything?

In a very short time Carl will be sealed up in a hood more blinding than that he has forced on Jean. He will lose himself in a rage without limits, which erases any difference he might have claimed separated his own sense of the world from Grimsrud's. When Grimsrud commits three murders in as many minutes with brutal, nerveless efficiency, the viewer might well be inclined to say that Carl is "out of his depth" with such a savage partner. Carl is a small-time crook who exhibits, by comparison with Grimsrud, a sociable nature, normal appetites, a capacity for acknowledging genuine horror, and a desire to preserve, as much as possible, balance and even civility. His warning to Jean in the backseat just as his car is stopped by the policeman seems to sum up his belief that he can remain, in the midst of crisis, a controlled individual, one mindful of others' feelings: "Let's keep still back there, lady, or we're gonna have to, ya know, to shoot you." The search for a considerate euphemism for the word "kill" at this juncture (which occurs during the pause at "ya know") implies that Carl regrets having to resort to threats and that the threat he makes now is in all probability an empty one, since he has no intention of doing her serious injury. His use of the word "lady" links him to criminals of an earlier, "simpler" time. When Carl eventually falls into his rage, however, a rage from which he never emerges, all of the civilizing restraints we have observed at work in him simply dissolve. He is at one with his fury, like a figure in allegory— and he is lost to any dimensions in the world confronting him that do not confirm or reinforce it.

One of Carl's last actions in the film is to bury close to a million dollars near a fence on an isolated stretch of highway. The money, which is his guarantee of future freedom and protection, is at this point expressive of everything decent or salvageable in him that he has abandoned in order to get himself here. He imagines that the money, like his more sensibly proportioned former life, will be waiting for him to return to when the time is right. He won't have much difficulty finding it because he has carefully marked the spot with a small snow scraper from his car. We look at the place where his treasure lies buried and then try, with him, to memorize its whereabouts. On either side of it a "regular line of identical fence posts stretches away against unblemished white."[13] It is one of those instances where the saving sense of difference, of distinctions that will hold and lead one back home to one's real purpose, have been undone by a white emptiness that extends as far as the eye can see. The landscape's features are reduced to endless self-repetition. Carl is satisfied that as long as others fail to notice the little signpost he has left behind, he has nothing to worry about. Though the marker is all but invisible even when he stands near it, he can't fail to recover it upon his return. He will find the money, he dazedly reasons, because it has cost him so much pain to get it. Some law of compensation must be at work. Carl has faith that his vision is still sufficiently reliable to guide him to what *belongs* to him. His eyes are a "currency," in Jean-Dominique Bauby's phrase, "strong enough to buy [his] freedom back."[14]

Jerry Lundegaard has a similar defining moment with a snow-scraper earlier in the film. We begin our approach to him with a high-angle view of what at first might be mistaken for an abstract painting with a predominantly white background. As our vision adjusts to identify another snow environment, this time an office building's parking lot, a tiny solitary figure in an otherwise motionless frame makes his way, like a persevering insect, through a pattern of boxed trees to the only car in sight. As we cut to ground level, Jerry and the distress that weighs him down suddenly snap into focus and regain their customary human-scale force. Jerry has just been humiliated by his father-in-law, Wade, who has taken one of Jerry's more intelligent moneymaking schemes out of his hands, and pointedly reminded him that a man without ready capital can make nothing of consequence happen. Jerry does not doubt the truth of Wade's gospel; he has, in fact, never thought otherwise.

When Jerry gets to his car, he discovers that the windows have frozen over in his absence and require scraping. As he distractedly sets about performing this familiar, irksome task, he meets unusually stiff resistance from the crust of ice settled on his windshield. Without warning, all the frustrations accumulated in him as a result of his defeats and general floundering erupt in a frenzy of ineffectual scraping, which in turn leads to an explosion of resentment. Once his violent fit has passed, however, the frozen windshield remains to be dealt with. There is no escaping the task at hand, if he desires to have adequate visibility for the drive home. He steps aside from the feelings that block the performance of his necessary work, and resumes, more methodically and patiently, his scraping. Jerry's efforts here do not, unfortunately, address the related visibility problems that cause his wife and son to be so completely hidden to him. Jerry's car is unyielding in its demands that one immediately attend to anything that will obstruct a clear view. There is no equivalently stern directive issued to the soul's gaze, when it clouds over. It is odd how many things can slip wholly out of sight without calling attention to the fact that they have gone missing. One's ability to move ahead in the face of an ever-more barren, depopulated visual field, without the *requirement* of alarm, is remarkable.

Let us go back for another glimpse at Carl hammering on his snowy television set, praying for a signal that will "plug" him into something that will assuage the fear of isolation. As if in answer to his appeal, the snowy screen is replaced with a clear one, where in extreme close-up a bark beetle is shown struggling to carry a worm to its nest. It may take us a few moments to figure out that we are watching an old, black-and-white television nature documentary, narrated by one of those bland, paternalistic voices that used to reassure us that all of nature's mysteries will gratefully surrender to the probing gaze of scientific authority. The signal that Carl has received, at first glance, seems to parallel his plight with the puny, futile exertions of an ephemera from the dregs of nature's kingdom. We are teased once again toward making an ironic judgment at a character's expense that he is too naive to make (or grasp) himself. We are meant to be startled, I think, by the additional revelation that it is not any longer Carl's television we are looking at but Marge and Norm Gunderson's. It is late in the evening, and only Marge is still awake to watch the show from her bed. Her husband is asleep beside her. Marge's perspective on the program is not distanced in the way that our first take on it encouraged ours to be. What holds her interest, in spite of her sleepiness, is the fact that the bark beetle is a mother, as Marge (with luck) will in just two more months be as well. She is perhaps struck by the bark beetle's efforts on behalf of her offspring, and the imposing struggle she undergoes, without hesitation, in order to feed them. This is the *true* part of the story, as she sees it, which doesn't need to be pried loose from the annoyingly official voice of the out-of-date narrator.

Marge doesn't require any reassurance about her status as a *human* mother in some indispensable hierarchy where the insect must occupy a lesser, lower place. If she were to dwell at all on the link between mothers, she would no doubt feel heartened rather than devalued by their mutual challenge. Truth, as Hannah Arendt often argued, is "not a result that comes at the end of a thought-process." On the contrary, truth "is always the beginning of thought; thinking is always result-less."[15] Marge Gunderson suggests through her quality of receptiveness how we might return to a useful point of beginning in order to reacquaint ourselves with truth. Perhaps her respect for truth, no matter how credulous, makes us curious about what it might mean once again to take the word seriously. Marge invariably starts with something small, as other characters for a variety of reasons forget to do, and demonstrates what a simple noting of attributes can bring to light in the way of value and satisfaction. One of her final observations to Norm is that his mallard painting—which has been chosen to appear on a new three-cent postage stamp rather than on a twenty-nine cent stamp, as he had hoped—will not be lost from view because, as he fears, people "don't much use the three-cent." She reminds him that the price of stamps is regularly raised, and because of that, people always "need the little stamps" to make up the difference. Marge's offhand tribute to the seeming throwaway stamp is, quite simply, satisfying—and not least as a way around the familiar taunt of the ingrained skeptic: "Just how little are you willing to settle for?"

Equally characteristic of Marge is her ability to keep things that are best left small from taking on a disproportionate weight and significance. The sort of small details that she is skilled at overlooking are behavioral transgressions and peculiarities that might seem to call for comment or rebuke or at times just private amusement. Perhaps Marge's most complex, beautifully tactful nonrecognition of a potentially troubling offense occurs during her meeting with Mike Yanagita in the hotel bar. Early in their conversation, Mike decides to make Marge aware of his romantic intentions by moving from his side of the booth to hers and, while drawing very close, placing his arm behind her. Marge promptly suggests that she would "prefer" him to be sitting across from her. Mike, sensing that he may have offended her, returns to his original seat and offers a sheepish apology. Marge then convincingly deflects his worry that she will hold his out-of-line conduct against him. She tells Mike, with no hint of reproach, that it is easier to converse with him if he is facing her, and, as a bonus courtesy, demonstrates how otherwise she would have to strain her neck to look at him. Marge betrays not the slightest sign of discomfort or injured feelings either to Mike or the viewer at any point in this exchange. She is so completely unreadable, in fact, that one could almost make a case that Mike's impertinence has escaped her notice. Here is an instance where Marge's reliably open demeanor takes us by surprise by becoming a perfect mask—designed to allow a former friend to save face. Marge demonstrates that she can be as resourceful as Jerry Lundegaard in making her expression a good hiding place, though the only advantage she hopes to gain is a preservation of mutual good will.

Marge's choice, in most situations, to refrain from calling others to account for their petty misconduct places her at the furthest possible remove from Wade Gustafson, Jerry's father-in-law, who is *Fargo*'s chief specialist in self-righteous browbeating. Wade consistently seizes on small infractions and bits of foolishness as a means of making those "guilty" of them *feel* small in relation to him. His arrogant scorekeeping sustains his large sense of himself as a man invariably in the right and entitled to all available privileges. (Even Jerry's deviousness and by-reflex obsequiousness acquire a certain emotional appeal—or at least greater acceptability—when juxtaposed with Wade's compulsive belittling.)

Wade's final undoing results from his confusion of his unbendable will with the natural order of things. He persuades himself that nothing opposed to his interests (that is, the natural order) can seriously challenge him. A situation where Wade must risk the loss of a huge sum of money to insure the safety of an asset (his daughter) that is rightfully his clearly makes no sense; no God with any notion of fair play would allow it. Everything that Wade is, and every Western he has ever seen, tell him that he must reject a deal whose terms he never agreed to and settle matters in person. He drives off at breakneck speed to settle with the kidnapper in place of Jerry, vehemently rehearsing his lines for the impending confrontation in a manner reminiscent of Jerry's, after his wife's disappearance. ("Goddam punk, where's my damn daughter?") Wade is absolutely certain that the "punk," pint-size fellow that he is, will fold up as soon as he can see the towering adversary he's up against. For Wade, not only the business world but the world as it exists *in itself* is obliged to recognize his superior standing and his massive presence. He is a natural extension of the towering office building where he works. The kidnappers may have felt they could get away with their crime (and the money) because they had hitherto confined their attention to Jerry, a nobody who is made for pushing around and who almost begs to be crushed. Wade, however, like Gary Cooper in *High Noon*, casts such a long shadow and possesses an aura of such invincible authority that he need only arrive on the scene and make himself visible to the small-fry kidnapper, and the latter, dismayed by his own presumption, will surrender both cash and daughter. Perhaps Wade will take a few lawful shots at his fleeing foe, to teach him a valuable life lesson.

Even as he places himself in extreme danger, Wade can't get past the idea of teaching yet another good-for-nothing a lesson. The viewer finds it next to impossible to form an image of Wade as an old man running a terrible risk out of love for his daughter. The implacable businessman is comically incapable of envisioning an outcome that will not ratify the *correctness* of his position. Chance and unforeseeable circumstances operate for lesser men; Wade is made safe by his knowing, here as always, that he is in the right.

When an enraged Carl, fresh from a merciless, "undeserved" thrashing at the hands of Shep Proudfoot, confronts the heroically puffed-up Wade on the parking ramp, he watches dumbfounded as a "pathetic geezer" launches into his rehearsed tough-guy routine. It is suddenly Wade's turn to be reduced, in an instant, to smallness. Far from being properly intimidated by his barked commands, Carl announces that this elderly stand-in for Jerry is no more than "a fuckin' joke," one which he hasn't the patience to laugh at. In Carl's mind, Wade is lumped together with the parking lot attendants, stupid accomplices, and "deaf," slow-service waiters that he has had to put up with since embarking on his miserable stint as a kidnapper. Wade is not differentiated, in fact, from any of the dozens of small irritants that have made Carl's job so needlessly complicated and unpleasant. Wade's unexpected appearance is just one frustration too many, and he is simply *not worth* arguing with.

Wade is movingly softened, for the first time in the film, as he is summarily stripped of status and then gunned down by a fed-up, distracted thug. He registers his astonishment at being shot in the gut with a peculiar half-smile, looking for a moment as though he were back in childhood, having to appease a grown-up he has made too angry through some inadvertent wrongdoing. Collapsing to the pavement, Wade clutches at the bullet hole in his parka from which tiny feathers rather than blood surprisingly flow. No sooner does he settle into his final role as an ill-prepared old-timer who has stumbled, touchingly, into death than it is Carl's turn, once again, to be made small. Reaching for Wade's briefcase, Carl casts a last contemptuous glance at the "fucking imbecile" who thought he could make trouble for him, and in so doing sees the dying man recover enough presence of mind to shoot *him* in the jaw. Carl echoes Wade's brief regression to a childlike state; his blood-smeared face is both frightening and amusingly suggestive of a prodigious nosebleed.

How often, especially in the late scenes of *Fargo*, characters' assured bids for power and for the high visual definition (icon status) that comes from being at one with a "hard" persona result in a radical diminishment of capacity. When we witness extravagant gestures collapse in the effort to magnify the personal, or to show that the personal indeed has some force, some majestic vigor, we are returned to the beginning of *Fargo*: the long, ironic view. The inhuman, unvarying terrain of the opening snowstorm reasserts itself and imparts a quality of mirage to all human striving. One figure after another makes his final mark, the only one that matters, as a spray of blood in the snow. In the words of Edmond Jabes, "And in that unbroken sameness of sky and [snow], you're nothing, absolutely nothing."[16]

When Marge, in the closing scene of the film, is discovered where we originally encountered her, in her cozy bedroom sanctuary with Norm, how satisfactorily does this setting (and the couple in it) work as a reply to the cumulative grisliness and comic degradation that have come before? Can we not almost hear the dreadful sound of the woodchipper or Jerry's animal scream upon being apprehended continuing faintly in the distance? And are we not, at least fleetingly, reminded of other ironic, "return to normal" film endings—chiefly, perhaps, *Blue Velvet*'s overlit kitchen in a suburban Lumberton bungalow, whose complacent occupants are surveyed by an artificial robin on a tree branch, with an ugly insect in its beak? There is, at present, something deeply suspect about closing a serious film with images of comfort and repose in the realm of middle-class domesticity. Tranquillity by fiat automatically sets us on edge and encourages ironic dismissal. To be at rest, after all, is not to be on the alert; and an intimacy that dispenses with sophistication and the need to be, in any telling way, remarkable, appears, surely, too straightforward, too *obvious*, when regarded as a point of closure for such an intricate film. The word "obvious" has its own enigmatic dimension, however, having not entirely shed its original meaning of "blocking the path" to something. Are Marge and Norm, huddled in bed together as they prepare for sleep, obscuring our view of more essential matters, or is our impatient itch to get past the mundane obvious that they stand for blocking our path to an available but not simple meaning?

Marge's last words to Norm are a repetition of *his* just offered phrase, "two more months." The couple are thinking about the small space of time that they must wait before their baby arrives and makes everything in their settled life together different. Perhaps the Coens intend for us to recall here the film's other child, the all-but-forgotten Scotty, who has suffered in swift, incomprehensible succession, the loss of his entire family. His terrible luck—and the concealed agony of his present, "exposed" situation—seem to put pressure on the whole idea of good fortune, and on Marge and Norm's trust (or hope) that *their* child will be spared undue affliction. If we remember to think about Scotty, is there still something worth dwelling on in this ordinary sight of a couple drawing close, watching television in bed, and trying to catch a glimpse of their future? What details help us focus the scene, before the image passes away?

Fargo is a film which reminds us, continually, of how easy and even likely it is for human beings to remain disconnected from each other, to squander the majority of chances they have to make the time they spend together *count*—count as time present, because of what is sensed or shared or made known. Marge and Norm's quiet, "small change" encounter may do no more than remind us what genuine human connection looks like, but that is perhaps not a negligible feat, if connection is so hard to come by in the world "out there." They provide a measure of solace, animal warmth, and tangible attentiveness to each other late at night; they are guiding each other to rest, and though neither is complaining about the strains of the day they've been through, they are mutually alleviating strain by talk that fits and suits them. Against the immense power of emptiness that *Fargo* often makes us feel is placed the low-level, heartbeat power of effective companionship. And though, as Thomas Browne declares in *Urne Buriall*, "the night of time far surpasseth the day,"[17] before daylight sense goes under we might reasonably consider this pair's unequivocal satisfaction at being together "for now" as improbable and miraculous as anything larger that could be revealed to us.

In one of his recent stories, "The Womanizer," Richard Ford has a character worry at considerable length whether now is the time to "take a true reading" of his life: "when the tide was out and everything exposed—including himself—as it really, truly was. *There* was the real life, and he wasn't deluded about it."[18] Ford has alerted us to be on our guard about this character's ability to arrive at a true reading, or recognize the moment (if there ever is one) when a true reading can be taken. He is, in short, ironic about his character's sense of himself within the situation, without using irony to secure a writerly vantage point that is morally outside the fray, in a *better position* to see what's what. A bit later the character gets closer to his own truth as he relinquishes the notion of a definitive true reading. In its place he posits the "crucial linkages of a good life," which "he *knew* were small and subtle and in many ways just lucky things that you hardly ever noticed" (my emphasis).[19] Marge's "naïveté," which *Fargo,* surprisingly, does not overturn or complicate, comes from a just appreciation of obvious, daily linkages, and from the good fortune, unaffected by the prevailing winds of irony, to notice them.

10

Drowning for Love: Jean-Claude Lauzon's *Léolo*

The image is fast fading out. The light that made it now dismantles it.

—Robin Robertson, "Camera Obscura"

It is hard / to understand how we could be brought here by love.

—Jack Gilbert

Synopsis: Jean-Claude Lauzon's second feature film, the autobiographical *Léolo*, presents episodes from the savage, baroque childhood of French-Canadian Leo Lauzon (Maxime Collin), in a phantasmagoric blend of memory and fantasy. The narrative does not allow us to make confident distinctions between what transpires in the boy's outer and inner life, but for purposes of preliminary summary I will hazard some guesses about the mutable facts of Leo's history. Leo lives with his parents, grandfather, brother, and two sisters in a cramped tenement in East Montreal, Quebec. Everyone in Leo's family, except for his mother (Ginette Reno) and himself, is afflicted with a severe, recurring mental disorder, at times resembling catatonia, which necessitates periods of confinement in a psychiatric ward. Leo's father (Roland Blouin), brutish and numb from his mindless job at the foundry, seems to have but one idea left in his head: proper bowel movements are the antidote to all of his family's health problems. Leo's first memories are of his mother's efforts to toilet train him in infancy and of his painful inability to satisfy her wishes.

Leo renames himself Léolo to mark the beginning of his self-awareness. He shouts his strong, new name to the winter night sky while he pees from his family's upstairs balcony. While still a very small child, he endeavors to dissociate himself from his family. He is determined to outwit the genetic fate that dooms all the Lauzons to a life of compliant wretchedness. Inspired by the single book (Réjean Ducharme's *L'avalée*

Léolo's grandfather (Julien Guiomar) nearly executed for his crimes against love in *Léolo*.

des avalés) that has somehow made its way into his otherwise art-bereft home, Leo begins to plan his escape from heredity and environment *through writing*, devoting a large part of each day to committing his thoughts and impressions to any scrap of paper he can find.[1] He learns what it means to be loyal to language for its own sake. He is sustained in this activity by his vision of a perfect reader, whom he calls the Word Tamer (Pierre Bourgault). Disguised by day as a derelict picking through garbage receptacles for salvage of all sorts, the Word Tamer lives by night in a candlelit heaven of lost and forgotten art objects. Leo's scraps of writing are carefully read, savored, and stored away by this imaginary elder patron. He is Leo's best hope that a meaningful alternative to his present situation exists *somewhere* and that the child's dreaming self points the way to it.

Leo is also intensely drawn to a teenaged Italian girl named Bianca (Giuditta del Vecchio), who lives in a neighboring flat. She embodies for him the innocence and joyful peasant vitality of a mythical Sicily. Though he never exchanges a word with Bianca, he plans to accompany her to Sicily one day, certain that he will find there his true spiritual homeland. Leo's older brother, Fernand (Yves Montmarquette), plots his own form of getaway from a life of daily humiliation. He commits himself totally to the religion of bodybuilding but is eventually defeated in his efforts to become a man whom others will fear and respect when he is given a beating by the same bully who had laid into him as a child. Leo witnesses his brother's defeat and sees him lose in an instant his belief that he has transformed himself into a different person.

As Leo approaches adolescence, his behavior becomes increasingly rash, self-destructive, and heartless. He attaches himself to a group of equally desperate young boys who experiment with any form of vice within reach: drugs, sex, animal torture. Leo attempts, unsuccessfully, to kill his grandfather (Julien Guiomar) with a meticulously planned scheme of hanging the old patriarch while he bathes. What prompts this ferocious attack is mainly his grandfather's persistent sexual exploitation of Bianca. Finally, having betrayed the best impulses of his childhood and lost touch with the truth that had once allowed him to forge a separate identity in his writing, he falls into a coma and is transferred to a hospital-asylum. By a strange paradox, the ending suggests that he succumbs to the family tragedy not because he has failed to cast his family off but because he has perhaps, in some inexpressible sense, been unworthy of them. The Word Tamer, however, continues to preserve all the fragments of Leo's attempts—as a writer—to give form and meaning to his tumultuous childhood experience.[2]

Léolo is the record of a struggle between two desires: the desire to face bravely and without shame all the ways in which Lauzon belongs to his strangely cursed family, and the desire to void his membership in this family. Lauzon revisits his childhood because this is the place where his memories of both subjection and love are strongest and least dismissable. Within memory, as Luis Buñuel once suggested, we find, if anywhere, "our coherence, our reason, our feeling, even our action."[3] The idea of our memory disappearing is terrifying because we know that our most intimate selfhood, salvaged bit by bit from the wreckage of our days, will vanish with it. Yet memories are never merely our benefactor. Holding painful ones at a manageable distance takes up much of our mental energy. Those that can't be moved from the glare of full consciousness or the dark of absolute denial are like tumors, and it seems scarcely an exaggeration to speak of their lethal power. Part of Lauzon's reason for making *Léolo*, then, is to make memory into a controllable structure, to become its author, if you like, so that it will somehow reconcile rather than exacerbate his warring desires.

Lauzon's method of looking back at his childhood reminds us that memory does not enjoy being literal, or taking even the most dire situations at face value. Memory does not move in straight lines, nor assemble things in proper sequence. We imagine what we experience, not only after the fact but while it is going on. That capacity is what steers whatever we undergo in a personal direction. Imagination, our best survival mechanism, refines the raw materials of our outward plight. As a conserving force, it helps memory decide what is worth holding onto when so much that happens passes so swiftly into oblivion. And as a curative, imagination lightens forms of affliction that would, in an unaltered state, prove unbearable.

For Lauzon, an imagination that operates passively and unrebelliously in collaboration with external forces will very early on lose its power to make a difference. The child, to put it simply, will stop seeing. Lauzon conceives the child that he was "once upon a time," balanced on the tightrope imagination has given him. This rope is stretched across a mind forever in danger of sinking into numbness or idiocy. If the rope breaks (an ever-present possibility), there will be no other. Lauzon believes he can only keep his imagination alive and strong by occupying it like a warrior. In order to take control of memory and construct anew his still festering childhood environment, he must begin by setting himself at odds with all the elements of reality that have been *assigned* to him by others. The world he inhabits shall be reduced to as few *givens* as possible.

For Lauzon, what counts as a given is anything that undermines the transforming power of dream and fantasy. The presumably natural first facts that set most life histories in motion—one's biological parents, the name on one's birth certificate—are, in Lauzon's view, so treacherous and steeped in fate that to concede their truth (as a settled matter) is already a death warrant. Lauzon's origin is as much a quandary and a playground for conjecture as Tristram Shandy's. The first story presented in *Léolo* tells us that Leo's true father is an anonymous Italian peasant who once upon a time insolently masturbated on a tomato marked for shipment to Canada. Some days later, this same tomato, by happy accident, became lodged in Leo's mother's womb long enough for her to be impregnated. Lauzon presents this buffoonish, squalid alternative to the "known facts" of his birth with as much giddy pride in his new status as if he had been revealed—fairy-tale fashion—to be the lost son of a king. It is as though any more lavish wish for a different lineage would be denied fulfillment because the imagination proved too greedy. The prospect of connecting himself to a better place (Sicily), and to a father who is at least sane, is so appealing to the child-author Lauzon that he willingly forgoes all thought of a higher class or any increase in privileges. In the kingdom of the unfortunate, the attention of the gods is not easily won, and one must keep one's demands not only modest but amusing to tempt their generosity. Lauzon revises his ancestry by placing himself as far beyond his father's genetic reach as a hard-nosed, peasant fable will permit. The semen-stained tomato can be viewed as a temperamental recoil from romantic gestures that are too high-flown, too withdrawn from the wormy, lower earth that powerfully feeds Lauzon's dream life. Though there is a fierce romantic strain in Lauzon's work, there is an equally intense need to weight every transcendent impulse with the mean refuse of poverty. However much contempt he feels for his family's enslavement to a life without curiosity, comfort, or art, Lauzon cannot betray that life by distancing himself, for any length of time, from its harsh materials. His heart lies down amidst harrowing things and knows itself to be at home *there,* despite the spirit's yearning to pitch its tent higher up.

Léolo is a film haunted by the difficulty of beginning. Lauzon doesn't want to think of his beginning as an irreversible first step, one which duplicates the mechanism of heredity and commits him (like a story arrived at its final form) to a determinist view of things. He aspires to dissolve, as much as possible, the constraints of filmic time and space, so he can hover above his life for a while, like an aircraft, and not belong to any image which too decisively identifies him. The effort to avoid discovery and naming suggests a fear of not being sufficiently protean in his sense of himself. To be discovered seems to carry with it the threat of being seen through and dismissed. And yet, Lauzon's drive to reveal himself—totally—is as great as his dread of being trapped in a too limited identity. To possess yourself with any force, he repeatedly suggests, you must not be afraid of losing anything to others' zeal for judging by appearances. So, how to begin?

Beginning properly means clearing a space large and indeterminate and fluid enough to allow the film's young protagonist to maneuver freely. The opening must not feel like a settled place, giving spectators the confidence to attach Leo to a background with certain tidy meanings. Lauzon is determined to outwit potential jailers of all sorts, whether they present themselves as family members or as movie viewers who assume that their decision to watch *Léolo* grants them some authority over its subject. Lauzon's anxiety about fixed starting points can only be relieved by the decision to have his narrative begin not once but many times, so often in fact that one quickly loses track of sequential order. Each new commencement attempts, by the force of its images and sounds, to loosen the grip of what has preceded it.

Lauzon protects his surrogate's own first appearances within the fearsome house of childhood by making the *viewers'* points of entry to this dwelling confusing and provisional, implying that every room comes equipped with a secret escape route. (The unstable narrative time frame, which overlaps several different periods of Lauzon's childhood with no obvious system, creates temporal escape routes to go along with the enticing domestic passageways the camera reveals to us.) The rhythm of the film is established immediately as a tug-of-war between images of enlargement and images of compression. The sudden widening out of conventional boundaries keeps pace with a ruthless litany of privations. Cramped rooms enlarge, natural vistas open up, time hangs luxuriously suspended in the dusty, somnolent air whenever freedom of any kind seems attainable. In those blessed intervals when the child's solitude appears like a fantastic jewel unmenaced by the clamor and contagious stupor of his kin, or by the sheer hardness of the world outside, Lauzon shows him effortlessly entering into realms bright with revelation. Light pours through an open closet door, a girl's voice rises in welcoming song and Leo, like Saul on the road to Damascus, is shaken by visions violent with love and ecstatic surrender—the rending nearness of fulfillment. Solitude, in its productive hours, is, in Bruno Schulz's phrase, "the catalyst that brings reality to fermentation."[4] But Lauzon is compelled to add: take care that you don't withdraw too deeply inside it. Ineluctably joined to solitude's beautiful fever is the steady threat of his family's hereditary madness. Haunting the heroic solitary in Lauzon is the specter of tiny, enfeebled destinies, beckoning to him in chains.

The rhythmic alternation between views of things opening up and closing down is tied to Lauzon's belief in reversal as the first law of narrative movement. I use the word "reversal" in the hope that it can be readily distinguished from its frequent companion, "negation." Unlike many reviewers of *Léolo* who were repelled by the film's apparent coldness and self-absorbed despair, I do not see Lauzon's main concern as the negation of possibilities. The frank depiction of childhood horrors might initially suggest an angry survivor's settling of accounts with those who have made him suffer. But vengeance recovers nothing of interest from reactivated "time past," as Lauzon well knows. Every window and door that memory yields to the man bent on retaliation turns out to be a wrong entrance. The rooms have no color, the air is poisonous, the time that he would relive is used-up time, where nothing but frozen, hyperbolic gestures remain.

To regard memory as the scene of a vast crime against yourself—even when the impulse seems justified—tends to make everything one retrieves impervious to clear light. Getting at the truth is confused with the fixation on wrongdoing. The moment of revelation is likely to mean catching someone in an unforgivable act—where the truth teller plays the part of the blameless victim. One of the terrible facts of life is that real victims, like persecutors, must live in time, which means moving past the moment where an event has a pure, unmistakable shape. Perhaps such moments are never fully available to consciousness. Going back to the evil done against you, however necessary in a court of justice or in a therapy session, requires one to play a role that was formerly messily lived, and it is never an exact fit. Often we damage ourselves, and our memory, by trying to make the fit exact. Remembered acts of others' cruelty and neglect can so easily become all-encompassing. A person who has done us injury can be reduced in memory to a single, defining gesture, performed by rote, like a mechanical figure on a clock who appears through a certain door whenever the hour of bitterness strikes.

Reversal, as Lauzon employs it, is an attempt to keep "yes" and "no" possibilities equally in play at all times, by moving us back and forth between the two poles with bewildering rapidity. "Yes" and "no"—what can be affirmed and negated in every situation—are pressed very close to each other throughout *Léolo*. Lauzon's framing, camera movement, editing, and elaborate voice-over narration all work to set antithetical values side by side, in intimate, quarrelsome relation, like the two brothers in the film (Leo and the mountainous Fernand) forced to share a single bed. Reversal, of course, is one of the most common devices in drama, and is fundamental to any successful film technique. What does Lauzon's formal and ethical approach to reversal require of us in this film?

Just as it is impossible for an actor to play two contrary intentions or feelings at the same moment, it is impossible for a movie spectator to occupy strong "yes" and "no" emotional positions (relative to a character) simultaneously. Both actors and spectators, however, have the ability to shift from one feeling to another very quickly. Only an instant or two is required to traverse large emotional distances, and to do so with remarkable precision. Every good film editor knows that the main function of a cut is to keep the emotion of a scene flowing, by fair means or foul, and that flow demands, paradoxically, a certain clash and tension between the images. One adds an image of "something else" to set what has come just before in relief. The "something else" applies some sort of "reversal" pressure to the preceding image that keeps alive viewer expectation and very often builds up a need to get back to what has been taken away from us, so we can see (and, the editor hopes, *feel*) what has altered in our brief absence from it. Prolonged camera movement is editing by other means, removing things from view to reveal other things, ideally in a manner that turns spectator feeling in a different direction. Things must forcefully strike the viewer's eye in passing to register at all on film. Each new element that appears should seem to separate sharply from what it replaces, so that it will gain some of its impact through its relation to what is no longer visible. In other words, one can be led to feel what is left behind as the camera goes forward, so that successive disclosures rustle with transience. There is a continual subtle revision of the emotional landscape in a well-planned tracking shot, like sunlight moving in and out of cloud cover. And the idea of objects taking over the light from other objects reminds us of photography's close kinship with death's slow dissolve.

Lauzon clearly understands how a camera's movement can remove things from view in an emotionally charged way. For him, the removal is most often allied with death and loss. When his camera tracks through the unfastened, banging windows of his parents' bedroom on a lightning-filled night, trying to make contact with his earliest memories, we seem to be floating through a kind of funeral in the brain. Instead of having the sense of a scene being restored to life, one feels that all signs speak of life slipping away. The room is lit by banks of candles, an angelic hymn swells up like a tide to make mourners of us as we slowly advance. Father is sprawled motionless on a bed, fully clothed, almost an apparition on the more solid mass of rumpled bedding. What is our destination? A cavernous bathroom, in which a small wailing child is held prisoner on a makeshift potty. All the forces conspiring against growth, freedom, rescue of any sort seem to greet the desolate camera visitor as it closes in on the bathroom. The fantastic array of candles with their permeating warm light do not work against the oppressiveness or provide any real shelter from the thunderstorm atmosphere. The candles seem tied to the crooning voice of mother, who faces her child— huge and inescapable as a Church service—from her own toilet seat, urging him to "push, my love" and to stop crying. She holds a flashlight which she points at him, like a prison searchlight. Here we have an honest but misguided expression of love, whose capacity to injure is vastly increased by its well-meaningness. Who can measure the price of love?

"Kind, gentle mama nails me to this pot each night, and if I am to please her I must empty myself. Whatever I give up, let go of, she tells me she can replenish with her hugs."

This episode, and others like it, introduce soft, gleaming, lavishly beautiful materials and then promptly reverse their pleasurable associations. A ravishing visual surface becomes our channel into bitter, corporeal hells. Horrific images, in Robert Lowell's celebrated line, "meathooked from the living steer,"[5] erupt from openings where something benevolent and healing seems poised to reveal itself. Occasions such as these bring forth the desperate, negative vein in Lauzon's visionary style; imagination and memory seem helplessly in thrall here to repudiation. The act of recollecting can so easily leave one stunned by the sheer quantity of things in life that cannot be undone. But if the camera, in its strange devil's pact with the world of appearances, can continually discover the monstrous within the beautiful, it also has an uncanny gift for resurrecting whatever it so firmly places in death's hands. The camera restores hope by the same means that it takes it away—once again, the simple act of *reversing* direction.

The time of a film is reversible time. Anything that enters the time sphere of a moving picture can be returned to, reclaimed for the attention "just as it was" (through a repeating shot) or slightly but crucially transformed (an alternate take). The reversal and pliability of time's motion is film's way of proclaiming, potently, that whatever is destroyed now is gone only conditionally. The whole of time, insofar as film can apprehend it, is "a mass of conjoint possibilities"[6] whose editing order again and again averts the inevitable. A camera's farewell to an image can be final or momentary. Movement away may eventually come full circle, and give anything back to us, shining with the full light of our first beholding. The dead can be restored to life, so that we may watch them turn their attention once more to interrupted tasks: washing themselves, opening the blinds to check the weather, coming down to breakfast. A gesture or phrase that never found its "proper" moment completes itself. Missing pieces are magically found, the child or parent given up for lost suddenly appears, moving up the path toward home. Robert Graves's lovely phrase, "past all hope where the kind lamp shone"[7] evokes the emotional space in any shot sequence where the forces of "no" unaccountably yield to widened boundaries of life.

In *Léolo*, scenes are often replayed with slight variations, at a later point in the narrative, reversing the significance of our first reading. Repetition can be traumatic, in film narratives as in nightmares, but it can also provide chances to approach the same set of binding conditions by different routes, and gradually to make them manageable. Repetition in *Léolo* also deliberately assumes the character of religious rituals. Brutal and profane elements are lifted—on their second and third appearances—into the realm of the sacred, and not merely for the sake of parody. Toxic images, which initially seem to express a scalding hopelessness, often come back to us as a place of renewal. Total prostration is often the nesting ground for rapturous mystery.

How does Lauzon intercede on behalf of the infant wailing on his potty in the depths of night? How does he turn the mother who regards her son's shit as the proof—indeed, the very image—of his love for her into a tenable provider of freedom, emotional ease, and self-possession? He accomplishes this transformation in two stages. While we are still looking at the distressed infant in close-up and listening to his cries, a space beside him opens in the frame, revealing the head of an elderly man, radiating benevolence, who is reading in his study. The camera moves into this new environment with such a smooth, gentle motion that the study becomes a wing of the bathroom, continuous with it in space and time. Candlelight of a less ominous sort is also the source of illumination here. The mother's grotesquely abortive efforts to soothe and encourage are translated in the old man's features into the quality of loving acceptance that they mean to be. The old man's voice repeats the fragment of narration that we have just heard spoken by Leo's adult self, who throughout the film softly reads to us from the child Leo's journal—his book of memory. The old man has somehow come into possession of the scraps of paper on which the toilet-training memory was first set down. He is a *second* reader, an ideal reader, one fully responsive both to what the writing directly conveys and to what it aims to express, without quite knowing how. He echoes the phrase "the smells and the light that solidified my first memories." He laughs with appreciation at Leo's reference to his grandmother's fervent belief in daily bowel movements as a cure-all.

Our brief contact with this sympathetic eavesdropper on Leo's anguished first memory begins to reverse its emotional meaning. We are reminded that the rawness and chill of the primal suffering are, to some degree, ameliorated by their passage into another medium—written language. More important, however, is the suggestion that the struggle to make sense of what happened is not merely another form of isolation. The rough notes the boy has composed, no matter how disjointed or incomplete, have found their way into safe hands. The old man, whom the narrator will later identify as the Word Tamer, takes each of Leo's tangled messages into his luminous understanding and surrounds them with his own healing quietness. He "tames words" in the same spirit that one might calm a frightened animal—stroking every phrase with his gentle voice, keeping close watch over Leo's feverish outpourings until the agitation shows signs of abating.

Lauzon's other attempt to redeem the endless night of potty captivity (stage two of the transformation) comes several scenes later, after we have watched an older Leo refuse to swallow the laxative that he and every member of his family gather to receive, like communion wafers, each day. When we return to the crying infant on his pot, lit by the same thunderstorm, with mother still intoning her grim instructions about "pushing" and "not crying," another observer has entered the scene. It is a turkey that the narrator tells us Leo's mother has won at a movie theater, resting in an adjoining bathtub. The turkey's head rises above the rim of the tub and meets the child's gaze with what feels like vehement alertness. Though the bird's foulness is stressed in the narration ("its remaining feathers were damp and stinky"), it functions in this context like an emissary from some delectable golden isle. It distracts the child from its misery enough so that he stops crying. The turkey then raises itself to an imposing height, and becomes through this act of resplendent, unchallengeable wildness the strongest presence in the room. Mother instantly loses her capacity to hold her son's mind "in custody" to his ordeal.

As she repeats the injunction "Do like mama," the camera follows the child's freshly liberated gaze into the dark mystery between her outspread legs on the toilet. Lauzon seems initially to have chosen an escape route from the scene that will only compound the obscenity of what transpires. It feels as though the child's eye is carrying us toward a destination that is clammily taboo: an engulfing womb steaming with the odor of defecation. But on the far side of this Stygian corridor an unexpected realm of marvels awaits us. A joyful tribal chant suddenly rings out on the soundtrack, summoning us to a celebration in the underworld. Two figures wearing illuminated miners' helmets move toward the camera from the far distance, in what appears to be a gigantic, drizzling cavern. The darkness glistens with light flaming up from free-standing torches. We soon identify Leo—here a young boy—as one of the two fearless travelers in the night world. His older companion is the Word Tamer. Both carry identical buckets, which serve, like the matching helmets, to link the pair together on a shared mission. Their breath is visible in the cold, but no discomfort registers.

Adversity has turned magical, as it so often does for children included in a grown-up adventure.

We cut away from this walking scene for a view of the Word Tamer's private museum, the camera tracking through a collection of beautiful art objects, in pleasing disarray. The Word Tamer is once again silently reading a manuscript. Who exactly is this man? What sort of reality does he dwell in, and how is it connected to the child's? The narrator tells us here that the old man spends his nights "digging in the garbage of the world. Only letters and photographs interest him." (In other words, he is drawn to documents imbued with feeling which actively seek out fellowship, along with pictures preserving odd bits of memory from extinction.) The narration continues: "He carried every smile, every glance, every word of love, every separation as if it was his own story." The Word Tamer's identity, as it gradually fills out for us, is that dimension of Leo's imagination which says "yes" to the world, despite all evidence of the world's frightening unresponsiveness. The Word Tamer keeps alive the dream that there is some presence on earth, however hidden from sight, that is passionately *for* us. He is the imagination's answer to prayer, a kindred soul who sees and sustains and encourages us in the very depths of our solitude. Our actions and thoughts do not rebound back on themselves like the remains of some idle fantasy. The power of our attentiveness to the world brings forth a similar force of attentiveness in things themselves. The process of opening ourselves unreservedly to an object may strengthen its ability to direct an answering light back to us. As in Rilke, the answering presence, or Word Tamer, moves closest to Leo when he is least acquisitive, when he is prepared to let everything, fear as well as security, go. "The serene/ countenance dissolved in night makes room for yours."[8]

When we leave the Word Tamer's museum we are once more outdoors, facing a bonfire before which Leo and the Tamer, still in their miners' helmets, are sitting. Leo takes an armful of irreplaceable letters and photographs that the old man offers him and, as he has been directed, drops them into the blaze. The camera—called to witness the death of its own powers—closes in as a number of poignantly old portrait photographs are consumed. How quickly the preserved, singular faces blur together, blacken, and vanish. The narration accompanying this sacrificial ceremony declares the Word Tamer's belief that "images and words must mingle with the ashes of the worms to be reborn in the imaginations of men." The fight with isolation that Leo wages throughout the film receives its purest but most difficult visualization of remedy in this scene. Only once in *Léolo* are Leo and the Word Tamer able to be together, as comrades unseparated by distance. While the narrator speaks of the Word Tamer's desire to be Leo's protector, we are granted a stunning long-shot view of the two of them on a tiny bit of dry land, tending their fire with a solitary tree behind them. On all sides are roaring cataracts, plunging to unseen depths. The sky above the lonely watch fire is threateningly dark. The narration links the torrential flow of water with the "black hole" of Leo's family, reminding us that this entire fantasy segment commenced as a journey "backward" into the mother's womb. The final image of the two of them yields many revelations at once. The forces of freedom have been mobilized; a child blossoms forth as an entity capable of withstanding the terrors of helplessness, able to make his own peace with a world that is not impossibly distant, not closed off. Leo entrusts his homelessness and habitual dread to someone fully attached to life and warmth, an old man who shares the boy's burden and shows him how to set it down, shows him that every external sign of his being becomes *more* real when it is moved inside him. Passing through fire and ashes does not necessarily result in death. The imagination needs to disintegrate the forms that it will later resurrect and consecrate. It is a secular version of Christ's summons: he who would save his life must first lose it.

In *Léolo* the camera takes instruction in how to see from the quiet, endlessly attentive and patient Word Tamer. Its vision strives to acknowledge "every smile, every glance, every word of love, every separation" as vital to its "own story," and regards every instance of neglect as a failure of the moral imagination. (I think it is fair to say that there is a will to coldness in Lauzon himself which he *needs* the camera to oppose.) When the Word Tamer dimension of Lauzon is in command, the camera endeavors neither to flatter nor abuse what it holds in view. Lauzon often seems to catch himself slighting the value of small, positive gestures in those scenes where cruelty and pathetic compulsions so fully dominate viewer attention that a meaningful compassion seems unthinkable. If Lauzon's family history often runs the risk of becoming a sterile, repetitive mechanism, the Word Tamer is the ethical force that moves this history *beyond* the mechanical. He divines the pause space in every stretch of filmic time when love or its possibility can manifest itself. He and his camera surrogate are forever on the lookout for "the space a man was meant for," as Brad Leithauser has termed it, "wrested from the drowning green and blue."[9]

We are made mindful of this space, and its spiritual contours, as early as the film's opening shot. The camera begins by showing us the top of a building with the year of its construction (1909) engraved like a headstone marking at its highest point. (Lauzon has acknowledged in interviews that the building is the actual house he grew up in.) As the narrator addresses us for the first time, identifying what we are seeing as "*my* place," in Mile End, Montreal, Canada, the camera gradually descends, passing a shabby-looking upstairs balcony containing some aluminum lawn chairs, and a long set of steps leading up to the house's entrance. Without pausing to settle on him, the camera notices a young boy in a cowboy hat seated on one of the steps, taking aim with a toy rifle at some unseen target in the distance and firing. It is crucial to the design of this shot that the camera passes over the boy and his initial flourish of bored, make-believe aggression, as though he were not what the viewer should focus on and validate. Before we go back to him, something larger than the child's immediate hostility needs to be located and embraced.

After Leo disappears from the frame—so casually observed that he cannot achieve point-of-view authority—our gaze comes to rest, and seemingly widens out, at ground level. We pause, in a way that feels effortless, in a space that is alive with ordinary beauty, altogether different from the drab markers of poverty and confinement with which the shot commenced. An open downstairs window catches our attention in the middle distance because its curtains ripple in the morning breeze with a lacy delicacy. Two bicycles rest in the grass, conveying a hopeful summons to adventure from the warmest summer recesses of childhood memory. When the camera halts in this enchanted corner of the yard and cleanly lifts us out of the shot's original feeling of stale hemmed-in-ness, one is reminded of how much the play of contingency determines the mood of vision. The duration of the camera's hold on this view is necessary for its soothing quality of interiority to sink in. Only in this spot, and perhaps only from this exact angle can the setting release its power to console, and possibly improve the lot of the child "doing time" here. But a tension arises from the fact that the boy with the rifle is so strikingly cut off from the camera's healing vantage point.

How does Leo partake of this authoritative first "outspreading" of vision? The answer arrives in the highlighted transition from this shot to the one that succeeds it. A slow lap-dissolve causes the mystery of the softly billowing curtains to generate a spectral afterimage, as if in reply to the question: "What good thing might lie within such an enticing window frame?" We sense almost a rustle of dim objects before we are able to make out an older version of the first child laboring at his writing desk. The voice-over phrase "Because I dream, I am not" is introduced as a knife-edge dividing line between the two realms—exterior and interior. The second moving camera shot (boy at writing desk) is subtly proposed as the creative source of the "memory" shot preceding it. Note once again how the camera reverses the direction (and meaning) of the earlier shot while seeming to expand upon it. The place of seeing becomes the boy who is committing words to paper. It is as though he were the hidden presence in the curtained window who is imaginatively recovering the one, easily overlooked point of equilibrium in his environment: the rescue point. It is the point where the scattered, unpromising materials of the boy's world come together and form a whole. We are granted access, as he is, to the ideal dreaming space, and thus have the sense of fitting the right key to the right door of the past. For the moment, at any rate.

"Because I dream, I am not." This oracular pronouncement returns again and again in the film's narration, as though Lauzon had managed to find just once his true home "in one sentence, concise, as if hammered in metal." (Czeslaw Milosz regards this securing of "home" in an unforfeitable "sentence" as the chief aim of his poetry, his best chance against "chaos and nothingness."[10]) How large does the "not" loom in Lauzon's trim credo, and what is left over when the force of negation has spent itself? The "not," I have argued, attaches itself to all the limiting labels and coercive alliances that form around the child without his consent and seek to hold him hostage. "I am *not* this man's son; I am *not* the same as these others; I am *not* mad; I am *not* ruled by fear or shame; I am *not* alone." The assertive "I dream" opposes itself to these and other ambushes of the vulnerable psyche. The waking dream resembles in its activity the routine survival mechanisms of most afflicted children: blotting out the source of distress by turning the inner gaze *elsewhere*, it hardly matters where. A television screen will serve as well as a drug, a favorite piece of music, a computer game, or a pet one might alternately hug and torture. Children, like everyone else, require a "beyond," and most of the time, again like their elders, they reach automatically for the one that lies closest.

The important questions to ask about escape routes, as Ernest Becker recommends in *The Denial of Death*, are: "What kind of beyond does [the] person try to expand in; and how much individuation does he achieve in it?"[11] Reading and, preeminently, imaginative writing are, of course, Leo/Léolo's chosen methods of attaining a meaningful beyond, but "what kind of beyond" do they afford access to, once denial and escape have done their utmost? Let us extend Becker's list of questions. Once Leo has found the courage to say "NO! in thunder"[12] to the soul-shriveling options others set before him, what does he find within and outside himself to accept and make his peace with? Are the glimpses of beauty that the observant child encounters in the most unlikely places and "catches" in language for the Word Tamer (as his sister catches pleasing insects in a jar)—are these glimpses adding up to some sort of progress of love? Is his rage against authority an insurmountable impediment to his desire to lay himself open to things? Does his longing for freedom move him (compulsively, self-protectively) in a different direction from his longing to love? Is there any chance of the two longings being revealed, in a gratifying denouement, as the same thing?

Surely the oddest feature of *Léolo*'s structure is its ultimate insistence that the child has failed in his project, that he has not proven strong enough to evade the "living death" sentence that has claimed most of the others in his family. Our last view of the boy in the film's *present* tense shows him harrowingly afloat in a hospital ice bath, his precious consciousness gone in a form of coma. The room he ends up in is a literal cage, as we viscerally discover when an attendant pulls a gate of bars across our field of vision to lock him in. This fiercely punitive end point seems to sever not only the spectator's empathic connection with Leo's heroic struggle (declaring it, for all intents and purposes, *over*) but Lauzon's as well. I think Lauzon is implying that whatever he has become in his own right as an adult cannot be made continuous with the radiant, perished potential of his former life as a child. The very existence of the film *Léolo* would seem to testify powerfully against such a view, but Lauzon refuses to see this gathering of words and images as a reconciling bridge between worlds. He conceives his film rather as "a strange half-bridge," in Jeanette Winterson's words, "drawn up (like the Rialto in Venice) to stop one half of this city from warring with the other. . . . Bridges join, but they also separate."[13]

The self-possessed, adult voice of *Léolo*'s narrator has misled us from the first. The mature survivor "looking back" is exposed as a counterfeit. It is not Leo we have been listening to in voice-over, but a phantom reader of Leo's recorded thoughts. Where does this leave Leo himself, suddenly shorn of his grown-up perspective and authority? Robert Lowell writes in *The Dolphin*, "Change I earth or sky I am the same,"[14] which painfully applies to the last images of the "dreaming" Leo, running in search of something he is not destined to find in the vast openness of a picture-book Italian countryside.

Lauzon expressed genuine perplexity in a 1992 interview with Carole Corbeil about why he included a line of narration, close to the end of the film, that links Leo's defeat (the disintegration of his dreaming self) with his failure to love.[15] I confess that the out-of-left-field jolt of this emphatic judgment, so at variance with my overall impression of Leo's sensitivity and indulgence of others' failings (especially within his family), seemed, at a level I could not immediately come to terms with, exactly the intuition required to bring my whole experience of the film together. Lauzon's effort to depict his childhood resilience in the face of towering adversity is not the dimension of his work that distinguishes it from other "portrait of the artist as a young man" narratives. What does seem unprecedented in *Léolo* is Lauzon's concern to balance the daily challenges of a turbulent, near-hopeless environment with the dismaying idea that one's growth in love, even as a child, is finally one's own responsibility.

No amount of kindness received from others can insure that love will find deep enough roots in one's heart to make love thrive. No amount of hardship relieves one of the obligation to press forward in whatever possible direction love's reality can be felt, in order to increase its presence in our inner life. It is truly a matter of survival. Love is the place where Lauzon's argument about childhood survival secretly begins and ends. In love's absence, *surviving* is reduced to what Eudora Welty once mockingly termed it: "perhaps the strangest fantasy of them all."[16] The creative dream-state only makes headway as a form of authentic revelation when its self-aggrandizing power plays, its natural impulse to possess and rule what it "takes in," are held in check by love's gift of patient surrender. Why does the voice of love so often counsel us to reduce our defenses, to relinquish our best hiding places, and to present ourselves to our enemies steeped in visible imperfections (learned by heart, as it were)? It is as though we were enjoined to consent repeatedly to our own unmasking, with no assurance of safety.

Lauzon's film asks to be judged, along with its child hero, according to the degree of "felt life" that has been attained in the right spirit. While it may sound unreasonable at first for the narrator to conclude that there was perhaps too little generosity and decency inside Leo, as well as outside him, to keep him "alive," in the full sense of that word, there is something memorably chastening about the thought that the child, as much or as little as anyone, is capable of crushing the heart's best gifts before they have ever been opened. Leo, like everyone, can give up on tenderness, and come abruptly to the end of trust. The child, as fully as the adult, can be a collaborator in world-emptying betrayals.

This is the key to the almost unwatchable scene when Leo makes common cause with a group of merciless boys at "play" who encourage the most unformed and insensible of their party to rape a declawed cat.

The narration accompanying this hideous ceremony coldly attempts to thrust the responsibility for what is done and passively witnessed to another quarter. The mother of the rapist is addressed (in her absence) as one who does not know her son or have any notion of what he is capable of doing. The narrator's voice swells, rather uncharacteristically, with contempt at her shameful blindness and the sheer quantity of facts she has kept herself ignorant of, as though this woman, and the society that she is accused of personifying, were the true agents of evil here. But the words that are generated to shed light on the offense fail to carry us away from what transpires in front of us, and the awful fact that Leo, at some deep, knowing level, embraces the deed that an outcast surrogate performs on his behalf. He says "yes" to the full flood of viciousness while pretending to stand back from it, as someone not there with the same *kind* of moral awareness as those "others" who crowd forward to get a good, close look. For the moment he experiments with the glassy excitement to be found in asphyxiating empathy, as though it were a justified response to everything he has been made to suffer himself.

The cat scene subtly parallels the earlier episode in which Leo's older brother Fernand has his long-awaited chance to get even with the street tough who terrorized him and broke his nose years earlier, when he was too weak and inexperienced to defend himself. Fernand's chief purpose in life, after the hour he is beaten up, is to make certain that he is never again found cowering in tears before an aggressor. He must never again be in a position of physical disadvantage. Fernand believes he has a sure means of putting himself beyond the reach of ordinary physical fear. With a ferocious single-mindedness he devotes every spare moment to bodybuilding. In little more than a blink of film time he has replaced his lean frame with one so massively imposing it is comic. (The transformation is conveyed by Lauzon through another remarkable tracking shot, in which years dissolve as a camera slowly circles a room, entranced by the deceptive play of a mirror reflection.) When Fernand is finally given his second chance, the chance to prove that he is larger than fear and to turn the tables on his by now mythic childhood adversary, he has his nose broken once again and again collapses against a wall, his useless bulk shaken by sobs.

Leo is the sole witness to both fights, and on each occasion reaches out with a pure sympathy for his brother, in which we detect no trace of shame or aversion, no inner recoil, no self-protective need to dissociate himself from the contagion of another's failure. The narrator declares as we watch Leo's commiseration that Fernand's core identity is fear, and that no amount of physical remolding could change what he was. It strikes me that in this instance, as in the cat scene, the narrator's emphasis is troublingly misplaced. His partial and bleak summing up of Fernand's emotional cave-in is reasonable as far as it goes, but it does not touch on the most important of the camera's revelations. The great mystery of the encounter, one that movies too seldom take up, has to do with how Fernand could prevail against the bully and not, in the process, become more like him. Brutality unimpeded by reflection is the natural vocabulary of the ruffian. It is the advantage he holds in conflicts like the one in *Léolo*. Fernand's adversary has his narrowly focused survivor's truth, and manages to live by it without the intrusion of competing instincts or sympathies. After his initial surprise at Fernand's muscle-flexing immensity, he moves into closer range and performs a quick, dispassionate assessment of Fernand's face and eyes. "Do I *see* in this expression someone resolved to take pleasure in harming me, someone who has practice in landing blows without flinching and who can rejoice at the sight of a victim's blood and pain?"

The alley fighter's brief time of calculation is the spectator's as well, though for the spectator the calculation may acquire a surprising moral weight. In the space of a few moments, we must decide not only whether Fernand has the resolve to demolish his foe (an outcome we have likely anticipated with some relish) but also whether we want him revealed to our gaze as the limited sort of creature who is "made for the job." To be this creature, he must let nothing appear on his face that compromises the will to vengeance, and we are lured, in a sense, to collaborate in the erasure of any giveaway signs of indecisiveness or softness. While it is undoubtedly horrifying to watch Fernand crumble in the ensuing assault, Lauzon makes it possible for us to see that what is best in Fernand (and most worth saving) is also what dictates the negative outcome and insures his paralysis. Fear plays a significant part, to be sure, in preventing him from striking back, but beyond that we are allowed to observe that he is not, in spite of all his efforts to achieve a fighter's appearance and mentality, a person who can *find himself* in acts of violence. The images of this gigantic child-man weeping have far more cathartic power, I would venture to say, than the freeze-dried mechanics of successful retaliation.

The main parallel I'd like to trace out with the cat scene has to do with the linked meanings of bodybuilding (for Fernand) and the building up of Leo's imagination through his daily immersion in writing and dreaming. Both Fernand and Leo suffer a major defeat, but Leo's is worse in the cat episode because it is soul-eroding: what Robert Lowell once called "dust in the blood."[17] It would be better for him to give himself over to fear in this setting than to harden himself against it. The violation of the cat marks the defeat of the whole imaginative process through an internal numbing that is somehow *chosen*. It also signals the imagination's complete severance from the discipline of love. What is the imagination good for, ultimately, if one arrives at such a testing ground and finds nothing more to dwell on than children repaying their families for failing to safeguard their innocence? Leo forgets that the justification for "dreaming" that he found with the Word Tamer's help has to do with the conduct of life. One dreams to keep alive the courage to act, in a manner that allows some triumph over one's baleful surroundings. One dreams to expand one's heart language and to hold on to images of what one's fellow-prisoners have it in them to be, through a perception infused with love—and clemency. Flannery O'Connor once memorably defined evil as the defective use of good,[18] which seems to put evil firmly in the realm of negligence, where a responsive spirit withers through lack of exercise. Confusing power relationships with the effort to love and assuming that the greater clarity of power proves it is more real than love can easily foul the well-spring of action and art.

Léolo pulses with the anxiety that the boy's proper love energy may be lethally contaminated by the energy of sexuality, aggression, and death. If there is a dominant fear in the film, it is the fear of an ever-encroaching coldness, fulfilled, if you like, by Leo's final coma bed of ice. The film's riotous profusion of candles is like a supplicant's appeal to every available visible expression of warmth. But candles, in such mournful, suffocating quantity, can equally attest (as we have seen) to a light without adequate heat—as though no amount of imported fire could assuage the child's core shivering. I am always struck by the image of Leo huddling in the darkness to read his first serious book early in the film. The secret light he finds to read by late at night is the light of an open refrigerator. He must pull a tuque over his head to protect himself from the chill that seems (here and elsewhere) the cost of illumination. What most intrigues me in this image is the suggestion that Leo is as much drawn to the refrigerator's bracing cold as to the light that accompanies it. It is the right temperature to learn by. As the narrator intones the passage from Réjean Ducharme's *L'avalée des avalés* that Leo is struggling to comprehend—"I find my only real joy is solitude. Solitude is my castle"—we see the boy feeling the icy integrity of this tempting fortress which, with the refrigerator as its gateway, rises up in fantasy against a bare, northern sky.

The quest for love gains its urgency in *Léolo* from Lauzon's equally strong attraction to a self-sufficient remoteness that will not thaw in the face of others' repellent needs and expectations. The film maps out devious pathways that momentarily link extremes of loving relationship with extremes of withdrawal, the latter very often bringing Leo close to death. This variation of "yes" and "no" fusion is most memorably accomplished in the film's two underwater scenes, where Leo is shown swimming effortlessly at a great depth, trying to put his hands on treasure no one else can see or reach. In the first scene, Leo experiences an ecstatic vision of a gleaming pirate's hoard at the bottom of the sea (with himself closing in on it) while his grandfather attempts to drown him in a plastic wading pool. Images of the boy pressing forward in slow motion closer and closer to the open sea chest gleaming with gold and jewels are intercut with shots of Leo's face struggling for air in the pool and shots of his mother leading him on visiting day through the dark corridors of the mental hospital. Candles from the Word Tamer's library are briefly superimposed on one image of the sunken treasure, and the Word Tamer becomes the final component of Leo's vision, reading in his safe haven about the boy's lack of fear as he approached the "white light" of death.

The various pieces of this "stop time" circling of death and beauty and love are held in suspension for a long interval until Leo's mother finally breaks it apart by her last-minute rescue of her flailing child. (She knocks his grandfather unconscious with a single blow to the head from an iron frying pan.) The strange bridge in the editing that is offered to us right *before* this resolution links up Leo's swimming toward death's alluring riches with a heartfelt declaration of the power of his mother's love for him. He reaches out to the jewels, and to his mother's living hand in the hospital corridor as though the two movements could somehow be reconciled into a single gesture. Leo kisses his mother's hand, which, in pulling him back from an intensely desired death, had replaced one sort of plenitude with another. In a lovely, unforced way, his mother is all at once transformed into the treasure. The metaphor of the underwater heaven, by the end of the sequence, seems as attached to her and the mystery of her simple, unalienated affection as it is to death's siren song. The gift of love—what humans can be and do for one another when they shake off their confusion—beckons Leo to "swim deeper" even more compellingly than the mirage at the furthest limit of solitude does. And the Word Tamer, who appears to live in some halfway house between the countries of the living and the dead, gently presides over Leo's struggle, hoping always that he will choose life but patient with each dark swerve and frantic mistake, as only one who lives beyond the reach of human turmoil can be.

So much of the visual design of *Léolo* is planned in terms of verticality. Leo's swimming to the bottom of the sea echoes or magnifies such pleasurable penetrations as the descent by stair and basement tunnel to sister Rita's insect and reptile sanctuary, or the dizzying climb, by secret airshaft, to a high bathroom window, through which Leo, disguised in a diver's mask, spies on his grandfather in the tub as he solicits peculiar sexual favors from the "girl next door." The Word Tamer's living quarters are eventually shown to include a maze of stairways, extending to a vast depth, where he keeps all his most precious documents and art objects in storage. Italy, Leo's "Fatherland" in his reveries of escape, is a verdant countryside with soaring hills and declivities, all warmly inviting a boy who dreams of unimpeded motion: endless climbing up and racing down. Finally, in a kind of parody of the transcendental urge, we are given a bird's-eye view of Leo stretched out on the floor of his bathroom, having fantasy sex with a raw chunk of liver he has sliced open, while he pages through a grimily earthbound skin magazine. The autoerotic is appropriately viewed here in terms of lifting and sinking: both a furious descent into the flesh and a vertiginous dream of sailing above it.

In the second underwater scene, Leo, once again outfitted in diving gear, is dropped from a high wall into a filthy Montreal canal in order to retrieve fishing lures from the seldom visited, infectious murk of its lower regions. As we have seen so often, the *event* of the scene consists largely of contrasts between an apparent will to die and a hunger for "deeper" life, gleaming intimations of which Leo snatches with Arabian Nights zest from a host of danger-filled hiding places. The fishing lures possess a palpable starlight power in the miasmal gloom of the stagnant canal. Everywhere the viewer's eye ventures here it is assailed by animal carcasses, rusty, slicing edges of things, and slime-coated consumer goods absurdly announcing their weighty uselessness. Bathtubs, refrigerators, and automobile torsos have usurped the places that rightfully belong to sunken galleons and the fabled spoils of piracy. The discarded possessions are somehow leprously imprinted with the rage and destitution of their former owners, who heaved them into the water as testimony of failure.

The operation that Leo performs, cutting each glittering lure loose from the object that has snagged it, is a replay of his routine scavenging of his graceless home for suitable poetic material. And just as his writing self prefers jumble to logical ordering and ephemera to what endures, so too his diving expedition builds its case for beauty on the recognition that the risk is pointless: the trifles collected have next to no value, and the impression of enchantment will not survive a return to land. In fact, the very act of cutting a lure loose and taking possession of it "kills" the precious image on the spot. What one owns is not the thing that filled one's gaze.

Wendy Lesser has found a nice term for the dramatic space of Lauzon's scenes that I am most interested in. She speaks of her predilection for "strange middle grounds because they help [one find] what's going on in seeming oppositions."[19] In the underwater search for lures the middle ground is Leo's resourceful, swift-moving body, undaunted by all impediments, asserting its dignity in the very midst of hell. The body seems so vulnerable to infection and wound, yet its refusal to take notice of, to be the least bit intimidated by, the encircling poisons feels like a remarkable shield against harm. The lures come out from hiding, like tiny lamps, as if to acknowledge and reward the sight of such exuberant, unself-conscious motion. And yet the impulse to dream our way into this landscape and make the young swimmer's freedom our own is held in check by some gathering pressure—perhaps something frightening in the *need* to stay under or the idea that vision is once more purchased at the expense of breathing.

The imagination is angling toward death (as in the first swimming scene). Death is the catalyst that will make things stand clear and glow with a pure light. Only in the danger zone, close to the bottom of the canal, do the lures come into magical focus and hold a value one can see and give one's heart to. Why return to the surface, where one knows the light is wrong and one's jewels will fade to rubbish? Like a pendulum, Leo's body—in this episode and many others—*overdoes* its movement because of an underlying drive to bring itself to rest. The pendulum's movement gives no outward sign that its basic desire is stillness. Leo's progressively more alarming physical excesses—by turns sexual and violent—seem impelled by the need to find a *point of no return,* which is a negative way of saying "coming to rest."

Follow the arc of most of Leo's fantasies and the end point is a version of being crushed under an enormous weight or being suffocated. To cite one of my favorite examples: he lies in bed one morning working his toe through a small hole in his blanket. He then imagines the amount of effort it will require to make the hole big enough for his whole body to fit through. (Once again, the route to freedom involves willing oneself into the cold. It is no small thing to make gaping holes in one's only blanket.) Yet as soon as Leo's imagination carries his twisting body, feet first, all the way through the rent fabric, he becomes convinced that his head won't make it. The hole will tighten to a noose around his neck at the moment of Houdini-triumphant getaway. The noose isn't simply posited as the last barrier to freedom; it insinuates itself, here and elsewhere, as freedom's most inviting purpose. *Léolo* manages to locate a common denominator of "gasping for breath" in nearly every form of love embrace and leads our attention inexorably back to the painful squeeze without release in Leo's Prussian school toilet training.

How does love get so mixed up with the body's most imperious and dismaying compulsions? Why is it so often the case that the urge to mistreat a loved one can coexist with a lucid awareness of the intended victim's appealing qualities? A clear-eyed sympathy is no guarantee that one will forswear vengeance or the bracing pleasures of cruelty. "What swells impels" is a medieval expression that proclaims the casual despotism of the libido in channeling male action, and, as Guido Ceronetti has noted, links the drive to procreate with the less exalted work of abscesses and pimples.[20] I can think of no film which lays greater stress on the body's peculiar and relentless demands for obedience than *Léolo*, but Lauzon's vision of the corporeal life neither celebrates nor grieves over our common servility. Thankfully there is no recourse to the empty utopianism of Bakhtin's "carnivalesque," a concept whose seemingly endless applications suggest not so much a daring and difficult regard for our subversive animal instincts as a sentimental replay of late sixties "let it all hang out" merrymaking. (For Bakhtin's Rabelais, substitute Woodstock and Elizabethan-style weddings in a meadow, and most of the pieces fall into place.)

When Leo makes his own version of the discovery that all our mansions are built on excrement, Lauzon resists the double temptation to declare the mansions illusory and to convert the excrement into something metaphorically (and metaphysically) more congenial. Lauzon stubbornly holds to the idea that if his imagination is to retain its faith in love as the highest human good, he must not seek to cleanse this love of its bodily embarrassments. Nor does he deny that his hunger for excess and pain may proceed from the same source as love's selfless expressions. Love finds its most compelling reflections in a mirror that also includes the body's stern will and love's mysterious Faustian wagers with death. The intimations of glory Lauzon shows to us are intermixed with uncouth discharges of all sorts, which declare their own truth without entering into some futile competition with the spiritual. The film, in other words, does not force us to choose between the Word Tamer and images of the out-of-control body. The authority of one does not emerge through the vanquishing of the other.

There is a cheap, potent glamour in all film assertions of the primacy of instinct and the exotic risks of surrendering to it. *Léolo* pursues the danger without believing for an instant that sexuality by itself is redemptive or a heroic response to chaos. Lauzon lacks any D. H. Lawrence-style crush on the male body's significance. He does not burden it with any more meaning than it deserves to carry. If Leo's body behaves immoderately, it is not because he lives within it more intensely or authentically than others but because immoderation is the natural fate of every emotion the body freely accepts: grief, dread, love. In our dreams and in our creaturely behavior, melodrama *is* our emotional realism.

Leo's drive to burst out of himself is what alternately moves him to enter compassionately the turmoil and despair of others and to court annihilation. Whether he presses in one direction or the other, he always comes up against the same inner tightness, as though love and dying both demanded the snapping of the same iron band. What he can never seem to attain, though he longs for it, is the spontaneous lightheartedness of young Bianca, a next-door neighbor who performs simple actions like hanging up laundry with such satisfaction that she can't help singing. Bianca faces at least as many difficulties in her life as Leo does. (Among other indignities, she is sexually preyed upon by Leo's grandfather.) And yet, whatever she has suffered, she holds on to an exuberance and a capacity for joy that Leo has barely touched in his life. Leo finds ample occasions for love, but he cannot sing about them. He consistently tries to secure images of beauty so strong that they will allow him to defy (briefly) the laws of gravity. But there is always a flaw that oppressively reminds him of what cannot be escaped, like the single flower in his bedroom with its "made in Hong Kong" sticker that he cannot bear to remove for fear of *improving* the illusion.

One last view of Leo as pure potential: he sits in his kitchen window overlooking the courtyard, watching Bianca sing with her unkillable delight, while behind him sits his family—miserably together—at supper. Leo cannot fully join Bianca, either physically or in largeness of spirit. Still, the reality of her presence in his world and the possibility of a "better heart" that her song awakens in him allow him to turn his attention back to his family not merely with regret but with a renewed interest in drawing near to them and finding out who they are. Bianca's music lowers the barriers to love, but not through its ideas or some quality of effort in its unfolding. Her song is "simply there, with no prior notice. . . . Nothing prepares for it," as if there could *be* preparation for the "pure poetry of good."[21] The song is not in search of love; it has found it, even if the form of love's object is not clear. All the accumulated tensions of Leo's mind and body, including the fact of his romantic longing for Bianca, are dissolved in the music, without the necessity of anything having to be denied. Momentarily unstuck from his usual place, between rebellion and shame, he begins to breathe. He looks at the members of his family one by one, not as figures to whom he is chained but as beings who will almost certainly be lost to him before they have even once come into proper focus. See them now, the film and the music call out to him. Until you learn how, you will be unable to see anything that lies beyond them.

11

From Archangel to Mandragora in Your Own Backyard: Collaborating with Guy Maddin

> But what the Man-Moth fears most he must do, although
> he fails, of course, and falls back scared but quite unhurt.
> —Elizabeth Bishop

I have been warned—by myself as well as others—not to sound too academic in my final chapter, as I try to discuss my work as a scriptwriter. My goal seems to be to impersonate a nonacademic for this one occasion. I have had to make some difficult decisions, in keeping with the stereotype of how academics are thought to sound, on just how much of my customary stuffiness I can safely remove at this late stage from my voice. Without the stuffing, can I speak above a whisper?

There are many good reasons not to know too much about how a story or script comes into being. One should simply feel grateful for those days when creative work of any sort is possible, and with sensible superstition, leave the "whys" and "hows" curled up in the dark. Attending too lucidly or probingly to the creative process can jeopardize it, as so many artists have testified. It is frighteningly easy for any evolving narrative to perish under the weight of excessive premeditation or analytic control—the wrong kind of knowing. The imagination is like an oversensitive friend, who can regard any form of inquiry into its secrets as a terrible slight, and who can go into hiding without any warning when it feels betrayed. So let me proceed here very gently, with the cunning and self-protective duplicity that seem preconditions for all discussions about how fictions are made. I'll have nothing to say about the phantasmagoria that envelops me (or any other writer) whenever a story starts moving forward of its own volition. Instead I shall strive for the nervous waking state that follows every happy enchantment, when one is obliged to wonder if any of it works. A potential viewer starts

Franz (Vince Rimmer) visited in his lonely attic room by the blind ghost of his father (Michael O'Sullivan) in *Careful.*

assailing me with a host of well-thought-out worries about story sense and whether the characters are worth bothering with. The flimsy edifice of dream teeters dangerously, even in this faint breeze. I steel myself for a discussion of meaning, which always turns into a cold, abstract lump when considered apart from a flow of images and sounds. How I wish I could evade at least the inner skeptic, whose only recommendations are that I become more self-conscious and properly ashamed of myself. The end of the first act of *Waiting for Godot* suggests the remedy I'm looking for.

> ESTRAGON: Shall we go?
>
> VLADIMIR: Yes, let's go. (They do not move.)[1]

When I began collaborating with Guy Maddin, the method I used to trick myself to open up a different channel for what might be termed unprotected expression was to pretend that I *was* Guy when I wrote.

"THERE MUST BE PEACE IN THIS HOME AGAIN."

Rivals for a mother's love: Johann (Brent Neale), Franz (Vince Rimmer), Grigorrs
(Kyle McCulloch), and Zenaida (Gosia Dobrowolska) in *Careful*.

The ideas and impulses that came to me were so much more deliciously
unsavory, unsightly, and extreme when I saw them swimming merrily
up from Guy's unconscious rather than my own. This simple but surprisingly effective form of self-deception helped all sorts of things I
wasn't ready to acknowledge in my own name get past the patrol dogs
of my still hyperactive, lapsed Catholic sense of guilt. Over time, it
became clear that few of my own sorry secrets (those, at least, not so
well hidden as to be hidden from me) continued to demand protection
from the Writer busily screening and sifting memories for good material.
I also began to worry less about the consequences if the secrets marked
"dangerous" not only slipped into a story but were recognized as my own
belongings. I gradually realized that my own autobiography, which
might reasonably strike outsiders as a small-town parade of unimpressive
incidents, was (unmetamorphosed) a quickly used up source of material.
A well-known, infected sliver of autobiography, however, when embel-
lished by a literature-fueled imagination, could often generate the kind
of wayward story ideas that Guy favors. His only firm requirements are
the following: Don't you dare bore me—or yourself. Be willing to tell
everything on yourself, but slantwise. We'll call what we're making fairy

tales, to put all but the most inquisitive off the scent. Don't be pretentious or you'll wake up one morning and see Peter Greenaway peering
back at you in the mirror. Never tell other people what you think they
already know or would be willing to vote for. Why would you need (or
want) a movie for that? Don't plot or think in a straight line. Keep the
dialogue fragrant, like honeyed wine. And finally, for God's sake, get
some comedy into it, but make sure the presentation is deadpan. (The
jokes should be as uncoercive and mysterious as Buster Keaton's face.)

Comedy. Perhaps the best way of explaining how Guy thinks about
the comic in relation to other attitudes toward experience is to discuss
a scene we both love from the Andrew Birkin film, *The Cement Garden*
(1992)—adapted from Ian McEwan's novel. A mother of four children,
who happens to be their only surviving relative, has just died after a long
illness in the bedroom of her London home. Her three older children—
a boy and girl in mid-to-late adolescence and a pre-adolescent girl—
discover the body. In addition to the shock of her passing away so quietly, when no one was present to be a witness or offer even small gestures
of comfort and assistance, the children instantly *know* (to their marrow)
that they are completely on their own. They have no grown-up anywhere
to turn to for consolation or protection. As soon as the mother's death
is reported to the proper authorities, the children will be divided up and
no doubt sent to various foster homes, or worse.

The two girls stand before the mother's bed, weeping helplessly
and hiding nothing of what they feel. The boy, perhaps envying their
abandon, remains silent. Julie, the eldest child, decides to draw the bedsheet over her mother's face, as though there might be a bit of protection
in any available ritual. But no sooner has she tugged the sheet to this
new position than her mother's large bare feet are left uncovered at the
other end. Noticing how grotesque and defenseless these bare feet look
with no owner to be solicitous about them, Jack, the brother, draws the
sheet back down to cover them, leaving her head exposed once more.
The sister pulls the sheet forward a second time, in line with her original
plan, then Jack a little more stubbornly yanks it away to honor his end
of the corpse. A small tug-of-war commences, which reduces both of
them to laughter. At this point, the fourth and youngest child, four-
year-old Tom, who still doesn't know what's happened to his mother,
enters the bedroom and quite reasonably asks,

> "What's so funny?"
> When his question goes unanswered he announces, "I
> want Mum."

"She's asleep. Look, you can see."

"Why were you laughing then? Anyway, she's not asleep, were you Mum?"

"She's very asleep," says the younger sister, at last finding a point of entry into her older siblings' "mature" air of frivolity.

Tom responds to the thickening atmosphere of secrecy and the sense that he is being unfairly left out of something by yelling his mother's name as he tries to climb onto her bed. Jack grabs his wrists and tells him, "You can't." Persevering and fiercely sure of himself, Tom kicks his brother and breaks free of him. He leaps onto the bed and pulls back his mother's bedsheet. Julie gently tries to extricate him from his mother's unresponsive form. "No, no," the boy squeals, holding fast to his mother's nightgown sleeve. Julie pulls once more, causing the corpse to pitch forward sideways, almost woodenly. Her head—in its new, peculiar thingliness—strikes a bedside table, sending a clock and glass of water crashing to the floor. Mother's head is now wedged between bed and table—and it is at this angle that Tom finally *sees* her and grasps that she is dead.

I'd like to dwell on that bedsheet for a few moments, as a means of clarifying how comedy can insinuate itself into the most terrible situations imaginable, without reducing or belittling the horror (in the self-congratulatory fashion typical of so much black comedy). The sheet initially functions as an expression of the natural human desire to have a unified, meaningful emotion that will fit its occasion smoothly and immaculately, like the sky fits its reflection on a still mountain lake. When your mother dies, and you have felt close to her, you simply grieve at the loss, and the assumption is that the action of grief happens spontaneously. One doesn't (or shouldn't) need a mourning etiquette manual to instruct one in how to grieve persuasively. Character becomes action. That is to say, here is one of those powerful instances where one is what one does. The bereaved one weeps, or (only slightly less ambiguously) he goes into shock. But *reality*, however we care to define it or cautiously bracket it with scare quotes, rarely allows us a bedsheet—even in as clear a case as the death of a parent—that is exactly the right size for the emotional situation. Comedy is our response to the wrong-size sheet we have to make do with. At first we may convince ourselves that it *is* the right size, appearances notwithstanding; then we struggle to make it work, ignoring the invincible limitation; then finally we are *caught* somehow in the recognition that the sheet won't stretch—and at this point it is not only the "mother's feet" that lie exposed but also something in us.

The comedy that most appeals to me is the sort that relieves, then reinforces, the pain in a dramatic predicament. The "soft" comedy temptation, if you like, promises a release from the demands of too pressure-filled an emotional involvement with what is going on. But suppose the release is a false one: it is not an escape, after all. The laughter, which for a moment or two increases our freedom to maneuver in relation to some anxiety, actually serves to make the predicament worse. It is as though our decision (or need) to laugh *just then* brings harm to the character who hasn't had our opportunity for defection but who instead continues to suffer. The mother's body and puppetlike head, wedged between bed and nightstand, seem weirdly *unable* to register the absurdity of being so suddenly inanimate, and therefore present an amusing spectacle. But Tom is not amused. It is left to him to really discover, at the crest of our laugh, that *this* is what's left of his mother. She's dead, Tom, and your pushing at her has caused her head to bump and get stuck in that dreadful position. You're too young to know any better, but still, how could you? The agony of his expression when the truth dawns on him is beyond question the real thing. His face is totally persuasive, but we are not *on the beat* with him. Our detour of laughter has left us behind somehow; we have to catch up. Comedy ideally is an elastic band firmly attached at one end to something troublingly messy. As the laugh pulls us away from the emotional mess (*elastically*) it also snaps us back: so we are returned full-force to Tom's face, having become (in our brief absence) invisible collaborators in his misfortune, his bereftness. He is doubly bereft—because in our comic escape we have abandoned him.

Guy is very interested in the sort of laugh that escapes from us without our quite meaning it, the laughter we would cancel or take back if we had a second chance. Overall, the scene from *The Cement Garden* creates what I take to be an exemplary form of comic impasse. The scene lacks a stable or normative figure whose responses we can comfortably share. Everyone connected to the scene—the characters, the audience, the writer, and the director—are equally on the hook, and the whole thing hinges on an imperative intimacy one would just as soon forgo. Guy has an aversion for jokes whose point seems to be the director's ethical superiority to one or more characters' behavior. Satire's "I know something that you don't" posture, with its commitment to judgment from above and assumption of correct answers always in the keeping of the morally healthy satirist, is anathema to Guy's comic perspective. He likes to steer his scenes through murky moral waters, where our ethical compass can't get a reading fast enough to let us decide what response we want. And, more important, he looks for situations where all the available perspectives on events (including his own) become suspect, where the mere fact of being present and gazing at something dirties you.

An excellent example of this strategic "dirtying" can be found in *Archangel* (1990), perhaps the least well known and, by common consent, most baffling of Guy's films. *Archangel* is a part-talkie whose narrative continuity matches Dreyer's *Vampyr* for opaqueness, and whose soundtrack is so starved of background noise that one can almost hear the ever-present mist and snow. Words, when they are spoken, rub against the silence like the sighs, creaks, and groans of an old house on a windy night. There is no tautological sound in this world. Instead we have amnesia sound, right down to the din of cannon and mortar shells, which seem not only spatially somewhat distant but temporally far away too. I recall one of Guy's notes on style for *Archangel*: sound should resemble, *if possible,* an ancient veteran's flickering recollections of his youthful apprenticeship in battlefield atrocities. The old warrior is almost capable, at this remove, of tenderly shrouding his worst experiences in the vapor of nostalgia. But a thin, irritating scratching noise persists in this mental fog, as though an unknown animal were clawing against the back door of memory, trying to get in. The setting of the film is that remote northern place in snowy Russia named in the title, where Frankenstein and his melancholy monster completed their wild pas de deux in Mary Shelley's novel. The time is the final days of the Russian chapter of World War I. In fact, the war is officially at an end here, but word hasn't yet reached the beleaguered combatants who have improbably traveled to this remote outpost from a great many countries, large and small. The fighters we observe in action pursue their bellicose tasks with the kind of distraction they might bring to a factory or mining job. The still-present dangers to life and limb seem to be concealed in a general atmosphere of forgetfulness. In the course of a long, aimless struggle, war has become increasingly difficult to separate from other phenomena; it is simply the mental weather into which all of the characters march off to do their duty. A penumbral fog moves along with them, seemingly hatched from their collective trance, and it is common for the soldiers to mislay their domestic identities and private memories there. Occasional battle fever, pitched at the same level as sexual fever, is the reward the characters hope for after so much tramping around and senseless waiting in the drizzle, mud, and snow.

In the *Archangel* scene I shall be looking at, we are in the home of one of the female soldiers, Danchak, during a combat intermission. Her husband, Jannings, who is a skulking stay-at-home whenever there is war work to be done, is regarded by Danchak, their twelve-year-old son, Geza, and everyone else who comes in contact with him during the movie as a coward because he can't find the strength to go into battle. He has no ethical reasons for staying out of the conflict. He is quite simply terrified of being killed—and even he doesn't see that as any kind of excuse for his unmanly derelictions. John Boles, a Canadian soldier (and amnesiac) billeted with this family, is the protagonist of the film. He tries to be sympathetic with his host's fear of various male duties, but he cannot avoid regretting that the valorous Danchak is saddled with such a spineless mate. Here is the relevant portion of the scene:

DANCHAK catches her son GEZA pocketing a piece of satin thread from her sewing box as a souvenir. With considerable embarrassment and remorse, she commands the repentant child to return the stolen thread. After he does so she sets out, with tears in her eyes, to make matters right by buckling GEZA's wrists to a special easel and then administering numerous blows with a switch to the boy's back. The necessity of this flogging, though visibly upsetting to DANCHAK, is nonetheless unquestioned by both parties. As the sounds of beating fill the air of the small cottage, JANNINGS quakes in the corner. Tactfully averting his gaze from the scene of corporal punishment, BOLES quietly approaches JANNINGS in an attempt to reason with him.

BOLES: Isn't it the *man's* place to discipline a wayward child?

JANNINGS (knowing Boles is right): I'm sorry.

JANNINGS slinks out of the room, conscious that his fear of disciplining his son is linked to his larger fear of facing the enemy.

GEZA: Please continue, mother.

BOLES: I'm not used to seeing a woman do a man's work. Do you mind?

BOLES takes the cane from DANCHAK and administers a good, Eton-style flogging to GEZA. When he is done, BOLES offers his hand in a gesture of forgiveness to the boy. GEZA looks up at BOLES through tearful eyes, and perhaps because of the moisture, BOLES appears to him in shimmering soft focus, as resplendent in his authority and military uniform as a god. ("Now, if *he* were my father . . . ") DANCHAK, whose thoughts are flowing in a similar vein, though with a connubial emphasis, also sheds a few tears as she and GEZA embrace.

BOLES: He's a good lad. You should be proud of him.

BOLES lights a cigarette, salutes the family and, spurs jingling brightly, departs the cottage for an evening excursion.

How might a viewer's feelings and judgments circulate and attempt to find closure in such an episode? The first thing to be said about the scene is that the characters are all in agreement about what the problem is and how to solve it. The cowering Jannings does not put forward an alternative point of view, and his total abjectness pretty much defeats a viewer's desire to identify with him. Danchak does not enjoy caning her son but regards it as an inescapable duty if Geza is to turn out to be a responsible grown-up. Boles *does* intervene midway through the punishment but not to protest anything but the distressing fact that it is not the mother's job to flog. Here is the scene's peculiar comedy aperture. My guess is that most movie and TV spectators are sufficiently well trained by now in the ways of patriarchal oafishness that whenever they hear the phrase, "Isn't this a man's job?" they know they are confronting the familiar sound of historic prejudice. How foolish, for example, those frontier men are to doubt that Dr. Quinn, Medicine Woman is the best damned sawbones in the West! Man's job, indeed. A woman can cane her child every bit as well as a man, if not better. No, wait—caning is something that men do because they have been socially constructed to be vile and warlike. Women *don't* (or shouldn't) do it, but it's not because they're incapable. They don't want to. But this boy—who is being whipped—looks up to his mother for doing what she would rather not do and assuming responsibility for the task shamefully neglected by deadbeat dad.

Boles, with a hero's self-possession, steps in at the last possible moment to save the situation, and perhaps our feelings are given one more twist at the sight of Danchak gratefully relinquishing the cane to the man who knows what the natural hierarchy is and how this thing is properly done. Boles takes no more pleasure in meting out the strokes than Danchak did. He is not a sadist. He performs the duty like Alan Ladd in *Shane* helping poor Van Heflin chop out that tree stump, while innocently aroused Jean Arthur (Heflin's wife) smiles encouragingly behind them. Like a well-treated guest, Boles is willing to lend a hand with the household chores. The fact that Danchak is slightly thrilled at the sight of him so efficiently taking charge is as invisible to him as Jean Arthur's response to Ladd's body in action is to both parties in *Shane*. Movie characters have a remarkably well-developed capacity not to be privy to the thoughts that are legible on their faces, if it is in the story's interests to preserve their uncomplicated goodness. Turning at last to the willing victim of Boles's gruesomely excessive punishment, is there not something truthful—at least not easily dismissable—in Geza's tearful admiration of the superhuman authority figure introducing some much-needed clarity to his moral universe?

It is at this moment that I, as the writer, find myself, piercingly, on the hook with the characters. I recall the complex mixture of pain and love I felt when my father offered me his hand after one of his spanking sessions. I found no anger in his expression, no evidence that he had gone out of control. I took his reluctant decision to resort to this uncommon mode of punishment as proof that there were firm rules in the world—all evidence of chaos notwithstanding—and that they made sense. My father gave every impression of knowing what the rules were, and part of what he was communicating through his blows was the desire that I become an equal sharer of this knowledge. He could imagine no better way of making the knowledge stick. Strangely, I felt more fully acknowledged by my father after these rare ceremonial summons to intimate violence than at most other times. I had succeeded in catching and holding his attention by my transgression of household law in a more complete fashion than my usually vague, out-of-focus filial presence could manage. We had made contact through his authority, and I welcomed it, in spite of the stiff price. Frighteningly often, I go back to these moments when I search for tangible memory proofs of my father's love for me. And though I believe, after failing in the same way myself as a father, that it is *never* right, *never* a good thing to physically discipline a child, I cannot rewrite my emotional history in keeping with this almost-too-late conviction, to make my experience simpler, less self-divided. Hence the scene from *Archangel*: laugh if you will.

Maurice Sendak was once asked during a visit to Berkeley why he thought Shakespeare would be drawn to so puerile a story as *The Winter's Tale*. "What's going on there?" his questioner cheerfully called out. I found Sendak's reply extremely suggestive. He touched upon something I've always wanted to believe about the potential of certain kinds of fantasy for film, even at this late date. "It seems to me," Sendak began, "[Shakespeare's] hiding something extraordinarily important, perhaps. And you hide it best in a fairy tale. Maybe I say that because I want to do that. But I think it's something too dangerous to talk about in a serious way, and so, paradoxically, you turn it on its head. Like some of the operas of Rossini, some of the operas of Mozart—comic operas that break your heart. He's telling you something very sere and severe, and it's kind of hidden in the fabric of this dopeyness.[2] I especially love the phrase: "something too dangerous to talk about in a serious way." It instantly puts me in mind of Nabokov's *Lolita*, where the reader's task is in part to find the reality of the girl, Dolores Haze, at an imaginative level that Humbert's voice works very hard to evade, in spite of the vast array of sexual/emotional/rhetorical optics he proposes for our consideration. Our wish to be serious about child-molesting must find a means to coexist honestly with our amusement and enchantment. A straightforward attempt to oppose Humbert in a voice of offended virtue runs the risk of denying our own pleasure in the book's aesthetic weave and in falsifying the nature of our disturbance. It is likely to be our too slippery, unstable involvement with Humbert rather than Humbert himself that accounts for our sense of menace in the book. Sendak's phrase also reminds me, at a much lower artistic altitude, of Guy Maddin's *Careful* (1992), where the fairy tale structure strikes me, at any rate, not as a refusal of the darkness of the incest and repression theme but as an attempt to keep the fear that naturally dwells in this darkness from becoming too sanitized and manageable—and thus, mere pretense.

Combining fairy tale with a comically extreme preoccupation with repression was a further move to insure that the slopes of our chosen subject would have, in Guy's phrase, "real avalanche potential." If *Careful* can accurately be termed a "pro-repression" movie, it is not because of any nostalgia on our part for Victorian strictures, with all their suffocating weight of duty and obedience. We are not pining for the revival of laws that breed submissive minds and deformed libidos. However, Freud was surely right to insist that whatever level of sanity any of us manage to retain depends, to a large degree, on our capacity for repression. Without effective psychic blocking mechanisms, would there be anything but God and drugs to keep us from the grip of terminal depression, on the one hand, or psychotic rage on the other? The term "pro-repression" can perhaps most interestingly be applied to art itself: art's necessary repression, if there is to be sufficient surprise and danger in the creative process, of its own deepest aims. I am almost persuaded that the *only* way for narrative art to approach anything consequential is by accepting the following intractable condition: that art can't fully illuminate anything without falsifying or destroying it. Its triumph always comes in the tension between what is made manifest and what the Orphean activity of bringing this much of something "into the clear" forces back into the darkness. Whatever a story most desires to reveal or "say" must remain half-buried, tantalizingly out of reach. And if this is true of art, I think it is equally true of the inner life, where so much depends on a tactful relationship with one's demons. Even our lifelong terrors and most private agonies can seem sadly diminished, and unconvincing, when we shine too much light on them. But bring back the nightwood and they writhe once again with their former power.

Quests in narratives typically begin like dreams, in which the quester knows neither the goal nor himself. The Russian folktale "Oom Razoom" explicates this situation nicely by assigning its average hero the rather daunting task of traveling to "I Know Not Where" to bring back "I Know Not What." Often, however—and in movies especially, far too often—there is an impatience to exchange at the earliest possible opportunity this mournful or exhilarating initial disorientation for a kind of false centeredness, which is usually a mimicry of some old-fashioned belief system that the story feigns allegiance to. The assumption seems to be that clarity is the basic requirement of both the quester's game plan and effective narrative closure. Purposeful story movement on-screen begins, screenwriting handbooks tell us, at that point where the quester knows where she is going and why. At the end of her journey, she will have an accumulation of insights to consider, which add up to better self-knowledge (the sort that changes one's life) and a sense of completion, in both the inner and outer world. What is one to do, however, if one believes that the most credible and intriguing questers are not decisive about goals but are, in effect, sleepwalkers? The fairy tale method would, at first, seem to guarantee, more than any other genre, a familiar quest order, an easy symmetry of rewards and punishments, and a final, out-of-time fulfillment for the simple hero when he returns home. In fact, however, fairy tales can, with only the slightest bending, yield inscrutable spells that cannot be broken, pain that cannot be healed, and a persistent forgetting of lessons learned. They can give us a sense of having drifted dangerously close to places where everything familiar and dear has either been taken away for good or transformed beyond recognition. Surely adult and child alike know that in "Hansel and Gretel" there is something irreversible and death-laden in the birds eating up Hansel's path of bread crumbs; the parental decision to abandon their children in the woods not once but twice means (like a word so wounding it can never be unsaid) that Hansel and Gretel are truly lost there forever, whatever illusions of escape present themselves later. What fairy tales present as their center of gravity is the renewable condition of being lost. Being lost is the price you pay for magic, and the magic can as easily increase your sense of not knowing where (or who) you are as lessen it.

The characters in *Careful* have struck many viewers as lacking in internal definition. Perhaps another way of putting this is to call them weightless. They are weightless, when we first encounter them, to the extent that they are not required to think about what they believe or how they intend to live their lives. They are comfortably obedient. Even nature declares, by unmistakable signs, that being cautious and treading lightly and never making a loud noise is one's only hope of survival. Nature and social indoctrination have but a single, wonderfully harmonized lesson to impart: keep the lid on. When, without warning, this inherited system fails the characters—when they wake up from it, as from a long, luxurious nap—they find in its place nothing but a sinister, unaccountable mood. From this time forward (though the characters' awakenings are staggered), their only form of knowledge will be mood-knowledge. However a passing mood capriciously paints their emotional and mental landscape at a given moment is all they have to go by. And when a different mood arrives, like a frenzied twilight thunderstorm, their whole sense of themselves is yanked into the midst of it, and they make whatever logic and rationality they have at their disposal somehow serve and validate the new mood.

Paradoxically, it is while the characters are filled with authoritative notions on how to behave and order their lives that they seem light as air. Once authority, which we normally think of as oppressively heavy, is taken away from them and quicksilver mood assumes the whole burden of knowledge, the characters appear to inhabit their thoughts and actions more substantially. In their former condition, they felt that those they were close to (family members, lovers, friends) shared with them an outlook, a set of values, a worldview. It seemed that such kinship made their minds transparent to one another. With the fading of other sorts of clarity, the subjectivity of anyone else starts to appear frighteningly impenetrable. One can no longer take even small things for granted in any relationship. Usually, the decision to trust one's instincts leads one to precisely the wrong conclusion or to a bizarrely foolish course of action. Ah, what torment there is in the ever-balked *need* to know what someone else truly thinks and feels. The rapid turnabouts in the motives and mind-sets of Johann, Grigorss, Klara, and Zenaida can seem purely comic, I suppose, if one regards one's own mind as better protected than theirs against such drift and veering. But perhaps radical discontinuity of mood is as plausible and compelling an approach to character inwardness as any other.

To Guy Maddin, every contemporary story that feels true is at bottom an amnesia story. And we needn't limit the importance of the amnesia dimension to current narratives. Returning to Sendak for a moment, Guy and I share his delight that the Queen of Night in *The Magic Flute*, "who seems so remarkably sensuous and beautiful and mournful and suffering in Act One," becomes inexplicably "as crazy as Leontes at the beginning of *The Winter's Tale* in Act Two."[3] And in the same opera, it seems wholly fitting to Sendak that Tamino can love a young woman intensely one minute and then not talk to her for the rest of the opera. Our best fictional surrogates at the beginning of the twenty-first century are by no means emotionally dead or ironed out flat by postmodernist disavowals of selfhood—any more than the characters in *The Magic Flute* are. They can still be filled up like a water balloon with an obsession, a hope, a benevolent impulse. The trouble comes when they (or we) try to hold on to those foggy transitions between each sovereign mood. What captivated me just yesterday can abruptly lose its power of definition and in an instant be replaced by a gloomy indifference. If only I could find or remember the bridge that led me from the first condition to the second. As Robert Musil once wrote of the mood swings in Robert Walser's prose: "the gravity of real conditions begins to drizzle along the thread" of every stray feeling.[4] But if there is cause for melancholy here, there is something amusing as well in the prospect of so many mood daybreaks and the jaunty confidence with which one goes out to meet them, one's memory strangely anesthetized to all but the very latest news.

Most of the time, viewers of *Careful* are encouraged to stand at a fair distance from the characters' dilemmas. (Is there not something distasteful about too many emotional solicitors coming to one's door in the course of a film?) Yet there are brief, crucial intervals where there is more direct pressure to feel something, at a personal depth. It's like entering one of those precious mountain node spaces where the citizens of Tolzbad can safely give vent to long-stifled impulses. One can never be sure, of course, whether subtle breaks in the tone or dominant "voice" of a film will be emotionally audible. Many of these "unguarded moments" in *Careful* have to do with Franz, the mute, paraplegic, all-but-forgotten eldest son who dwells helplessly in a foliage of cobwebs in the Bernholtz attic. He is visited early on by the blind ghost of his father, enjoining him to actions he cannot possibly perform, and can barely understand. Quite late in the film, Franz is magically reconciled to his mother, who had incomprehensibly abandoned him to his utterly isolated domestic outpost at an early age. Soon after that, he is asked by his mother in a tender voice to watch her hang herself, as though it has somehow been the impossible act of forgiving him and trying to love him that has destroyed her.

What made Franz seem the right figure to bring the film's perhaps too well-buried emotional life out in the open is that he has no voice, no capacity to act or injure, and no direct stake in the story's events. It is almost as easy for the spectator to forget about him as it is for the other characters. Taken literally, his plight is extravagantly absurd. And yet his face consistently reflects suffering (compliant, bewildered suffering) in an unstylized way. He has just enough presence of mind to be forever in touch with his own anguish—in a manner that seems pure, since neither words nor action can discharge or falsify it. *Careful* is shy about making any emotional claims on the spectator where the nature of the petition can be clearly specified.

At the end of the movie, Grigorss returns to his beloved Klara's icy, furnished cave (originally designed by her as a lovers' sanctuary for herself and her emotionally distant father). Having finally attained an isolation as pristine as Franz's, Grigorss retires to a frozen bed and, while gazing blankly at the cave ceiling, releases a single tear. In the preternatural stillness, the tear sets off an echo when it lands on the stone floor that prompts a whole series of rebound echoes, gaining steadily in resonance and volume. The sound builds to the point where one last tiny avalanche is created, sealing Grigorss into the cave. No one but his mother's consoling shade will be able to reach him there. She does arrive, however, bearing neither reproach nor any suggestion that things might be amiss. She tucks him in, checks his forehead for fever, and smiles at him, her face once more radiant with unconditional love, as he perishes in the cold. The scene strives for the wit of one of those densely knotted metaphysical love poems, a wit whose function is to hold the film's last spasm of feeling in some sort of check. What does the scene express? I can't say, but I know that it reminds me of a story Guy once told me about his blind, ninety-year-old grandmother fraily singing "Happy Birthday" to his mother from her musty downstairs room. She had to lift her head to sing into a heating duct so her voice would carry to the upstairs parlor where she guessed her daughter would be sitting. The warm air of the duct faintly carried the tune aloft and Guy's mother couldn't be sure whether she was hearing or imagining this greeting from her parent's dark, lonely anchorhold.

I'd like to close with a description by William Gass, typically and satisfyingly baroque, of Robert Walser's prose style. This description catches, better than anything I've ever read or managed to formulate for myself, the way that *Careful* might work in a world of ideal spectators and unimpeded communication from heart to heart:

> It is as if, holding in one's hand a postcard picturing, let
> us say, a pretty Swiss scene—perhaps an inn at the edge
> of a snowy village with the Alps (as they ought to be)
> above, blue lake below—one were in the same look to

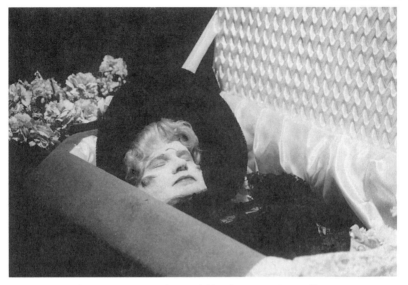

The mother of Count Knotkerss (George Toles) lying in her coffin in *Careful.*

sense behind the little window with its painted pot the shadow of a weeping woman, while in the other room of the inn there was loneliness as cold as the window glass, cruelty in the severely scraped and shoveled walk, death in the depths of the lake, a cloud of callousness about the mountain peaks; and then with nary a word about what one had seen—about bitterness, sadness, deprivation, boredom, defeat, failure added to failure—yet having seen these things, sensed these things, felt them like a cinder in the shoe, one were nevertheless to write . . . an apparently pleasant description of the pretty Swiss inn on its pretty site, colors as bright as printed paint, surfaces as shiny and slick as ice, smoke as fixed and frozen in its coils as on the quarter-a-copy card, with its space for any message, provided the message is trite and true, gay and brief.[5]

NOTES

Introduction

1. Sven Birkerts, "States of Reading," in *Readings* (St. Paul, Minn.: Graywolf Press, 1999), p. 108.
2. George Levine's introduction to the collection of essays *Aesthetics and Ideology* (New Brunswick: Rutgers University Press, 1994) is entitled "Reclaiming the Aesthetic."
3. Donald Barthelme, "Not-Knowing," *Georgia Review* 39, no. 3 (Fall 1985): 522.
4. Wittgenstein raises a question which precisely captures my sense of rigid boundary divisions in aesthetic discussions. "Isn't the concept with blurred edges just what we want—especially in ethics and aesthetics?" Geoffrey Galt Harpham makes compelling use of this question from *Philosophical Investigations* in his essay, "Aesthetics and the Fundamentals of Modernity," in *Aesthetics and Ideology*, pp. 135–38. See also J. Hillis Miller's "Word and Image" (especially his discussion of Ruskin's and Heidegger's theories of art) in *Illustration* (Cambridge: Harvard University Press, 1992), pp. 61–96.
5. R. P. Blackmur, introduction to Henry James, *The Aspern Papers* and *The Spoils of Poynton* (New York: Dell Publishing, 1975), p. 5.
6. Willa Cather, *My Antonia* (Boston: Houghton Mifflin Sentry Edition, 1961), p. 258.
7. Charles Taylor, *Sources of the Self* (Cambridge: Harvard University Press, 1989), p. 418.
8. Mary Wollstonecraft, *A Vindication of the Rights of Woman*, ed. Carol H. Poston (New York: Norton, 1975), p. 140.
9. Peter Brooks, "What Happened to Poetics?" in *Aesthetics and Ideology*, p. 165.
10. Edward Snow, *Inside Bruegel: The Play of Images in "Children's Games"* (New York: North Point Press, 1997), p. 8.
11. Friedrich Nietzsche, quoted by Snow in *Inside Bruegel*, p. 8.
12. Mary Gaitskill, "Orchid," in *Because They Wanted To* (New York: Simon and Schuster, 1997), p. 74.
13. Luiz de Camoes, quoted in *Quincas Borba* by Joaquim Maria Machado de Assis, trans. Gregory Rabassa (New York: Oxford University Press, 1998), p. 13.
14. Quoted by T. J. Clark in "God Is Not Cast Down" from *Farewell to an Idea: Episodes from an History of Modernism* (New Haven: York University Press, 1999), p. 228.
15. Henry James, *The Art of the Novel: Critical Prefaces*, ed. R. P. Blackmur (New York: Charles Scribners, 1934), p. 46.

Chapter 1

This chapter is a revised version of an essay that originally appeared in *Raritan: A Quarterly Review* 13, no. 2 (1993). Grateful acknowledgment is made to the editors for granting permission to reprint it here.

1. Roland Barthes, "The Face of Garbo," reprinted in *Film Theory and Criticism: Introductory Readings,* ed. Leo Braudy and Marshall Cohen (New York: Oxford University Press, 1999), p. 536.
2. Jorge Luis Borges, "The Wall and the Books," in *Labyrinths: Selected Stories and Other Writings.* (New York: New Directions, 1964), p. 188.
3. Rudyard Kipling, "Mrs. Bathurst," in *Short Stories, Volume I: A Sahib's War and Other Stories* (New York: Penguin, 1982), p. 85.
4. Ibid., p. 86.
5. Ibid., p. 87.
6. Anne Hollander, *Moving Pictures* (New York: Alfred A. Knopf, 1989), p. 22.
7. See Stephen Snyder's superb reading of *Spirit of the Beehive* in *The Transparent I: Self/subject in European Cinema.* (New York: Peter Lang, 1994), pp. 111–23.
8. Quoted in Frank Kermode, *The Romantic Image* (New York: Vintage, 1957), p. 124.
9. F. Gonzalez-Crussi, *The Five Senses* (New York: Vintage, 1980, p. 152.
10. Ibid., p. 153.
11. Ibid., p. 154.

Chapter 2

This chapter is a revised version of an essay that originally appeared in *North Dakota Quarterly.* Grateful acknowledgment is made to the editors for granting permission to reprint it here.

1. The following series of quotes are all taken from the "Days of Victory" articles in the August 27, 1945, issue of *Life* magazine.
2. The phrase is Paul Goodman's.
3. Grace Paley, *Enormous Changes at the Last Minute* (New York: Farrar, Straus, Giroux, 1974), p. 86.
4. Franz Kafka, *Diaries: 1914–1923,* ed. Max Brod, trans. Martin Greenberg (New York: Schocken Books, 1971), p. 195.
5. Paul Goodman, *Creator Spirit Come: The Literary Essays of Paul Goodman,* ed. Taylor Stoehr (New York: Free Life Editions, 1977), p. 105.
6. C. S. Lewis, "On Stories," in *Essays Presented to Charles Williams,* ed. C. S. Lewis (Grand Rapids: William B. Eerdmans Publishing, 1977), p. 105.
7. Frank Capra, *The Name Above the Title* (New York: Macmillan, 1971), p. 377.
8. Robert Harbison, *Eccentric Spaces* (New York: Alfred A. Knopf, 1977), p. 133.
9. Walter Pater, "Style," in *Essays on Literature and Art,* ed. Jennifer Uglow (Totowa, N.J.: Rowan and Littlefield, 1973), p. 71.
10. John Updike, *Assorted Prose* (New York: Alfred A. Knopf, 1965), p. 301.

11. James Richardson, *Thomas Hardy: The Poetry of Necessity* (Chicago: Quadrangle Books, 1972), p. 83–84.
12. Vernon Young, *On Film: Unpopular Essays on a Popular Art* (Chicago: Quadrangle Books, 1972), p. 3.
13. Donald C. Willis, *The Films of Frank Capra* (Metheun, N.J.: Scarecrow Press, 1974), p. 105.
14. I am deliberately echoing Orson Welles's narration of George Minafer's "last walk home" in *The Magnificent Ambersons.*
15. W. B. Yeats, *Selected Criticism,* ed. A. Norman Jerrares (London: Macmillan, 1970), pp. 215–26.
16. The connection between the cigar lighter and the bannister knob was suggested to me by Michael Silverblatt, who read an earlier draft of this essay.
17. The conspicuous flow of money undeniably has a share in the magic of the film's ending, perhaps reminding us unwelcomely of the more sinister implications of Karl Marx's claim that "money is the externalization of all the capacities of humanity." How is the steady heaping up of bills and coins on the table near the Bailey Christmas tree prevented from achieving a disproportionate weight in a ceremony designed to honor other forms of reciprocity as well? The emphasis in this "gift economy" is not George Bailey's final right to turn a profit in Bedford Falls. The newly bestowed wealth hovers ambiguously in its status between gift and loan. The dynamic of the film, here as always, is to foster a productive disequilibrium where, in the words of I. Morris, "the aim is never to have debts paid off but to preserve (unoppressively) a situation of personal indebtedness." Bailey's financial progress, in the closing minutes, is merely a return to the break-even point. The money arrives in time to head off a disaster that George has already fully confronted and found the peace of mind to accept.
    Uncle Billy has lost the company funds through a failure of memory. It is important to bear in mind that the actual whereabouts of the money George has set aside to pay his bills—Potter's office—is never discovered, never recollected, never even suspected by anyone in the community. The money which makes up for the loss reverberates powerfully as a counterbalancing instance of memory working well: Bedford Falls's collective memory of George Bailey, successfully awakened. When George wanders through Pottersville in the vain attempt to find someone, anyone, who knows or remembers him, it is as though the entire meaning of community is plausibly condensed into the ability to hold others fast in one's mind. The absolute failure of those in Pottersville to make a place for George (or for each other) in their memory, creates a mounting dramatic pressure not only for George but for the whole of Bedford Falls— after its temporary obliteration—to recall effortlessly the true nature of their connectedness and, by extension, their indebtedness. Can we imagine, without undue strain, a situation where the act of reckoning fairly what one owes to others could be construed as a cause for rejoicing?
    The contagion of good will among George's friends, released by a group willingness to recognize his need and all the saved details of his history in their midst, reverses the force of the earlier bank panic, where Mary calms a desperate

crowd by holding before them, as a pledge of good faith, George's modest life savings. Once Mary brings the money out into the open, it becomes theirs for the asking. Capra is highly knowledgeable about the unavoidably mixed feelings attaching to monetary display, whether the motive is giving, getting, or flaunting. On the one hand, showing money to others can express the relief of letting go, the unexpected loosening of money's often terrible grip. On the other hand, display can readily excite the hoarder's impulse to retrieve and cover up. The act of exhibiting money in movies is as likely to be accompanied by embarrassment as arrogance. It so often feels like an unseemly invitation to stare at another's nakedness. The endlessly repeated crime film scene, for example, in which a briefcase full of clean, stacked bills is opened up for another's approval is customarily played as though it were the proud unzipping of one's fly.

The pure happenstance of Uncle Billy's misplacement of the Building and Loan money in the first place—and its *useless* arrival literally in Potter's lap—where further hoarding and concealing automatically commence, seems to make more dramatically feasible the later mysterious truce in everyone else's hoarding instinct. Why is this the case? An exorbitant incident of accidental loss, within the system of narrative checks and balances, somehow makes provision for an equivalently exorbitant incident of retrieval, especially since the net result of the compensating rescue leaves George, materially, pretty much where he was at the beginning of the day. He is again simply (or, in Capra's vision, not so simply) holding his own.

Potter's negative force of accumulation is not very far removed from the small gifts positively accumulating in the Bailey living room. The money that appears magically, impulsively from all the human places where it typically hides is, on one level, a mere consolidation of Potter's successful theft. In this Christmas carol, Scrooge intriguingly undergoes no conversion. Nothing tempts him to relent, not for a moment. George's regained eight thousand dollars sharply depletes the reserves of the assembled group. Viewers are surely more conscious of this drain than the characters appear to be. The spirited emptying of the neighbors' pockets means that Potter has found yet another way to enrich himself at their expense, and one might be troubled that everyone remains blind to that fact. To see the ending in this fashion (exclusively) could well lead one to experience George's ongoing entrapment more intensely than the sensations of release I have been describing. The weight of the money/loan on the table is not of necessity pleasurable gift weight; it can also be regarded as extending the duration of George's "perfect" (because unbroken) confinement in Bedford Falls. The crowd in George's home, following this logic, can be taken to literalize the sad renewal of unending obligations. George is completely hemmed in by these obligations—neighbors whose gratitude is a subtle demand for an even fuller show of commitment to their interests in the future. (Most of the parodies of the *Wonderful Life* ending fasten on the extreme precariousness of any group's elation at one person's good fortune. This reasonable suspicion of the frailty of the community's allegiance to George, when joined with the idea that he is condemned to stay in his town, by his own submission to happiness, if you like, suggests a wholesale triumph of delusion.)

My sense of the ending is that it vanquishes the skeptic in me by legitimate means, rising exultantly above what my skepticism is sure of with respect to these people, but not by banishing the skeptic's misgivings and negative knowledge from the room. My giddy kinship with George's newfound spirit is spurred on by the fact that it is only now, for the first time, that he achieves the emotional freedom to receive something from others unself-consciously, without question or defense. The fact that this freedom seems hard-won causes some spectators, and I am one of them, to wish to emulate it. The throng that lines up to honor George with gifts is highly reminiscent of the throng that earlier lined up at his office, to reduce him, just as impetuously and with a similar pressing need, to his last two dollars. On both occasions, it is more a matter of people facing each other than the financial transaction itself: of people unequivocally showing their faces at a time when these faces are at one with the actions being performed by their owners. Billy's impulse during the bank run was to lock the doors and hide himself; George and Mary overcome the same impulse and throw open the doors, admitting a crowd driven by fear and distress just minutes after their wedding. Instead of a bridal bouquet, Mary lifts the couple's entire savings before her troubled guests, and in effect tosses it into the air. According to Aristotle, "this is the essence of *charis*: the necessity to repay a grace done to oneself and also to initiate gracious action on one's own." The giving of money is converted to grace by the givers being there (fully there) in person. The gift escapes the curse of commodity by being reflected through the looks passing without barrier between giver and recipient. The truth of the light in the faces, on both sides of the giving "border," certifies the presence of Aristotelian grace. I shall have still more to say about the efficacious power of the sentiment in Capra's final scene in my *Random Harvest* chapter.

(The quotes from Marx, Morris, and Aristotle, as well as the inspiration for this lengthy ramble on money matters are drawn from Anne Carson's discussion of the alleged miser poet, Simonides of Keos, in *Economy of the Unlost* (Princeton: Princeton University Press, 1999), pp. 10–22.)

I would also like to direct readers interested in Capra to two searching, deeply informed interpretations of *It's a Wonderful Life:* Raymond Carney's "American Dreaming: *It's a Wonderful Life*," in *American Vision: The Films of Frank Capra* (New York: Cambridge University Press, 1986), pp. 377–435; and Leland Poague's "'To Be or Not to Be': *It's a Wonderful Life*," in *Another Frank Capra* (New York: Cambridge University Press, 1994), pp. 187–222.

Chapter 3

Grateful acknowledgment is made to the Arizona Board of Regents for granting permission to reprint this essay that originally appeared in the *Arizona Quarterly*.

1. T. S. Eliot, *Four Quartets* (New York: Harcourt, Brace and World, 1943), p. 30.
2. See Mary Ann Doane, *The Desire to Desire: The Woman's Film of the 1940s* (Bloomington: Indiana University Press, 1987), pp. 70–95. For an impressive

range of responses to the problem of sentiment in film, see Christina Gledhill, ed., *Home Is Where the Heart Is: Studies in Melodrama and the Woman's Film* (London: British Film Institute, 1987). Also, William Rothman, *The "I" of the Camera: Essays in Film Criticism, History, and Aesthetics* (Cambridge: Cambridge University Press, 1988), especially his chapters on *Stella Dallas* and *City Lights.*

3. Robert Walser, *Jacob von Gunten,* trans. Christopher Middleton (New York: Vintage Books, 1973), p. 128.

4. Ingmar Bergman, "Why I Make Movies," reprinted in Lewis Jacobs, *The Emergence of Film Art* (New York: Norton & Company, 1979), pp. 296–304.

5. Donald Carveth, "Some Reflections on Lacanian Theory in Relation to Other Currents in Contemporary Psychoanalysis," paper presented to the Toronto Psychoanalytic Society, Mar. 4, 1987, p. 23.

6. Ibid., p. 28.

7. A variation of Harold Brodkey's wonderful sentence about reading and writing. "If the reader is not at risk, he is not reading. And if the writer is not at risk he is not writing." From "Reading: The Most Dangerous Game," in Harold Brodkey, *Sea Battles on Dry Land* (New York: Metropolitan Books, 1999), p. 320.

8. Trans. Erich Heller. Quoted in Heller, *The Importance of Nietzsche* (Chicago: University of Chicago Press, 1988), p. 61.

9. Charles Affron, *Cinema and Sentiment* (Chicago: University of Chicago Press, 1982), p. 52.

10. Ovid, *The Metamorphoses,* trans. Mary Innes (Baltimore: Penguin Books, 1962), p. 92.

11. Stanley Cavell, *The World Viewed,* enlarged edition (Cambridge: Harvard University Press, 1979), p. 190. Cavell's finest essay on film sentiment, in my view, is "'Ugly Duckling, Funny Butterfly:' Bette Davis and *Now, Voyager,*" in Stanley Cavell, *Contesting Tears: The Hollywood Melodrama of the Unknown Woman* (Chicago: University of Chicago Press, 1996), pp. 115–48.

12. Alice Miller, *The Drama of the Gifted Child,* trans. Ruth Ward (New York: Basic Books, 1981), p. 57.

13. Ibid., p. 58.

14. Cavell, *World Viewed,* p. 67.

15. Ibid., p. 17.

16. James Hilton, *Random Harvest* (Boston: Little Brown and Company, 1941), pp. 203–4. Subsequent quotes are taken from this edition.

17. Alfred Kazin, *On Native Grounds: An Interpretation of Modern American Prose Literature* (Garden City, N.Y.: Doubleday and Company, 1956), p. 405.

18. Kaja Silverman, *The Acoustic Mirror: The Female Voice in Psychoanalysis and Cinema* (Bloomington: Indiana University Press, 1988), pp. 211–12.

19. Mary Ann Doane, "The Voice of the Cinema: The Articulation of Body and Space," *Yale French Studies* 6 (1980): 33–50.

20. Ovid, *Metamorphoses,* p. 91.

21. Ibid., p. 93.

22. Alice Miller, *Drama of the Gifted Child,* p. 21.

23. Quoted by Roland Barthes in *Camera Lucida* (New York: Hill and Wang, 1981), p. 40.
24. Barthes, *Camera Lucida*, pp. 45, 49.
25. Rainier Maria Rilke, *Where Silence Reigns: Selected Prose*, trans. by G. Craig Huston (New York: New Directions, 1978), pp 34–35.
26. *The Selected Poetry of Rainier Maria Rilke*, The Eighth Duino Elegy, trans. Stephen Mitchell (New York: Vintage, 1984), p. 193.
27. Ibid., p. 195.

Chapter 4

This chapter also appears as an essay in Vittorio de Sica: Contemporary Perspectives, edited by Howard Curle and Stephen Snyder (Toronto: University of Toronto Press, 2000). Grateful acknowledgment is made to the University of Toronto Press for granting permission to reprint it here.

1. Irving Massey, *Find You the Virtue: Ethics, Image, and Desire in Literature* (Fairfax, Va.: George Mason University Press, 1987), p. 33.
2. Hugo von Hofmannsthal, "The Letter of Lord Chandos," in *Selected Prose*, trans. Mary Hottinger, Tania Stern, and James Stern, Bollingen Series 33 (New York: Pantheon Books, 1952), p. 138.
3. Hofmannsthal, "Colours," in *Selected Prose*, pp. 153–54.
4. Ibid., p. 145.
5. Percy Bysshe Shelley, "A Defence of Poetry" in *Shelley's Poetry and Prose*, selected and ed. Donald H. Reiman and Sharon B. Powers (New York: W. W. Norton, 1977), 487–88. "The great secret of morals is Love; or a going out of our own nature, and an identification of ourselves with the beautiful which exists in thought, action, or person, not our own. A man, to be greatly good, must imagine intensely and comprehensively; he must put himself in the place of another and of many others; the pains and pleasures of his species must become his own. The great instrument of moral good is the imagination; and poetry administers to the effect by acting upon the cause."
6. Cesare Zavattini, *sequences from a cinematic life*, trans. William Weaver (Englewood Cliffs, N.J.: Prentice-Hall, 1970), p. 9. All subsequent page citations for Zavattini quotes refer to this work.
7. Quoted by Marina Warner in *L'Atalante* (London: British Film Institute, 1993), p. 77.
8. Quoted by Gale Carrithers in "Loren Eiseley and the Self as Search," *Arizona Quarterly* 50, no. 1 (Spring 1994): 81.
9. Jiri Weil, *Life With a Star*, trans. by Rita Klimova and Roslyn Schloss (New York: Penguin, 1989), p. 23.
10. Ibid., p. 114.
11. Benjamin Bennett, *Hugo von Hofmannsthal: The Theatres of Consciousness* (Cambridge: Cambridge University Press, 1988), p. 118.

12. The linking of William James's *Pragmatism* with Wittgenstein's idea of language going on holiday was suggested by Arthur Danto in *Connections to the World* (New York: Harper and Row, 1990), p. 12.
13. Massey, *Find You the Virtue*, p. 84.
14. Rainer Maria Rilke, *Where Silence Reigns: Selected Prose*, trans. G. Craig Huston (New York: New Directions, 1978), p. 5.
15. Rilke, *Letters to a Young Poet*, trans. by Stephen Mitchell (New York: Vintage, 1986), p. 87.
16. Paul Coates, *The Story of the Lost Reflection* (London: Verso, 1985), p. 49.
17. Quoted by Gilberto Perez in "A Man Pointing: Antonioni and the Film Image," *Yale Review* 82, no. 3 (July 1994): 55.
18. The phrase "moral occult" is Peter Brooks's.
19. Elizabeth Bishop, "Sandpiper," in *The Complete Poems* (New York: Farrar, Straus and Giroux, 1970), p. 153.
20. Ethan Canin, "City of Broken Hearts," in *The Palace Thief* (New York: Random House, 1994), p. 151.
21. Robert Hass, *Praise* (New York: Ecco, 1979), p. 47.

Chapter 5

This chapter is a revised version of an essay that originally appeared in *New Literary History* (Spring 1984). Grateful acknowledgment is made to the editors for granting permission to reprint it here.

1. Ronald Barthes, "The Metaphor of the Eye," in *Critical Essays*, trans. Richard Howard (Evanston, 1972), p. 239. See also Roland Kuhn, "The Attempted Murder of a Prostitute," in *Existence: A New Dimension in Psychiatry and Psychology*, ed. Rollo May, Ernest Angel, and Henri F. Ellenberger (New York, Basic Books, 1958), pp. 365–425.
2. Edgar Allan Poe, "Berenice," in *Complete Tales and Poems* (New York: Modern Library, 1965), p. 645.
3. Daniel Hoffman, *Poe Poe Poe Poe Poe Poe Poe* (New York: Doubleday, 1972), pp. 234–35.
4. Georges Bataille, *Story of the Eye*, trans. Joachim Neugraschel (New York, 1977), p. 56.
5. Georges Bataille, *Manet*, trans. Austryn Wainhouse and James Emmons (Cleveland: Skira, 1955), p. 82.
6. Sanford Schwartz, "Reflections: (The Mystery and Melancholy of a Career)," *New Yorker*, June 28, 1982, p. 93.
7. V. F. Perkins, *Film as Film* (Baltimore: Penguin, 1972), p. 106.
8. Garrett Stewart, "Keaton through the Looking Glass," *Georgia Review* 33 (Summer 1979): 365.
9. John Russell Taylor, *Hitch: The Life and Times of Alfred Hitchcock* (New York, Pantheon, 1978), p. 256.
10. James Naremore, *Filmguide to Psycho* (Bloomington: Indiana University Press, 1973), p. 36.

11. Stevie Smith, "Not Waving But Drowning," in *The Norton Anthology of Poetry*, rev. ed. (New York: W. W. Norton, 1975), p. 1097.
12. Irving Massey, *The Gaping Pig: Literature and Metamorphosis* (Berkeley and Los Angeles: University of California Press, 1976), p. 8.
13. For a discussion of a similar search in Poe's "The Purloined Letter" (nearly as famous as that in *Psycho*), see Jacques Lacan, "Seminar on 'The Purloined Letter,'" *Yale French Studies* 41 (1972): 38–72.
14. Massey, *Gaping Pig*, p. 6.

Chapter 6

This chapter is a revised version of an essay that originally appeared in *boundary 2* (Winter/Spring 1989). Grateful acknowledgment is made to the editors for granting permission to reprint it here.

1. See Eric Rohmer and Claude Chabrol, *Hitchcock*, trans. Stanley Hochman (New York: Frederick Ungar, 1979), pp. 122–28; Robin Wood, *Hitchcock's Films* (New York: A. C. Barnes, 1977), pp. 68–76; Raymond Durgnat, *The Strange Case of Alfred Hitchcock* (Cambridge: MIT Press, 1974), pp. 188–201. Among the provocative more recent examinations of *Rear Window* are Roberta Pearson and Robert Stam's "Hitchcock's *Rear Window*; Reflexivity and the Critique of Voyeurism," *Enclitic* 7 (Spring 1983): 136–45; John Belton, "The Space of *Rear Window*," in *Hitchcock's Re-released Films*, ed. Walter Raubicheck and Walter Srebnick (Detroit: Wayne State University Press, 1991), pp. 76–94; and Dana Brand, "Rear-View Mirror: Hitchcock, Poe, and the Flaneur in America," in *Hitchcock's America*, ed. Jonathan Freedman and Richard Millington (New York: Oxford University Press, 1999), pp. 123–34. For a meticulous shot-by-shot breakdown of *Rear Window*, with resolutely unadventurous but sometimes illuminating commentary, see Stefan Sharff, *The Art of Looking in Hitchcock's Rear Window* (New York: Limelight Editions, 1997).
2. My thinking on the psychology of urban perception has been influenced by Philip Fisher's essay, "City Matters: City Minds," which suggestively links comic descriptions in Dickens with the landscapes of Eliot's early poems: Harvard English Studies 6, *The Worlds of Victorian Fiction*, ed. Jerome Buckley (Cambridge: Harvard University Press, 1975), pp. 371–89.
3. Fisher, "City Matters: City Minds," p. 375.
4. Paul Fry, *The Reach of Criticism* (New Haven: Yale University Press, 1983). See especially "The Instance of Walter Benjamin: Distraction and Perception in Criticism," pp. 168–205.
5. William Gass, "The Habitations of the Word," *Kenyon Review* 6, no. 4 (Fall 1984): 99.
6. J. M. Coetzee, *In the Heart of the Country* (New York: Penguin, 1977), p. 41.
7. John Berger, *Ways of Seeing* (London, Penguin, 1982), p. 149. Of course, it is also possible for a feminist to view Hitchcock's female characters in *Rear Window* sympathetically and still have legitimate concerns about his representation of (and attitudes toward) women. See Tania Modleski, "The Master's Doll-

house: *Rear Window,*" in *The Women Who Knew Too Much: Hitchcock and Feminist Theory* (New York: Routledge, 1988), pp. 73–85.

8. Nathaniel Hawthorne, *The Blithedale Romance* (New York: Penguin, 1983), p. 69.

9. Ibid., p. 157

10. Peter Brooks, *Reading for the Plot: Design and Intention in Narrative* (New York: Vintage, 1985), p. 91.

11. Albert Cook, "The Wilderness of Mirrors," *Kenyon Review* 7, no. 3 (Summer 1986): 90.

12. Leo Steinberg, "Picasso's Sleepwatchers," *Other Criteria: Confrontation with Twentieth-Century Art* (New York: Oxford University Press, 1972), p. 99.

13. Ibid., p. 104. The phrase comes from the Spanish poet Quevedo.

14. Michael Murrin, *The Veil of Allegory: Some Notes Toward a Theory of Allegorical Rhetoric in the English Renaissance* (Chicago: University of Chicago Press, 1969), p. 15.

15. Ibid., p. 15.

16. Ibid., p. 11.

17. Paul de Man, *Blindness and Insight: Essays in the Rhetoric of Contemporary Criticism* (New York: Oxford University Press, 1971), pp. 136, 139.

18. The question has been raised, on numerous occasions, by Wim Winders. Can a film which contains scenes of violence, say, be against violence?

19. Iris Murdoch, *Acastos: Two Platonic Dialogues* (London: Chatto and Windus, 1986), p. 55.

20. For a fuller discussion of this episode, see Susan Sontag, "Persona: The Film in Depth," rpt., in *Ingmar Bergman: Essays in Criticism*, ed. Stuart M. Kaminsky (New York: Oxford University Press, 1975), pp. 253–69.

21. Paul de Man, *Allegories of Reading: Figural Language in Rousseau, Nietzsche, Rilke, and Proust* (New Haven: Yale University Press, 1979), p. 205.

22. The phrase is Robert Stam's. See his *Reflexivity in Film and Literature: From Don Quixote to Jean Luc Godard* (Ann Arbor: UMT Research Press, Studies in Cinema, 1985), p. 44. Stam draws the by now de rigueur parallel between Foucault's description of cells in the panopticon (viewed from the warden's position) and the rear window complex: ("so many small cages, so many small theatres, in which each actor is alone, perfectly individualized and constantly visible" [p. 48]).

23. Charles Altieri, "Plato's Performance Sublime and the Ends of Reading," *New Literary History* 16, no. 2 (Winter 1985): 259.

Chapter 7

1. Laura Mulvey, "Visual Pleasure and Narrative Cinema," *Screen* 16, no. 2 (1975): 6–18. Raymond Bellour analyzed the implications of the male gaze in Hitchcock in very similar terms in a series of influential essays that appeared in France and North America between 1969 and 1977. Bellour and Mulvey, together, are chiefly responsible for consolidating "first wave" thinking about how the gaze

works in Hitchcock films. See Raymond Bellour, "*Les Oiseaux:* analyse d'une séquence," *Cahiers du Cinéma* 216 (1969): 24–38; Bellour, "Hitchcock, the Enunciator," *Camera Obscura* 1 (Fall 1977): 66–91; Bellour, "Psychosis, Neurosis, Perversion," *Camera Obscura* 3–4 (1979). Reprinted in *A Hitchcock Reader,* ed. Marshall Deutelbaum and Leland Poague (Ames: Iowa State University Press, 1986), pp. 311–31. Tania Modleski, in her book *The Women Who Knew Too Much: Hitchcock and Feminist Theory* (New York: Routledge, 1989), desires to open up a space for the female gaze in Hitchcock, thus departing from Mulvey's original position, but seems determined to regard Hitchcock's own "misogynist" and "patriarchal" intentions as necessarily in opposition to her own. Modleski wants to hold onto Mulvey's conception of Hitchcock's guilt (and the guilt of his male characters) while arguing for the apparent "innocence" of many of Hitchcock's women characters on those narrative occasions when their point of view is (almost accidentally) represented. In her conclusion, she writes: "Though our monstrous father may have made us fear our own image of ourselves, he has also (no doubt against his will) given us reason to hope that we will be able to survive patriarchy's attacks" (120–21). My emphasis and conclusions are quite different from Modleski's, but I have learned a great deal from her book, especially her chapters on *Blackmail, Rebecca,* and *Notorious.*

2. Franz Kafka, "In the Penal Colony," in *The Complete Stories and Parables,* ed. Nahum Glatzer (New York: Quality Paperback Book Club, 1983). "For I was the former Commandant's assistant in all penal matters and know more about the apparatus than anyone. My guiding principle is this: Guilt is never to be doubted" (p. 145).

3. William Rothman, *Hitchcock—The Murderous Gaze* (Cambridge: Harvard University Press, 1982). See also Rothman, "Alfred Hitchcock's *Notorious,*" *Georgia Review* 39, no. 4 (1975): 884–927; and the essays on *Vertigo* and *North by Northwest* in Rothman, *The "I" of the Camera: Essays in Film Criticism, History, and Aesthetics* (New York: Cambridge University Press, 1988).

4. Roland Barthes, quoted by Lionel Gossman in *Between History and Literature* (Cambridge: Harvard University Press, 1990), p. 254.

5. Jenny Diski, *Skating to Antarctica* (London: Granta Books, 1997), p. 174.

6. Kaja Silverman, *The Acoustic Mirror: The Female Voice in Psychoanalysis and Cinema* (Bloomington: Indiana University Press, 1988). Elizabeth Weis's book, *The Silent Scream: Alfred Hitchcock's Sound Track* (Rutherford, N.J.: Fairleigh Dickinson University Press, 1982), while offering detailed examinations of Hitchcock's use of sound in many films, engages only slightly with feminist or gaze theorist concerns. Also, she does not work with the sounds of particular actors' voices—their vocal *presence,* if you like.

7. Terry Eagleton, *William Shakespeare* (Oxford: Basil Blackwell, 1986), p. 72.

8. My skepticism about things Lacanian is reserved mainly for theory-by-rote, formulaic readings of film and literary texts swearing fealty to an efficient psychoanalytic system. I am well aware that my own reflections on the migrating "eye" in *Psycho* and the apparitional "rope" in *Rope* owe a substantial debt to Lacan. Furthermore, I think there is no interpreter of Hitchcock at present who seems to me more discerning and wittily provocative than the dazzlingly multi-

faceted Lacanian, Slavoj Zizek. See, for example, *Enjoy Your Symptom! Jacques Lacan in Hollywood and Out* (Routledge: New York, 1992).

9. Ivan Turgenev, *First Love*, trans. by Isaiah Berlin (London: Hunt Barnard, 1965), pp. 64–65.

10. Brigitte Werneburg, "Ernst Junger and the Transformed World," trans. by Christopher Hill, *October* 62 (1992): 52–53.

11. Maria Flook, "You Are Here," in *You Have the Wrong Man* (New York: Pantheon Books, 1996), p. 85.

12. Francois Truffaut, with the collaboration of Helen Scott, *Hitchcock* (New York: Simon and Schuster, 1984), pp. 308–9.

13. Raymond Durgnat, *The Strange Case of Alfred Hitchcock* (Cambridge: MIT Press, 1974), p. 208.

14. Scottie, in his last dialogue with Judy-Madeleine in the bell tower, expresses his bewilderment about the meaning of her earlier scream there, which he heard as he struggled to climb up the tower stairs to rescue her. For him the scream somehow failed to offer a credible protest against the real Mrs. Ellster's death and his own subsequent pain, and her need to scream in no way mitigates the fact that she abandoned him. Scottie remains oddly certain that he has identified the sound of Judy's scream correctly. He is quite insistent about it. The scream *belonged* to her more conclusively, in his mind, than anything else she has said or done. He *knows* the difference between the sound of her scream and Mrs. Ellster's as surely as he knows Judy to be guilty, at every level. But he confesses his uncertainty about what the scream signifies. In a few moments, when she falls to her death, he will hear the scream once more. What does it mean this time?

15. Robert Browning, "Porphyria's Lover," in *The Poetical Works of Robert Browning*, Cambridge Edition (Boston: Houghton Mifflin, 1974), p. 286.

16. Lesley Brill helpfully reminded me of yet another precursor of the rope in *Rope* from Hitchcock's British period: the murderous raincoat belt used by the Drummer Man to strangle his female victim in the generally "light" *Young and Innocent* (1937). The Drummer Man briefly escapes his incriminating facial twitch through laughter, during his final confession: "What did I do with the belt? (Laughs) I twisted it round her neck and choked the life out of her." Brill further commented on the fact that no one but Erica believes in the existence of the missing raincoat, providing another instance of a female character's resistance to neat, "conclusive," controlling masculine explanations.

I am also indebted to Lesley for the suggestion that Brandon in *Rope* is a demonic version of Margaret Brown's runaway bunny. If the "complementary desires that drive the narrative" of *Rope* are, as I argue, "successfully hiding something" and "desiring to be found out in one's clever duplicity," then Brandon might be said to reenact the Brown nursery story, with Rupert cast in the role of mother.

17. Robert G. Goulet, "Life With(out) Father: The Ideological Masculine in *Rope* and Other Hitchcock Films," in *Hitchcock's Rereleased Films: From Rope to Vertigo*, ed. Walter Raubicheck and Walter Srebnick (Detroit: Wayne State University Press, 1991), p. 251.

18. Malcolm Bowie, *Proust among the Stars* (New York: Columbia University Press, 1998), p. 51.
19. Hitchcock's gaze was so thoroughly identified and implicated with this character's that he believed the actress playing her, Tippi Hedren, would have no choice but to recognize him as one who, before all others, had the right to love her and to expect love in return. Hedren's unequivocal rejection of Hitchcock, ironically, "spoiled" the ending of *Marnie* for both of them.

Chapter 8

This chapter is a revised version of an essay that originally appeared in *Film Quarterly* 48, no. 4 (1995). Grateful acknowledgment is made to the journal editors and the Regents of the University of California for granting permission to reprint it here.

1. Wim Wenders, "Impossible Stories," in *The Logic of Images: Essays and Conversations,* trans. Michael Hoffman (Boston: Faber and Faber, 1991), p. 53.
2. Quoted in Christopher Williams, ed., *Realism and the Cinema: A Reader* (London: Routledge and Kegan Paul, 1980), p. 253.
3. Gustav Janouich, *Conversations with Kafka,* trans. Goronwy Rees (New York: New Directions, 1971), p. 144.
4. Quoted in Susan Sontag, *On Photography* (New York: Farrar, Straus and Giroux, 1977), p. 184.
5. Roberto Calasso, *The Marriage of Cadmus and Harmony,* trans. Tim Parks (New York: Alfred A. Knopf, 1993), p. 102.
6. André Bazin, "De Sica: Metteur en Scene" in *What Is Cinema?* vol. 2, trans. Hugh Gray (Berkeley and Los Angeles: University of California Press, 1972), p. 62.
7. Sontag, *On Photography,* p. 168.
8. Elias Canetti, *Crowds and Power,* trans. Carol Stenkorf (New York: Penguin, 1987), p. 376.
9. Herman Melville, "Cock-a-Doodle-Doo! or the Crowing of the Noble," in *Great Short Works of Herman Melville* (New York: Harper and Row Perennial, 1966). "Of fine mornings, / We fine lusty cocks begin our crows in gladness; / But when eve does come we don't crow / quite so much, / For then cometh despondency and madness" (p. 40).

Chapter 9

This chapter originally appeared in *Michigan Quarterly Review* (Fall 1999) volume xxxviii, Number 4. Grateful acknowledgment is made to the journal editors for granting permission to reprint it here.

1. Ethan Coen and Joel Coen, *Fargo* (Boston: Faber and Faber, 1996), p. x.
2. Czeslaw Milosz, "Ars Poetica?" in *The Collected Poems 1931–87* (Hopewell, N.J.: Ecco Press, 1992), p. 211.

3. Edith Wharton, *The Valley of Decision* (New York, 1902), II, p. 94.
4. Penelope Fitzgerald, *The Blue Flower* (New York: Houghton Mifflin Company, 1997), p. 135.
5. Richard Poirier, *Robert Frost: The Work of Knowing* (New York: Oxford University Press, 1979), p. 15.
6. The phrase is Francis Bacon's, from his celebrated description of what a reader becomes through the habit of engaged reading.
7. Osip Mandelstam, "Fourth Prose," in *The Noise of Time*, trans. Clarence Brown (New York: Penguin, 1993), p. 189.
8. Mary Oliver, "First Snow," in *New and Selected Poems* (Boston: Beacon Press, 1992), pp. 150–51.
9. Herman Melville, *Moby-Dick; or, The Whale*, ed. Alfred Kazin (Boston: Houghton Mifflin Company, 1956), p. 163.
10. Ibid., p. 162.
11. Ibid., p. 163.
12. Coen and Coen, *Fargo*, p. 34
13. Ibid., p. 91.
14. Jean-Dominique Bauby, *The Diving Bell and the Butterfly* (New York: Alfred A. Knopf, 1997), p. 132.
15. Hannah Arendt, *Between Friends: The Correspondence of Hannah Arendt and Mary McCarthy, 1949–1975*, ed. Carol Brightman (New York: Harcourt Brace and Company, 1995), p. 24.
16. Edmond Jabes, quoted in John Berger, *Keeping a Rendezvous* (New York: Vintage, 191), p. 64.
17. Thomas Browne, "Hydriotaphia or Urne Buriall," in *The Prose of Thomas Browne*, ed. Norman J. Endicott (New York: Norton, 1972), p. 282.
18. Richard Ford, "The Womanizer," in *Women with Men* (New York: Alfred A. Knopf, 1997), p. 31.
19. Ibid., p. 57.

Chapter 10

This essay also appears in *Canada's Best Features*, edited by Gene Walz (Amsterdam: Rodopi, 2001). Grateful acknowledgment is made to the editors for granting permission to reprint it here.

1. Réjean Ducharme, *L'avalée des Avalés* (Paris: Gallimard, 1966). Also, *The Swallower Swallowed*, translation of *L'avalée des Avalés* by Barbara Bray (London: Hamish Hamilton, 1968).
2. Lauzon's only other feature film is *Un Zoo, la nuit* (1987). It combines two stories, the first (and more compelling) a quasi-autobiographical account of a son's relationship with his dying father, and the second a *policier* plot in which this same son, in his profession as drug dealer, attempts to evade capture by repellent law officers. The film received thirteen Genie awards.
3. Luis Bunuel, *My Last Sigh*, trans. Abigail Israel (New York: Vintage, 1984), p. 5.

4. Bruno Schulz, *The Street of Crocodiles*, trans. Celina Wieniewska (New York: Penguin, 1977), p. 22.
5. Robert Lowell, quoted in Mark Rudman, *Robert Lowell: An Introduction to the Poetry* (New York: Columbia University Press, 1983), p. 144.
6. Jean Cocteau, *Cocteau on the Film: Conversations with Jean Cocteau*, trans. Vera Traill (New York: Dover, 1972), p. 129.
7. Robert Graves, writing about W. H. R. Rivers's study room in Cambridge. "For that was the place I longed to be / And past all hope where the kind lamp shone." Quoted by Rosemary Dinnage in "Death's Gray Land," *New York Review of Books* (Feb. 15, 1996), p. 19.
8. Rainer Maria Rilke, *Uncollected Poems*, trans. Edward Snow (New York: Farrar, Straus and Giroux, 1996), p. 57.
9. Brad Leithauser, *The Mail from Anywhere* (New York: Alfred A. Knopf, 1990), p. 6.
10. Cszeslaw Milosz, *The Collected Poems, 1931–1987* (Hopewell, N.J.: Ecco Press, 1988), author's note on back cover.
11. Ernest Becker, *The Denial of Death* (New York: Free Press, 1975), p. 170.
12. Herman Melville, "Letter to Nathaniel Hawthorne, April 16?, 1851," in *The Norton Anthology of American Literature*, vol. 1 (New York: Norton and Company, 1979), p. 2072.
13. Jeanette Winterson, *The Passion* (New York: Vintage, 1989), p. 61.
14. Quoted in David Laskin, *A Common Life: Four Generations of American Literary Friendship and Influence* (New York: Simon and Schuster, 1994), p. 346.
15. Carole Corbeil, "The Indiscreet Charm of Jean-Claude Lauzon," *Saturday Night* 107, no. 10 (Dec. 1992): 60.
16. Laskin, *Common Life*, p. 265.
17. Ibid., p. 320.
18. Flannery O'Connor, *The Habit of Being*, ed. Sally Fitzgerald (New York: Farrar, Straus and Giroux, 1979), p. 144.
19. Wendy Lesser, "Bodies at Motion and Bodies at Rest," *Threepenny Review* 66 (Summer 1996): 23.
20. Guido Ceronetti, *The Silence of the Body*, trans. Michael Moore (New York: Farrar, Straus and Giroux, 1993), p. 8.
21. Irving Massey, *Find You the Virtue: Ethics, Image, and Desire in Literature* (Fairfax, Va.: George Mason University Press, 1987), pp. 115, 127.

Chapter 11

This chapter is a revised version of an essay that originally appeared in *Post Script: Essays in Film and the Humanities* 18, no. 2 (Winter/Spring 1999). Special issue: Canadian Cinema, edited by Barry Keith Grant. Grateful acknowledgment is made to the editors for granting permission to reprint it here.

1. Samuel Beckett, *Waiting for Godot* (New York: Grove Press, 1954), p. 36.
2. Maurice Sendak, "Symposium: Sendak's Rabbis, Mozart, and Shakespeare," in *Threepenny Review* 17, no. 2 (Summer 1996): 35.

3. Ibid., p. 34
4. Robert Musil, "The Stories of Robert Walker," in *Robert Walker Rediscovered: Stories, Fairy-Tale Plays, and Critical Responses,* ed. Mark Harmon (Hanover: University Press of New England, 1985), p. 142.
5. William Gass, *Finding a Form* (New York: Alfred A. Knopf, 1996), pp. 69–70.

INDEX

absence, 44, 48, 49, 83–84, 108, 112, 118, 134, 143, 153, 165, 202, 203, 208, 212, 217, 224; in *It's a Wonderful Life*, 58, 70, 71, 73–74; in "Mrs. Bathurst," 33–36; in *Spirit of the Beehive*, 42–43
absorption. *See* transfixion
Acoustic Mirror, The, 192
aestheticism, 14, 17, 21, 78, 85, 86, 87
aesthetic response in Hitchcock, 143–46
Aesthetics and Ideology, 335n. 2
Affron, Charles, 89–90
aging, 86, 119, 127; of actors, 236–37; of film, 30–31
Alfred Hitchcock Presents, 214
Altieri, Charles, 182
America: in *Fargo*, 259–60; postwar, 51–56; small-town life in, 59, 61; in WWII, 96
American Vision: The Films of Frank Capra, 339n. 17
amnesia. *See* forgetting
angel: in *It's a Wonderful Life*, 54–56, 75; images as angels, 233–34. *See also* revelation
Anna Karenina, 61
Antonioni, Michelangelo, 130, 172
apparition, 40, 108, 116, 202, 204, 206, 208, 210, 213, 222, 224, 227, 230, 332; Bedford Falls as, 72–73
Archangel, 325–28
Arendt, Hannah, 264, 287
Aristotle, 339n. 17
arrival, 24, 37, 117; in "Mrs. Bathurst," 32–35
Ars Poetica?, 262
Arthur, Jean, 327

Art of Looking in Hitchcock's Rear Window, The, 343n. 1
Astaire, Fred, 57
L'Atalante, 116
audience. *See* spectator
Austen, Jane, 263
authority, 14, 47, 85, 162, 168, 171, 182, 184, 187, 193, 197–99, 204, 206, 208, 223, 224, 226, 229, 230, 239, 251, 255, 279, 289, 297, 327–28, 331
L'avalée des avalés, 293, 312
awakening, 44, 92, 105, 107, 113, 116, 123, 273, 331
awe. *See* enchantment; magic

Bacon, Francis, 348n. 6
Bakhtin, Mikhail, 316
Balzac, Honoré de, 201
Barrie, James M., 202
Barthelme, Donald, 15
Barthes, Roland, 31, 108, 130, 138, 188
Bataille, Georges, 137–42, 146, 152
Bauby, Jean-Dominique, 285
Bazin, André, 15, 233–34, 237, 238, 241, 257
beauty, 201, 233, 235–36, 273–74, 301, 317; and truth, 235–36
Becker, Ernest, 16, 307–8
Bellour, Raymond, 186, 344n. 1
Belton, John, 343n. 1
Benjamin, Arthur, 212
"Berenice," 137–39, 142, 144, 157
Berger, John, 167
Bergman, Ingmar, 83–84, 180
Bergson, Henry, 283
Best Years of Our Lives, The, 241–44

Books in the
CONTEMPORARY FILM AND TELEVISION SERIES